W9-DDL-081

POLICIES OF PUBLISHERS:

A Handbook for Order Librarians

1989 edition

by
DAVID U. KIM
and
CRAIG A. WILSON

THE SCARECROW PRESS, INC.
Metuchen, N.J., & London
1989

The authors invite comments, criticisms, and suggestions for new
format or inclusion of additional information, from both
librarians and publishers. Such communications should be
addressed to: David U. Kim, Assistant Director, Sam Houston State
University Libraries, Huntsville, TX 77341 or Craig A. Wilson,
Assistant Director for Collection Development, Oregon State
University Libraries, Corvallis, OR 97331.

Policies of Publishers: A Handbook for Order Librarians is
intended to help librarians find information concerning publishers
from whom they often order. The authors believe that the
information enables librarians to prepare appropriate library
orders which will in turn benefit publishers. The authors reserve
the right to exclude listing of any publisher, or add other
statements which are considered necessary by the authors. The
publisher and the authors have sought accuracy in collecting and
preparing the information included in this book, but do not
assume, and hereby disclaim, any liability to any party for any
loss or damage caused by use of this book.

British Library Cataloguing-in-Publication data available

Library of Congress Cataloging-in-Publication Data

Kim, Ung Chon, 1932-
    Policies of publishers.

    1. Acquisitions (Libraries)--Handbooks, manuals, etc.
2. Libraries and publishing--Handbooks, manuals, etc.
3. Publishers and publishing--United States--Directories.
I. Wilson, Craig A., 1946-   . II. Title.
Z689.K55   1989   025.2'3   89-6406
ISBN 0-8108-2233-4

```
******************************
        TABLE OF CONTENTS
******************************
```

The policies of some publishers, dealing with discounts, prepayment requirements, return procedure, invoicing and shipping, backorders, and available standing orders, may be found in scattered places within their catalogs and announcements. Sometimes these policies are announced separately in printed letters, found among a pile of daily mail directed to librarians from publishers. Yet, in many cases, such information is not conveniently available anywhere.

The main purpose of this book is to provide, in a single source, the information that is needed by librarians in placing direct orders. The information contained in the present book is mostly derived from questionnaires completed by approximately 800 publishers. Other sources of information include the current editions of The Publishers' Trade List Annual, the Literary Market Place, previous editions of the Policies of Publishers, weekly issues of the Publishers Weekly, and recent catalogs and announcements of the publishers.

The present edition of Policies of Publishers: A Handbook for Order Librarians includes listings of approximately 600 publishers' policies and cross references from about 780 publishers. As in the 1982 edition, all the publishers' names, including cross references, are arranged in one alphabetical sequence. The policies of all publishers referred to apply to those referred from, whether there is a subsidiary, distributorship, or imprint relationship.

The authors would like to acknowledge the assistance of Mary Steckel who proofread the final copy of the manuscript.

David U. Kim
Craig A. Wilson

```
***********************************************************
```
FACTORS TO BE CONSIDERED IN PLACING DIRECT ORDERS
```
***********************************************************
```

In order to accomplish their most important duty--purchasing library material in the most prompt and economical way possible--order librarians have to select appropriate vendors. Whether a library prefers generally to place most of its orders with publishers or with wholesalers, all need at some time to place some orders directly with publishers. In order to acquire books speedily, librarians find direct orders effective in most cases. Libraries receive a smaller discount from many publishers than from reliable wholesalers; however, by placing orders with certain publishers, libraries do find it possible to purchase some books more economically. Librarians should know the policies of individual publishers and use direct orders selectively. [See Ung Chon Kim, "Purchasing Books from Publishers and Wholesalers," Library Resources & Technical Services, 19:133-147 (Spring 1975).]

Many factors need to be considered when a librarian decides on vendors for his/her orders. These factors include: (1) promptness of delivery, or length of time the library has to wait until it receives the material; (2) discount that the library can expect; (3) special requirements with orders, such as prepayment; (4) charges other than the actual prices of books, such as shipping, billing, or service charges; (5) convenience of returning materials received in error or mistakenly ordered by the library; (6) accurate and prompt reports of titles currently unavailable; (7) automatic shipments of backordered items; and (8) availability of a standing order or approval plan which provides special convenience and saving for the library.

PROMPTNESS OF SUPPLY: In general, libraries receive shipments of material much faster from a publisher than from any other source, usually within two to three weeks, unless the ordered title is unavailable at the time of order. There are some differences in time lag depending on the publisher and on the location of the publisher's warehouse and the receiving library. In order to receive a book as soon as possible, libraries should send the orders to the appropriate address.

Addresses immediately following publishers' names herein are usually those of the main or central offices. Many publishers, however, have

different offices for receiving and processing orders. Since this address
is of primary importance to order librarians, the ADDRESS FOR ORDERS is also
noted. When the address for orders is the same as that given before, "Same
as above" is indicated. If a publisher has a distinct address for certain
kinds of correspondence--such as writing to report shorts or wrong titles,
or requesting permission to return, etc.--the address is shown under the
heading, ADDRESS FOR CORRESPONDENCE. For address of returns, see the
discussion under RETURN POLICY.

PREPAYMENT: Because of the high cost of billing and maintaining
accounts with libraries, many publishers specify terms of cash-with-order
for libraries which place only a few orders. Orders totalling less than a
set amount, or all orders from certain publishers, must be accompanied by
payment. Otherwise, the orders are returned unfilled, causing delays for
libraries in receiving books and inconvenience to publishers.

DISCOUNT POLICY: A publisher's library discount policy is an
important factor when considering direct orders. While some publishers
provide a favorable discount to libraries, others allow only a small one,
and some, no discount to libraries. Since many publishers provide a more
generous discount to library wholesalers than to libraries themselves,
especially when the wholesalers buy multiple copies, some wholesalers can
pass on to the library some part of the discount they get from publishers.
Consequently, libraries often receive a larger discount from well-selected
wholesalers than from publishers. Only from certain publishers may
libraries receive more discount than from wholesalers. Also, the discount
rate is often dependent on the size of an order a library is placing.
Librarians should know the discount policies of individual publishers.

In determining the volume of orders, some publishers go by number of
copies per title, while others count the number of assorted books in one
order. Publishers often classify their output into several categories.
"Long discount" items, which include trade titles, receive more discount
than "short discount" items, and long discount rates usually grow with the
number of books ordered. The rate for short discount items, which include
technical and text books, is usually fixed and does not increase regardless
of the number of copies ordered. These discount rates are for ordinary
(firm) orders unless otherwise noted. Some publishers apply a different
rate for shipments on an approval plan or for standing orders. This special
rate is sometimes applied to orders for all backlist titles and reorders for
additional copies from the libraries having a standing order or approval
plan.

RETURN POLICY: Librarians should be aware of the circumstances involved in cases when they have to return books to a publisher. Returns may be caused either by an error of the publisher in shipping or manufacturing, or by a mistake by the ordering library. Although a careful check prior to ordering reduces the number of library errors, librarians often have to send out orders without final verification, since a primary requirement is to obtain books for readers as soon as possible. They cannot delay the orders for a long period of time simply to eliminate all possible errors. For this reason, an order librarian needs to consider the possibility or the convenience of returns when placing an order.

Publishers' policies regarding the requirement of prior written permission for returns are noted. When there is no specific instruction, librarians are advised to apply Guidelines for Handling Library Orders for In-Print Monographic Publications (Chicago: American Library Association, 1973). In general, when an unordered or defective book is received, it may be returned automatically. If the error is caused by the ordering library, prior permission to return is generally required.

Some other return restrictions imposed by publishers are also noted. These include types of non-returnable titles, if there are any, acceptable physical condition of the books to be returned, and time limits set by the publisher. Librarians should pay special attention to the address returned books are sent to since many publishers have a special address for this purpose. When books are returned to a wrong address, the publisher must forward them to their warehouse facilities. This not only causes delay in adjustment to libraries, but an inconvenience to publishers. Some publishers credit less than the purchase price for books returned to their editorial offices in order to compensate for the transferring cost. Whether a librarian should return books to the order address or to a different address is noted for most publishers.

SHIPPING AND BILLING POLICY: There is a variety of shipping and billing practices among publishers. Many publishers charge for shipping and add this amount to the invoice. Some publishers pay shipping costs for libraries. There are quite a few publishers who charge libraries the shipping cost when they bill, but pay the shipping for prepaid orders. There are a few publishers who have two different discount rates according to who pays the shipping charge. Some publishers charge billing or handling costs in addition to postage. This charge is normally less than $2.00, but is sometimes much higher. Librarians need to consider the amount of actual discount they are getting from a certain publisher.

On routine orders where billing is necessary, publishers either enclose the invoice with the shipment, or send the shipment with a packing slip (list) and mail the invoice separately to the billing address. Most publishers usually honor a library's request to send invoices and shipments to two different addresses.

BACK ORDER POLICY: When books are currently unavailable but are expected to be published or re-stocked within a set period of time, many publishers usually report the expected date of availability and back order the books which are then automatically shipped upon their availability. The length of back order period differs from publisher to publisher; some follow the time-limit set by the ordering library. Other publishers immediately cancel all titles that cannot be filled at the time of the order and advise the library of the expected date of a book's availability. In such cases, libraries have to keep the orders on file and reorder at the appropriate time. Libraries' instructions are followed by many publishers, and it is advisable to indicate the action desired to be taken by the publisher if titles ordered are not immediately available.

STANDING ORDERS/SPECIAL PLANS: Libraries can expect several advantages from placing a standing order or by joining a special plan offered to libraries by publishers. By placing a carefully selected standing order/special plan, libraries can receive quality titles automatically upon publication (sometimes before publication date) without going through routine selection and ordering processes. Many publishers provide a special discount for standing orders and/or special order shipments, thus enabling libraries to save substantially. The publishers' policies stated in this book are brief summaries, and libraries planning to place a standing order or to join a special plan are advised to contact the publisher for more details and an application form. Detailed discussion of the advantages and disadvantages of various standing orders and special plans may be found in the library literature.

DISTRIBUTION/IMPRINTS: The merging of two or more publishers and the purchase or sale of one publisher by another is one of the characteristics of the contemporary publishing industry. When they merge or are purchased, some publishers retain their identity and keep their independent sales function. Except for their names, others completely lose their identity and follow entirely the policies of the new parent company. Another trend today is for a publisher, in order to cut costs, to arrange with another publisher the distribution of all its publications. In addition to the publishers with listings of policies, this book includes cross references from publishers whose books are often published and announced independently but are actually sold under the policies of the parent organization or of the publisher to whom they have given distribution rights. The addresses for orders, returns policies, etc. are also those of the referred-to publishers, with only few exceptions.

```
*****************************************
              POLICIES OF PUBLISHERS
*****************************************
```

AARP BOOKS see LITTLE, BROWN AND COMPANY

ABC-CLIO

2040 A.P.S.
Box 4397
Santa Barbara, California 93140
Telephone: 805-963-4221
          800-422-2546
          800-824-2103 (Calif.)

ADDRESS FOR ORDERS:

Same as above.

PREPAYMENT:

Not required.

DISCOUNT POLICY:

Libraries receive a 15% discount on
standing orders only.

RETURN POLICY:

Return permission must be requested in
advance. The original invoice number
must be cited on the written request and
the packing slip. Returns must be in
clean, unmarked, and salable condition.
Returns must be made within one year from
the date of original billing. Only
titles which remain in print may be
returned for credit.

Imperfect books must be accompanied by
an indication of the imperfection.
Returns can only be accepted for credit.
Any return not complying with the above
policy will be returned to sender at
sender's expense.

SHIPPING AND BILLING POLICY:

Libraries pay shipping charge. The
amount of shipping charge is determined
by weight and destination of freight.

Invoices are enclosed with shipment
unless otherwise instructed.

BACK ORDER POLICY:

Titles not currently available are either
cancelled or back ordered according to
library's instruction.

SPECIAL ORDER PLAN:

Publisher accepts standing orders for
books in series at a 15% discount.

AMPHOTO see WATSON-GUPTILL PUBLICATIONS

ASA INC. see AVIATION BOOK COMPANY

ASTM see AMERICAN SOCIETY FOR TESTING AND
MATERIALS

AVI see VAN NOSTRAND REINHOLD COMPANY

ABBOT COMPANY see AVIATION BOOK COMPANY

ABINGDON PRESS

---

201 Eighth Avenue South
Nashville, Tennessee 37202
Telephone: 615-749-6451

ADDRESS FOR ORDERS:

Same as above.

DISTRIBUTION/IMPRINT:

Festival

PREPAYMENT:

Not required.

DISCOUNT POLICY:

Libraries receive a 25% discount regardless of number of books ordered.

RETURN POLICY:

Publisher requests libraries obtain written permission before shipping returns. Address for returns and orders is the same.

SHIPPING AND BILLING POLICY:

Libraries pay postage. There is no handling or billing charge. Invoices are sent separately after shipments. Packing slips are enclosed in shipments.

BACK ORDER POLICY:

Titles not currently available are either back ordered or cancelled according to library instructions.

ABLEX PUBLISHING CORPORATION

---

355 Chestnut Street
Norwood, New Jersey 07648
Telephone: 201-767-8450

ADDRESS FOR ORDERS:

Same as above.
Telephone: 201-767-8455

PREPAYMENT:

Prepayment is required if library does not have an open account.

DISCOUNT POLICY:

20% discount to libraries.

RETURN POLICY:

Returns in salable condition are accepted within one year from invoice date.

SHIPPING AND BILLING POLICY:

Libraries are charged shipping (Book Rate) plus handling ($1.00 for 1-3 books; $1.50 for 4-6 books; $2.00 for 7-9 books; $2.50 for 10 books or more) except on prepaid orders which are shipped free. Invoices are sent with shipments unless the library specifies otherwise.

BACK ORDER POLICY:

Publisher back orders unavailable titles and ships books when they become available, or queries after six months.

SPECIAL PLANS:

Standing orders are available for serial publications.

ACADEMIC PRESS

1250 Sixth Avenue
San Diego, California 92101
Telephone: 619-699-6345

ADDRESS FOR ORDERS:

Academic Press
465 S. Lincoln Drive
Troy, Missouri 63379
Telephone: 800-321-5068

PREPAYMENT:

Not required if an account is established with the Credit Department.

DISCOUNT POLICY:

10% discount to libraries.

RETURN POLICY:

Permission is not required. Returns are accepted within 18 months. Returns should be sent with postage prepaid to: Academic Press Returns Dept/465 S. Lincoln Dr/Troy, MO 63379.

SHIPPING AND BILLING POLICY:

Shipping is free on prepaid orders; $2.00 handling charged is included with shipping charge on billed orders. Invoices are sent separately after shipments.

BACK ORDER POLICY:

Items are held on back order for up to six months.

SPECIAL PLANS:

Library standing order plan is available through publisher's representatives.

ACADEMIC THERAPY PUBLICATIONS, INC.

20 Commercial Boulevard
Novato, California 94949
Telephone: 415-883-3314

ADDRESS FOR ORDERS:

Same as above.

DISTRIBUTION/IMPRINTS:

Libraries should contact publisher for list.

PREPAYMENT:

Prepayment required on orders under $15.00.

DISCOUNT POLICY:

No discount to libraries.

RETURN POLICY:

Returns are accepted within 3 months. Written permission is required, and requests must include the invoice number.

SHIPPING AND BILLING POLICY:

Libraries are charged handling of $1.50 on orders under $15.00 and 10% on all others. Invoices are sent separately after shipments.

BACK ORDER POLICY:

Publisher back orders unavailable titles and ships books when they become available.

ACADEMY BOOKS see CHARLES E. TUTTLE COMPANY, INC.

ACADEMY EDITIONS see ST. MARTIN'S PRESS

ACOMA BOOKS

P.O. Box 4
Ramona, California 92065-0004
Telephone: 619-789-1288

ADDRESS FOR ORDERS:

Same as above.

PREPAYMENT:

Prepayment is required on orders of less than $25.00.

DISCOUNT POLICY:

0-4 books: no discount
5 or more: 20%

RETURN POLICY:

No returns are accepted except for defective books.

SHIPPING AND BILLING POLICY:

Libraries are charged shipping plus handling ($1.50 for the first books and $0.50 for each additional book). Invoices are always sent with shipments.

BACK ORDER POLICY:

Orders for titles that are out of stock are cancelled.

ADDISON-WESLEY PUBLISHING CO.

Reading, Massachusetts 01867
Telephone: 800-447-2226

ADDRESS FOR ORDERS:

Same as above.

PREPAYMENT:

Not required.

DISCOUNT POLICY:

Libraries receive a 25% discount on all General Books regardless of number of books ordered.

RETURN POLICY:

No return permission is required. Returns are limited to one year from the date of purchase. The address for returns is: Addison-Wesley Publishing Company, 5851 Guion Road, Indianapolis, IN 46254.

SHIPPING AND BILLING POLICY:

Libraries pay postage. There is no handling or billing charge. Invoices are sent separately after shipments.

BACK ORDER POLICY:

Publisher back orders titles currently unavailable and reports approximate availability dates. If library requests, publisher cancels back orders and advises on availability date.

SPECIAL ORDER PLAN:

On Standing Order Plan, libraries receive automatic shipments of new books on categories requested by libraries.

_____

AGATHON PRESS, INC.
_____

111 Eighth Avenue
New York, New York 10011
Telephone: 212-741-3087

ADDRESS FOR ORDERS:

Same as above.

PREPAYMENT:

Not required except for journals.

DISCOUNT POLICY:

No discount to libraries except for occasional special offers.

RETURN POLICY:

Returns are accepted for damaged or defective books only.

SHIPPING AND BILLING POLICY:

Publisher pays postage on prepaid orders; otherwise, libraries are charged

shipping at Fourth Class Book Rate plus a handling charge of $0.50 for the first book, $0.20 for each of the next four books, and $0.10 per book thereafter. Invoices are sent with shipments unless the library specifies otherwise.

BACK ORDER POLICY:

Orders are held until the book is available unless there is a time limit on the library's order; in either event, the library is notified of the delay or asked to reorder when the book is published.

SPECIAL PLANS:

A standing order is available for Higher Education Handbook at a 15% discount. No returns are accepted.

_____

AGLOW PUBLICATIONS
_____

P.O. Box 1548
Lynnwood, Washington 98020

ADDRESS FOR ORDERS:

Same as above.

PREPAYMENT:

Not required.

DISCOUNT POLICY:

30% discount to libraries.

RETURN POLICY:

Returns are accepted within one year from invoice date. Addresses for returns: (for UPS) 7821 224th S.W./Edmonds, WA 98020; (for parcel post) Parcel Post/Box I/Lynnwood, WA 98046.

SHIPPING AND BILLING POLICY:

Libraries are charged actual shipping on billed orders; prepaid orders are charged 15% of sale (maximum of $7.00) plus tax, if applicable. Invoices are sent after shipments.

BACK ORDER POLICY:

Publisher back orders unavailable titles and ships books when they become available. An account can be programmed for no back orders if library prefers.

SPECIAL PLANS:

A standing order plan for publisher's magazines is available at 30% discount.

AIR AND SPACE COMPANY see AVIATION BOOK COMPANY

AIRGUIDE PUBLICATIONS see AVIATION BOOK COMPANY

ALABAMA REVIEW see UNIVERSITY OF ALABAMA PRESS

ALADDIN BOOKS see MACMILLAN PUBLISHING COMPANY, INC.

ALASKA GEOGRAPHIC see ALASKA NORTHWEST PUBLISHING COMPANY

ALASKA NORTHWEST PUBLISHING COMPANY

130 Second Avenue South
Edmonds, Washington 98020
Telephone: 206-744-4111

ADDRESS FOR ORDERS:

Same as above.

DISTRIBUTION/IMPRINT:

Alaska Northwest Publishing Company distributes publications of Alaska Geographic.

PREPAYMENT:

Not required.

DISCOUNT POLICY:

Libraries receive a 20% discount on all orders.

RETURN POLICY:

No prior permission is necessary to return books. However, returns are limited to after 90 days but within one year from invoice date. The address for returns is the same as for orders.

SHIPPING AND BILLING POLICY:

Publisher charges shipping costs to libraries. There is no other handling charge. Invoices are sent with shipment.

BACK ORDER POLICY:

Publisher back orders unavailable titles if requested by library.

ALBA HOUSE COMMUNICATIONS see ALBA HOUSE PUBLISHERS

ALBA HOUSE PUBLISHERS

Society of St. Paul
2187 Victory Boulevard
Staten Island, New York 10314
Telephone: 212-698-2759

ADDRESS FOR ORDERS:

Same as above.

DISTRIBUTION/IMPRINTS:

Distributes: Daughters of St. Paul; Alba House Communications; Alba House (Sydney)

PREPAYMENT:

Not required.

DISCOUNT POLICY:

$10.00-$24.99:   10% discount
$25.00 and over: 20%

RETURN POLICY:

Returns of defective books only are accepted within 90 days.

SHIPPING AND BILLING POLICY:

Libraries are charged shipping. Invoices are sent with shipments unless the library specifies otherwise.

BACK ORDER POLICY:

Publisher back orders unavailable titles and ships books when they become available.

SPECIAL PLANS:

A standing order plan is available.

ALFRED PUBLISHING COMPANY, INC.

16380 Roscoe Boulevard
P.O. Box 10003
Van Nuys, California 91410-0003
Telephone: 818-891-5999

ADDRESS FOR ORDERS:

Same as above.

DISTRIBUTION/IMPRINTS:

Distributes: Cherry Lane; Lawson-Gould; Dover.

PREPAYMENT:

Prepayment is required for orders under $100 unless the library has an open account. Publisher requires a minimum order of $20.00.

DISCOUNT POLICY:

10% discount to libraries.

RETURN POLICY:

All publications are sold on a non-returnable basis. Short shipments and defective books are reshipped at publisher's expense within 30 days. Misshipments are reshipped and rebilled, and credit is issued upon return. Address for returns: Alfred's Distribution Center/5166 Commercial Drive/Yorkville, NY 13495-0205.

SHIPPING AND BILLING POLICY:

Libraries are charged shipping. Invoices are sent with shipments.

BACK ORDER POLICY:

Publisher back orders all publications unless instructed otherwise.

OTHER:

Publisher prefers that libraries order through wholesalers

ALGOL PRESS see BORGO PRESS

ALGONQUIN BOOKS see TAYLOR PUBLISHING COMPANY

ALICE JAMES BOOKS

---

33 Richdale Avenue
Cambridge, Massachusetts 02140
Telephone: 617-354-1408

ADDRESS FOR ORDERS:

Same as above.

PREPAYMENT:

Not required.

DISCOUNT POLICY:

Discounts on cloth editions for
libraries: 2-3 books: 10%
            4-9 books: 15%
            10 or more: 20%

RETURN POLICY:

Returns are accepted within one year if they are in salable condition. Prior written permission is required.

SHIPPING AND BILLING POLICY:

Orders are shipped postpaid. Invoices are sent with books unless otherwise requested.

BACK ORDER POLICY:

All books not in stock are shipped as soon as they are received.

STANDING ORDER PLANS:

Standing orders accepted for the four books published, in pairs, each year. 10% discount offered.

ALLEN & UNWIN, INC.

8 Winchester Place
Winchester, Massachusetts 01890
Telephone: 617-729-0830
        800-547-8889

ADDRESS FOR ORDERS:

Same as above.

DISTRIBUTION/IMPRINTS:

Distributes Priority Press Publications.
Pandora Press (Imprint)

PREPAYMENT:

Not required.

DISCOUNT POLICY:

20% discount on orders of 5 or more
titles.

RETURN POLICY:

Returns of books in salable condition
and still in print are accepted without
written permission. Address for returns:
Allen & Unwin/c/o Publishers Storage &
Shipping Corp/231 Industrial Park/
Fitchburg, MA 01420.

SHIPPING AND BILLING POLICY:

Libraries are charged shipping. Invoices
are sent with shipments.

BACK ORDER POLICY:

Publisher will back order for one year.

SPECIAL PLANS:

Standing orders for series are
available.

OTHER:

Publisher prefers that libraries order
through wholesalers.

ALTA RESEARCH see AVIATION BOOK COMPANY

ALYSON PUBLICATIONS

40 Plympton Street
Boston, Massachusetts 02118
Telephone: 617-542-5679

ADDRESS FOR ORDERS:

Same as above.

DISTRIBUTION:

Distributes publications of GMP
Publishers Ltd. (London)

PREPAYMENT:

Not required.

DISCOUNT POLICY:

No discount to libraries.

RETURN POLICY:

Full credit for books returned within
one year of purchase. Written permission
is not required.

SHIPPING AND BILLING POLICY:

Shipping costs are billed to the
library. Invoices are sent with
shipments unless otherwise requested.

BACK ORDER POLICY:

Books not in stock are automatically
back ordered unless the library
requests otherwise.

AMADEUS PRESS see TIMBER PRESS

AMERICAN ACADEMY IN ROME see PENNSYLVANIA
STATE UNIVERSITY PRESS

AMERICAN ANTIQUARIAN SOCIETY see
UNIVERSITY PRESS OF VIRGINIA

AMERICAN ASSOCIATION FOR THE ADVANCEMENT
    OF SCIENCE (AAAS)

1333 H Street, NW
Washington, DC 20005
Telephone: 202-326-6450

ADDRESS FOR ORDERS:

AAAS Product Distribution Center
P.O. Box 10982
Des Moines, Iowa 50340
Telephone: 515-246-6857

PREPAYMENT:

Required for orders under $10.00 or over $150.00.

DISCOUNT POLICY:

Discounts apply only to bulk quantities of the same item ordered at the same time and are valid only for non-member rates:

1-4 copies: no discount;
5-19 copies: 20%; etc.

RETURN POLICY:

Books in salable condition can be returned within 30 days. Prior permission is not required. Return to Iowa address.

SHIPPING AND BILLING POLICY:

Shipping costs plus $2.00 handling charge per order billed to the library. Invoices are sent separately after shipments.

BACK ORDER POLICY:

Out-of-print books may be obtained from University Microfilms International.

_____

AMERICAN ASSOCIATION OF RETIRED PERSONS see LITTLE, BROWN AND COMPANY

_____

AMERICAN ATHEIST PRESS
_____

P.O. Box 2117
Austin, Texas 78768-2117
Telephone: 512-458-1244

ADDRESS FOR ORDERS:

Same as above.

DISTRIBUTION/IMPRINTS:

Gustav Broukal Press (Imprint)

PREPAYMENT:

Prepayment is required on all orders.

DISCOUNT POLICY:

20% discount to libraries.

RETURN POLICY:

All books in salable condition can be returned for full credit within six months of invoice date. The packing slip accompanying the returns must show invoice number and date. No prior permission is required.

SHIPPING AND BILLING POLICY:

Libraries are charged shipping of $1.00 for orders under $20.00 or $2.50 for orders over $20.00. Invoices are sent with shipments unless the library specifies otherwise.

BACK ORDER POLICY:

Publisher returns payment and informs the library when the material is again available.

OTHER:

Libraries should request publisher's list since many materials available through AAP are not available elsewhere.

_____

AMERICAN BAR ASSOCIATION see INDEPENDENT PUBLISHERS GROUP

_____

_____

AMERICAN CHEMICAL SOCIETY
_____

1155 Sixteenth Street, NW
Washington, DC 20036
Telephone: 202-872-4363

ADDRESS FOR ORDERS:

American Chemical Society
Distribution Office
1155 Sixteenth Street, NW
Washington, DC 20036

PREPAYMENT:

Prepayment, credit card, and institutional purchase orders are accepted.

DISCOUNT POLICY:

List prices are net for library orders.

RETURN POLICY:

Written authorization is required before returning books. There is a 30 day review period for all books. 100% credit is given for all books returned in resalable condition within one year of invoice date. The address for returns is: Maple Press Distribution Center, Returns Department, 60 Grumbacher Road, 1-83 Industrial Park, P.O. Box M100, Yor, PA 17405.

SHIPPING AND BILLING POLICY:

Publisher pays 4th class postage for domestic prepaid orders. Shipping/handling charge is added to unpaid orders. Invoices are sent separately from shipments.

SPECIAL ORDER PLAN:

Primary Access to Chemical Titles is a standing order plan for American Chemical Society Advances in Chemistry Series, American Chemical Society Symposium Series, and American Chemical Society Monograph Series. Libraries may place a standing order for selected subject categories or for all subjects from the above mentioned series. All books are shipped immediately upon publication and billed on a 30-day approval. Libraries may return unwanted titles for credit.

OTHER INFORMATION:

Rush orders can be placed by:

    Toll free 1-800-227-5558
    Telex No. 440159
    Cable JIECHEM
    FAX 202-872-4615

AMERICAN DIALECT SOCIETY see UNIVERSITY OF ALABAMA PRESS

AMERICAN ENTERPRISE INSTITUTE see UNIVERSITY PRESS OF AMERICA

AMERICAN GEOGRAPHIC see FALCON PRESS PUBLISHING COMPANY

AMERICAN HISTORY PRESS see CONSERVATORY OF AMERICAN LETTERS

AMERICAN INSTITUTE OF AERONAUTICS AND ASTRONAUTICS

370 L'Enfant Promenade S.W.
Washington, D.C. 20024
Telephone: 202-646-7400

ADDRESS FOR ORDERS:

Same as above.

PREPAYMENT:

Required for orders under $50.00.

DISCOUNT POLICY:

No discount to libraries.

RETURN POLICY:

Returns are accepted within 15 days; prior permission is not required.

SHIPPING AND BILLING POLICY:

$4.50 shipping charge per library order. Invoices are sent separately only.

BACK ORDER POLICY:

Order is held if book will be available; otherwise, publisher will notify.

STANDING ORDER PLANS:

Standing orders are available for Education Series and Progress Series.

AMERICAN INSTITUTE OF CHEMICAL ENGINEERS

345 East 47th Street
New York, New York 10017
Telephone: 212-705-7321

ADDRESS FOR ORDERS:

Address book orders to:

AIChE
Publications Sales
345 East 47th Street
New York, NY 10017
Telephone: 212-705-7657
Telex: 710 581 5267 ASME NY
Fax: 212-752-3294

Address periodicals orders to:

AIChE
Subscriptions Department
345 East 47th Street
New York, NY 10017
Telephone: 212-705-7663

PREPAYMENT:

Payment must accompany all orders. U.S.
standing order subscribers accepting
publisher's no return policy are the only
exceptions to the prepayment requirement.

Check or money order must accompany all
U.S. orders not paid by credit card.

DISCOUNT POLICY:

Special discounts are available on
multiple copy orders of books. Special
discounted package plans (for books and
journals) are also offered. Contact the
publisher for detail.

RETURN POLICY:

All publication sales are final. Order
carefully.

SHIPPING AND BILLING POLICY:

There is no charge for postage or
handling on U.S. orders when prepaid and
shipped surface or bookrate. When faster
service is required, specify "First Class
Mail" and add $2 postage to the price of
each book. For "Air Mail" postage,
contact AIChE to determine cost.

SPECIAL ORDER PLAN:

Publisher accepts standing orders for
AIChE Symposium & Monograph Series,
Center for Chemical Process Safety
publications, Chemical Engineering
Faculties and Meetings Papers on
Microfiche.

AMERICAN LIBRARY ASSOCIATION

Publishing Services
50 East Huron Street

Chicago, Illinois 60611
Telephone: 312-944-6780
          800-545-2433 (in US)
          800-545-2444 (in IL)
          800-545-2455 (in Canada)

ADDRESS FOR ORDERS:

Same as above.

DISTRIBUTION/IMPRINTS:

Distributes the publications of: Library
Association Publishing, Ltd. (London);
Clive Bingley, Ltd. (London).

PREPAYMENT:

Institutions may order on account.

DISCOUNT POLICY:

10% discount to members of American
Library Association.

RETURN POLICY:

All returns must be authorized in
writing within nine months from invoice
date. Requests should be addressed to
Customer Service.

SHIPPING AND BILLING POLICY:

Shipping and handling charges ($1.00 for
orders up to $20.00; $2.00 for orders of
$20.01 - $50.00; $3.00 for orders of
$50.01 - $100.00; $4.00 for orders of
$100.01 - $200.00; $5.00 for orders over
$200.00) are added to billed orders
only. Invoices are sent separately after
shipments only.

BACK ORDER POLICY:

Titles will remain on back order for as
long as the library specifies.

SPECIAL PLANS:

Publisher offers 18 different approval
categories with return privileges.
Divisional publications are not
included. Interested libraries should
contact publisher for details.

AMERICAN LIFE BOOKS

P.O. Box 349
Watkins Glen, New York 14891
Telephone: 607-535-4737

ADDRESS FOR ORDERS:

Same as above.

DISTRIBUTION/IMPRINTS:

Library of Victorian Culture (Imprint)

PREPAYMENT:

Not required.

DISCOUNT POLICY:

No discount to libraries.

RETURN POLICY:

Books may be returned within 60 days for a refund or cancellation of the invoice.

SHIPPING AND BILLING POLICY:

Publisher pays shipping charges. Invoices are sent with shipments.

BACK ORDER POLICY:

Orders are cancelled for material that is not available.

AMERICAN LITERARY ASSOCIATION see PACIFIC INFORMATION INC.

AMERICAN MATHEMATICAL SOCIETY

P.O. Box 6248
Providence, Rhode Island 02940
Telephone: 401-272-9500

ADDRESS FOR ORDERS WITH REMITTANCE:

American Mathematical Society
P.O. Box 1571. Annex Station
Providence, RI 02901-9930

ADDRESS FOR CORRESPONDENCE:

American Mathematical Society
P.O. Box 6248
Providence, RI 02940

PREPAYMENT:

Prepayment is required.

DISCOUNT POLICY:

Libraries of institutional members of the society who order directly from the society are granted a 20% discount on most books published by the society and on back numbers of the journals. No discount to non-member libraries.

RETURN POLICY:

Publisher requires written permission for returns. Book returns are limited to one year from the date of invoice for non-members. The address for returns is: AMS Warehouse, 201 Charles Street, Providence, RI 02904.

SHIPPING AND BILLING POLICY:

Books are sent via surface mail unless air delivery is requested. The shipping and handling charge is $2 for the first book, $1 for each additional books, up to $25.

BACK ORDER POLICY:

Titles currently unavailable are reported and back ordered.

SPECIAL ORDER PLAN:

Standing orders are accepted for books in a series. Journal subscriptions must be prepaid and renewed annually.

AMERICAN PHILOSOPHICAL SOCIETY

---

104 South Fifth Street
Philadelphia, Pennsylvania 19106
Telephone: 215-627-0706

ADDRESS FOR ORDERS:

Academic Services
c/o P.O. Box 40098
Philadelphia, PA 19106
Telephone: 617-828-8450

PREPAYMENT:

Prepayment is required.

DISCOUNT POLICY:

No discount to libraries.

RETURN POLICY:

Invoices should accompany returns. Written permission is not required.

SHIPPING AND BILLING POLICY:

Publisher pays postage on prepaid orders. Invoices are sent separately prior to shipment.

BACK ORDER POLICY:

Checks are held until items are available.

SPECIAL PLANS:

Standing orders are available for publisher's Proceedings, Memoirs (20% discount), and Transactions (30-40% discount).

AMERICAN PHOTOGRAPHIC BOOKS PUBLISHING COMPANY see WATSON-GUPTILL PUBLICATIONS

AMERICAN POETRY AND LITERATURE PRESS

P.O. Box 2013
Upper Darby, Pennsylvania 19082
Telephone: 215-352-5438

ADDRESS FOR ORDERS:

Same as above.

PREPAYMENT:

Not required.

DISCOUNT POLICY:

25% discount to libraries.

RETURN POLICY:

Returns are accepted for full credit or refund. Written permission is not required, and there is no time limit for returns. Return address (UPS): Building B, Number 206/Long Lane & Bradford Rd/ Upper Darby, PA 19082.

SHIPPING AND BILLING POLICY:

Libraries are charged actual Book Rate postage. Invoices are sent with shipments unless the library specifies otherwise.

AMERICAN PSYCHIATRIC PRESS, INC.

1400 K Street NW, Suite 1101
Washington, D.C. 20005
Telephone: 202-682-6262

ADDRESS FOR ORDERS:

Same as above.
Telephone: 800-368-5777

PREPAYMENT:

Not required with purchase order.

DISCOUNT POLICY:

Members of Mental Health Librarian's Association receive a 15% discount.

RETURN POLICY:

Returns of damaged books or books sent incorrectly do not require permission; otherwise write to Ms. Helena Jones for permission, within 15 days if possible.

SHIPPING AND BILLING POLICY:

Libraries are charged actual shipping (UPS) on all orders. Invoices are sent with shipments.

BACK ORDER POLICY:

Back orders are accepted.

AMERICAN QUILTERS SOCIETY see COLLECTOR BOOKS

AMERICAN SCHOOL OF CLASSICAL STUDIES

Publications Committee
Institute for Advanced Study
Princeton, New Jersey 08543-0631
Telephone: 601-734-8386

ADDRESS FOR ORDERS:

Same as above.
Telephone: 601-734-8387

PREPAYMENT:

Not required.

DISCOUNT POLICY:

Discounts of 10% (hardcover) and 20% (booklets) are offered to libraries that belong to universities that are cooperating institutions of the ASCSA.

RETURN POLICY:

Hardcover books may be returned for credit. Booklets are not returnable. Libraries pay return postage.

SHIPPING AND BILLING POLICY:

Libraries are charged actual shipping on all orders. Invoices are sent with shipments unless the library specifies otherwise.

BACK ORDER POLICY:

All titles are available.

SPECIAL PLANS:

A standing order is available upon request in writing. Pre-publication prices apply to standing orders.

AMERICAN SCIENCES PRESS

20 Cross Road
Syracuse, New York 13224-2144
Telephone:

ADDRESS FOR ORDERS:

Same as above.

PREPAYMENT:

Orders are Pro-forma.

DISCOUNT POLICY:

No discount to libraries.

RETURN POLICY:

Returns are accepted within six months. Prior written authorization is required.

SHIPPING AND BILLING POLICY:

Shipping and handling are added to invoices.

BACK ORDER POLICY:

Back orders are accepted.

SPECIAL PLANS:

Standing orders are accepted.

AMERICAN SHOWCASE see WATSON-GUPTILL PUBLICATIONS

AMERICAN SOCIETY FOR TESTING AND MATERIALS (ASTM)

1916 Race Street
Philadelphia, Pennsylvania 19103
Telephone: 215-299-5400

ADDRESS FOR ORDERS:

ASTM Customer Service
1916 Race Street
Philadelphia, PA 19103
Telephone: 215-299-5585

PREPAYMENT:

Not required.

DISCOUNT POLICY:

10-20% discount, depending on publication, to ASTM members.

RETURN POLICY:

Written permission is required unless the order was improperly filled or the book has been damaged.

SHIPPING AND BILLING POLICY:

Libraries pay shipping/handling charges of 7% ($1.50 minimum) on billed orders; there is no shipping/handling charged on prepaid orders. Invoices are sent separately.

BACK ORDER POLICY:

Publisher will back order items that have been priced.

SPECIAL PLANS:

Standing orders are available.

AMERICAN UNIVERSITY IN CAIRO PRESS see
COLUMBIA UNIVERSITY PRESS

AMERICAN UNIVERSITY OF BEIRUT see
SYRACUSE UNIVERSITY PRESS

ANALYTIC PRESS see LAWRENCE ERLBAUM
ASSOCIATES

ANCHOR FOUNDATION see PATHFINDER PRESS

ANCHORAGE PRESS

P.O. Box 8067
New Orleans, Louisiana 70182
Telephone: 504-283-8868

ADDRESS FOR ORDERS:

Same as above.

PREPAYMENT:

Not required.

DISCOUNT POLICY:

No discount to libraries.

RETURN POLICY:

Books ordered by libraries are not
returnable.

SHIPPING AND BILLING POLICY:

Libraries are charged shipping plus
$1.00 handling charge. Invoices are sent
as directed on purchase order.

BACK ORDER POLICY:

All titles not immediately available are
back ordered, and the library is
notified of the approximate date of
availability.

SPECIAL PLANS:

Publisher offers standing orders for all
new publications.

OTHER:

Anchorage Press publishes plays for
Children's Theatre and textbooks for
drama and theatre.

AND BOOKS

702 S. Michigan
South Bend, Indiana 46618
Telephone: 219-232-3134

ADDRESS FOR ORDERS:

The Distributors
702 South Michigan
South Bend, Indiana 46618
Telephone: 219-232-8500

PREPAYMENT:

Required until an account is
established.

DISCOUNT POLICY:

1-4 copies: 10%
5-14 copies: 30%
over 15:   40%

RETURN POLICY:

Books in salable condition may be
returned for full credit after three
months and before one year of invoice
date. If the original invoice does not
accompany the returns, credit will be at
the minimum discount. Calendars are non-
returnable after January 31. Send
returns to The Distributors.

SHIPPING AND BILLING POLICY:

Libraries are charged shipping (UPS) on
all orders. Invoices are sent with
shipments.

BACK ORDER POLICY:

Back orders are placed until cancelled
or book arrives.

SPECIAL PLANS:

Publisher offers standing orders to
various series at a 20% discount. As
each new title is received, the library

is billed, and the book is shipped under the above return policy.

AND/OR PRESS, INC.

Box 2246
Berkeley, California 94702
Telephone: 415-548-2124

ADDRESS FOR ORDERS:

Same as above.

PREPAYMENT:

Prepayment is required for orders of fewer than 5 copies.

DISCOUNT POLICY:

5 copies: 25%
over 5:   40%

RETURN POLICY:

Returns are accepted within nine months. Written permission is required. Address for returns: 11A Commercial Blvd/Novato, California 94947.

SHIPPING AND BILLING POLICY:

Libraries are charged actual shipping. Invoices are sent with shipments.

BACK ORDER POLICY:

Back orders are cancelled after six months.

ANGEL BOOKS see DUFOUR EDITIONS, INC.

ANGUS & ROBERTSON see SALEM HOUSE PUBLISHERS

ANN ARBOR SCIENCE see TECHNOMIC PUBLISHING COMPANY

ANNUAL REVIEWS, INC.

4139 El Camino Way
P.O. Box 10139
Palo Alto, California 94303-8097
Telephone: 415-493-4400

ADDRESS FOR ORDERS:

Same as above.

PREPAYMENT:

Not required as long as the library has an established credit account.

DISCOUNT POLICY:

No discount to libraries.

RETURN POLICY:

Written permission is required.

SHIPPING AND BILLING POLICY:

Postage via Fourth Class Book Rate is included in the base price of books. Libraries are charged only for special handling, etc. at their request. Invoices are sent separately in all cases.

BACK ORDER POLICY:

Back orders are placed, and books are shipped when available.

SPECIAL PLANS:

Publisher offers a standing order plan for each annual publication. 10% pre-publication discount is offered for standing orders provided that payment is received 30 days prior to publication.

ANTHROPOSOPHIC PRESS

Bells Pond, Star Route
Hudson, New York 12534
Telephone: 518-851-2054

ADDRESS FOR ORDERS:

Same as above.

DISTRIBUTION/IMPRINTS:

Distributes publications of Rudolf
Steiner Press (London).

PREPAYMENT:

Prepayment is required for orders of
fewer than ten books.

DISCOUNT POLICY:

No special discount for libraries.

RETURN POLICY:

Returns in salable condition and with
postage prepaid and accompanied by
invoice information are accepted within
one year. Written permission is
required. Claims for books received in
damaged condition must be made within 30
days of receipt.

SHIPPING AND BILLING POLICY:

Libraries are charged shipping charge of
3% (USPS) or 4.4%-8.8% (UPS, depending
upon zone). Invoices are sent with UPS
shipments or separately for USPS unless
the library specifies otherwise.

BACK ORDER POLICY:

Books in the process of being printed or
which are in transit to publisher are
back ordered unless library requests
otherwise.

SPECIAL PLANS:

A standing order plan for all new titles
is available at a 40% discount.

OTHER:

Publisher plans to have over 350 volumes
of Rudolf Steiner in English completed
by 2000.

APPALACHIAN CONSORTIUM PRESS

University Hall
Appalachian State University
Boone, North Carolina 28608
Telephone: (704) 262-2064

ADDRESS FOR ORDERS:

Same as above.

PREPAYMENT:

Not required.

DISCOUNT POLICY:

No discount to libraries.

RETURN POLICY:

Returns, in resalable condition, are
accepted no sooner than 90 days and no
later than one year from date of
receipt. Prior written permission is
required. Library pays shipping.

SHIPPING AND BILLING POLICY:

Shipping is charged at fourth class mail
rate. Invoices are sent with shipments.

BACK ORDER POLICY:

Back orders are held and cancelled only
upon request.

STANDING ORDER PLANS:

Available upon special request.

APPALACHIAN MOUNTAIN CLUB BOOKS

---

5 Joy Street
Boston, Massachusetts 02108
Telephone: 617-523-0636

ADDRESS FOR ORDERS:

Same as above.

PREPAYMENT:

No prepayment required after the first
order.

DISCOUNT POLICY:

1 book/map	no discount
2 or more books/maps	20%

RETURN POLICY:

Books and maps may be returned for 100%
credit between 3 months and 1 year from
date of invoice. Items must be prepaid
and in salable condition. Without
original invoices or invoice numbers,
returns will be credited at 50% of retail
value. Damaged books and maps are
returnable up to 60 days from date of

invoice. Written permission is not
required. The address for returns is the
same as for orders.

SHIPPING AND BILLING POLICY:

Publisher pays shipping cost on prepaid
orders. Invoices are sent separately
after shipment.

BACK ORDER POLICY:
Publisher notifies libraries of back
ordered items, and ships the items as
soon as they become available, unless
requested to cancel by library.

APPLETON AND LANGE PUBLISHING COMPANY

25 Van Zant Street
E. Norwalk, Connecticut 06855
Telephone: 203-838-4400

ADDRESS FOR ORDERS:

Appleton and Lange
c/o Prentice Hall
200 Old Tappan Road
Old Tappan, New Jersey 07675
Telephone: 800-922-0579
        201-767-5937

PREPAYMENT:

Not required.

DISCOUNT POLICY:

20% discount to libraries.

RETURN POLICY:

Returns are accepted within 30 days
after billing. Shrink-wrapped items that
have been opened are not returnable. No
written permission is required. Address
for returns: PH Distribution
Center/Route 59 and Brookhill Drive/ W.
Nyack, NY 10994.

SHIPPING AND BILLING POLICY:

Libraries pay shipping and handling
except on prepaid orders. Invoices are
sent separately after shipments.

BACK ORDER POLICY:

Back orders will be placed for items
that have been assigned an ISBN or if
the material is to be reprinted unless
the library requests otherwise.

SPECIAL PLANS:

A standing order plan for all new titles
is available as well as for specific
titles (Surgery Annual; Pathology
Annual; Urology Annual; and Current
Medical Diagnosis and Treatment).

APPLETON-CENTURY-CROFTS see PRENTICE-HALL

APPLEWOOD BOOKS see GLOBE PEQUOT PRESS

AQUARIAN PRESS see STERLING PUBLISHING
COMPANY, INC.

ARABESQUE BOOKS see BLACK SPARROW PRESS

ARCHITECTURAL HISTORY FOUNDATION BOOKS
see MIT PRESS

ARCHITECTURAL PRESS see VAN NOSTRAND
REINHOLD COMPANY

ARCHON BOOKS see SHOE STRING PRESS, INC.

ARCO PUBLISHING see PRENTICE-HALL

ARCTURUS BOOKS see SOUTHERN ILLINOIS
UNIVERSITY PRESS

ARIEL PRESS

P.O. Box 30975
4082 Clotts Road
Columbus, Ohio 43230
Telephone: 800-336-7769 (outside OH)
          800-336-7768 (in OH)

ADDRESS FOR ORDERS:

Same as above.

DISTRIBUTION/IMPRINTS:

Brindabella Books (Subsidiary)

PREPAYMENT:

Prepayment is required for orders of
fewer than five books.

DISCOUNT POLICY:

20% discount to libraries.

RETURN POLICY:

Books in salable condition are fully
returnable after six months. Libraries
should call or write for permission.

SHIPPING AND BILLING POLICY:

Publisher pays shipping on prepaid
orders; shipping is added to the bill
for billed orders. Invoices are sent
with shipments unless the library
specifies otherwise.

BACK ORDER POLICY:

Publisher back orders until the material
is available.

ARMS AND ARMOR see STERLING PUBLISHING
COMPANY, INC.

ART DIRECTION BOOK COMPANY

---

10 East 39th Street, 6th Floor
New York, New York 10016
Telephone: 212-889-6500

ADDRESS FOR ORDERS:

Same as above.

DISTRIBUTION/IMPRINTS:

Infosource Publications Inc. (Imprint)

PREPAYMENT:

Not required.

DISCOUNT POLICY:

20% discount to libraries.

RETURN POLICY:

Returns are accepted within one year.
Written permission is required.

SHIPPING AND BILLING POLICY:

Libraries are charged actual shipping
for whatever method of shipment is used
(parcel post, UPS). Invoices are sent
separately only.

BACK ORDER POLICY:

Back orders are shipped when available.

SPECIAL PLANS:

Standing orders are available for books
in series.

ART INSTITUTE OF CHICAGO MUSEUM STUDIES
see UNIVERSITY OF CHICAGO PRESS

ASHTON TATE see MCGRAW-HILL BOOK COMPANY

ASIA SOCIETY see CHARLES. E. TUTTLE
COMPANY, INC.

ASSOCIATED FACULTY PRESS, INC.

---

19 West 36th Street
New York, New York 10018
Telephone: 212-307-1300

ADDRESS FOR ORDERS:

Same as above.

DISTRIBUTION/IMPRINTS:

Kennikat Press (Imprint)

National University Publications
(Imprint)
Ira J. Friedman (Imprint)

PREPAYMENT:

Libraries are billed on open account.

DISCOUNT POLICY:

No discount to libraries.

RETURN POLICY:

Publisher does not accept returns when
books are shipped as ordered. To return
defective books, libraries should write
for return label.
SHIPPING AND BILLING POLICY:

Shipping charges are $2.25 for the first
book and $0.75 for each additional book.
Invoices are sent with shipments unless
the library specifies otherwise.

BACK ORDER POLICY:

Unavailable titles are back ordered; if
order is cancelled or expires, publisher
will write to library before shipping.

ASSOCIATED UNIVERSITY PRESSES

---

440 Forsgate Drive
Cranbury, New Jersey 08512
Telephone: 609-655-4770

ADDRESS FOR ORDERS:

Same as above.

DISTRIBUTION/IMPRINT:

Balch Institute for Ethnic Studies
Bucknell University Press
Cornwall Books
University of Delaware Press
Fairleigh Dickinson University Press
Folger Shakespeare Library
Lehigh University Press
Moravian Music Foundation
Ontario Film Institute
Susquehanna University Press
Virginia Center for the Creative Arts
Western Research Historical Society

PREPAYMENT:

Not required.

DISCOUNT POLICY:

There is a 10% discount for libraries.

RETURN POLICY:

Publisher requests that libraries write
for written permission before sending
return shipments. Returns are limited to
one year, and subscription publications
are not returnable.

SHIPPING AND BILLING POLICY:

Libraries pay shipping costs. The amount
is the actual freight charge.

BACK ORDER POLICY:

Publisher back orders unavailable titles
on request of libraries.

ASSOCIATION FOR ASIAN STUDIES see
UNIVERSITY OF ARIZONA PRESS

ASSOCIATION OF DEPARTMENT OF ENGLISH see
MODERN LANGUAGE ASSOCIATION OF AMERICA

ASSOCIATION OF DEPARTMENT OF LANGUAGES
see MODERN LANGUAGE ASSOCIATION OF
AMERICA

ATHENEUM PUBLISHERS see MACMILLAN
PUBLISHING COMPANY, INC.

ATHLETIC INSTITUTE see STERLING
PUBLISHING COMPANY, INC.

ATLANTIC MONTHLY PRESS see LITTLE, BROWN
AND COMPANY

AUBURN HOUSE PUBLISHING COMPANY

---

14 Dedham Street
Dover, Massachusetts 02030-0658

Telephone: 617-785-2220

ADDRESS FOR ORDERS:

Same as above.

PREPAYMENT:

Orders for single copies must be prepaid.

DISCOUNT POLICY:

No discount to libraries.

RETURN POLICY:

Books are not returnable from library accounts.

SHIPPING AND BILLING POLICY:

Libraries are charged shipping/handling of $3.00 for the first book and $1.00 for each additional book on all orders. Invoices are sent separately only.

BACK ORDER POLICY:

Books not yet published or temporarily out of stock are automatically back ordered unless library instructs otherwise.

SPECIAL PLANS:

Standing orders can be arranged; interested libraries should contact publisher.

AUDEL BOOKS see MACMILLAN PUBLISHING COMPANY, INC.

AUGUST HOUSE, INC.

P.O. Box 3223
Little Rock, Arkansas 72203
Telephone: 501-663-7300
         800-527-0924

ADDRESS FOR ORDERS:

Same as above.

DISTRIBUTION/IMPRINTS:

August House (Imprint)

American Folklore Series (Series)

PREPAYMENT:

Not required.

DISCOUNT POLICY:

10% discount for 5 copies or more;
25% to subscribers of American Folklore
 Series;
33% for approval plans.

RETURN POLICY:

Returns are accepted as long as the book is in print. Invoice numbers should accompany returns. Written permission is not required. Address for returns: August House/1820 Fair Park Blvd/Little Rock, AR 72204.

SHIPPING AND BILLING POLICY:

Libraries are charged actual shipping on all orders. Invoices are always sent with shipments, but an additional copy is sent if the billing address is different.

BACK ORDER POLICY:

Libraries are informed of back order status and estimated shipping date.

SPECIAL PLANS:

An approval plan with return privileges is available at a 33% discount.

AVE MARIA PRESS

Notre Dame, Indiana 46556-0428
Telephone: 219-287-2831

ADDRESS FOR ORDERS:

Same as above.

DISTRIBUTION/IMPRINTS:

Distributed also by Spring Arbor Distributors.

PREPAYMENT:

Prepayment is required on orders under $10.00.

DISCOUNT POLICY:

Orders of $25.00:   10% discount
$50.00 orders: 15%
$100.00 orders: 20%
$500.00 orders: 25%

RETURN POLICY:

Returns in resalable condition and
accompanied by invoice number, date, and
discount are accepted within 90 days.
Written permission is required.

SHIPPING AND BILLING POLICY:

Libraries are charged actual shipping on
billed orders; prepaid orders are
shipped free. Invoices are sent
separately and as the library specifies.

BACK ORDER POLICY:

All titles are available immediately or
within 2-3 weeks.

AVERY PUBLISHING GROUP, INC.

350 Thorens Avenue
Garden City Park, New York 11040
Telephone: 516-741-2155

ADDRESS FOR ORDERS:

Order Department at above address.

DISTRIBUTION/IMPRINTS:

Distributes: Prism Press (U.K.)

PREPAYMENT:

Not required.

DISCOUNT POLICY:

No discount to libraries.

RETURN POLICY:

Returns in salable condition are accepted
within 6 months. Written permission is
required.

SHIPPING AND BILLING POLICY:

Libraries are charged shipping on all
orders. Invoices are sent with shipments
unless the library specifies otherwise.

BACK ORDER POLICY:

Publisher back orders unavailable titles
and ships books when they become
available.

AVIATION BOOK COMPANY

1640 Victory Boulevard
Glendale, California 91201
Telephone: 818-240-1771

ADDRESS FOR ORDERS:

Same as above
Telephone: 800-423-2708
  In California: 800-542-6657
Minimum order: $10.

DISTRIBUTION/IMPRINT:

Abbot Company
Air and Space Company
Airguide Publications
Alta Research
Asa Inc.
Avcom International
Aviation Computing Research
Aviation Publications
Baja Bush Pilots Inc.
Buckeye Aviation Book Company
Career Advancement Publications
Cockpit Management
Edo-Aire Seaplane Division
Emergency Response Institute
Fletcher Aircraft Company
General Aviation Press
Goldstar Enterprises
Grand Canyon Balloon Adventures
Haldon Books
Heritage Press
HJC Software
International Helicopter Financial
Services
Multi-Vision Inc.
Optima Publications
Osborne Publications
Pilot Publications
RGR Publications
Skyprints Corp.
TCA Productions
Tuskegee Airmen Inc.
Video Training Aids
Village Press
Vogel Aviation
Watosh Publishing
World War Two Publications

DISCOUNT POLICY:

Discounts are based upon the total
quantity of books shipped to one address.
Titles can be mixed. Discount rate
varies depending on the price code shown
in publisher's catalog.

No discount on "n" items.

"w", "v", "f" books:

1 to 4 books	20%
5 to 24 books	40%
25 or more books	42%

"t" books:

1 to 4 books	20%
5 to 24 books	35%
25 or more	40%

"a" books:

1 to 4 books	20%
5 to 24 books	30%
25 or more	35%

"b" books:

1 to 4 books	15%
5 to 24 books	25%
25 or more	30%

"c" books:

1 to 4 books	10%
5 to 24 books	20%
25 or more	25%

"x" books:

1 to 4 books	5%
5 to 24 books	15%
25 or more	20%

"s" books:

1 to 4 books	none
5 to 24 books	10%
25 or more	15%

"z" books:

1 to 4 books	none
5 to 24 books	5%
25 or more	10%

RETURN POLICY:

Current editions can be returned for 85% credit anytime from 3 months to 12 months after purchase. Library must request and receive written authorization and "return label" prior to making shipment. The request must include date of purchase, invoice number, quantity and title to be returned, and reason. If all this information is not supplied, credit will be allowed at maximum discount rate.

Returned books must be current editions, free of marks or labels, and in undamaged condition.

Permission is not required to return defectively manufactured books.

SHIPPING AND BILLING POLICY:

Libraries pay shipping charges. Invoice is generally sent with shipment.

BACK ORDER POLICY:

Publisher back orders unavailable titles unless library requests otherwise.

ON APPROVAL PLAN:

Publisher accepts on approval orders from libraries. These orders must be marked "on approval". Unsatisfactory items can be returned within 30 days for full credit.

AVON BOOKS

---

105 Madison Avenue
New York, New York 10016

ADDRESS FOR ORDERS:

Address orders to Education Department.

DISTRIBUTION/IMPRINT:

Publisher has two imprints: Avon Flare; Avon Camelot.

PREPAYMENT:

Required for all orders for less than 24 copies.

DISCOUNT POLICY:

25 - 499 copies: 40% discount.

RETURN POLICY:

All books are sold on a non-returnable basis.

SHIPPING AND BILLING POLICY:

40% discounted orders are shipped at no charge; $1.00 per book to a maximum of $3.00 for orders for less than 25 copies. Invoices are sent with shipments.

OTHER INFORMATION:

Publisher prefers that libraries use a wholesaler unless they prepay.

BNA BOOKS

1231 25th Street, NW
Washington, DC 20037
Telephone: 202-452-4276

ADDRESS FOR ORDERS:

BNA Books Distribution Center
300 Raritan Center Parkway
CN 94
Edison, New Jersey 08818
201-225-1900

PREPAYMENT:

Not required.

DISCOUNT POLICY:

Publisher offers a 20% discount
regardless of the number of books ordered
to public, government, and university
libraries.

RETURN POLICY:

Books are returnable within 14 days of
receipt for full credit. A copy of the
invoice or packing slip should be
enclosed. The address for returns is:
BNA Books, Building 424, Raritan Center,
80 Northfield Avenue, Edison, New Jersey
08837.

SHIPPING AND BILLING POLICY:

All orders are shipped via UPS unless
library specifies another method of
shipment. For prepaid orders, library
should include the cost of the books,
state's sales tax, and shipping charges
of $3 for the first book and $1 for each
additional book. For billed orders, the
invoice will include the cost of the
books, state's sales tax, actual
shipping charges, and a $2 handling fee.

BACK ORDER POLICY:

Titles currently unavailable are back
ordered unless the library instructs
otherwise.

BALCH INSTITUTE FOR ETHNIC STUDIES see
ASSOCIATED UNIVERSITY PRESSES

BALLANTINE BOOKS see RANDOM HOUSE, INC.

BALLINGER PUBLISHING COMPANY

BANKS-BALDWIN LAW PUBLISHING COMPANY

University Center, P.O. Box 1974
1904 Ansel Road
Cleveland, Ohio 44106
Telephone: 216-721-7373
          800-362-4500 (in OH)
          800-221-2630 (in KY)

ADDRESS FOR ORDERS:

Same as above.

PREPAYMENT:

Not required.

DISCOUNT POLICY:

Discounts available on multiple copy
orders.

RETURN POLICY:

Publications in salable condition and
accompanied by either the original
invoice or a note listing account
number, invoice number, and reason for
return are accepted for full credit
within 30 days of invoice date.
Publications involving photocopied
material are not returnable. Written
permission is not required.

SHIPPING AND BILLING POLICY:

Shipping and handling charges are added
to all orders. The handling charge on
regular orders is $2.00, or $6.50 for
special orders (photocopied material).
Invoices are usually sent separately;
invoices are sent with material on
standing order.

BACK ORDER POLICY:

If material is unavailable at the time
of order, the library is notified and
the order held until the material is
available.

SPECIAL PLANS:

Since most publications are updated with
supplements, most orders are placed on
standing order. Libraries may request
automatic shipment of updates or
notification prior to shipment.

A. S. BARNES see OAK TREE PUBLICATIONS

BARNES AND NOBLE BOOKS see LITTLEFIELD, ADAMS, AND COMPANY

BARRON'S EDUCATIONAL SERIES, INC.

250 Wireless Boulevard
Hauppauge, New York 11788
Telephone: 516-434-3311

ADDRESS FOR ORDERS:

Same as above.

PREPAYMENT:

Prepayment is required on orders of less than $50.00.

DISCOUNT POLICY:

Libraries receive 20% discount on all orders submitted on an official purchase order.

RETURN POLICY:

Returns, in original condition, are accepted within 30 days from invoice date. Written permission from Customer Services Department is required after 30 days from invoice date. Bargain titles are not returnable.

SHIPPING AND BILLING POLICY:

Libraries are charged actual shipping costs which are prepaid and added to the invoice. Invoices are sent separately after shipments unless the library specifies otherwise.

BACK ORDER POLICY:

Unavailable titles are back ordered for 3 months after which time they are cancelled.

BASIC BOOKS see HARPER AND ROW, PUBLISHERS, INC.

BATTELLE PRESS

505 King Avenue
Columbus, Ohio 43201-2693
Telephone: 614-424-6393
          800-451-3543

ADDRESS FOR ORDERS:

Same as above.

PREPAYMENT:

Not required.

DISCOUNT POLICY:

There is a 10% discount to libraries.

RETURN POLICY:

Returns are accepted within 14 days with invoice information enclosed. Written permission is not required. Returns should be sent with postage prepaid.

SHIPPING AND BILLING POLICY:

Libraries are charged shipping at the following rate: $3.50 for the first book; $0.75 for each additional book. Free shipping on orders of 5 or more books. Invoices are sent with shipments unless the library specifies otherwise.

BACK ORDER POLICY:

Publisher back orders unavailable titles and ships books when they become available.

WILLIAM L. BAUHAN, INC.

Old County Road
P.O. Box 158
Dublin, New Hampshire 03444
Telephone: 603-563-8020

ADDRESS FOR ORDERS:

Same as above.

PREPAYMENT:

Not required.

DISCOUNT POLICY:

10% discount to libraries.

RETURN POLICY:

Books in salable condition may be returned within one year. Written permission is required.

SHIPPING AND BILLING POLICY:

Libraries are charged actual postage at Library Rate. Invoices are sent with shipments unless the library specifies otherwise.

BACK ORDER POLICY:

Orders are held, and books are shipped when available.

BAY BOOKS see SALEM HOUSE PUBLISHERS

BAYLOR UNIVERSITY PRESS

Box 547
Waco, Texas 76798
Telephone: 817-755-3164

ADDRESS FOR ORDERS:

Baylor Book Store
P.O. Box 6325
Waco, TX 76706
Telephone: 817-755-2161, ext. 6971

DISTRIBUTION/IMPRINTS:

Markham Press Fund (Imprint)

PREPAYMENT:

Prepayment is required for orders of less than $10.00.

DISCOUNT POLICY:

20% discount to libraries.

RETURN POLICY:

Written permission for returns is required. Returns should be sent to the Baylor Book Store.

SHIPPING AND BILLING POLICY:

Libraries are charged shipping plus handling charges of $2.50 for the first book and $0.50 for each additional book on all orders. Invoices are sent with shipments unless the library specifies otherwise.

BACK ORDER POLICY:

Publisher does not maintain back orders.

BEACON MUSIC see HAL LEONARD PUBLISHING CORPORATION

BEACON PRESS see HARPER AND ROW, PUBLISHERS, INC.

BEAUTIFUL AMERICA PUBLISHING COMPANY

9725 South West Commerce Circle
Wilsonville, Oregon 97070
Telephone: 503-682-0173

ADDRESS FOR ORDERS:

P.O. Box 646
Wilsonville, OR 97070

PREPAYMENT:

Not required.

DISCOUNT POLICY:

1-5:   25%
Over 5: 40%

RETURN POLICY:

Returns are accepted within one year. Written permission is not required, and return postage is paid.

SHIPPING AND BILLING POLICY:

Libraries are charged shipping on all orders. Invoices are sent with shipments unless the library specifies otherwise.

BACK ORDER POLICY:

Publisher follows the library's requests as stated on the purchase order.

PETER BEDRICK BOOKS, INC.

---

125 East 23rd Street
New York, New York 10010
Telephone: 212-777-1187

ADDRESS FOR ORDERS:

Publishers Group West
P.O. Box 8843
Emeryville, California 94552
Telephone: 415-658-3453

DISTRIBUTION/IMPRINTS:

Distributes children's books only of Blackie & Son, Ltd (Glasgow & London).

Bedrick/Blackie (Imprint)

PREPAYMENT:

Not required.

DISCOUNT POLICY:

Trade Titles:

1-4 copies:	20%
5-9 copies:	25%
10-34 copies:	30%
35 or more:	35%

Short Discount Titles:

1-9 copies:	10%
10 or more:	20%

RETURN POLICY:

Written authorization is required for all returns; request must include invoice number (otherwise credited at maximum discount), discount, title, and quantity. Defective copies will be exchanged; defects should be noted. Books must be in clean, salable condition and still in print. Address for returns: Peter Bedrick Books/c/o Publishers Group West/4064 Holden Street/Emeryville, CA 94608.

SHIPPING AND BILLING POLICY:

Libraries are charged shipping on all orders.

BACK ORDER POLICY:

Publisher will back order unless library requests that order be cancelled.

SPECIAL PLANS:

Libraries should write to: Muriel Gundersen Bedrick/Director of School and Library Services/125 East 23rd St./New York, NY 10010 for information on services.

BEEKMAN PUBLISHERS, INC.

P.O. Box 888
Woodstock, New York 12498
Telephone: 914-679-2300

ADDRESS FOR ORDERS:

Same as above.

PREPAYMENT:

Not required except for Canadian libraries.

DISCOUNT POLICY:

No discount to libraries.

RETURN POLICY:

Books may be returned within 6 months of invoice date only if they are in mint condition. Written permission is required. Address for returns (UPS): Rt.1, Box 506/Woodstock, NY 12498.

SHIPPING AND BILLING POLICY:

Libraries are charged shipping plus handling (usually $2.00 for the first book and $0.50 for each additional book) on all orders. Invoices are sent with shipments unless the library specifies otherwise.

BACK ORDER POLICY:

Publisher notifies library immediately if book is out of stock or being reprinted.

BEGINNER BOOKS see RANDOM HOUSE, INC.

BEHAVIORAL PUBLICATIONS see HUMAN SCIENCE PRESS, INC.

BELLEROPHON BOOKS

36 Anacapa Street
Santa Barbara, California 93101
Telephone: 805-965-7034

ADDRESS FOR ORDERS:

Same as above.

DISTRIBUTION:

None

PREPAYMENT:

Required for orders under $50.00 and for orders qualifying for 40% discount.

DISCOUNT POLICY:

24 - 99 books: 40% discount;
over 100 books: 50%.

RETURN POLICY:

"Why would libraries want to return books?"

SHIPPING AND BILLING POLICY:

Libraries charged actual freight; for $1.00 shipping charge, publisher will pay postage on prepaid orders. Invoices are sent with shipments; invoice can be sent separately on orders over $50.00.

BACK ORDER POLICY:

Back orders are placed for 6 or more books; balance is cancelled unless requested otherwise.

ROBERT BENTLEY, INC.

1000 Massachusetts Avenue
Cambridge, Massachusetts 02138
Telephone: 617-547-4170
         800-423-4595

ADDRESS FOR ORDERS:

Same as above.

PREPAYMENT:

Not required.

DISCOUNT POLICY:

No discount to libraries.

RETURN POLICY:

Only defective books may be returned. Address for returns: Robert Bentley, Inc./ c/o PSSC/231 Industrial Park/Fitchburg, MA 01420.

SHIPPING AND BILLING POLICY:

Libraries pay shipping on all orders. Invoices are sent separately after confirmation of shipment is received from publisher's warehouse.

BERGIN & GARVEY see INDEPENDENT PUBLISHERS GROUP

BERKLEE PRESS see HAL LEONARD PUBLISHING CORPORATION

BERKSHIRE TRAVELLER PRESS

Pine Street
Stockbridge, Massachusetts 01262
Telephone: 413-298-3636
         413-298-3778

ADDRESS FOR ORDERS:

Same as above.

DISTRIBUTION/IMPRINTS:

Distributed by Harper & Row Publishers.

PREPAYMENT:

Not required.

DISCOUNT POLICY:

50% discount - no returns.

RETURN POLICY:

No returns are allowed unless books have been damaged in transit in which case publisher must be notified within 7 days after shipment.

SHIPPING AND BILLING POLICY:

Libraries are charged actual postage (Library Rate or UPS). Invoices are sent separately after shipments unless the library specifies otherwise.

BACK ORDER POLICY:

Books not in stock at time of order will be shipped as soon as they are available.

BETTER HOMES AND GARDENS BOOKS

1716 Locust Street
Des Moines, Iowa 50336
Telephone: 515-284-2363

ADDRESS FOR ORDERS:

Same as above.

PREPAYMENT:

Not required.

DISCOUNT POLICY:

1-4 copies, assorted: 20%
over 5:   40%

RETURN POLICY:

Returns are accepted at any time except for out-of-print titles which are returnable within one year after they go out of print. Return labels are sent upon request for return. Address for returns: Meredith Distribution Services/ 2301 Fleur Dr/Des Moines, Iowa 50315.

SHIPPING AND BILLING POLICY:

Libraries are charged shipping on all orders. Invoices are sent separately after shipments.

BACK ORDER POLICY:

Publisher back orders unavailable titles unless the library instructs otherwise.

SPECIAL PLANS:

Standing order plan offers automatic shipment of new titles twice a year at a 40% discount.

BETTERWAY PUBLICATIONS, INC.

P.O. Box 219
Crozet, Virginia 22932
Telephone: 804-823-5661

ADDRESS FOR ORDERS:

Same as above.

PREPAYMENT:

Not required.

DISCOUNT POLICY:

1 book: no discount
2-9 books: 20%
10-24 books: 25%
25-49 books: 30%
50 or more: 40%

RETURN POLICY:

Books, in salable condition, may be returned for full credit as long as the book is in print. Permission is not required if the customer's account is current and the invoice is clearly marked on the package. Address for returns (UPS): Rt.2, Box 180/ Charlottesville, VA 22901. Address for returns (USPS): same as order address.

SHIPPING AND BILLING POLICY:

Prepaid orders are shipped free; actual shipping charges (FOB Charlottesville) are added to billed orders. Invoices are sent with shipments unless the library specifies otherwise.

BACK ORDER POLICY:

Books that are out of stock or not yet published are back ordered and shipped when available.

OTHER:

One of publisher's criteria is that
their books be good library books. Most
are reviewed by Booklist or Library
Journal.

BEYNCH PRESS see METAMORPHOUS PRESS, INC.

BIBLICAL INSTITUTE PRESS see LOYOLA
UNIVERSITY PRESS

BIBLIOGRAPHICAL SOCIETY OF AMERICA see
UNIVERSITY PRESS OF VIRGINIA

BILLART PUBLISHING see STACKPOLE BOOKS

BILLBOARD BOOKS see WATSON-GUPTILL
PUBLICATIONS

BINFORD & MORT PUBLISHING

1202 N.W. 17th Avenue
Portland, Oregon 97209
Telephone: 503-221-0866

ADDRESS FOR ORDERS:

Same as above.

DISTRIBUTION/IMPRINTS:

Metropolitan Press (imprint)

PREPAYMENT:

Not required.

DISCOUNT POLICY:

1-4 Books   10%
5-24 Books   15%

RETURN POLICY:

Books may be returned within one year

from purchase date if in salable
condition (not stamped, stickered, or
shop-worn). Prior permission is
required.

SHIPPING AND BILLING POLICY:

Library pays shipping costs at library
rate. Invoices are sent with shipments,
but preferences will be considered.

BACK ORDER POLICY:

Titles not currently available are back-
ordered and customer is advised when
books are available.

OTHER:

Direct orders are shipped within 24
hours. Libraries may also order from
wholesalers.

BITS PRESS

Department of English
Case Western Reserve University
Cleveland, Ohio 44106
Telephone: 216-795-2810

ADDRESS FOR ORDERS:

Same as above.

PREPAYMENT:

Not required.

DISCOUNT POLICY:

20% discount to libraries.

RETURN POLICY:

Returns accompanied by order number and
date are accepted within 8 months of
invoice date. Written permission is not
required. An $0.85 charge per book is
made against credit or cash refunds.
Limited, signed editions are not
returnable.

SHIPPING AND BILLING POLICY:

Libraries are charged actual shipping.
Invoices are sent with shipments unless
the library specifies otherwise.

SPECIAL PLANS:

A standing order is available for the biennial, Light Year.

BLACK SPARROW PRESS

---

24 Tenth Street
Santa Rosa, California 95401
Telephone: 707-579-4011

ADDRESS FOR ORDERS:

Same as above.

DISTRIBUTION/IMPRINTS:

Arabesque Books (Imprint)

PREPAYMENT:

Not required.

DISCOUNT POLICY:

No discount on library orders.

RETURN POLICY:

Only damaged or defective books that are still in print are accepted for return.

SHIPPING AND BILLING POLICY:

Libraries are charged shipping, at Library Rate unless otherwise requested. Invoices are sent with shipments unless the library specifies otherwise.

SPECIAL PLANS:

Libraries with standing orders are assured receiving signed limited editions or deluxe limited editions.

BASIL BLACKWELL, INC.

---

432 Park Avenue South, Suite 1503
New York, New York 10016
Telephone:

ADDRESS FOR ORDERS:

Harper & Row Publishers
Keystone Industrial Park
Scranton, PA 18512
Telephone: 800-242-7737

DISTRIBUTION/IMPRINTS:

Harper & Row handles warehousing, distribution and billing.

Polity Press (Division)
Andre Deutsch (Imprint)

PREPAYMENT:

Prepayment is required on any order from a library which does not have an account with Harper & Row.

DISCOUNT POLICY:

No discount to libraries except for special offers.

SHIPPING AND BILLING POLICY:

Libraries are charged shipping.

BACK ORDER POLICY:

Orders are held until a book is restocked unless the library specifies otherwise.

SPECIAL PLANS:

Standing order plans are available.

BLACKWELL SCIENTIFIC PUBLICATIONS see C. V. MOSBY COMPANY

JOHN F. BLAIR, PUBLISHER

1406 Plaza Drive
Winston-Salem, North Carolina 27103
Telephone: 800-222-9796 (outside NC)
          919-768-1374 (in NC)

ADDRESS FOR ORDERS:

Same as above.

PREPAYMENT:

Not required.

DISCOUNT POLICY:

20% discount to libraries regardless of quantity.

RETURN POLICY:

Damaged books may be returned for replacement or credit.

SHIPPING AND BILLING POLICY:

Libraries are charged shipping costs on all orders. Invoices are sent with shipments unless the library specifies otherwise.

BACK ORDER POLICY:

Publisher back orders titles unless instructed otherwise or until library cancels.

BLANFORD PRESS see STERLING PUBLISHING COMPANY, INC.

BLOODAXE BOOKS see DUFOUR EDITIONS, INC.

BLUE MOUNTAIN ARTS

P.O. Box 4549
Boulder, Colorado 80306
Telephone: 800-525-0642

ADDRESS FOR ORDERS:

Same as above.

PREPAYMENT:

Not required.

DISCOUNT POLICY:

5 books or less: 30%
More than 5 books: 43%

RETURN POLICY:

Call for return authorization. Address for returns: 2845 29th St./Boulder, CO 80301.

SHIPPING AND BILLING POLICY:

Free shipping on prepaid orders. Invoices are sent separately after shipment unless the library specifies otherwise.

BACK ORDER POLICY:

Back orders are shipped when ready.

BOB JONES UNIVERSITY PRESS

1700 Wade Hampton Boulevard
Greenville, South Carolina 29614
Telephone: 803-242-5100, ext. 4311
         800-845-5731

ADDRESS FOR ORDERS:

Same as above.

PREPAYMENT:

Prepayment is required unless a credit account has been established.

DISCOUNT POLICY:

25% discount to libraries on most trade books and student texts.

RETURN POLICY:

Publisher charges a 10% restocking fee for returns (25% for computer software, video cassettes, and drama scripts). Books returned after 60 days from invoice date also receive a 10% credit reduction each month thereafter. No written permission is required. Address for returns: Bob Jones University Press Warehouse/41 Karen Drive/Greenville, SC 29607.

SHIPPING AND BILLING POLICY:

Libraries are charged shipping (UPS unless otherwise requested) on all orders plus $0.85 handling per box. Invoices are sent separately after shipments unless the library specifies otherwise.

BACK ORDER POLICY:

Back ordered items are noted on packing list and are sent when available unless library requests otherwise.

BODLEY HEAD see RANDOM HOUSE, INC.

BOLCHAZY-CARDUCCI PUBLISHERS

44 Lake Street
Oak Park, Illinois 60302
Telephone: 312-386-8360

ADDRESS FOR ORDERS:

Same as above.

DISTRIBUTION/IMPRINTS:

Distributes: Teubner (Leipzig); Georg
Olms (W. Germany).

PREPAYMENT:

Not required; terms are 30 days net.

DISCOUNT POLICY:

No discount to libraries.

RETURN POLICY:

Returns are accepted within 6 months.
Written permission is required.

SHIPPING AND BILLING POLICY:

Libraries are charged shipping on all
orders. Invoices are sent with shipments
unless the library specifies otherwise.

BONNER PRESS see INDEPENDENT PUBLISHERS
GROUP

BONNEVILLE BOOKS see UNIVERSITY OF UTAH
PRESS

BOOKS ON THE SQUARE see HIVE PUBLISHING
COMPANY

BOOKWRIGHT see FRANKLIN WATTS, INC.

BORGO PRESS

Box 2845
San Bernardino, California 92406
Telephone: 714-884-5813

ADDRESS FOR ORDERS:

Same as above.

DISTRIBUTION/IMPRINTS:

Distributes: A&A Infos; Aardvark House;
Algol Press; Aquarian Press (selective);
Arcline Publications; Brownstone Books;
CFPR Publications; Cathedral Books;
William K. Cavanaugh Books; Cosmos
Literary Agency; Dast Books; Daystar;
Doodly Squat Press; Drumm Books; Fandom
Unlimited; Fax Collectors Editions;
Fellowship of St. Alban & St. Sergius;
Fictioneer Books; G.T. International;
Galliard Press; Greenbriar Books;
Greystoke Mobray Ltd; Hunter House; IBS
Press; K.R.I. Pubs; Kundalini Research
Inst; Frances Nelson; Newcastle Pub. Co.;
Pandora's Books; Paperback Quarterly
Books; Pauper's Press; Ramira Press;
SFBRI; St. Willibrord's Press; Servire;
Sidewinder Press; Spiritual Community
Pubs; Starmont House; Sufi; Sun Dance
Press; Thorsons Publishers (selective);
Xenos Books.

PREPAYMENT:

Not required.

DISCOUNT POLICY:

10-19 books:	10%
20-29:	15%
30 or more:	20%

RETURN POLICY:

Returns, in salable condition and
accompanied by invoice number and with
postage prepaid, are accepted at any
time for credit or cancellation of the
invoice. Written permission is required.

SHIPPING AND BILLING POLICY:

Libraries are charged actual shipping on
billed orders; prepaid orders are
shipped free. Invoices are sent with
shipments unless the library specifies
otherwise and pays for additional
postage.

BACK ORDER POLICY:

Publisher will back order indefinitely or as instructed by library.

SPECIAL PLANS:

Publisher accepts standing orders for any series or multiple-edition reference books at a 10% discount.

BOSTON CHILDREN'S MUSEUM see MOYER BELL LIMITED

BOULTON PUBLISHING see INDEPENDENT PUBLISHERS GROUP

BOWERS & MERENA GALLERIES, INC. see VESTAL PRESS, INC.

R.R. BOWKER COMPANY

245 West 17th Street
New York, New York 10011
Telephone: 800-521-8110
 (In NY, AK, HI: 212-337-6934)
 (In Canada: 800-537-8416)

ADDRESS FOR ORDERS:

R.R. Bowker
Order Department
P.O. Box 762
New York, NY 10011

For Forthcoming Books, Forthcoming Children's Books, ALD Update, Weekly Records, and ABPR Monthly:

R.R. Bowker
P.O. Box 14080
Newark, NJ 07198

For Publishers Weekly:

P.O. Box 1979
Marion, OH 43302

For School Library Journal:

P.O. Box 1978
Marion, OH 43302

For Library Journal:

P.O. Box 1977
Marion, OH 43302

For Reviews on Cards:

P.O. Box 444
Mt. Morris, IL 61054

In Canada:

Butterworth and Company
2265 Midland Avenue
Scarborough, Ontario M1P 4S1

PREPAYMENT:

Not required.

DISCOUNT POLICY:

No discount is allowed for library orders, except on selected titles which carry a quantity discount.

RETURN POLICY:

Libraries may return books with a copy of the invoice within 30 days. Publisher will credit library's account or provide a complete refund if so requested. Microfiche editions are nonreturnable. Returned books must be unmarked and in saleable condition. Returns must be addressed to: The Bowker Warehouse, c/o Mercedes Distribution Center, 62 Imlay Street, Brooklyn, NY 11231.

SHIPPING AND BILLING POLICY:

Shipping and handling charge will be added to each order at 5% of net invoice amount. Minimum shipping and handling charge is $3.50.

BACK ORDER POLICY:

Publisher back orders titles that are not currently available unless library instructs otherwise.

SPECIAL ORDER PLAN:

Any book can be placed on standing order. Many Bowker titles periodically undergo revision and are published on an annual, biennial, or triennial basis. All books are sold on 30-day approval and can be returned after examination for full credit within this time if in perfect and resalable condition.

BRADBURY PRESS see MACMILLAN PUBLISHING COMPANY, INC.

BRADFORD BOOKS see MIT PRESS

BRADY see APPLETON AND LANGE PUBLISHING COMPANY

CHARLES T. BRANFORD COMPANY

P.O. Box 41
Newton Center, Massachusetts 02159
Telephone: 617-964-2441

ADDRESS FOR ORDERS:

Same as above.

DISTRIBUTION/IMPRINTS:

Distributes: B. T. Batsford, Ltd; Dryad Press, Ltd.

PREPAYMENT:

Not required.

DISCOUNT POLICY:

20% discount to libraries.

RETURN POLICY:

Returns are accepted within 6 months. Written permission is required. Address for returns: Publishers Storage & Shipping Corp/231 Industrial Park/ Fitchburg, MA 01420.

SHIPPING AND BILLING POLICY:

Libraries are charged actual shipping costs. Invoices are sent with shipments unless the library specifies otherwise.

BACK ORDER POLICY:

Back orders are placed and filled as soon as possible.

BREAKWATER see INDEPENDENT PUBLISHERS GROUP

BREITENBUSH BOOKS see SYRACUSE UNIVERSITY PRESS

BRINDABELLA BOOKS see ARIEL PRESS

BRITISH FILM INSTITUTE see UNIVERSITY OF ILLINOIS PRESS

PAUL H. BROOKES PUBLISHING COMPANY

P.O. Box 10624
Baltimore, Maryland 21285
Telephone: 301-337-9580

ADDRESS FOR ORDERS:

Same as above.
Telephone: 800-638-3775

DISTRIBUTION/IMPRINTS:

Distributes selective publications of: Croom Helm, Ltd (England).

PREPAYMENT:

Not required.

DISCOUNT POLICY:

No discount to libraries.

RETURN POLICY:

Returns, in unmarked and undamaged condition, sent postpaid, and accompanied by a copy of the original invoice, are accepted within six months of invoice date. Defective books may be returned for replacement or full credit. Address for returns: Returns Department/The Maple Press Distribution Center/York County Industrial Park, M100/York, PA 17405.

SHIPPING AND BILLING POLICY:

Publisher pays shipping on prepaid orders; libraries pay shipping and handling charges of $1.00 (1-2 books), $2.00 (3-5 books), $3.00 (6-10 books), or $5.00 (over 10 books). Invoices are sent with shipments.

BACK ORDER POLICY:

Orders are held, and the library is notified of date of availability.

BROOKING INSTITUTION

1775 Massachusetts Avenue, NW
Washington, DC 20036
Telephone: 202-797-6215

ADDRESS FOR ORDERS:

Brooking Institution
Publications Office
1775 Massachusetts Avenue, NW
Washington, DC 20026

PREPAYMENT:

Not required.

DISCOUNT POLICY:

See Special Order Plan for standing order discounts.

RETURN POLICY:

Returns must be made between 90 days and one year from date of invoice. Pamphlets are not returnable. A copy of the invoice, or a listing showing invoice number, title, quantity, discount, and list price should accompany the return package. The address for returns is the same as for orders.

SHIPPING AND BILLING POLICY:

Libraries pay shipping charges. Invoices are sent with shipment if billing and shipping addresses are the same.

BACK ORDER POLICY:

Titles not currently available are placed on back order unless library requests cancellation of order.

SPECIAL ORDER PLAN:

Publisher offers three different automatic shipment plans.

Standing Order Plan: Libraries receive new publications of all or selected fields at 20% discount, plus postage and handling. Libraries on Standing Order Plan are entitled to a 20% discount on all reorders of new books or books ordered from the back list.

Annual Subscriptions: For an annual fee ($425 in 1988) an institution may become an annual subscriber, receiving a copy of each new Brookings book and reprint in the General Series and the Technical Series published during the year. In addition, the annual subscriber receives Brookings Review, Brookings Papers on Economic Activity, and other publications describing the Institution's research and educational activities.

Reprint Series Subscription: For an annual fee of $20, an institution may become a reprint series subscriber, receiving a copy of each General Series reprint published during the year. Subscription may be started at any time; they must be renewed each year by the expiration date.

BROOKSIDE PRESS see INDEPENDENT PUBLISHERS GROUP

GUSTAV BROUKAL PRESS see AMERICAN ATHEIST PRESS

WM. C. BROWN COMPANY, PUBLISHERS

College Division
2460 Kerper Boulevard
Dubuque, Iowa 52001
Telephone: 319-588-1451

ADDRESS FOR ORDERS:

Same as above
Telephone: 800-338-5578

DISTRIBUTION/IMPRINTS:

Wm. C. Brown Company, RED Division (Division);
Kendall-Hunt Publishing Company (Separate Company);
Championship Books (Imprint)

PREPAYMENT:

Not required.

DISCOUNT POLICY:

No discount to libraries.

RETURN POLICY:

Books, in excellent condition and accompanied by the original packing slip or invoice, are accepted without written permission for up to 12 months from the date of order.

SHIPPING AND BILLING POLICY:

Libraries are charged shipping/handling of approximately 4% or $2.00 per book (if only one or two books are ordered) on all orders. Invoices are sent with shipments unless the library specifies otherwise.

BACK ORDER POLICY:

Libraries are notified of the date of availability for items placed on back order.

BROWNSTONE BOOKS see BORGO PRESS

BRUNNER/MAZEL, INC.

---

19 Union Square West
New York, New York 10003
Telephone: 212-924-3344

ADDRESS FOR ORDERS:

Same as above.

DISTRIBUTION/IMPRINTS:

Publisher supplies books in the mental health sciences from all publishers.

Magination Press (Imprint)

PREPAYMENT:

Not required.

DISCOUNT POLICY:

10% discount on Brunner/Mazel or Magination Press titles. Distributed books are not discounted.

RETURN POLICY:

Books, accompanied by the invoice or invoice information, may be returned within 90 days. No written permission is required. Videotapes and audiotapes cannot be returned after 10 days.

SHIPPING AND BILLING POLICY:

Libraries are charged shipping ($1.75 minimum per shipment). Invoices are sent with shipments unless the library specifies otherwise.

BACK ORDER POLICY:

Publisher will hold back orders for as long as the library requests.

SPECIAL PLANS:

All books are available for examination and return within 90 days. Standing orders are available for series.

OTHER:

Publisher stocks over 2,000 different titles in the mental health sciences.

BRYCE-WATERTON see INDEPENDENT PUBLISHERS GROUP

BUCKEYE AVIATION BOOK COMPANY see AVIATION BOOK COMPANY

BUCKNELL UNIVERSITY PRESS see ASSOCIATED UNIVERSITY PRESSES

BULLETIN OF THE ATOMIC SCIENTISTS see UNIVERSITY OF CHICAGO PRESS

BUSINESS & LEGAL REPORTS

---

64 Wall Street
Madison, Connecticut 06443
Telephone: 203-245-7448
         800-553-4569

ADDRESS FOR ORDERS:

Same as above.

PREPAYMENT:

Not required.

DISCOUNT POLICY:

No discount to libraries.

RETURN POLICY:

Books, accompanied by invoice or invoice copy, are accepted within 30 days. No written permission is required.

SHIPPING AND BILLING POLICY:

Publisher pays shipping/handling on prepaid orders; libraries pay shipping and handling of 15% (maximum of $5.99) on books. Shipping charges for films are based on weight. Invoices are sent with shipments unless next day shipment is requested, in which case the invoice follows the shipment and a $15.00 charge is incurred in addition to shipping.

BACK ORDER POLICY:

Orders are held until items become available.

BYREN HOUSE see INDEPENDENT PUBLISHERS GROUP

CARE see PRENTICE-HALL

CBP PRESS

P.O. Box 179
St. Louis, Missouri 63166
Telephone: 800-351-2665
         800-451-2665 (in MO)

ADDRESS FOR ORDERS:

Same as above.

PREPAYMENT:

Prepayment is required on orders under $10.00.

DISCOUNT POLICY:

20% discount is offered.

RETURN POLICY:

Returns are accepted within one year of invoice date. Written permission is required. Seasonal pamphlets are not returnable. Address for returns: 2711 Olive St/St. Louis, MO 63103.

SHIPPING AND BILLING POLICY:

Libraries are charged actual postage on all orders. Invoices are sent separately.

BACK ORDER POLICY:

Back orders are held, and the books are shipped when available.

CQ PRESS see CONGRESSIONAL QUARTERLY, INC.

CTO ASSOCIATES see DELMAR PUBLISHERS, INC.

CADMUS EDITIONS see CITY LIGHTS BOOKS

CAEDMON

1995 Broadway
New York, New York 10023
Telephone: 212-580-3400

ADDRESS FOR ORDERS:

Caedmon, Harper & Row Publishers, Inc.
Keystone Industrial Park
Scranton, PA 18512
Telephone: 800-C-HARPER

DISTRIBUTION/IMPRINTS:

Caedmon is a division of Harper & Row.

PREPAYMENT:

Payment is required with order unless customer is a member of Caedmon Library Subscription Plan.

DISCOUNT POLICY:

No discount except for Library Subscription Plan.

RETURN POLICY:

Returns should be sent to the Harper & Row address.

SHIPPING AND BILLING POLICY:

Libraries are charged shipping plus handling of $1.50 for the first title and $0.50 for each additional title.

BACK ORDER POLICY:

Orders are held until material is available.

SPECIAL PLANS:

Library Subscription Plan offers 40% discount on new cassette releases and 40% discount on backlist titles. The plan has 4 options: Children's Plays (max. 15 new cassettes per year); Small Budget Children's Plays (max. 8 cassettes); Student/Adult Plan (max. 10 cassettes); Complete Plan (max. 25 cassettes).

OTHER:

Caedmon specializes in spoken audio recordings including the 1988 Voices & Visions series.

CALEDONIA

P.O. Box 245
Racine, Wisconsin 53401
Telephone:

ADDRESS FOR ORDERS:

Same as above.
Telephone orders are not accepted.

PREPAYMENT:

Not required with purchase order.

DISCOUNT POLICY:

No discount to libraries.

RETURN POLICY:

Damaged or imperfect books are accepted for return not later than 30 days after receipt.

SHIPPING AND BILLING POLICY:

Publisher pays shipping on prepaid orders; otherwise, libraries pay actual Library Rate postage or UPS. Invoices are sent with shipments unless the library specifies otherwise.

BACK ORDER POLICY:

Publisher will hold orders and fill them when items become available up to the time limit specified on the purchase order.

CALIFORNIA INSTITUTE OF PUBLIC AFFAIRS

P.O. Box 10
Claremont, California 91711
Telephone: 714-624-1486

ADDRESS FOR ORDERS:

Same as above.

PREPAYMENT:

Not required.

DISCOUNT POLICY:

No discount to libraries.

RETURN POLICY:

Written permission is required. Returns, in salable condition, are accepted within 60 days.

SHIPPING AND BILLING POLICY:

Billed orders only pay shipping and handling of $2.00. Invoices are sent with shipments unless the library specifies otherwise.

CAMBRIDGE UNIVERSITY PRESS

32 East 57th Street
New York, New York 10022
Telephone: 212-688-8888

800-221-4512

ADDRESS FOR ORDERS:

510 North Avenue
New Rochelle, New York 10801
Telephone: 800-872-7423 (in US)
          800-227-0247 (in NY)

PREPAYMENT:

Not required for established accounts.

DISCOUNT POLICY:

Discount schedules are available upon
request.

RETURN POLICY:

Returns in salable condition and
accompanied by a copy of the invoice are
accepted without permission within 18
months. Returns should be sent via UPS.
Address for returns: 19 Winthrop Ave/
New Rochelle, NY 10801.

SHIPPING AND BILLING POLICY:

Libraries are charged shipping (Book
Rate normally) except on prepaid orders
which are shipped free. Invoices are
sent with shipments and as the library
requests.

BACK ORDER POLICY:

Publisher back orders unavailable titles
and ships books when they become
available unless the library cancels the
order.

SPECIAL PLANS:

Standing orders are available for all
publisher's series. In addition,
publisher offers a Library Standing
Order Plan (LSOP) which enables
libraries to select from one or all of
publisher's categories and by level
(undergraduate or graduate). LSOP books
are shipped twice each month. Returns
are accepted in accordance with above
return policy. Cancellation can be made
by a telephone call.

CAP AND GOWN PRESS

Box 58825
Houston, Texas 77258
Telephone: 409-763-3410

ADDRESS FOR ORDERS:

Same as above.

PREPAYMENT:

Not required.

DISCOUNT POLICY:

No discount to libraries.

RETURN POLICY:

Returns are accepted within 60 days of
receipt for damaged books or books
incorrectly sent only. Prior permission
is required. Address for returns:
Receiving Dept/Cap and Gown Press,
Inc/4519 Woodrow Ave/Galveston, TX
77551.

SHIPPING AND BILLING POLICY:

Shipping costs are added to invoices on
all orders. Invoices are sent with
shipments unless the library specifies
otherwise.

BACK ORDER POLICY:

Back orders are usually filled within 60
days. Notification that a book is on
back order is sent promptly to the
library.

SPECIAL PLANS:

Special order plans are under
development.

JONATHAN CAPE see RANDOM HOUSE, INC.

CAPRA PRESS

Box 2068
Santa Barbara, California 93120
Telephone: 805-966-4590

ADDRESS FOR ORDERS:

Same as above.

DISTRIBUTION/IMPRINTS:

Distributes: Perseverance Press;
Garland/Clarke Editions.

PREPAYMENT:

Not required.

DISCOUNT POLICY:

10% discount to libraries.

RETURN POLICY:

Books in salable condition and
accompanied by invoice number and date
will be accepted for return for credit
only after three months but before one
year from invoice date. Permission is
not required.

SHIPPING AND BILLING POLICY:

Publisher charges shipping costs except
on prepaid orders. Invoices are sent
with shipments unless the library
specifies otherwise.

BACK ORDER POLICY:

Libraries are notified of back orders.

SPECIAL PLANS:

Standing order plan for category books
is available at 20% discount.

_____

CARAVAN BOOKS see SCHOLARS' FACSIMILES &
REPRINTS

_____

CAREER ADVANCEMENT PUBLICATIONS see
AVIATION BOOK COMPANY

_____

CAREER PUBLISHING, INC.

_____

910 Main Street
P.O. Box 5486
Orange, California 92613-5486
Telephone: 714-771-5155
          800-854-4014

ADDRESS FOR ORDERS:

Same as above.

DISTRIBUTION/IMPRINTS:

Distributes: Video Professor; Morris
Video; Instructional Aids.

PREPAYMENT:

Not required.

DISCOUNT POLICY:

No discount to libraries.

RETURN POLICY:

Returns are accepted within 60 days.
Videos are non-returnable. Written
permission to return is required.

SHIPPING AND BILLING POLICY:

Libraries are charged shipping plus a
$1.00 handling charge per order.
Invoices are sent separately only.

BACK ORDER POLICY:

Library is notified when a back order is
placed. Orders are filled when publisher
receives the material.

_____

CAREER PUBLISHING COMPANY see WILLIAMSON
PUBLISHING COMPANY

_____

CAROLRHODA BOOKS, INC.

_____

241 1st Avenue N.
Minneapolis, Minnesota 55401
Telephone: 612-332-3344
          800-328-4929

ADDRESS FOR ORDERS:

Same as above.

PREPAYMENT:

Not required.

DISCOUNT POLICY:

No discount to libraries.

RETURN POLICY:

Returns in salable condition are accepted within one year. Prior permission, preferably by telephone, is required. Invoice numbers should be quoted on boxes.

SHIPPING AND BILLING POLICY:

Libraries are charged shipping/handling on billed orders; prepaid orders are shipped free, at Fourth Class Book Rate. Invoices are sent separately but can be sent with shipments as well.

BACK ORDER POLICY:

Publisher back orders unavailable titles and ships books when they become available unless the library instructs otherwise or cancels, preferably by telephone.

CARRIAGE HOUSE PRESS

Carriage Lane
Barnes Landing
East Hampton, New York 11937
Telephone: 516-267-8773

ADDRESS FOR ORDERS:

Same as above.

PREPAYMENT:

Not required.

DISCOUNT POLICY:

No discount to libraries.

RETURN POLICY:

Libraries must obtain written permission before returning books. A 25% penalty on all returns. No returns accepted after one year. Credit balance held against future orders. No refunds. Single copy is not returnable.

SHIPPING AND BILLING POLICY:

Libraries pay shipping and handling charge. The amount is $2 for the first book, $.25 for each additional book.

BACK ORDER POLICY:

Publisher back orders and fills temporarily out-of-stock titles.

CARROLL & GRAF PUBLISHERS, INC.

260 Fifth Avenue
New York, New York 10001
Telephone: 212-889-8772

ADDRESS FOR ORDERS:

Publishers Group West
P.O. Box 8843
Emeryville, CA 94662
Telephone: 800-982-8319

DISTRIBUTION/IMPRINTS:

Distributed by Publishers Group West.

PREPAYMENT:

Prepayment is required until an account is established.

DISCOUNT POLICY:

1-4:	20%
5-9:	25%
10-34%:	30%
35 or more:	35%

RETURN POLICY:

Returns, in salable condition, still in print, and accompanied by invoice information, are accepted not sooner than 90 days. Written permission is required. Claims for damaged books, misshipments, or non-receipts must be made within 60 days of invoice date. Address for returns: Publishers Group West/4064 Holden St/Emeryville, CA 94608.

SHIPPING AND BILLING POLICY:

Libraries are charged shipping on all orders. Invoices are sent separately unless the library specifies otherwise.

BACK ORDER POLICY:

Back orders will be placed unless the library specifies otherwise.

CASSELL see STERLING PUBLISHING COMPANY, INC.

CATHEDRAL BOOKS see BORGO PRESS

CATHOLIC HEALTH ASSOCIATION OF THE U.S.

4455 Woodson Road
St. Louis, Missouri 63134
Telephone: 314-427-2500

ADDRESS FOR ORDERS:

Same as above.
Attn: Books/AV Department
Telephone: 800-327-0541 (outside MO)
          800-338-1312 (in MO)

PREPAYMENT:

Prepayment is required for orders of $15.00 or less.

DISCOUNT POLICY:

No discount to libraries.

RETURN POLICY:

Returns in resalable condition, accompanied by invoice number and date, and sent with postage prepaid are accepted within 6 months of invoice date. Prior permission is required except for defective books. Out-of-print titles and audiovisual items are not returnable.

SHIPPING AND BILLING POLICY:

Libraries are charged actual shipping except on prepaid orders which are shipped free. Invoices are sent separately.

BACK ORDER POLICY:

Back orders are accepted.

CATHOLIC UNIVERSITY OF AMERICA PRESS

---

620 Michigan Avenue, NE
Washington, D.C. 20064
Telephone: 202-635-5052

ADDRESS FOR ORDERS:

CUA Press
P.O. Box 4852, Hampden Station
Baltimore, Maryland 21211
Telephone: 301-338-6953

PREPAYMENT:

Not required.

DISCOUNT POLICY:

No discount to libraries.

RETURN POLICY:

Returns accompanied by the reason for return and invoice number are accepted within one year. Written permission is not required. Address for returns: CUA Press Warehouse/2200 Girard Ave/ Baltimore, MD 21211.

SHIPPING AND BILLING POLICY:

Libraries are charged actual shipping on billed orders only. Invoices are sent with shipments unless the library specifies otherwise.

BACK ORDER POLICY:

Publisher back orders unavailable titles and notifies library.

SPECIAL PLANS:

Standing orders are available at a 20% discount; 40% is offered on an approval plan if 15 or more titles are purchased.

CELESTIAL ARTS see TEN SPEED PRESS

CENTENNIAL see WATSON-GUPTILL PUBLICATIONS

CENTER FOR AGRICULTURAL PUBLISHING AND DOCUMENTATION see UNIPUB

CENTER FOR APPLIED RESEARCH IN EDUCATION
see PRENTICE-HALL

CENTER FOR INTERNATIONAL STUDIES, OHIO
UNIVERSITY see OHIO UNIVERSITY/SWALLOW
PRESS

CENTER FOR MIGRATION STUDIES see JEROME
OZER, PUBLISHERS

CENTER FOR STRATEGIC AND INTERNATIONAL
STUDIES see UNIVERSITY PRESS OF AMERICA

CENTER FOR THE STUDY OF LANGUAGE AND
INFORMATION see UNIVERSITY OF CHICAGO
PRESS

CHAMPIONSHIP BOOKS see WILLIAM C. BROWN,
PUBLISHERS

CHANDLER & SHARP PUBLISHERS, INC.

11A Commercial Boulevard
Novato, California 94949
Telephone: 415-883-2353

ADDRESS FOR ORDERS:

Same as above, or:
c/o Publishers Services
P.O. Box 2510
Novato, CA 94948

PREPAYMENT:

Prepayment required unless the library
has a standing account.

DISCOUNT POLICY:

Libraries pay list price.

RETURN POLICY:

Returns, for credit only, are accepted
within one year of invoice date. Prior
written permission is required. Returns
should be sent to Commercial Boulevard
address.

SHIPPING AND BILLING POLICY:

Libraries are charged shipping costs on
all orders. Invoices are sent with
shipments unless the library specifies
otherwise.

BACK ORDER POLICY:

Publisher will back-order for a time
limit specified by the library.

CHATTO & WINDUS see RANDOM HOUSE, INC.

CHELSEA PUBLISHING COMPANY, INC

15 East 26th Street
New York, New York 10010
Telephone: 212-889-8095

ADDRESS FOR ORDERS:

Same as above.

PREPAYMENT:

Not required.

DISCOUNT POLICY:

10% on orders of $40.00 or more.

RETURN POLICY:

Books shipped in accordance with order
are not returnable. A return label is
required for all returns.

SHIPPING AND BILLING POLICY:

Libraries are charged shipping. Invoices
are sent with shipments unless the
library specifies otherwise.

BACK ORDER POLICY:

Publisher back orders unavailable titles
and notifies library when they become
available.

CHERRY LANE see ALFRED PUBLISHING, INC.

CHICAGO REVIEW PRESS see INDEPENDENT PUBLISHERS GROUP

CHIDVILAS

P.O. Box 17550
Boulder, Colorado 80308
Telephone: 303-665-6611

ADDRESS FOR ORDERS:

Same as above.
Telephone: 800-777-7743 (orders only)

DISTRIBUTION/IMPRINTS:

Distributes: Rebel Publishing.

PREPAYMENT:

Not required.

DISCOUNT POLICY:

Books, Discourse Audiotapes, Tarot
Decks:
1-2:   20%
3-4:   30%
5-29:   40%
30-49:   41%, etc.

Music Cassettes: 40%

Videotapes: 30%

RETURN POLICY:

Returns are accepted for in-print books
and tapes in resalable condition and are
credited at 50% discount off the retail
price.

SHIPPING AND BILLING POLICY:

Libraries are charged actual shipping
costs on all orders. Invoices are sent
separately unless the library specifies
otherwise.

BACK ORDER POLICY:

Items are placed on back order unless
library instructs otherwise.

CHILDRENS PRESS

5440 North Cumberland Ave.
Chicago, Illinois 60656
Telephone: 312-693-0800 (800-621-1115)

ADDRESS FOR ORDERS:

Same as above.

PREPAYMENT:

Not required.

DISCOUNT POLICY:

Childrens Press prices to schools and
libraries. Libraries should see
publisher's checklist and order form for
library prices.

RETURN POLICY:

Publisher requires written permission for
returns. Returns are limited to three
months from receipt of book. The address
for returns is: Ware-Pak, Childrens
Press, 2427 Bono Street, University Park,
Illinois 60466.

SHIPPING AND BILLING POLICY:

Publisher pays postage. Invoices are
sent after shipment within 48 hours.
Packing slips are enclosed in shipments.

BACK ORDER POLICY:

Titles not currently available are
reported and back ordered unless library
instructs otherwise.

CHRISTOPHER PUBLISHING HOUSE

106 Longwater Drive
Norwell, Massachusetts 02061
Telephone: 617-878-9336

ADDRESS FOR ORDERS:

Same as above.

PREPAYMENT:

Not required.

DISCOUNT POLICY:

15% discount to libraries.

RETURN POLICY:

Returns are accepted within one year. Written permission is required.

SHIPPING AND BILLING POLICY:

Libraries are charged shipping. Invoices are sent as the library requests.

BACK ORDER POLICY:

Publisher back orders unavailable titles and ships books when they become available, within 90 days.

CHRONICLE GUIDANCE PUBLICATIONS, INC.

P.O. Box 1190, Aurora Street
Moravia, New York 13119-1190
Telephone: 315-497-0330

ADDRESS FOR ORDERS:

Same as above.

PREPAYMENT:

Prepayment is requested for orders under $35.00, plus shipping and handling.

DISCOUNT POLICY:

Libraries receive "School Price" as indicated in publisher's price list.

RETURN POLICY:

Returns are accepted within 30 days of shipping date. Prior permission is required, and libraries should telephone publisher for details.

SHIPPING AND BILLING POLICY:

Shipping and handling charges are prepaid by publisher and added to invoices. Charges are: $1.00 minimum on orders up to $10.00; 10% on orders from

$10.01 to $400.00; 8% on orders over $400.00. Invoices are sent after shipments.

BACK ORDER POLICY:

Publisher holds back orders until they can be filled. Library is notified in case of long delays or if books go out of print.

SPECIAL PLANS:

Standing orders are available. Items of $100.00 or more may be ordered on 30-day approval. If returned, item must be in resalable condition.

CISTERCIAN PUBLICATIONS, INC.

WMU Station
Kalamazoo, Michigan 49008
Telephone: 616-387-5090

ADDRESS FOR ORDERS:

Same as above.

DISTRIBUTION/IMPRINTS:

Distributes publications of: Peregrina Press (Saskatoon, Saskatchewan); Fairacres Press (Oxford, England - selected titles only).

PREPAYMENT:

Prepayment is required on all orders except for standing orders and orders from established customers.

DISCOUNT POLICY:

No discount to libraries.

RETURN POLICY:

Returns must be arranged within 90 days of purchase. Written permission is required.

SHIPPING AND BILLING POLICY:

Libraries are charged shipping plus handling charge of 6% for postal shipments or 8% UPS on small orders. Pro forma invoice is sent on receipt of order, and book is shipped upon receipt of payment.

BACK ORDER POLICY:

Publisher back orders and notifies the library. When the book is available, library will be advised and asked for confirmation.

SPECIAL PLANS:

Standing order customers receive an automatic 15% discount. Occasional returns are accepted; frequent returns result in the cancellation of the standing order.

CITY LIGHTS BOOKS

261 Columbus Avenue
San Francisco, California 94133

ADDRESS FOR ORDERS:

Subterranean Company
P.O. Box 10233
Eugene, Oregon 97440
Telephone: 503-343-6324

DISTRIBUTION/IMPRINTS:

Distributed by Subterranean Company.

Distributes: Grey Fox Press; Four Seasons Foundation; Turtle Island Foundation; Tombouctou Books; Cadmus Editions.

PREPAYMENT:

Not required.

DISCOUNT POLICY:

No discount to libraries.

RETURN POLICY:

Returns, accompanied by invoice number and date, are accepted after 90 days but before one year. Permission is not required. Address for returns: 1327 W. 2nd St/Eugene, OR 97402.

SHIPPING AND BILLING POLICY:

Libraries are charged shipping on all orders. Invoices are sent with shipments only.

BACK ORDER POLICY:

Back orders are placed and the library notified.

OTHER:

Publisher prefers that libraries order through wholesalers.

CLARION BOOKS see HOUGHTON MIFFLIN COMPANY

ARTHUR H. CLARK COMPANY

P.O. Box 230
Glendale, California 91209
Telephone: 213-254-1600

ADDRESS FOR ORDERS:

Same as above.

DISTRIBUTION/IMPRINTS:

Distributes the publications of: Prosperity Press; Summit Press.

PREPAYMENT:

Not required.

DISCOUNT POLICY:

No discount for library orders.

RETURN POLICY:

Books may be returned for full credit within 10 days; after 10 days, books are credited at 90% of invoice. Prior permission is required except for approval books. Address for returns: 5025 Sierra Villa Dr/Los Angeles, CA 90042.

SHIPPING AND BILLING POLICY:

Prepaid orders are shipped FOB destination. Shipping and handling ($1.50 for the first book and approximately $0.75 for each additional book, or $0.50 over postage) are added to billed orders. Invoices are sent with shipments unless the library specifies otherwise.

BACK ORDER POLICY:

Orders will be held for up to 90 days.

SPECIAL PLANS:

Publisher offers standing order, approval, and other special plans. Interested libraries should contact publisher.

CLARKSON POTTER, INC. see CROWN PUBLISHERS, INC.

CLEVELAND MUSEUM OF ART see INDIANA UNIVERSITY PRESS

CLINICAL NEUROSCIENCE PRESS see LAWRENCE ERLBAUM ASSOCIATES

CLOUD 10 PUBLICATIONS see TRILLIUM PRESS, INC.

CLYMER PUBLICATIONS see WESTERN MARINE ENTERPRISES

COCKPIT MANAGEMENT see AVIATION BOOK COMPANY

COFFEE HOUSE PRESS

P.O. Box 10870
Minneapolis, Minnesota 55440
Telephone: 612-338-0125

ADDRESS FOR ORDERS:

Same as above or that of distributor.

DISTRIBUTION/IMPRINTS:

Distributed by: Consortium Books Sales & Distribution/213 E. 4th St/St. Paul, MN 55101.

Toothpaste Press (previous name of Coffee House Press)

PREPAYMENT:

For this and other policies, libraries should contact the distributor.

COLLECTOR BOOKS

P.O. Box 3009
Paducah, Kentucky 42002-3009
Telephone: 502-898-6211

ADDRESS FOR ORDERS:

Same as above.
Telephone: 800-626-5420

DISTRIBUTION/IMPRINTS:

American Quilters Society (Division)

PREPAYMENT:

Not required.

DISCOUNT POLICY:

1-4 books: no discount
5 or more: 25%

RETURN POLICY:

Books are accepted for return not before 6 months or after one year. Written permission is required; requests should include a list of books to be returned, quantities, and invoice numbers and dates. Address for returns: Collector Books/5801 Kentucky Dam Rd/Paducah, KY 42001.

SHIPPING AND BILLING POLICY:

Libraries are charged shipping. Invoices are sent separately unless the library specifies otherwise.

BACK ORDER POLICY:

Publisher will back order and ship as soon as items become available.

COLLEGE ART ASSOCIATION see PENNSYLVANIA STATE UNIVERSITY PRESS

COLLEGE BOARD

45 Columbus Avenue
New York, New York 10023-6992
Telephone: 212-713-8000

ADDRESS FOR ORDERS:

College Board Publications
Box 886
New York, New York 10101-0886
Telephone: 212-713-8165 (telephone
orders are not accepted)

DISTRIBUTION/IMPRINTS:

Publications of the College Board are
distributed by its program service
offices and its test program offices.

PREPAYMENT:

Prepayment is requested for orders under
$10.00.

DISCOUNT POLICY:

20% discount is offered on orders of 5
or more copies of a single title or
package unless publisher's catalog
states otherwise.

RETURN POLICY:

Books, in salable condition and
currently in print, are accepted for
return, postpaid, within 30 days of
receipt. A copy of the original invoice
and the stated reason for return must
accompany the books; otherwise, prior
permission must be obtained from the Box
886 address. All claims concerning
damaged or missing shipments must be
received within 45 days of invoice.

SHIPPING AND BILLING POLICY:

Publisher pays postage (Fourth Class
Book Rate) on prepaid orders; library
pays postage on billed orders or for
faster shipment. Handling is charged
only on some orders. Invoices are sent
with shipments unless the library
specifies otherwise.

BACK ORDER POLICY:

Only titles out of stock or not yet
published will be placed on back order.

SPECIAL PLANS:

No standing orders are accepted.

COLLIER BOOKS see MACMILLAN PUBLISHING
COMPANY, INC.

COLLINE LITURGICAL PUBLICATIONS see
HARPER AND ROW, PUBLISHERS, INC.

COLONIAL WILLIAMSBURG see UNIVERSITY
PRESS OF VIRGINIA

COLORADO ASSOCIATED UNIVERSITY PRESS

1344 Grandview Avenue
Campus Box 480
Boulder, Colorado 80309
Telephone:

ADDRESS FOR ORDERS:

Same as above.

PREPAYMENT:

Not required.

DISCOUNT POLICY:

10% discount to libraries.

RETURN POLICY:

Returns are accepted within one year of
purchase order date. Claims for damaged
books must be made immediately upon
receipt.

SHIPPING AND BILLING POLICY:

Libraries are charged shipping (Library
Rate) and handling (for UPS only).
Invoices are sent as specified by the
library.

SPECIAL PLANS:

Standing order plans are available.

COLUMBIA PUBLISHING COMPANY see VANGUARD PRESS, INC.

COLUMBIA UNIVERSITY PRESS

562 West 113th Street
New York, New York 10025
Telephone: 212-316-7100

ADDRESS FOR ORDERS:

Columbia University Press
136 South Broadway
Irvington-On-Hudson, NY 10533

DISTRIBUTION/IMPRINT:

New York University Press
University of Edinburgh Press
University of Tokyo Press
Free Association Press
Printer Publishers
American University in Cairo Press

PREPAYMENT:

Not required.

DISCOUNT POLICY:

Publisher allows a 15% discount on blanket standing orders. There is no discount on regular library orders.

RETURN POLICY:

Publisher requires written permission for returns. No book may be returned before 90 days nor after one year from invoice date. All books must be returned in new and salable condition. Books out-of-print longer than one year are not returnable. Books received from the publisher in damaged or imperfect condition must be returned within 30 days of receipt. The address for returns is the same as for orders.

SHIPPING AND BILLING POLICY:

Libraries pay postage. Invoices are either sent with shipments or separately according to library instructions. All shipments are f.o.b. Irving-On-Hudson, NY 10533.

BACK ORDER POLICY:

Titles not currently available are reported and back ordered unless instructed otherwise by library.

SPECIAL ORDER PLAN:

On the publisher's Standing Order Plan, all new books are sent as they appear at a 15% discount. Paperbacks, reprints, and NBER series are excluded.

COLUMBINE see RANDOM HOUSE, INC.

COMMERCE CLEARING HOUSE, INC.

2700 Lake Cook Road
Riverwoods, Illinois 60015
Telephone: 312-940-4600

ADDRESS FOR ORDERS:

Commerce Clearing House, Inc.
4025 W. Peterson Avenue
Chicago, Illinois 60646
Telephone: 312-940-4600
          312-583-8500

PREPAYMENT:

Not required.

DISCOUNT POLICY:

School libraries are allowed a discount on a selected number of loose-leaf publications available on subscription and a 20% discount off single-copy list price for books.

RETURN POLICY:

Loose-leaf publications and books may be returned at the purchaser's expense with an explanation of the reason for return. Books should be returned with 15 days after receipt; loose-leaf publications would be returned within 30 days after the effective subscription date. Cancellation charges may apply to the return of loose-leaf publications. Returns should be sent to Peterson Avenue address.

SHIPPING AND BILLING POLICY:

There are no shipping or handling charges for loose-leaf publications available on subscription or prepaid orders for books shipped Fourth Class.

There is a $1.00 charge for each book for billed orders. Invoices are sent with shipments of books and after loose-leaf publications on subscription.

BACK ORDER POLICY:

Back orders are accepted.

COMMUNICATION CREATIVITY

Box 213 (County Road FF38)
Saguache, Colorado 81149
Telephone: 303-589-8223
          303-589-5995

ADDRESS FOR ORDERS:

Same as above.

DISTRIBUTION/IMPRINTS:

Distributes: Drelwood Publications; Smart Luck.

PREPAYMENT:

Not required.

DISCOUNT POLICY:

1-4 copies: no discount
5 or more: 20%

RETURN POLICY:

Returns in salable condition are accepted for full credit within six months. No prior authorization is necessary if the returns are accompanied by a copy of the original invoice or packing list with invoice information.

SHIPPING AND BILLING POLICY:

Prepaid orders are shipped free; library pays shipping on billed orders. Invoices are sent with shipments unless the library specifies otherwise.

BACK ORDER POLICY:

If a book is not in print when ordered, it is permanently out of print.

COMMUNICATIONS PRESS

1705 Desales Street, NW
Washington, DC 20036
Telephone: 202-659-2340

ADDRESS FOR ORDERS:

Same as above.

PREPAYMENT:

Not required.

DISCOUNT POLICY:

No library discounts.

RETURN POLICY:

Publisher requests that libraries obtain written permission. A request must include invoice number of original shipment, titles, quantities, and price paid. Return is limited to one year. There is no non-returnable title except out-of-print books. The address for returns is the same as for orders.

SHIPPING AND BILLING POLICY:

There is a shipping/handling charge for billed orders of $2 for the first book, $1 per book thereafter. Invoice is included with shipment unless library requests otherwise.

BACK ORDER POLICY:

Publisher back orders unavailable titles if delivery of out-of-stock item is expected within three months.

COMPACT BOOKS see FREDERICK FELL PUBLISHERS, INC.

COMPCARE PUBLICATIONS

2415 Annapolis Lane
Minneapolis, Minnesota 55441
Telephone: 612-559-4800

ADDRESS FOR ORDERS:

Same as above.
Telephone: 800-328-3330

PREPAYMENT:

Not required.

DISCOUNT POLICY:

No discount to libraries.

RETURN POLICY:

Publisher does not accept returns from libraries.

SHIPPING AND BILLING POLICY:

Libraries pay shipping and handling which vary with each order. Invoices are sent separately only.

BACK ORDER POLICY:

Orders are held, and items are shipped when available.

COMPUTER SCIENCE PRESS see W. H. FREEMAN AND COMPANY

COMSTOCK PUBLISHING ASSOCIATES see CORNELL UNIVERSITY PRESS

CONDUCE see WARREN H. GREEN, INC.

CONFERENCE BOARD, INC.

---

845 Third Avenue
New York, New York 10022
Telephone: 212-759-0900

ADDRESS FOR ORDERS:

Publication Sales
The Conference Board, Inc.
845 Third Avenue
New York, New York 10022

PREPAYMENT:

Publisher requires prepayment for library orders.

DISCOUNT POLICY:

1-9 copies	no discount
10-24 copies	25% discount
25-99 copies	50% discount
100 and more	60% discount

RETURN POLICY:

Book returns are not accepted from nonmembers. The address for returns is the same as for orders.

SHIPPING AND BILLING POLICY:

Publisher pays postage. There is no handling charge to libraries. Invoices are sent with shipments.

BACK ORDER POLICY:

Orders for titles not currently available are returned to libraries.

CONGRESSIONAL QUARTERLY, INC.

1414 22nd Street, NW
Washington, DC 20037
Telephone: 202-887-8621

ADDRESS FOR ORDERS:

Same as above.

DISTRIBUTION/IMPRINTS:

Publisher imprints: CQ; CQ Press.

PREPAYMENT:

Not required.

DISCOUNT POLICY:

No scheduled discount to libraries.

RETURN POLICY:

Returns are accepted within 30 days unless there are extenuating circumstances. Written permission is not required. Invoice information must accompany returns.

SHIPPING AND BILLING POLICY:

Libraries are charged shipping/handling on billed orders only; prepaid orders are shipped free. Shipping/Handling charges are assessed as follows: $1.95 on orders under $50.00; $3.50 on orders from $50.00-100.00; 5% of total on orders over $100. Invoices are sent with shipments except for single titles that are prepackaged.

BACK ORDER POLICY:

Publisher back orders unavailable titles and ships books when they become available.

SPECIAL PLANS:

Standing order plans are available for publisher's 12 serial publications.

CONSERVATION FOUNDATION

1250 24th Street, N.W.
Suite 500
Washington, D.C. 20037
Telephone: 202-293-4800

ADDRESS FOR ORDERS:

Same as above.

DISTRIBUTION/IMPRINTS:

Publisher imprints: World Wildlife Fund.

PREPAYMENT:

Prepayment is required on all orders.

DISCOUNT POLICY:

1-4 books: no discount
5-9 books: 20% discount
10-99 books: 25% discount
over 100 books: 40% discount

No discount is offered on research papers.

RETURN POLICY:

No returns for libraries.

SHIPPING AND BILLING POLICY:

Shipping charges are $1.00 per book, with a minimum of $2.00 and a maximum of $5.00 charged for fourth-class shipping.

CONSERVATORY OF AMERICAN LETTERS

P.O. Box 88
Thomaston, Maine 04861
Telephone: 207-354-6550

ADDRESS FOR ORDERS:

Conservatory of American Letters
P.O. Box 123
South Thomaston, Maine 04858
Telephone: 207-354-6550

DISTRIBUTION/IMPRINTS:

Northwoods Press (Division)
Dan River Press (Division)
American History Press (Division)

PREPAYMENT:

Not required but appreciated.

DISCOUNT POLICY:

1 book: no discount
% discount (for 2 or more) = number of
    books ordered X 2.

RETURN POLICY:

No returns accepted except for damaged books which must be returned within 24 hours of receipt. Returns should be sent to P.O. Box 123 address.

SHIPPING AND BILLING POLICY:

Libraries pay shipping of $1.25 for the first book plus $0.50 for the next five books and $0.20 for each additional book. Invoices are sent with shipments.

BACK ORDER POLICY:

Orders are held until the books become available.

CONSULTANT PRESS see PHOTOGRAPHIC ARTS CENTER, LTD.

CONSUMER GUIDE PUBLICATIONS INTERNATIONAL, LTD.

7373 North Cicero Avenue
Lincolnwood, Illinois 60646
Telephone: 312-676-3470

ADDRESS FOR ORDERS:

Same as above.

PREPAYMENT:

Prepayment is required only for orders of
small amounts.

DISCOUNT POLICY:

20% discount to libraries.

RETURN POLICY:

Publisher does not accept returns.

SHIPPING AND BILLING POLICY:

Libraries are charged actual shipping
costs. Invoices are sent as specified by
the library.

BACK ORDER POLICY:

Publisher will advise library if a title
is out of stock and try to give an
availability date.

CONSUMER REPORTS BOOKS

---

110 E. 42nd Street, Suite 1301
New York, New York 10017
Telephone: 212-682-9280

ADDRESS FOR ORDERS:

Same as above.
Telephone: 800-242-7737

DISTRIBUTION/IMPRINTS:

Distributes selected publications of
Consumers' Association of Great Britain.

PREPAYMENT:

Not required.

DISCOUNT POLICY:

1-5 assorted copies: no discount
6 or more: 20%

RETURN POLICY:

Returns are accepted within one year of
invoice date. Written permission is not
required. Address for returns: Harper &
Row/Key Distribution Center/Reeves
St/Dunmore, PA 18512.

SHIPPING AND BILLING POLICY:

Libraries are charged shipping at
Library Rate. Invoices are sent with
shipments unless the library specifies
otherwise.

BACK ORDER POLICY:

Publisher back orders unavailable titles
and ships books when they become
available.

SPECIAL PLANS:

A standing order plan for annuals and
biennials is available at 20% discount
and free postage and handling.
Interested libraries should write to: 540
Barnum Ave/Bridgeport, CT 06608.

CONTEMPORARY DRAMA SERVICE see MERIWETHER
PUBLISHING, LTD.

CONTINUUM see HARPER AND ROW, PUBLISHERS,
INC.

COORDINATING RESEARCH COUNCIL see SOCIETY
OF AUTOMOTIVE ENGINEERS

COPPER CANYON PRESS

P.O. Box 271
Port Townsend, Washington 98368
Telephone:

ADDRESS FOR ORDERS:

Same as above.

DISTRIBUTION/IMPRINTS:

Distributed by: Consortium/213 East 4th Street/St. Paul, MN 55101. Telephone: 612-221-9035.

PREPAYMENT:

Not required.

DISCOUNT POLICY:

10% discount on all orders.

RETURN POLICY:

Books may be returned within one year for full credit as long as they are in salable condition and accompanied by the invoice number. Limited edition books cannot be returned. No prior permission is required. Returns should be sent to the address from which the books were ordered.

SHIPPING AND BILLING POLICY:

Libraries are charged shipping (Library Rate) plus a handling charge of $0.50 per order on all orders. Invoices are sent with shipments unless the library specifies otherwise.

BACK ORDER POLICY:

Back orders are filled when a book is available. Libraries are notified of the due date.

SPECIAL PLANS:

Standing orders for trade or limited editions or both are available at a 15% discount.

CORNELL MARITIME PRESS, INC.

306 E. Water Street
P.O. Box 456
Centreville, Maryland 21617
Telephone: 800-638-7641
          301-758-1075

ADDRESS FOR ORDERS:

Same as above.

DISTRIBUTION/IMPRINTS:

Tidewater Publishers (Imprint)

PREPAYMENT:

Accounts are automatically opened for public libraries.

DISCOUNT POLICY:

No discount to libraries.

RETURN POLICY:

Books, in salable condition and accompanied by invoice number and date, are accepted for return within one year. Written permission is not required.

SHIPPING AND BILLING POLICY:

If the order is prepaid, the shipping cost is included in the quoted price; for billed orders, postage plus handling ($0.10 for every $20.00) will be added to the quoted price. Invoices are sent with shipments unless the library specifies otherwise.

BACK ORDER POLICY:

Unless publisher notes otherwise, titles not yet published or out of stock are automatically back ordered.

CORNELL PAPERBACKS see CORNELL UNIVERSITY PRESS

CORNELL/PHAIDON BOOKS see CORNELL UNIVERSITY PRESS

CORNELL UNIVERSITY PRESS

124 Roberts Place
Ithaca, New York 14853
Telephone: 607-277-2211

ADDRESS FOR ORDERS:

Same as above.

DISTRIBUTION/IMPRINT:

Comstock Publishing Associates
Cornell/Phaidon Books
Cornell Paperbacks

PREPAYMENT:

Not required.

DISCOUNT POLICY:

Library orders are filled at list price. Special discount for blanket standing orders for all new books is 20%. Standing orders for all books within a series receive a 10% discount.

RETURN POLICY:

Books may be returned at any time, without prior permission, as long as they are in print as listed in the latest PTLA. Books must be in resalable condition and be accompanied by a packing slip showing quantities, discounts, and invoice number. If no invoice information is given, credit will be issued at a maximum discount allowable.

SHIPPING AND BILLING POLICY:

Publisher pays postage for prepaid orders. Libraries pay shipping for billed orders. Invoices are sent with shipment unless library instructs otherwise.

BACK ORDER POLICY:

Titles not currently available are reported and back ordered unless otherwise instructed by library.

SPECIAL ORDER PLAN:

On the Standing Order Plan, libraries automatically receive all books published within a particular series as specified by library, at a discount of 10%. On the Blanket Standing Order Plan, all new books published by the publisher are automatically sent and libraries receive a 20% discount.

CORNERSTONE BOOKS see CROSSWAY BOOKS

CORNWALL BOOKS see ASSOCIATED UNIVERSITY PRESSES

CORONA PUBLISHING COMPANY

1037 S. Alamo
San Antonio, Texas 78210
Telephone: 512-227-1771, x1977.

ADDRESS FOR ORDERS:

Texas Monthly Press
P.O. Box 1569
Austin, Texas 78767
Telephone: 800-288-3288

PREPAYMENT:

Not required.

DISCOUNT POLICY:

1 copy: no discount
2-9:   20%
10 or more: 30%

RETURN POLICY:

Permission is not required. Address for returns: Texas Monthly Press/3800 Drosett Drive #H/Austin, TX 78744.

SHIPPING AND BILLING POLICY:

Libraries are charged actual shipping on all orders. Invoices are sent separately.

BACK ORDER POLICY:

Publisher back orders unavailable titles unless the library instructs otherwise.

SPECIAL PLANS:

Library Standing Order Plan is available at a maximum 40% discount.

COSMOS LITERARY AGENCY see BORGO PRESS

COTTAGE PRESS see WILLIAMSON PUBLISHING COMPANY

COUNCIL OAKS BOOKS see INDEPENDENT PUBLISHERS GROUP

COURAGE BOOKS see RUNNING PRESS BOOK
PUBLISHERS

COWARD-MCCANN see PUTNAM PUBLISHING GROUP

COWLEY PUBLICATIONS

980 Memorial Drive
Cambridge, Massachusetts 02138
Telephone: 617-876-3507

ADDRESS FOR ORDERS:

Same as above.

PREPAYMENT:

Not required.

DISCOUNT POLICY:

All books ordered direct are eligible for
a 10% discount.

RETURN POLICY:

Books must be in resalable condition and
should be returned within one year of
invoice date.

SHIPPING AND BILLING POLICY:

Libraries are charged shipping plus
$1.00 handling charge. Invoices are sent
with shipments unless the library
specifies otherwise.

BACK ORDER POLICY:

Publisher will back order any book
currently unavailable.

SPECIAL PLANS:

A standing order plan for new titles
(approximately 10 per year) is available
at a 20% discount. Libraries may cancel
at any time with a written notice.

CRAFTSMAN BOOK COMPANY

6058 Corte del Cedro
Box 6500
Carlsbad, California 92009
Telephone: 619-438-7828

ADDRESS FOR ORDERS:

Same as above.

PREPAYMENT:

Not required.

DISCOUNT POLICY:

5% discount on 24 or more titles.

RETURN POLICY:

Books may be returned at any time for
full credit.

SHIPPING AND BILLING POLICY:

Publisher pays shipping on prepaid
orders; library pays shipping on billed
orders. Invoices are sent with
shipments.

BACK ORDER POLICY:

Publisher ships when books are available
and sends the bill in advance.

CRAIN BOOKS see NATIONAL TEXTBOOK COMPANY

CRANE RUSSAK see TAYLOR & FRANCIS GROUP

CREATIVE EDUCATION

P.O. Box 227
Mankato, Minnesota 56002-0227

ADDRESS FOR ORDERS:

Same as above.

PREPAYMENT:

Prepayment is required for orders under
$25.00.

DISCOUNT POLICY:

30% discount from list price on library orders.

RETURN POLICY:

Returns, with written permission, are accepted within 90 days.

SHIPPING AND BILLING POLICY:

Libraries are charged shipping/handling of 9.2% ($2.00 minimum). Invoices are sent separately unless the library specifies otherwise.

BACK ORDER POLICY:

Publisher will back order titles that are temporarily out of stock.

CREATIVE JOYS, INC. (PARACLETE PRESS)

P.O. Box 1568
Orleans, Massachusetts 02653
Telephone: 617-255-4685
          800-451-5006

ADDRESS FOR ORDERS:

Same as above.

PREPAYMENT:

Prepayment is required for all first-time orders.

DISCOUNT POLICY:

15% discount to libraries.

RETURN POLICY:

With written permission, books, in salable condition, may be returned for credit no sooner than three months and no later than twelve months after the invoice date. There is a 10% restocking fee.

SHIPPING AND BILLING POLICY:

Libraries pay shipping (UPS) plus a handling charge of from $1.00 to $3.00 depending on the amount of the order. Invoices are sent separately, but special arrangements could be made.

BACK ORDER POLICY:

Unavailable titles are placed on back order until they are available.

CRESTWOOD HOUSE, INC.

Highway 66 South
P.O. Box 3427
Mankato, Minnesota 56002-3427
Telephone: 507-388-1616
          800-535-4393

ADDRESS FOR ORDERS:

Same as above.

PREPAYMENT:

Not required.

DISCOUNT POLICY:

1-24 books: no discount
25-99 books: 10%
100 or more: 15%

RETURN POLICY:

Returns are accepted. Libraries should telephone or write for a return label.

SHIPPING AND BILLING POLICY:

Prepaid orders are shipped free; others are charged 5% shipping/handling. Invoices are normally sent separately after shipments unless the library specifies otherwise.

BACK ORDER POLICY:

Any books not currently in stock are automatically back ordered unless library specifies otherwise.

CROSSING PRESS

Box 1048
22-D Roache Road
Freedom, California 95019
Telephone: 408-722-0711

ADDRESS FOR ORDERS:

Same as above.

PREPAYMENT:

Publisher usually requires prepayment for library orders.

DISCOUNT POLICY:

20% discount to libraries.

RETURN POLICY:

Returns are accepted within one year from invoice date. Prior written permission is required.

SHIPPING AND BILLING POLICY:

Libraries are charged actual shipping costs. Invoices are sent with shipments unless the library specifies otherwise.

BACK ORDER POLICY:

Publisher back orders according to library's specifications.

OTHER:

Publisher fills most orders in 2-3 days.

CROSSROAD see HARPER AND ROW, PUBLISHERS, INC.

CROSSWAY BOOKS

9825 W. Roosevelt Road
Westchester, Illinois 60153
Telephone: 800-323-3890

ADDRESS FOR ORDERS:

Same as above.

DISTRIBUTION/IMPRINTS:

Crossway Books (formerly Cornerstone Books) is a division of Good News Publishers.

PREPAYMENT:

Not required.

DISCOUNT POLICY:

30% discount to libraries.

RETURN POLICY:

Returns accompanied by original invoice number, purchase date, and which are still in print are accepted within 9 months. Written permission is required. Send returns to Returns Department at the address above.

SHIPPING AND BILLING POLICY:

Libraries are charged actual shipping. Invoices are sent separately.

BACK ORDER POLICY:

Publisher automatically back orders unavailable titles.

OTHER:

Publisher releases titles twice a year and will place interested libraries on its mailing list to receive new title information.

CROWN PUBLISHERS, INC.

---

225 Park Avenue South
New York, New York 10003
Telephone: 212-254-1600

ADDRESS FOR ORDERS:

Same as above.

DISTRIBUTION/IMPRINTS:

Distributes: Harmony Books; Clarkson Potter, Inc; Orion Books; Outlet Book Company.

PREPAYMENT:

Not required.

DISCOUNT POLICY:

20% flat rate discount except on Outlet Books.

RETURN POLICY:

Returns, accompanied by the invoice, are accepted at any time without written permission. Return address: Crown Publishers/34 Englehard Ave/Avenel, NJ 07003.

SHIPPING AND BILLING POLICY:

Libraries are charged shipping. Invoices are sent separately after shipments.

BACK ORDER POLICY:

Publisher back orders titles that are not yet published.

CRUISING CLASSROOM see WESTERN MARINE ENTERPRISES

CUADRA/ELSEVIER see ELSEVIER SCIENCE PUBLISHING COMPANY, INC.

CUTTER TABLES, INC. see LIBRARIES UNLIMITED

DEC BOOKS see DIGITAL PRESS

DALCROZE SOCIETY see PRINCETON BOOK COMPANY, PUBLISHERS

DALLAS INSTITUTE PUBLICATIONS see SPRING PUBLICATIONS, INC.

DANCE NOTATION BUREAU see PRINCETON BOOK COMPANY, PUBLISHERS

JOHN DANIEL, PUBLISHER

P.O. Box 21922
Santa Barbara, California 93121
Telephone: 805-962-1780

ADDRESS FOR ORDERS:

Same as above.

DISTRIBUTION/IMPRINTS:

Distributes the publications of: Naris Publications; Atlas Signs.

Fithian Press (Division/Imprint)

PREPAYMENT:

Not required.

DISCOUNT POLICY:

10% discount to libraries.

RETURN POLICY:

Books still in print may be returned for credit. Permission to return is required. Address for returns: 629 State St #220/Santa Barbara, CA 93101.

SHIPPING AND BILLING POLICY:

Libraries are charged shipping at Library Rate. Invoices are sent with shipments unless the library specifies otherwise.

BACK ORDER POLICY:

Publisher will back order unless instructed otherwise.

DAST BOOKS see BORGO PRESS

DAUGHTERS OF ST. PAUL see ALBA HOUSE PUBLISHERS

DAVID & CHARLES see STERLING PUBLISHING COMPANY, INC.

HARLAN DAVIDSON, INC.

3110 No. Arlington Heights Road
Arlington Heights, Illinois 60004-1592
Telephone: 312-253-9720

ADDRESS FOR ORDERS:

Same as above.

DISTRIBUTION/IMPRINTS:

Imprints: Crofts Classics; Goldentree Bibliographies.

PREPAYMENT:

Not required.

DISCOUNT POLICY:

10% discount to libraries.

RETURN POLICY:

Returns, in salable condition and accompanied by invoice numbers, dates and quantities, are accepted within 12 months of invoice date. Written permission is required.

SHIPPING AND BILLING POLICY:

Libraries are charged shipping plus a handling charge of $1.50 for fewer than five books. Invoices are sent separately after shipments.

BACK ORDER POLICY:

Back orders are placed for items temporarily out of stock or not yet published unless the library instructs otherwise.

F. A. DAVIS COMPANY

1915 Arch Street
Philadelphia, Pennsylvania 19103
Telephone: 215-568-2270

ADDRESS FOR ORDERS:

Same as above.

PREPAYMENT:

Not required with purchase order.

DISCOUNT POLICY:

0-29 books: No discount (FOB destination)
30 or more: 10% plus postage (FOB Philadelphia)

RETURN POLICY:

Returns accepted within 30 days of receipt. If a copy of the invoice is enclosed with returns, prior permission is not required; otherwise, permission is required. Out-of-print books or books with superseded editions are non-returnable. Address for returns: F. A. Davis Company/5600 Paschall Avenue/Philadelphia, PA 19143.

SHIPPING AND BILLING POLICY:

Shipping costs depend upon discount (see above). No handling charge for purchase orders. Invoices are sent separately unless the library specifies otherwise.

BACK ORDER POLICY:

Items are back ordered according to the terms of the purchase order. Items that have been back ordered are indicated on the invoice. If an item has been on back order for longer than three months, publisher sends letter requesting confirmation of order prior to shipping.

SPECIAL PLANS:

Standing order is available on above terms.

DAVIS PUBLICATIONS, INC.

50 Portland Street
Worcester, MA 01608
Telephone: 800-533-2847
          617-754-7201

ADDRESS FOR ORDERS:

Same as above.

PREPAYMENT:

Not required.

DISCOUNT POLICY:

All books are sold at list price.

RETURN POLICY:

Returns, in salable condition, are accepted within three months. Prior written permission is required.

SHIPPING AND BILLING POLICY:

Libraries are charged shipping/handling of $1.75 for the first book and $0.50 for each additional book. Invoices are sent after shipments only.

BACK ORDER POLICY:

Items out of stock are placed on back order and are shipped when available.

OTHER:

Publisher prefers that libraries order through a wholesaler.

DAWNWOOD PRESS see STERLING PUBLISHING COMPANY, INC.

DAYSTAR see BORGO PRESS

ALDINE DE GRUYTER see WALTER DE GRUYTER

MOUTON DE GRUYTER see WALTER DE GRUYTER

WALTER DE GRUYTER, INC.

---

200 Saw Mill River Road
Hawthorne, New York
Telephone: 914-747-0110

ADDRESS FOR ORDERS:

Same as above.

DISTRIBUTION/IMPRINTS:

Mouton de Gruyter (Division)
Aldine de Gruyter (Division)

PREPAYMENT:

Not required.

DISCOUNT POLICY:

No discount to libraries.

RETURN POLICY:

Only books shipped on approval are considered for return. Prior written permission and a return label are required. Time limit: 12 months.

SHIPPING AND BILLING POLICY:

Libraries are charged shipping on all orders. Invoices are sent with shipments unless the library specifies otherwise.

BACK ORDER POLICY:

Titles out-of-stock will be back ordered, reported, and supplied within the time specified.

SPECIAL PLANS:

Standing orders are available for subscriptions to journals, yearbooks, and serial publications.

OTHER:

Publisher supplies direct as well as through wholesalers. A complete stock is available in Hawthorne.

JUAN DE LA CUESTA - HISPANIC MONOGRAPHS

---

270 Indian Road
Newark, Delaware 19711
Telephone: 302-453-8699

ADDRESS FOR ORDERS:

Same as above.

PREPAYMENT:

Not required.

DISCOUNT POLICY:

10% discount if more than one book is ordered; 15% discount for standing orders.

RETURN POLICY:

Returns, with an explanation, are accepted within three months.

SHIPPING AND BILLING POLICY:

Libraries are charged shipping on all orders. Invoices are sent with shipments unless the library specifies otherwise.

BACK ORDER POLICY:

Back orders are shipped when available.

B. C. DECKER see C. V. MOSBY COMPANY

DEL REY see RANDOM HOUSE, INC.

DELMAR PUBLISHERS, INC.

---

2 Computer Drive West
P.O. Box 15-015
Albany, New York 12212
Telephone: 800-347-7707

ADDRESS FOR ORDERS:

Same as above.

DISTRIBUTION/IMPRINTS:

Distributes publications of:
Lawrenceville Press; Motor Publications;
CTO Associates.

PREPAYMENT:

Not required.

DISCOUNT POLICY:

10% discount to libraries.

RETURN POLICY:

Books, in salable condition, may be returned within one year from invoice date to: Book Distribution Center/7625 Empire Dr/Florence, KY 41042. Permission is not required. Software, videos, slides, and films are not returnable.

SHIPPING AND BILLING POLICY:

Billed orders pay shipping (FOB Kentucky) plus a 2 1/4% handling charge. Prepaid orders are shipped free. Invoices are sent separately only.

BACK ORDER POLICY:

Publisher will hold orders until an item is in stock.

DEMBNER BOOKS see W. W. NORTON AND COMPANY, INC.

DENLINGER'S PUBLISHERS, LTD.

P.O. Box 76
Fairfax, Virginia 22030
Telephone: 703-830-4646

ADDRESS FOR ORDERS:

Same as above.

PREPAYMENT:

Prepayment is required for orders under five titles; these orders receive a 25% discount and are shipped free.

DISCOUNT POLICY:

1-4 titles:	25% (prepaid)
5-99:	40%
100 or more:	50%

RETURN POLICY:

Returns in salable condition are accepted at any time. Written permission is required. UPS returns should be sent to: 14016 West View Dr/Centreville, VA 22020.

SHIPPING AND BILLING POLICY:

Libraries are charged actual shipping except on prepaid orders. Invoices are sent separately.

BACK ORDER POLICY:

Publisher back orders unavailable titles and informs library when titles are available.

DENVER CENTER THEATER COMPANY see JOHNSON BOOKS

DESALES PROGRAM see TABOR PUBLISHING

DESTINY BOOKS see INNER TRADITIONS

DETAIL & SCALE see TAB BOOKS

ANDRE DEUTSCH see E. P. DUTTON

DEVIN-ADAIR PUBLISHERS

6 North Water Street
Greenwich, Connecticut 06830
Telephone: 203-531-7755

ADDRESS FOR ORDERS:

Same as above.

DISTRIBUTION/IMPRINTS:

Distributes the publications of: Flag
Press; Patriot Press; Irish-American Book
Society.

PREPAYMENT:

Publisher prefers prepayment on orders
under $25.00.

DISCOUNT POLICY:

20% discount to libraries.

RETURN POLICY:

Written permission to return is
required. Requests should include
titles, quantities, and invoice numbers.
All returns must be prepaid and in
salable condition.

SHIPPING AND BILLING POLICY:

Libraries are charged shipping of $1.75
per order. Invoices are sent with

shipments unless the library specifies
otherwise.

BACK ORDER POLICY:

Libraries are notified when an item on
back order becomes available.

SPECIAL PLANS:

Publisher offers a single title order
plan (STOP) and a library standing order
plan.

DIGITAL PRESS

12 Crosby Drive
Bedford, Massachusetts 01730
Telephone: 617-276-1498

ADDRESS FOR ORDERS:

Digital Press Order Fulfillment
12A Esquire Road
Billerica, MA 01862

DISTRIBUTION/IMPRINTS:

Imprints: Digital Press; DECBooks;
Digital Equipment Corporation Handbooks;
Digital Technical Journal.

PREPAYMENT:

Prepayment is required on orders of
$50.00 or less.

DISCOUNT POLICY:

1:	no discount
2-9:	5%
10-49:	10%
50-249:	15%
500-749:	25%

RETURN POLICY:

Returns in resalable condition are
accepted within one year. Permission is
required either by telephone (617-663-
4152) or in writing to Esquire Road
address to which the returns should be
sent also.

SHIPPING AND BILLING POLICY:

Libraries are charged shipping (UPS) on
billed orders; prepaid orders are
shipped free. Invoices are sent
separately only.

BACK ORDER POLICY:

As long as a book has an ISBN and a DEC part number, it can be back ordered at any time.

OTHER:

Publisher encourages libraries to order through wholesalers.

DILLON PRESS, INC.

242 Portland Avenue South
Minneapolis, Minnesota 55415
Telephone: 612-333-2691
          800-328-8322, x687

ADDRESS FOR ORDERS:

Same as above.

DISTRIBUTION/IMPRINTS:

Imprint: Gemstone Books

PREPAYMENT:

Not required.

DISCOUNT POLICY:

No discount to libraries.

RETURN POLICY:

Returns in salable condition are accepted for credit within one year. Written or verbal permission is required. Address for returns: Dillon Press/c/o Dillon Warehouse/521 Washington Avenue South/Minneapolis, MN 55415.

SHIPPING AND BILLING POLICY:

Libraries are charged shipping on all orders. Invoices are sent separately after shipments.

BACK ORDER POLICY:

Publisher back orders out-of-stock titles unless the library specifies otherwise.

SPECIAL PLANS:

Libraries should contact the Marketing Department for information about special order plans.

DIOSCORIDES PRESS see TIMBER PRESS

ED DOBSON TRADERS PRESS see LAMBERT GANN PUBLISHING COMPANY

DOCUMENTTEXT see MCPHERSON & COMPANY

DODD, MEAD AND COMPANY, INC.

71 Fifth Avenue
New York, New York 10003
Telephone: 212-627-8444

ADDRESS FOR ORDERS:

Same as above.

PREPAYMENT:

Not required.

DISCOUNT POLICY:

Library discount schedule is:

1 to 9 copies	10%
10 to 24 copies	20%
25 to 99 copies	25%
100 and more	30%

RETURN POLICY:

Damaged or defective books are returnable for full credit or replacement including transportation both ways. The address for returns is: Dodd, Mead and Company, 6 Ram Ridge Road, Spring Valley, NY 10977.

SHIPPING AND BILLING POLICY:

Libraries pay postage. There is no other handling charge. Invoices are sent separately from shipments; packing slips are enclosed in shipments.

BACK ORDER POLICY:

Titles not currently available are either back ordered or cancelled as library requests.

SPECIAL ORDER PLAN:

Individual arrangement to ship in special categories, i.e., best plays, mysteries, adult, can be made by writing the publisher. Library will be billed at 20% off the list price for each title plus postage.

There are no return privileges. However, damaged or defective books will be exchanged promptly. The only titles which will not be included are those books published for a small, specific non-library market, reissue of older titles, and slightly revised editions. Invoices are rendered with each shipment and the terms are 30 days net.

Formal contracts are not necessary. Library's letter agreeing to these arrangements is all that is necessary to commence service as would a letter to terminate library's participation.

In addition to the Standing Order Plan, Dodd, Mead has a Greenaway Plan. Books are not returnable unless damaged or defective. Invoices are rendered with each shipment, terms 30 days net. The plan can be terminated at any time by written notice.

DOLMEN PRESS see DUFOUR EDITIONS, INC.

DOODLY SQUAT PRESS see BORGO PRESS

DORSEY PRESS see RICHARD D. IRWIN, INC.

DOVER see ALFRED PUBLISHING COMPANY, INC.

DOVER PUBLICATIONS, INC.

31 East Second Street
Mineola, New York 11501
Telephone: 516-294-7000

ADDRESS FOR ORDERS:

Same as above.

PREPAYMENT:

All orders under $7.50 (without postage) must be prepaid.

DISCOUNT POLICY:

Publisher allows a 25% discount for orders of $35 or more. A 10% discount is given for orders of less than $35 only if library orders 25 or more copies of the same title.

RETURN POLICY:

All items may be returned within 30 days of purchase. No prior permission is required. The address for returns is the same as for orders.

SHIPPING AND BILLING POLICY:

Libraries pay postage and handling charges. For prepaid orders, the amount of postage and handling is $1.25 for one book and $2.50 for two or more books, or a flat fee of $3.00 for UPS.

BACK ORDER POLICY:

Publisher back orders only for prepaid orders. Orders for billed orders are cancelled and returned to library.

DOW JONES-IRWIN see RICHARD D. IRWIN, INC.

DOWN EAST BOOKS

P.O. Box 679
Camden, Maine 04843
Telephone: 207-594-9544
        800-432-1670 (Maine only)

ADDRESS FOR ORDERS:

Same as above.

PREPAYMENT:

Not required for libraries.

DISCOUNT POLICY:

No discount to libraries.

RETURN POLICY:

Books, in resalable condition, can be returned no sooner then 90 days from order and no later than one year. Prior written permission is required. Calendars are non-returnable.

SHIPPING AND BILLING POLICY:

All orders are FOB Camden. Most shipments are UPS unless library requests otherwise. There are no additional billing charges. Invoices are sent with shipments unless library requests otherwise.

BACK ORDER POLICY:

Back orders are accepted and held until the material is available.

DRAMATIC PUBLISHING COMPANY

---

311 Washington Street
P.O. Box 109
Woodstock, Illinois 60098
Telephone: 815-338-7170

ADDRESS FOR ORDERS:

Same as above.
Telephone: 800-448-7469

PREPAYMENT:

Not required.

DISCOUNT POLICY:

No discount to libraries.

RETURN POLICY:

Returns are not accepted.

SHIPPING AND BILLING POLICY:

Libraries are charged shipping on all orders. Invoices are sent separately only.

BACK ORDER POLICY:

Publisher back orders indefinitely.

DRELWOOD PUBLICATIONS see COMMUNICATION CREATIVITY

DRUMM BOOKS see BORGO PRESS

DRYAD PRESS see CHARLES T. BRANFORD COMPANY

DRYDEN PRESS see HOLT, RINEHART AND WINSTON PUBLISHERS

DUFOUR EDITIONS, INC.

P.O. Box 449
Chester Springs, Pennsylvania 19425-0449
Telephone: 215-458-5005

ADDRESS FOR ORDERS:

Same as above.

DISTRIBUTION/IMPRINTS:

Distributes: Angel Books; Bloodaxe Books, Ltd; Canongate Publishing, Ltd; Dolmen Press; Norvik Press; Peter Owen, Ltd; Poetry Wales Press, Ltd; Seron Books; Polygon Books; Raven Arts Press, Ltd; Shepherd-Walwyn, Ltd; Soho Book Company, Ltd; Colin Smythe, Ltd; Spokesman Press; Stanley Thornes, Ltd; Wilfion Books; Hulton Educational Publications.

PREPAYMENT:

Not required.

DISCOUNT POLICY:

10% discount plus shipping.

RETURN POLICY:

Books may be returned without permission within 18 months of invoice date. Claims for damaged books must be reported immediately. Defective books should be returned promptly with a clear indication of the defect. Street address for returns is: Byers Road.

SHIPPING AND BILLING POLICY:

Libraries are charged shipping on all orders. Invoices are sent with shipments unless the library specifies otherwise.

BACK ORDER POLICY:

Back orders are recorded forever unless cancelled by the library.

SPECIAL PLANS:

An approval plan is available whereby the library specifies subjects, etc. of books to be sent. Books are sent automatically upon publication at 15% discount and free freight. Unwanted books must be returned, at library's expense, within 75 days.

DUKE UNIVERSITY PRESS

6697 College Station
Durham, North Carolina 27708
Telephone: 919-684-2173

ADDRESS FOR ORDERS:

Same as above.
Telephone: 919-684-6837

PREPAYMENT:

Not required with purchase order; journal subscriptions must be prepaid.

DISCOUNT POLICY:

No discount to libraries.

RETURN POLICY:

Returns in salable condition are accepted within one year of invoice date. Written permission is required. Return to Shipping Department at above address.

SHIPPING AND BILLING POLICY:

Libraries are charged shipping on all orders. Invoices are sent with shipments unless the library specifies otherwise.

BACK ORDER POLICY:

Publisher automatically back orders

unavailable titles unless the library instructs otherwise.

SPECIAL PLANS:

Standing orders are available.

DUQUESNE UNIVERSITY PRESS

600 Forbes Avenue
Pittsburgh, Pennsylvania 15282
Telephone: 412-434-6610

ADDRESS FOR ORDERS:

Duquesne University Press
Order Department
Box 675
Holmes, PA 19043
Telephone: 800-345-8112

PREPAYMENT:

Not required.

DISCOUNT POLICY:

15% from the catalog price on all quantities.

RETURN POLICY:

Returns accepted within six months. Prior written permission is required from the Forbes Avenue address. Address for returns: Duquesne University Press/1260 Woodland Avenue/Springfield, PA 19064.

SHIPPING AND BILLING POLICY:

Libraries are charged shipping costs on all orders plus approximately $1.50 handling charge per order. Invoices are sent with shipments.

BACK ORDER POLICY:

Titles not currently available are back ordered and filled when ready.

E.P. DUTTON

2 Park Avenue
New York, New York 10016

Telephone: 212-725-1818

ADDRESS FOR ORDERS:

New American Library
120 Woodbine Avenue
Bergenfield, NJ 07621
Telephone: 201-387-0600
            800-526-0275 (For
  established account)
FAX Number: 201-385-6521

DISTRIBUTION/IMPRINT:

Andre Deutsch
Dial Books for Young Readers
Lodestar Books
New American Library
Stillpoint Publishing

PREPAYMENT:

Not required.

DISCOUNT POLICY:

The following schedule of discounts
applies to all school, college, special
and public libraries.

Single or assorted orders for all
hardcover and paperback titles from
Dutton or the publishers for which it
distributes:

1 to 4 copies   none
5 to 24 copies   35%
25 or more copies   40%

Library editions:

1 to 4 copies   none
5 or more copies   20%

RETURN POLICY:

Any trade book purchased from New
American Library may be returned for any
reason provided it is in salable
condition and in print. All returns will
be credited at the price paid and must be
sent to: Publishers Warehouse and
Shippers, Inc., 34 Engelhard Drive,
Cranbury, NJ 08512. A copy of the
original invoice must be enclosed.

SHIPPING AND BILLING POLICY:

Libraries pay shipping charges on all
orders. Invoices are sent separately
after shipment.

BACK ORDER POLICY:

Publisher fellows library's instruction.

SPECIAL ORDER PLAN:

Dutton Advance Copy Review Plan is a
Greeenaway plan available to very large
library systems which purchase multiple
copies of books. There are separate
plans for each of the publishers for whom
Dutton distributes and the plans can be
divided into adult and juvenile.

Publisher will ship one copy of each new
book with a consumer price of under $35
as it is released by publisher's
warehouse before publication. Libraries
receive invoices with shipments but pay
on statements for the previous six months
issued in June and December. The number
of titles sent per year is approximately
300. Books received under the plan
cannot be returned.

EDC PUBLISHING

P.O. Box 470663
Tulsa, Oklahoma 74146
Telephone: 800-331-4418
            918-662-4522 (collect in OK)

ADDRESS FOR ORDERS:

Same as above.

DISTRIBUTION/IMPRINTS:

Publisher is a division of Educational
Development Corporation.

Usborne Publishing (Imprint)

PREPAYMENT:

Not required.

DISCOUNT POLICY:

No discount to libraries.

RETURN POLICY:

Returns are accepted within one year.
Prior written permission is required.
Math workbooks are non-returnable.
Address for returns: EDC
Publishing/10302 East 55th Place/Tulsa,
OK 74146.

SHIPPING AND BILLING POLICY:

Libraries are charged shipping plus a
handling charge of approximately 15%.
Shipping is free on orders of 25 books
or more. Invoices are sent separately
unless the library specifies otherwise.

BACK ORDER POLICY:

Back orders are shipped when ready.

EAST-WEST CENTER see UNIVERSITY OF HAWAII PRESS

ECCO PRESS see W. W. HORTON AND COMPANY, INC.

EDICIONES UNIVERSAL

P.O. Box 450353 (Shenandoah Station)
Miami, Florida 33145
Telephone: 305-642-3234

ADDRESS FOR ORDERS:

Same as above.

DISTRIBUTION/IMPRINTS:

Distributes publications of Playor (Spain).

PREPAYMENT:

Not required.

DISCOUNT POLICY:

No discount on small orders. On large orders, the discount depends on the titles requested but is usually 10%.

RETURN POLICY:

Returns are accepted within 3 months. Prior written permission is required. Books imported especially for a library are non-returnable. Address for returns: Ediciones Universal/3090 S.W. 8th St./ Miami, Florida 33135.

SHIPPING AND BILLING POLICY:

Libraries are charged a flat rate of $2.00 shipping per order. Invoices are sent with shipments unless the library specifies otherwise.

BACK ORDER POLICY:

Publisher tries to obtain an item on back order no matter how long it takes or from where the item is obtained.

SPECIAL PLANS:

Publisher has a Spanish Books on Approval Plan. Every one or two months, books will be shipped free, and the library may return any that it does not wish to purchase and be billed for the others. The plan may be refined by subject, amount per fiscal year, original language, geographical location (Peninsular Spain, Latin America, Cuba), etc.

OTHER:

Publisher offers free catalogs to libraries. Most of its titles are imports from Spain and Latin America.

EDINBURGH REVIEW see MCPHERSON & COMPANY

EDITORIAL EXPERTS, INC.

---

85 S. Bragg Street, Suite 400
Alexandria, Virginia 22312
Telephone: 703-642-3040

ADDRESS FOR ORDERS:

Same as above.

PREPAYMENT:

Not required with a purchase order.

DISCOUNT POLICY:

No specials discounts for libraries.

RETURN POLICY:

Returns are accepted within one year from purchase date. Prior written permission is required. The current Directory of Editorial Resources is not returnable after October.

SHIPPING AND BILLING POLICY:

Libraries are charged shipping/handling of $2.00 per book. Actual shipping only is charged on orders for 5 or more copies. Invoices are sent with shipments.

BACK ORDER POLICY:

Publisher notifies libraries when a
reprinting is scheduled and gives them
the option of waiting or reordering
later.

EDO-AIRE SEAPLANE DIVISION see AVIATION
BOOK COMPANY

WILLIAM B. EERDMANS PUBLISHING COMPANY

---

255 Jefferson, SE
Grand Rapids, Michigan 49503
Telephone: 616-459-4591
          800-253-7521

ADDRESS FOR ORDERS:

Same as above.
Telephone: 800-633-9326 (orders only)

PREPAYMENT:

Not required.

DISCOUNT POLICY:

20% discount to libraries regardless of
quantity.

RETURN POLICY:

Defective books will be replaced at no
charge. Returns are accepted up to 12
months of invoice date for titles still
in print. Returns will be accepted free
provided that: library has written for
and received permission to return; a
copy of the invoice is included (or the
invoice number, date, customer number,
and packing slip). Returns not meeting
the above conditions will be credited at
90% of invoice.

SHIPPING AND BILLING POLICY:

Libraries are charged actual shipping,
and shipping charges are included on the
invoice. Invoices are sent separately.

BACK ORDER POLICY:

Publisher will back order all
unavailable titles unless the library

requests otherwise. Back orders are
shipped prepaid.

SPECIAL PLANS:

Standing orders are available for any
series.

ELEUTHERIAN-MILLS HAGLEY FOUNDATION see
UNIVERSITY PRESS OF VIRGINIA

ELSEVIER APPLIED SCIENCE see ELSEVIER
SCIENCE PUBLISHING COMPANY, INC.

ELSEVIER SEQUOIA see ELSEVIER SCIENCE
PUBLISHING COMPANY, INC.

ELSEVIER SCIENCE PUBLISHING CO., INC.

---

52 Vanderbilt Avenue
New York, New York 10017
Telephone: 212-370-5520

ADDRESS FOR ORDERS:

Same as above.

DISTRIBUTION/IMPRINT:

Elsevier
North-Holland
Excerpta Medica
Elsevier Sequoia
Elsevier Applied Science
MEPC
Cuadra/Elsevier

PREPAYMENT:

Not required.

DISCOUNT POLICY:

List prices are net to library orders,
except on series standing orders and for
approval plans.

RETURN POLICY:

Written permission to return books must be submitted prior to the return. 100% return privileges apply on all titles in print and in salable condition. Books may be returned up to 18 months from date of invoice to qualify for full credit. All returns must be shipped UPS or insured mail to Elsevier Distribution Center, 160 Imlay Street, Brooklyn, NY 11231.

SHIPPING AND BILLING POLICY:

Libraries pay postage and handling charge. Invoices are sent with the shipments. If requested by library, invoices can be sent to a different address.

BACK ORDER POLICY:

Titles not currently available are either back ordered or cancelled according to library instructions.

SPECIAL ORDER PLAN:

Except for several short discount series, publisher offers a Series Standing Order Plan for most series at either subscription price or 10% discount. A special discount rate of 15% applies when standing orders for 10 or more series are placed directly with the publisher. Approval Plan is available and offers a 15% discount. Libraries may obtain additional information from the publisher.

EMERGENCY RESPONSE INSTITUTE see AVIATION BOOK COMPANY

EMPIRE STATE BOOKS see HEART OF THE LAKE PUBLISHERS

ENGLISH FOLK DANCE & SONG SOCIETY see PRINCETON BOOK COMPANY, PUBLISHERS

ENTELEK

P.O. Box 1303
Portsmouth, New Hampshire 03801
Telephone: 603-436-0439

ADDRESS FOR ORDERS:

Same as above.

PREPAYMENT:

Prepayment is required for orders of less than $100.00.

DISCOUNT POLICY:

Libraries are charged list price.

RETURN POLICY:

Books may be returned within 90 days. Written permission is required. Dated indexes are non-returnable.

SHIPPING AND BILLING POLICY:

Libraries are charged shipping costs on all orders plus a handling charge of 10% of the invoice amount. Invoices are sent separately after shipments.

BACK ORDER POLICY:

Publisher does not back order.

EPISCOPAL RADIO-TV FOUNDATION PUBLICATIONS see MOREHOUSE-BARLOW COMPANY

EPOCH PRESS see WARREN H. GREEN, INC.

EQUAL PARTNERS, INC. see JALMAR PRESS

PAUL S. ERICKSON see INDEPENDENT PUBLISHERS GROUP

ERIDANOS PRESS see RIZZOLI INTERNATIONAL PUBLICATIONS, INC.

LAWRENCE ERLBAUM ASSOCIATES

365 Broadway
Hillsdale, New Jersey 07642
Telephone: 201-666-4110

ADDRESS FOR ORDERS:

Same as above.

DISTRIBUTION/IMPRINTS:

Distributes: Clinical Neuroscience
Press.

Subsidiary: Analytic Press.

PREPAYMENT:

Not required.

DISCOUNT POLICY:

No discount to libraries.

RETURN POLICY:

Returns in salable condition are
accepted for credit within one year.
Prior authorization from Customer
Service Department is required. Damaged
items or short shipments must be claimed
within two weeks of receipt. Invoice
information must accompany returns which
should be sent with postage prepaid. A
$1.00 restocking fee per copy returned
is assessed.

SHIPPING AND BILLING POLICY:

Libraries are charged shipping according
to UPS schedule except for prepaid
orders which are shipped free. Invoices
are sent with shipments.

BACK ORDER POLICY:

Back orders are held until library
cancels.

ETHICS AND PUBLIC POLICY CENTER

1030 15th Street N.W., Suite 300
Washington, D.C. 20005
Telephone: 202-682-1200

ADDRESS FOR ORDERS:

Ethics and Public Policy Center
Order Department
4720 Boston Way
Lanham, MD 20706
Telephone: 301-459-3366

DISTRIBUTION/IMPRINTS:

Distributed by: University Press of
America.

PREPAYMENT:

Prepayment is required for all orders.

DISCOUNT POLICY:

10% discount to libraries; 30% discount
on standing orders.

RETURN POLICY:

Books, in salable condition, postage-
paid, well-packed, and marked "returns",
are accepted within one year of invoice
date. When books are received, the
library is issued a credit memo, but no
credit is allowed on books returned in
poor condition. Prior permission is
required. Address for returns:
University Press of America/8705 Bollman
Place/Savage, MD 20763.

SHIPPING AND BILLING POLICY:

Libraries are charged shipping plus a
handling charge of $1.25 for the first
book and $0.50 for each additional
books. Invoices are sent separately
after shipments only.

BACK ORDER POLICY:

Unavailable titles are placed on back
order for as long as necessary.

SPECIAL PLANS:

A standing order is available at a 30%
discount. Books are billed and shipped
quarterly. Requests should specify paper
or cloth edition.

ETHICS IN A CHANGING WORLD see UNIVERSITY
OF UTAH PRESS

EXECUTIVE REPORTS CORPORATION see
PRENTICE-HALL

FAO see UNIPUB

F & W PUBLICATIONS

1507 Dana Avenue
Cincinnati, Ohio 45207
Telephone: 513-531-2222

ADDRESS FOR ORDERS:

Same as above.
Telephone: 800-543-4644 (outside OH)
800-551-0884 (in OH)

DISTRIBUTION/IMPRINTS:

Publisher distributes:
Rockport Publications
Vacation Workbooks

Writer's Digest Books (Division)
North Light Books (Division)

PREPAYMENT:

Orders for 1-2 books must be prepaid.

DISCOUNT POLICY:

1-2 books: no discount
3-9 books: 20%
10-24 books: 25%
over 25:   30%

RETURN POLICY:

Returns are not accepted.

SHIPPING AND BILLING POLICY:

Publisher pays postage on prepaid orders
only. Invoices are sent with shipments
unless the library specifies otherwise.

BACK ORDER POLICY:

Publisher notifies library on the
invoice when a book is expected and
ships when it is available.

SPECIAL PLANS:

A Greenaway Plan is available;
interested libraries should contact
publisher for details.

FABER & FABER, INC.

50 Cross Street
Winchester, Massachusetts 01890
Telephone: 617-721-1427

ADDRESS FOR ORDERS:

AIDC
2 Acorn Lane
Sunderland Park, VT 05446
Telephone: 800-445-6638

DISTRIBUTION/IMPRINT:

Victoria & Albert Museum
Lorrimer Screenplays

PREPAYMENT:

Not required.

DISCOUNT POLICY:

Libraries receive a 20% discount.

RETURN POLICY:

Return permission is not required for
returns from 6 to 12 months after invoice
date. Credits will be at 47% discount
unless a copy of the original invoice is
furnished. Books judged to be ineligible
or in unsalable condition will be
returned to the library at its expense.
Annual Travel Guides will be declared
out-of-print in January and returns will
be accepted for 6 months, or until the
end of June. The address for returns is
the same as for orders.

SHIPPING AND BILLING POLICY:

Libraries pay shipping charge. There is
no handling or billing charge. Invoices
are sent separately after shipments.

BACK ORDER POLICY:

Publisher notifies library of unavailable
titles and ships as they become
available.

SPECIAL ORDER PLAN:

On Single Title Order Plan, publisher
sends prepaid single-copy orders at a 40%
discount.

FABER MUSIC LTD. see HAL LEONARD
PUBLISHING CORPORATION

FACTS ON FILE, INC.

---

460 Park Avenue South
New York, NY 10016
Telephone: 212-683-2244
           800-322-8755

ADDRESS FOR ORDERS:

Same as above.

PREPAYMENT:

Not required.

DISCOUNT POLICY:

Library discount schedule is as follows.
Clothbound and paperbound editions,
single and assorted titles, and new and
backlist titles can be combined for
quantity discount. All books must be
shipped to a single address.

Long/short/academic books:

1 to 2 books	0%
3 to 5 books	10%
6 to 9 books	15%
10 to 49 books	20%
50 to 99 books	25%
100 or more books	30%

Special discount books:

1 to 9 books	0%
10 to 49 books	10%
50 to 99 books	15%
100 or more books	20%

RETURN POLICY:

Libraries may return books to publisher's
warehouse located in Illinois. Books
should not be returned to New York office
unless the book is defective or damaged.
Credit will be applied to the library's
account only when publisher receives
confirmation from the warehouse that the
books were received in good salable
condition. The address for returns is:
Facts on File Returns Department, c/o
Warepak, Inc., 2427 Bond Street,
University Park, IL 60466.

SHIPPING AND BILLING POLICY:

On prepaid orders, publisher pays postage
and handling charges; if order is billed
on invoice, library pays postage and
handling cost. The amount is based on
the weight of the order. Invoices are
sent separately after shipment unless
library requests otherwise.

BACK ORDER POLICY:

Publisher back orders unavailable titles.
Back orders are held until cancelled by
library.

SPECIAL ORDER PLAN:

On Advance Order Plan, one copy of each
new title is sent to the library
automatically as soon as bound books are
available. Library can eliminate books
with list prices of more than $60.

Books can be examined for 60 days
without obligation. Additional copies
may be ordered through a wholesaler or
directly from the publisher. If a book
received is not suitable for the library,
it can be returned to the publisher in
salable condition and the invoice will be
cancelled automatically.

Titles sent to libraries under the
Advance Order Plan will be billed at a
40% discount. If the library wishes to
cancel subscription to the plan, it may
do so by giving publisher a 30 day's
notice.

FAIRCHILD BOOKS & VISUALS/PROFESSIONAL
  PRESS BOOKS

---

7 E. 12th Street
New York, New York 10003
Telephone: 212-741-4280

ADDRESS FOR ORDERS:

Same as above.

DISTRIBUTION/IMPRINTS:

Distributes: Retail Reporting Bureau;
National Textbook Co.

PREPAYMENT:

Not required with official purchase
order.

DISCOUNT POLICY:

20% discount to school libraries.

RETURN POLICY:

Returns in salable condition and accompanied by a copy of the invoice are accepted within 10 days of receipt. Address for returns: W.A. Books/26 Ranick Rd/Hauppauge, NY 11787. Video cassettes and floppy disks are non-returnable.

SHIPPING AND BILLING POLICY:

Libraries are charged shipping/handling (minimum of $4.00) on billed order; prepaid orders are shipped free at Book Rate. Invoices are sent with shipments.

BACK ORDER POLICY:

Publisher has no particular back order policy.

SPECIAL PLANS:

Standing orders are available for publisher's business information sources (some at pre-publication discount) and Fact File series (no discount) with normal return privileges.

RETURN POLICY:

Returns are accepted within one year. Written permission is requested but not required. Address for returns: Falcon Press/14 N. 24th St/Billings, MT 59102.

SHIPPING AND BILLING POLICY:

Libraries are charged shipping plus $1.00 handling except on prepaid orders. Invoices are sent as library requests.

BACK ORDER POLICY:

Back orders are accepted, and the library is notified. Back orders are cancelled at the library's request.

SPECIAL PLANS:

A standing order plan is available.

OTHER:

All orders are shipped within three days, or publisher will notify library of delay.

FAIRLEIGH DICKINSON UNIVERSITY PRESS see ASSOCIATED UNIVERSITY PRESSES

FALMER PRESS see TAYLOR & FRANCIS GROUP

FALCON PRESS PUBLISHING COMPANY

P.O. Box 279
Billings, Montana 59103
Telephone: 406-245-0550

ADDRESS FOR ORDERS:

Same as above.
Telephone: 800-582-2665 (in US)
          800-592-2665 (in MT)

DISTRIBUTION/IMPRINTS:

Distributes: Utah Geographic Series; American Geographic; Montana Magazine.

PREPAYMENT:

Not required, but prepaid orders are shipped free.

DISCOUNT POLICY:

20% discount to libraries.

FAWCETT see RANDOM HOUSE, INC.

FEARON EDUCATION see DAVID S. LAKE PUBLISHERS

FEARON TEACHER AIDS see DAVID S. LAKE PUBLISHERS

FREDERICK FELL PUBLISHERS, INC.

2131 Hollywood Boulevard, #204
Hollywood, Florida 33020
Telephone: 305-925-5242

ADDRESS FOR ORDERS:

Publishers Distribution Center

25 Branca Road
East Rutherford, NJ 07073

DISTRIBUTION/IMPRINTS:

Publisher uses an independent
commissioned sales force.

Compact Books (Imprint)

PREPAYMENT:

Prepayment is required on orders of four
or fewer books.

DISCOUNT POLICY:

No discount to libraries.

RETURN POLICY:

Library should contact, within 60 days,
either a sales representative or the
Florida office for information regarding
returns.

SHIPPING AND BILLING POLICY:

Libraries are charged actual postage
plus $0.50 handling. Invoices are sent
with shipments.

BACK ORDER POLICY:

Publisher keeps orders on file until
titles are available.

FERNHURST see INTERNATIONAL MARINE
PUBLISHING COMPANY

FESTIVAL PUBLICATIONS

P.O. Box 10180
Glendale, California 91209
Telephone: 818-718-8494

ADDRESS FOR ORDERS:

Same as above.

PREPAYMENT:

Not required.

DISCOUNT POLICY:

Libraries should contact publisher for
discounts on large orders.

RETURN POLICY:

Returns in resalable condition are
accepted within one year.

SHIPPING AND BILLING POLICY:

Libraries are charged shipping/handling
of $1.75 for the first book and $0.50
for each additional book. Invoices are
sent with shipments unless the library
specifies otherwise.

BACK ORDER POLICY:

Publisher back orders all unavailable
titles.

FICTIONEER BOOKS see BORGO PRESS

FIESTA PUBLISHING CORP.

6360 N.E. 4th Court
Miami, Florida 33138
Telephone: 305-751-1181

ADDRESS FOR ORDERS:

Same as above.

DISTRIBUTION/IMPRINTS:

Distributes all Spanish language
publishers from Spain and Mexico.

PREPAYMENT:

Not required with purchase order.

DISCOUNT POLICY:

"Special Package Offers" extend a 10-30%
discount and are subject to additional
discounts on dollar-volume orders:
orders of $400.00 or more receive 10%
discount, and orders of $1000.00 or more
receive 15% discount.

RETURN POLICY:

Any book may be returned within 10 days
for full refund, credit, or replacement.

SHIPPING AND BILLING POLICY:

Libraries are charged shipping of 6% of net cost. Invoices are sent with shipments as well as separately, or as the library specifies.

BACK ORDER POLICY:

Publisher accepts back orders.

SPECIAL PLANS:

Budget Allotment Plan: library indicates total allotment and percentage of that allotment to be devoted to each of 10 broad types and several categories of books. Upon receipt of the data, publisher sends a pro-forma invoice which the library confirms, revises, or rejects. Books are shipped within 7 days of confirmation.

FILM REVIEW PUBLICATIONS see JEROME S. OZER, PUBLISHERS

FINANCIAL PUBLISHING COMPANY

82 Brookline Avenue
Boston, Massachusetts 02215
Telephone: 617-262-4040

ADDRESS FOR ORDERS:

Same as above.

PREPAYMENT:

Not required.

RETURN POLICY:

Returns are accepted within 45 days without permission.

SHIPPING AND BILLING POLICY:

Libraries are charged shipping (UPS) plus $0.50 handling on all orders. Invoices are always sent with shipments.

FIRESIDE see SIMON & SCHUSTER, INC.

FIRESIDE BOOKS see WARREN H. GREEN, INC.

FIRST AVENUE EDITIONS see LERNER PUBLICATIONS COMPANY

FITHIAN PRESS see JOHN DANIEL, PUBLISHERS

FLAG PRESS see DEVIN-ADAIR PUBLISHERS

FLEET ACADEMIC EDITIONS, INC. see FLEET PRESS CORPORATION

FLEET PRESS CORPORATION

160 Fifth Avenue, Suite 719
New York, New York 10010
Telephone: 212-243-6100

ADDRESS FOR ORDERS:

Same as above.

DISTRIBUTION/IMPRINTS:

Subsidiary: Fleet Academic Editors, Inc.

PREPAYMENT:

Libraries are billed on open account.

DISCOUNT POLICY:

1-5 copies: 15%
6 or more: 18%

RETURN POLICY:

Returns in salable condition and with postage prepaid are accepted for credit within four months from invoice date. Written permission and return label are required. Requests must list invoice information. Claims for short shipments or damaged books must be made within 8 days of receipt. No returns on prepaid single-copy orders.

SHIPPING AND BILLING POLICY:

Libraries are charged shipping. Invoices are sent with shipments unless the library specifies otherwise.

BACK ORDER POLICY:

Publisher back orders any title if library so requests.

FLETCHER AIRCRAFT COMPANY see AVIATION BOOK COMPANY

FLINT, INC. see METAMORPHOUS PRESS, INC.

FLORIDA A & M UNIVERSITY PRESS see UNIVERSITY PRESSES OF FLORIDA

FLORIDA ATLANTIC UNIVERSITY PRESS see UNIVERSITY PRESSES OF FLORIDA

FLORIDA INTERNATIONAL UNIVERSITY PRESS see UNIVERSITY PRESSES OF FLORIDA

FLORIDA STATE UNIVERSITY PRESS see UNIVERSITY PRESSES OF FLORIDA

FODOR'S see RANDOM HOUSE, INC.

FOLGER SHAKESPEARE LIBRARY see ASSOCIATED UNIVERSITY PRESSES

FOOD AND AGRICULTURE ORGANIZATION OF THE UNITED NATIONS see UNIPUB

FOREST PRESS

85 Watervliet Avenue
Albany, New York 12206-2082
Telephone: 518-489-8549

ADDRESS FOR ORDERS:

Same as above.

PREPAYMENT:

Prepayment is preferred.

DISCOUNT POLICY:

25-49 copies of sets of one title: 5%
50 or more: 10%
(Policy may change in 1989)

RETURN POLICY:

Returned books must be postpaid and in salable condition and are accepted within six months of invoice date unless an extension is requested. A service charge of $1.00 for each volume is assessed. Superseded editions and special sale items are not returnable. Prior permission is required.

SHIPPING AND BILLING POLICY:

Shipping and handling costs are charged on all orders. Invoices are sent separately.

BACK ORDER POLICY:

Library is notified of status, and the order is held until available.

FORTRESS PRESS

2900 Queen Lane
Philadelphia, Pennsylvania 19129
Telephone: 800-367-8737

ADDRESS FOR ORDERS:

Same as above.

DISTRIBUTION/IMPRINTS:

Distributes: T&T Clark (Edinburgh); SCM Press (London); dissertations and Theological Studies of the Harvard Divinity School.

PREPAYMENT:

Prepayment is required for orders under $25.00.

DISCOUNT POLICY:

20% discount to libraries.

RETURN POLICY:

Returns are accepted within one year. Written permission is required. Sale books and out-of-print books are not returnable.

SHIPPING AND BILLING POLICY:

Libraries are charged shipping plus $1.00 handling per package on all orders. Invoices are sent after shipments only.

BACK ORDER POLICY:

Publisher back orders unavailable titles and ships books when they become available unless the library instructs otherwise.

SPECIAL PLANS:

Standing orders are available for any series.

OTHER:

Publisher publishes "Handbook for Church Librarians".

FOUR SEASONS FOUNDATION see CITY LIGHTS BOOKS

FOREIGN AND COMPARATIVE STUDIES see SYRACUSE UNIVERSITY PRESS

FORUM PRESS, INC.

3110 N. Arlington Heights Road
Arlington Heights, Illinois 60004-1592
Telephone: 312-253-9722

ADDRESS FOR ORDERS:

Same as above.

PREPAYMENT:

Not required.

DISCOUNT POLICY:

10% discount to libraries.

RETURN POLICY:

Returns, for credit only, in salable condition are accepted within 12 months of the invoice date. Prior written permission is required; requests must include invoice number, date, and quantity.

SHIPPING AND BILLING POLICY:

Libraries are charged shipping plus a handling charge of $1.50 for an order of fewer than 5 books. Invoices are sent separately after shipments.

BACK ORDER POLICY:

Items that are temporarily out-of-stock or not-yet-published are back ordered unless the library instructs otherwise.

FOUNDATION PRESS, INC.

615 Merrick Avenue
Westbury, New York 11590-6607
Telephone: 516-832-6950

ADDRESS FOR ORDERS:

Same as above.
Telephone: 516-832-6954

PREPAYMENT:

Not required.

DISCOUNT POLICY:

20% discount on all titles ordered in quantities of five or more.

RETURN POLICY:

All library orders are non-returnable except under extenuating circumstances.

SHIPPING AND BILLING POLICY:

Libraries are charged normal shipping on all orders. Invoices are sent just prior to shipments.

BACK ORDER POLICY:

All titles in publisher's catalog are in stock; old editions are not available.

SPECIAL PLANS:

Selected standing orders are available to law libraries only.

FRANCISCAN HERALD PRESS

1434 W. 51st Street
Chicago, Illinois 60609
Telephone: 312-254-4466

ADDRESS FOR ORDERS:

Same as above.

PREPAYMENT:

Not required.

DISCOUNT POLICY:

30% discount to libraries.

RETURN POLICY:

Returns in mint condition are accepted at any time. Written permission is required.

SHIPPING AND BILLING POLICY:

Libraries are charged shipping on all orders. Invoices are ordinarily sent separately unless the library specifies otherwise.

BACK ORDER POLICY:

Publisher back orders unavailable titles and ships books when they become available.

GORDON FRASER see MOYER BELL LIMITED

FRASER RESEARCH BOOKS see WILLIAMSON PUBLISHING COMPANY

FREE ASSOCIATION PRESS see COLUMBIA UNIVERSITY PRESS

FREE PRESS see MACMILLAN PUBLISHING COMPANY, INC.

W. H. FREEMAN AND COMPANY

41 Madison Avenue
New York, New York 10010
Telephone: 212-576-9400

ADDRESS FOR ORDERS:

W. H. Freeman and Company
4419 West 1980 South
Salt Lake City, Utah 84104
Telephone: 801-973-4660

DISTRIBUTION/IMPRINTS:

Imprints: Scientific American Books; W. H. Freeman and Company; Computer Science Press.

PREPAYMENT:

Not required.

DISCOUNT POLICY:

No discount to libraries.

RETURN POLICY:

Returns are accepted within one year of invoice date provided that reference is made to original invoice number and that books have not been superseded by new editions.

SHIPPING AND BILLING POLICY:

Libraries are charged shipping on all orders. Invoices are sent separately.

BACK ORDER POLICY:

Publisher back orders unavailable titles and ships books when they become available.

OTHER:

Publisher prefers that libraries order through wholesalers.

FREER GALLERY OF ART see SMITHSONIAN INSTITUTION PRESS

FRENCH FORUM, PUBLISHERS, INC.

P.O. Box 5108
Lexington, Kentucky 40505
Telephone: 606-299-9530

ADDRESS FOR ORDERS:

Same as above.

DISTRIBUTION/IMPRINTS:

Distributes: Harvard Studies in the Romance Languages (Department of Romance Languages, Harvard University).

PREPAYMENT:

Not required.

DISCOUNT POLICY:

No discount to libraries.

RETURN POLICY:

Returns are accepted within 6 months. Permission is required.

SHIPPING AND BILLING POLICY:

Libraries are charged actual shipping. Invoices are sent with shipments unless the library specifies otherwise.

BACK ORDER POLICY:

All temporarily unavailable titles are placed on back order.

SPECIAL PLANS:

Publisher offers standard approval plans and standing orders.

IRA J. FRIEDMAN see ASSOCIATED FACULTY PRESS, INC.

FRIENDS UNITED PRESS

101 Quaker Hill Drive
Richmond, Indiana 47374
Telephone: 317-962-7573
         800-537-8838 (outside Indiana)

ADDRESS FOR ORDERS:

Same as above.

PREPAYMENT:

Not required.

DISCOUNT POLICY:

10% discount for libraries.

RETURN POLICY:

Returns are accepted within one year if in salable condition and accompanied by invoice.

SHIPPING AND BILLING POLICY:

Libraries pay shipping charges. Invoices are sent with shipments.

BACK ORDER POLICY:

Titles not currently available are back-ordered for up to two months.

SPECIAL PLANS:

Publisher's standing order available at 10% discount.

FROMM INTERNATIONAL PUBLISHING
CORPORATION

560 Lexington Avenue
New York, New York 10022
Telephone: 212-308-4010

ADDRESS FOR ORDERS:

Kampmann & Company
9 East 40th Street
New York, New York 10016
Telephone: 212-685-2928
            800-526-7626

DISTRIBUTION/IMPRINTS:

Publisher is distributed by Kampmann &
Company

PREPAYMENT:

Prepayment is required for all orders.

DISCOUNT POLICY:

1-4 copies: 30%
5-9 copies: 40%
10-24 copies: 41%
25-49 copies: 42%
50-99 copies: 43%
etc.

RETURN POLICY:

Permission to return must be obtained
from Kampmann & Company.

FUTURA PUBLICATIONS

P.O. Box 330
Mount Kisco, New York 10549
Telephone: 914-666-7528

ADDRESS FOR ORDERS:

Same as above.

DISTRIBUTION/IMPRINTS:

Distributed by: Futura Publishing Co./900
Passaic Ave/E. Newark, NJ 07029.

PREPAYMENT:

Prepayment is required for orders of
$50.00 or less.

DISCOUNT POLICY:

No discount to libraries.

RETURN POLICY:

Returns are accepted after six months
from the invoice date but before 18
months. Publisher must be notified of
damaged books within two weeks of date
of receipt. Prior authorization is
required. Address for returns: Futura
Publishing Co., Inc./295 Main St./Mount
Kisco, NY 10549.

SHIPPING AND BILLING POLICY:

Without specific instructions, all
orders are sent via regular surface
post, and shipping charges are paid by
the library.

FUTURE PACE see METAMORPHOUS PRESS, INC.

GATT see UNIPUB

GABRIEL MICROGRAPHICS see MEDIA MARKETING
GROUP

GALE RESEARCH INC.

Book Tower
Detroit, Michigan 48277-0748
Telephone: 313-961-2242
            800-223-Gale
FAX: 313-961-6241

ADDRESS FOR ORDERS:

Same as above.

PREPAYMENT:

Not required.

DISCOUNT POLICY:

Publisher offers a 5% discount on
standing orders.

RETURN POLICY:

Libraries need not request permission to return Gale books. Books in salable condition may be returned with a copy of invoice and reason for the return.

SHIPPING AND BILLING POLICY:

Publisher pays postage and handling for prepaid orders. Libraries pay shipping charges when billed. Invoices are sent with shipment, or separately to billing address if it is different from shipping address.

BACK ORDER POLICY:

Titles not currently available are back ordered unless library requests otherwise.

SPECIAL ORDER PLAN:

Publisher accepts standing orders for any titles of continuing nature, i.e., new editions, new volumes in a series, periodicals, etc. Standing orders may be cancelled at any time. Libraries receive a 5% discount on standing orders.

All Gale books are sent on approval, and the libraries have 30 days to return books that are not suited to their needs.

GALLAUDET UNIVERSITY PRESS

800 Florida Avenue, NE
Washington, D.C. 20002
Telephone: 201-651-5499
         800-672-6720 ext. 5488

ADDRESS FOR ORDERS:

Same as above.

DISTRIBUTION/IMPRINTS:

Kendall Green Publications (Imprint)
Clerc Books (Imprint)

PREPAYMENT:

Not required.

DISCOUNT POLICY:

Libraries receive a 10% discount on all trade discount and textbook discounted items.

RETURN POLICY:

If specific authorization is obtained in advance, books and other materials will be accepted for return within three months of invoice date. Invoice number must be included with request. Books and materials must be current editions and returned in resalable condition. Defective books and materials will be replaced upon receipt of merchandise.

SHIPPING AND BILLING POLICY:

Libraries pay actual postage plus $2.00 handling fee. Invoices are sent separately without exception.

BACK ORDER POLICY:

A back order will be placed on a book that is unavailable; the book will be shipped when available.

SPECIAL PLANS:

Standing orders are available at a 20% discount.

GALLIARD PRESS see BORGO PRESS

GARDEN WAY see HARPER AND ROW, PUBLISHERS, INC.

GARDNER PRESS, INC.

19 Union Square West
New York, New York 10003
Telephone: 212-924-8293

ADDRESS FOR ORDERS:

Gardner Press, Inc.
c/o M & B Fulfillment Center
540 Barnum Avenue
Bridgeport, CT 06608
Telephone: 203-366-1900

DISTRIBUTION/IMPRINTS:

Gardner Press Trade Books (Division) are distributed by Kampmann & Company.

Gestalt Institute of Cleveland Press (Division)

PREPAYMENT:

Not required.

DISCOUNT POLICY:

No discount to libraries.

RETURN POLICY:

Returns are accepted within one year from invoice date. Written permission is required. Send returns to M & B Fulfillment.

SHIPPING AND BILLING POLICY:

Libraries are charged shipping costs plus handling charges of $1.75 for the first books and $0.75 for each additional book on all orders. Invoices are sent with shipments unless the library specifies otherwise.

BACK ORDER POLICY:

Back orders are placed indefinitely.

GARLAND/CLARKE EDITIONS see CAPRA PRESS

GAY SUNSHINE PRESS & LEYLAND PUBLICATIONS

P.O. Box 40397
San Francisco, California 94140
Telephone: 415-824-3184

ADDRESS FOR ORDERS:

Same as above.

PREPAYMENT:

Not required.

DISCOUNT POLICY:

Discount policy for mixed titles:
Up to 4 copies: No discount
4-9 copies: 10%
10 or more: 20%

RETURN POLICY:

Returns accepted within 60 days of

receipt for defective books only; other titles are not returnable.

SHIPPING AND BILLING POLICY:

Libraries are charged shipping except for prepaid orders which are shipped free. Invoices are sent with shipments unless the library specifies otherwise.

BACK ORDER POLICY:

Publisher accepts back orders if a title is going to be reprinted.

SPECIAL PLANS:

Publisher offers a 30% discount with postage paid for a standing order for all titles published (cloth library editions).

GENEALOGICAL PUBLISHING COMPANY

1001 N. Calvert Street
Baltimore, Maryland 21202
Telephone: 301-837-8271

ADDRESS FOR ORDERS:

Same as above.

DISTRIBUTION/IMPRINTS:

Imprints: Regional Publishing Co; Southern Books Co.

PREPAYMENT:

Prepayment is required on initial orders only.

DISCOUNT POLICY:

10% discount to libraries.

RETURN POLICY:

Written permission is required and should be requested immediately.

SHIPPING AND BILLING POLICY:

Libraries are charged shipping/handling of $2.00 for the first book and $0.75 for each additional book or $1.25 first and $0.50 additional on orders of $10.00 or less. Invoices are sent separately only.

BACK ORDER POLICY:

Publisher will keep back orders in their computer and notify library at time of reissue.

GENERAL AGREEMENT ON TARIFFS AND TRADE
see UNIPUB

GENERAL AVIATION PRESS see AVIATION BOOK COMPANY

GENERAL HALL, INC.

---

5 Talon Way
Dix Hills, New York 11746
Telephone: 516-243-0155

ADDRESS FOR ORDERS:

Same as above.

PREPAYMENT:

Not required.

DISCOUNT POLICY:

No discount to libraries.

RETURN POLICY:

Returns are accepted within 90 days. Prior written pemission is required.

SHIPPING AND BILLING POLICY:

Libraries are charged shipping/handling of $2.25 for the first book and $0.75 for each additional book. Publisher pays all charges on prepaid orders. Invoices are sent with shipments.

BACK ORDER POLICY:

Back orders are accepted.

GEOLOGICAL SOCIETY OF AMERICA

P.O. Box 9140
3300 Penrose Place
Boulder, Colorado 80301
Telephone: 303-447-2020
          800-472-1988

ADDRESS FOR ORDERS:

Same as above.

PREPAYMENT:

Prepayment required.

DISCOUNT POLICY:

Geological Society of America is a nonprofit organization and does not give discounts except for standing orders to the member.

RETURN POLICY:

Written requests to return must be filed within 45 days from date of the invoice. Later requests will be denied. Returns made without prior permission will be refused and sent back at buyer's expense.

SHIPPING AND BILLING POLICY:

There are no shipping & handling charges. GSA pays shipping charges at the most economical surface rate.

BACK ORDER POLICY:

Titles currently unavailable are back ordered unless library instructs otherwise.

SPECIAL ORDER PLAN:

Under Regular Standing Order Plan, GSA publications in series are shipped immediately upon publication along with the invoice, which is payable upon receipt. Libraries are expected to accept all new publications issued in each series library ordered for at least one year. Discount for GSA members is 25%; all others, 15%. Publications shipped under standing order plan are not returnable.

Standing order plan can be cancelled on 30 day's notice after one year. Only titles published after the effective date of the standing order agreement are covered by the plan. Products damaged in transit will be replaced if returned within 30 days after receipt (60 days if outside the continental limits of the U.S.)

GEORGETOWN UNIVERSITY PRESS

Intercultural Center, Room 111
Georgetown University
Washington, D.C. 20057
Telephone: 202-687-6063

ADDRESS FOR ORDERS:

Order Department
Same as above.

DISTRIBUTION/IMPRINTS:

Distributes the Annual of the Society of
Christian Ethics as well as the history
of the Society which was published by
Religious Ethics, Inc.

PREPAYMENT:

Not required.

DISCOUNT POLICY:

10% discount to libraries.

RETURN POLICY:

Returns of hardcover books in salable
condition are accepted, with postage
prepaid, within three months. Written
permission is required. Defective books
may be returned without permission but
should be accompanied by invoice
information and a description of the
defect. Claims for shorts or
misshipments must be made within 30
days. Unless defective, paperbacks are
not returnable. Send returns to Customer
Service at the above address.

SHIPPING AND BILLING POLICY:

Libraries are charged shipping plus
$1.00 handling on all orders. Invoices
are sent with shipments unless bill to
and ship to addresses are different.

BACK ORDER POLICY:

The library will be informed on the
invoice of a title's availability. When
the titles becomes available, library
will be contacted by telephone for
confirmation of order.

SPECIAL PLANS:

Standing orders are offered for two
annuals: Georgetown University Round
Table on Languages & Linguistics (GURT);

Annual of the Society of Christian
Ethics. Annuals are shipped upon
publication, and the invoice follows.
Standing orders should be placed with
the Business Manager.

OTHER:

Libraries may order direct by mail or
telephone; accounts are opened with the
first order.

GESTALT INSTITUTE OF CLEVELAND PRESS see
GARDNER PRESS, INC.

C. R. GIBSON COMPANY

32 Knight Street
Norwalk, Connecticut 06856
Telephone: 203-847-4543

ADDRESS FOR ORDERS:

Same as above.
Telephone: 800-243-6004

PREPAYMENT:

Prepayment is required for orders under
$50.00.

DISCOUNT POLICY:

50% discount on a minimum of three copies
for one title; otherwise, no discount is
offered.

RETURN POLICY:

Damaged or defective books only are
accepted for return within 10 days.

SHIPPING AND BILLING POLICY:

Libraries are charged shipping. Invoices
are sent separately.

BACK ORDER POLICY:

Back orders are placed for orders over
$20.00.

OTHER:

Publisher strongly recommends that
libraries order through wholesalers.

GLOUCESTER PRESS see FRANKLIN WATTS, INC.

GLENBOW MUSEUM see UNIVERSITY OF CHICAGO PRESS

GNOMON PRESS

GLOBE PEQUOT PRESS

P.O. Box 475
Frankfort, Kentucky 40602-0475
Telephone: 502-223-1858

138 West Main Street
Box Q
Chester, Connecticut 06412
Telephone: 203-526-9571

ADDRESS FOR ORDERS:

Same as above.

ADDRESS FOR ORDERS:

PREPAYMENT:

Same as above.
Telephone: 800-243-0495 (in US)
            800-962-0973 (in CT)

Not required.

DISTRIBUTION/IMPRINTS:

DISCOUNT POLICY:

Distributes Applewood Books.

No discount to libraries.

PREPAYMENT:

RETURN POLICY:

Not required.

Returns, in resalable condition, are
accepted within six months from invoice
date. Written permission is required.

DISCOUNT POLICY:

SHIPPING AND BILLING POLICY:

20% discount for library orders of any
quantity.

Libraries are charged actual shipping
(at Library Rate) on billed orders;
prepaid orders are shipped free.
Invoices are sent with shipments.

RETURN POLICY:

Books may be returned for full credit if
sent with postage prepaid between three
months and one year of invoice date, in
salable condition, and accompanied by
invoice numbers. Address for returns:
Shipping Department/Globe Pequot Press
Warehouse/10 Denlar Dr/Chester, CT
06412.

BACK ORDER POLICY:

If a title is out of stock for more than
3 months after an order has been
received, publisher will notify library
before shipping.

SHIPPING AND BILLING POLICY:

SPECIAL PLANS:

Libraries are charged shipping/handling
which averages 3% of net. Invoices are
sent with shipments.

Standing orders are available and are
shipped free.

BACK ORDER POLICY:

Libraries are informed of titles on back
order; availability dates are given, if
known. Back orders are held
indefinitely.

GOLDEN QUILL PRESS AND MARSHALL JONES CO

Avery Road
Francestown, New Hampshire 03043
Telephone: 603-547-6622

ADDRESS FOR ORDERS:

Same as above.

PREPAYMENT:

Not required.

DISCOUNT POLICY:

20% discount to libraries.

RETURN POLICY:

Publisher will replace defective books returned within 30 days; otherwise, returns are not accepted.

SHIPPING AND BILLING POLICY:

Libraries are charged actual postage. Invoices are sent with shipments unless the library specifies otherwise.

RETURN POLICY:

Returns of current editions in salable condition are accepted within 6 months after purchase date. Written permission is required. Invoice information must accompany returns which should be sent insured.

SHIPPING AND BILLING POLICY:

Libraries are charged shipping of 7% on all orders. Invoices are sent with shipments unless the library specifies otherwise.

BACK ORDER POLICY:

Publisher will hold orders if books are expected within 8-12 weeks; if not, publisher will notify library.

GOLDENTREE BIBLIOGRAPHIES see HARLAN DAVIDSON, INC.

GOLDSTAR ENTERPRISES see AVIATION BOOK COMPANY

GOODHEART-WILLCOX COMPANY, INC.

---

123 W. Taft Drive
South Holland, Illinois 60473
Telephone: 312-333-7200

ADDRESS FOR ORDERS:

Same as above.

DISTRIBUTION/IMPRINTS:

Distributes: Workbench Magazine project books.

PREPAYMENT:

Prepayment is required on all orders unless library establishes an account.

DISCOUNT POLICY:

No discount to libraries.

GORSUCH SCARISBRICK, PUBLISHERS

8233 Via Paseo del Norte, Suite #F-400
Scottsdale, Arizona 85258
Telephone: 602-991-7881

ADDRESS FOR ORDERS:

Same as above.

DISTRIBUTION/IMPRINTS:

Prospect Press (Imprint)
Quantum Editions (Imprint)

PREPAYMENT:

Not required with purchase order.

DISCOUNT POLICY:

20% discount on orders of 3 or more books.

RETURN POLICY:

Returns are limited to 20% of the quantity ordered within twelve months of the invoice date. Books must be returned in perfect condition for resale. Written permission is required. Returns of computer floppy discs are not accepted.

SHIPPING AND BILLING POLICY:

Libraries are charged shipping on all orders. Invoices are sent with shipments unless the library specifies otherwise.

GOSPEL PUBLISHING HOUSE

1445 Boonville Avenue
Springfield, Missouri 65802
Telephone: 800-641-4310

ADDRESS FOR ORDERS:

Same as above.

PREPAYMENT:

Required unless the library has an account with the publisher.

DISCOUNT POLICY:

None offered to libraries.

RETURN POLICY:

Returns of books that are still in print are accepted within 30 days. Prior written permission is necessary.

SHIPPING AND BILLING POLICY:

Postage is charged according to the following scale: add 15% for orders of less than $10.00; 10% for orders of $10.00-$24.00; 9% for orders of $25.00-$49.99; 7% for orders of $50.00 or more. Invoices are sent separately.

BACK ORDER POLICY:

Titles not currently available are back ordered and billed when they are shipped.

GRAND CANYON BALLOON ADVENTURES see AVIATION BOOK COMPANY

GRAND RAPIDS INTERNATIONAL PUBLISHERS see KREGEL PUBLICATIONS

GRAPHIC ARTS CENTER PUBLISHING COMPANY

P.O. Box 10306
Portland, Oregon 97210
Telephone: 800-452-3032

ADDRESS FOR ORDERS:

Same as above.

PREPAYMENT:

Not required, but publisher pays postage on prepaid orders.

DISCOUNT POLICY:

25% regardless of quantity.

RETURN POLICY:

Returns for credit are allowed on books still in print and in salable condition. Prior permission is not required. Calendars are not returnable after March 25.

SHIPPING AND BILLING POLICY:

Libraries are charged shipping except on prepaid orders. A late charge is assessed at 1 1/2% per month on overdue invoices. Invoices are sent separately.

BACK ORDER POLICY:

Titles not currently available are back ordered and shipped when available.

WARREN H. GREEN, INC.

8356 Olive Boulevard
St. Louis, Missouri 63132
Telephone: 314-991-1335

ADDRESS FOR ORDERS:

Same as above.

DISTRIBUTION/IMPRINTS:

Zeus Publishers (Division)
Fireside Books (Division)
Pioneer Press (Division)
Epoch Press (Division)
Conduce (Division)

PREPAYMENT:

Not required.

DISCOUNT POLICY:

10% discount to libraries.

RETURN POLICY:

Libraries should request permission to return within 120 days from invoice date.

SHIPPING AND BILLING POLICY:

Libraries are charged approximately $1.50 shipping and handling on single book orders and actual cost on larger orders. Invoices are sent with shipments unless the library specifies otherwise.

BACK ORDER POLICY:

Publisher offers standing order and approval plan with return privileges at special discounts.

GREEN TIGER PRESS see ZONDERVAN PUBLISHING HOUSE

GREENBRIAR BOOKS see BORGO PRESS

STEPHEN GREENE PRESS see VIKING PENGUIN, INC.

GREENFIELD BOOKS see PIERIAN PRESS, INC.

GREENHAVEN PRESS, INC.

---

577 Shoreview Park Road
St. Paul, Minnesota 55126
Telephone: 612-482-1582

ADDRESS FOR ORDERS:

Same as above.
Telephone: 800-231-5163

PREPAYMENT:

Prepayment is required only on orders under $10.00.

DISCOUNT POLICY:

No discount to libraries.

RETURN POLICY:

Returns, with postage prepaid, are accepted within six months. Written permission is not required.

SHIPPING AND BILLING POLICY:

7% shipping/handling/insurance charge applies to all orders. Invoices are sent separately only.

BACK ORDER POLICY:

Titles are back ordered according to the library's preference.

SPECIAL PLANS:

A standing order program is available for major series: Opposing Viewpoints; Great Mysteries; and Sources. Libraries will receive new titles as they are published, be invoiced upon their delivery, and have full return privileges.

GREENWOOD PRESS, INC.

---

88 Post Road West
Box 5007
Westport, Connecticut 06881
Telephone:

ADDRESS FOR ORDERS:

Same as above.

DISTRIBUTION/IMPRINTS:

Quorum Books (Imprint)
Praeger Publishers (Division)

PREPAYMENT:

Not required with purchase order from libraries.

DISCOUNT POLICY:

No discount to libraries.

RETURN POLICY:

Books, in salable condition, may be returned for full credit within twelve months. Prior written permission is required. Address for returns: The Academic Building/Saw Mill Road/ West Haven, CT 06516.

SHIPPING AND BILLING POLICY:

Shipping costs are charged to libraries except for prepaid orders which are shipped free of charge at Fourth Class Book Rate only. Invoices are sent separately.

BACK ORDER POLICY:

Out-of-stock books are placed on back order.

SPECIAL PLANS:

Standing orders to publisher's series are available at a 15% discount.

GREGG PRESS see G. K. HALL & COMPANY

GREGORIAN UNIVERSITY PRESS see LOYOLA UNIVERSITY PRESS

GREY FOX PRESS see CITY LIGHTS BOOKS

GROLIER CLUB see UNIVERSITY PRESS OF VIRGINIA

GROLIER EDUCATIONAL CORPORATION

Sherman Turnpike
Danbury, Connecticut 06816
Telephone: 203-792-1200

ADDRESS FOR ORDERS:

Same as above.

PREPAYMENT:

Not required.

DISCOUNT POLICY:

Publisher offers discounts from the list price of major reference sets, such as Encyclopedia Americana. However, there is no fixed percentage discount. Such discounts vary from 20% to 30%. Publisher also offers quantity discounts for purchases of more than one unit, but these also vary in terms of percentage.

RETURN POLICY:

Publisher requires library to write for written permission before shipping returns. The address for permission is as above.

SHIPPING AND BILLING POLICY:

Libraries pay postage on most Grolier merchandise. Invoices are sent separately after shipment. Order numbers are shown on shipping labels.

BACK ORDER POLICY:

Libraries are advised of titles currently unavailable and may either cancel or keep them on back order.

GROSSET AND DUNLAP, INC. see THE PUTNAM PUBLISHING GROUP

GRUNE & STRATTON see W. B. SAUNDERS COMPANY

GUILFORD PUBLICATIONS, INC.

---

72 Spring Street
New York, New York 10012
Telephone: 212-431-9800

ADDRESS FOR ORDERS:

Same as above.

Telephone: 800-221-3966 (outside NY)

DISTRIBUTION/IMPRINTS:

Distributed in Canada by: Copp Clark Pitman/495 Wellington West/Toronto, Ontario, M5V 1E9.

Imprints: BMA Audio Cassettes; Guilford Press.

PREPAYMENT:

Not required except for occasional special offers.

DISCOUNT POLICY:

No discount to libraries except for occasional special offers.

RETURN POLICY:

Returns in salable condition are accepted within 30 days from date of receipt. Invoice information must accompany returns which should be sent to: Guilford Publications/62 Imlay St/ Brooklyn, NY 11231. Audio and video tapes and journals are not returnable.

SHIPPING AND BILLING POLICY:

Libraries are charged shipping. Invoices are sent with shipments unless the bill to and ship to addresses are different.

BACK ORDER POLICY:

Orders are generally held for one year unless the library requests otherwise.

SPECIAL PLANS:

A standing order is available for the Review of Behavior Therapy at a 20% discount. Other plans for series and subjects are available; interested libraries should contact publisher.

GUINNESS SUPERLATIVES see STERLING PUBLISHING COMPANY, INC.

GULF PUBLISHING COMPANY BOOK DIVISION

Post Office Box 2608
Houston, Texas 77252-2608
Telephone: 713-529-4301

ADDRESS FOR ORDERS:

Same as above.

DISTRIBUTION/IMPRINT:

Pacesetter Press
Lone Star Books

PREPAYMENT:

Not required.

DISCOUNT POLICY:

Publisher offers a 10% discount to libraries for orders of 4 or more books.

RETURN POLICY:

Publisher requires written permission for returns. The address for returns is the same as for orders.

SHIPPING AND BILLING POLICY:

Libraries pay postage and handling charges. Amount charged depends on quantity and weight of books shipped. Invoices are included with shipment unless library instructs otherwise.

BACK ORDER POLICY:

Titles not currently available are either back ordered or cancelled according to library instructions.

HRD see HUMAN RESOURCES DEVELOPMENT PRESS

HACKER ART BOOKS, INC.

---

54 West 57th Street
New York, New York 10019
Telephone: 212-757-1450

ADDRESS FOR ORDERS:

Same as above.

PREPAYMENT:

Not required.

DISCOUNT POLICY:

No discount to libraries.

RETURN POLICY:

Returns are accepted within 30 days. Written permission is not required.

SHIPPING AND BILLING POLICY:

Libraries are charged shipping. Invoices are sent after shipments.

BACK ORDER POLICY:

Back orders are accepted.

HALDEN BOOKS see AVIATION BOOK COMPANY

G. K. HALL & COMPANY

70 Lincoln Street
Boston, Massachusetts 02111
Telephone: 614-423-3990

ADDRESS FOR ORDERS:

Same as above.
Telephone: 800-343-2806

DISTRIBUTION/IMPRINTS:

Twayne Publishers (Division)
Gregg Press (Defunct division)

PREPAYMENT:

Not required, but prepaid orders receive free shipping and handling.

DISCOUNT POLICY:

No discount to libraries.

RETURN POLICY:

Books may be returned no sooner than 90 days or later than 365 days from purchase. Audio titles are non-returnable. Written permission is required. Address for returns: G. K. Hall & Co./70 Finnell Dr./Weymouth, MA 02188.

SHIPPING AND BILLING POLICY:

Shipping and handling charges total approximately 5% of the total order. Free shipping and handling is offered on prepaid orders. Invoices are sent with shipments unless the library specifies otherwise.

BACK ORDER POLICY:

Titles, if out-of-stock or not-yet-published (within 3 months of due date), will remain on back order for 365 days unless the library requests otherwise.

SPECIAL PLANS:

Publisher offers several standing order plans, including: Large Print; Twayne; Audio; Critical Essays; Hall Bibliographic Guides.

OTHER:

Written confirmation of telephone orders is not necessary.

HAMMOND INCORPORATED

515 Valley Street
Maplewood, New Jersey 07040
Telephone: 201-763-6000

ADDRESS FOR ORDERS:

Same as above.

DISTRIBUTION/IMPRINTS:

Distributes: Bartholomew Maps (Edinburgh - selected titles); Times (London - Times Atlas of World History; Times Concise Atlas of World History.

PREPAYMENT:

Not required with purchase order.

DISCOUNT POLICY:

15% discount from list price to libraries for all trade titles.

RETURN POLICY:

Books as sold are non-returnable unless there is a problem with the order in which case written permission is required.

SHIPPING AND BILLING POLICY:

Libraries are charged shipping of 7% of total order. Invoices are sent separately after shipments.

BACK ORDER POLICY:

Publisher will back order until the library cancels the order.

OTHER:

Catalog card kits are available at $0.50 for most titles.

HANGING LOOSE PRESS

231 Wyckoff Street
Brooklyn, New York 11217
Telephone: 212-206-8465 (days)
          718-643-9559 (evenings)

ADDRESS FOR ORDERS:

Same as above.

DISTRIBUTION/IMPRINTS:

Publisher does its own distribution but is distributed as well by Bookslinger; Small Press Distribution; Inland.

PREPAYMENT:

Not required.

DISCOUNT POLICY:

No discount is offered.

RETURN POLICY:

Written permission is required but routinely granted if book is in good condition. 90 days time limit for returns. Hard cover books are not returnable.

SHIPPING AND BILLING POLICY:

Libraries are charged shipping at Library Rate plus handling ($1.00 for the first two titles and $0.25 for each additional title). Invoices are sent with shipments.

BACK ORDER POLICY:

All catalogue titles are kept in print, and all materials are available unless a title is not yet published or being reprinted.

HANNA-BARBERA see TABOR PUBLISHING

HAPPY HOUSE see RANDOM HOUSE, INC.

HARBINGER HOUSE, INC.

3131 N. Country Club, Suite 106
Tucson, Arizona 85716
Telephone: 602-326-9595

ADDRESS FOR ORDERS:

Same as above.

PREPAYMENT:

Not required.

DISCOUNT POLICY:

20% discount to libraries.

RETURN POLICY:

Returns in salable condition and accompanied by a copy of the original invoice are accepted within one year. Prior permission is not required. Posters and calendars are not returnable.

SHIPPING AND BILLING POLICY:

Publisher pays shipping on all orders from libraries. Invoices are sent separately unless the library specifies otherwise.

BACK ORDER POLICY:

Publisher automatically back orders unavailable titles unless the library instructs otherwise.

HARLE HOUSE see LARKSDALE

HARMONY BOOKS see CROWN PUBLISHERS, INC.

HARPER AND ROW, PUBLISHERS, INC.

10 East 53rd Street
New York, New York 10022
Telephone: 212-593-7000

ADDRESS FOR ORDERS:

Harper and Row, Publishers, Inc.
Scranton, PA 18512
Telephone: 800-242-7737
        800-982-4377 (in PA)

DISTRIBUTION/IMPRINT:

Alfred van der Marck Editions
Ballinger Publishing Company
Basic Books
Beacon Press
Collins Liturgical Publications
Crossroad
Ungar
Continuum
Garden Way
Storey Publishing
Harper & Row San Francisco
Kodansha International
Newmarket Press
Scala Books
Newbury House Publishers

PREPAYMENT:

Not required.

DISCOUNT POLICY:

Discount schedule for schools and
libraries are:

Trade editions:

1 to 9 books	10%
10 to 49 books	35%
50 or more books	40%

Library editions: 10%

College textbooks: None

RETURN POLICY:

Trade Books and Library Editions are
returnable as long as they are in print.

Returns of College Textbooks are limited
to one year from invoice date.

SHIPPING AND BILLING POLICY:

Libraries pay shipping charges. Invoices
are sent separately after shipments;
packing slips are enclosed in shipments.

BACK ORDER POLICY:

Titles not currently available are either
back ordered or cancelled as library
requests.

HARPER & ROW SAN FRANCISCO see HARPER AND
ROW, PUBLISHERS, INC.

HARPSWELL PRESS

132 Water Street
Gardiner, Maine 04345
Telephone: 207-582-1899

ADDRESS FOR ORDERS:

Same as above.

DISTRIBUTION/IMPRINTS:

Distributes: Kennebec River Press; TBW
Books.

PREPAYMENT:

Not required.

DISCOUNT POLICY:

20% discount to libraries.

RETURN POLICY:

Books to be returned must be in salable
condition and still in print. Written
permission is required.

SHIPPING AND BILLING POLICY:

Libraries are charged shipping at either
Library Rate or UPS depending upon
quantity. Invoices are sent with
shipments unless the library specifies
otherwise.

BACK ORDER POLICY:

Back orders are placed for titles that are temporarily out of stock, and books are shipped as soon as they are available.

HARVARD BUSINESS SCHOOL PRESS

Harvard Business School
Boston, Massachusetts 02163
Telephone: 617-495-6700

ADDRESS FOR ORDERS:

Harvard Business School Press
P.O. Box 1542
Hagerstown, MD 21741
Telephone: 800-638-3030

DISTRIBUTION/IMPRINTS:

Publications are distributed by Harper & Row Publishers.

PREPAYMENT:

see Harper & Row for this and other policies.

HARVARD STUDIES IN ROMANCE LANGUAGES see FRENCH FORUM, PUBLISHERS, INC.

HARVARD UNIVERSITY PRESS

79 Garden Street
Cambridge, Massachusetts 02138
Telephone: 617-495-2600

ADDRESS FOR ORDERS:

Same as above.

PREPAYMENT:

Not required.

DISCOUNT POLICY:

Libraries receive no discount except on blanket standing orders. Blanket standing order shipments are billed at a 10% discount.

RETURN POLICY:

Libraries must enclose a checklist showing: titles, quantity, and the original invoice number and date. The address for returns is: Harvard University Press, c/o Uniserv, Inc., 525 Great Road, Littleton, Massachusetts 01460.

SHIPPING AND BILLING POLICY:

Libraries pay shipping charges. There is no handling charge. Invoices are sent with shipments.

BACK ORDER POLICY:

Titles not currently available are reported and back ordered.

SPECIAL ORDER PLAN:

Under Library Blanket Standing Order Plan, Harvard University Press supplies each library with one copy of all new publications. Each month, shipments are made in one lot from books that have arrived in the warehouse the preceding month. Special discount of 10% applies to blanket standing order shipments. Libraries may exclude a limited number of subject classifications such as Law and Medicine. Occasional returns are permitted, but publisher does not establish a standing order with the understanding that each and every book is subject to return. A blanket standing order may be set up on a trial basis and cancelled at any time.

HARVEST HOUSE PUBLISHERS

1075 Arrowsmith
Eugene, Oregon 97402
Telephone: 503-343-0123

ADDRESS FOR ORDERS:

Same as above.
Telephone: 800-547-8979

PREPAYMENT:

Prepayment is required for the first order; subsequent orders sold on a credit basis.

DISCOUNT POLICY:

20% discount to libraries on all orders.

RETURN POLICY:

Returns in salable condition are accepted within one year. Written permission is required. Invoice information must accompany returns which should be sent with postage prepaid. Claims for damaged or defective material or short shipments must be made within 60 days.

SHIPPING AND BILLING POLICY:

Libraries are charged shipping plus handling (approximately $0.35) on billed orders; prepaid orders are shipped free. Invoices are sent separately after shipments.

BACK ORDER POLICY:

Publisher back orders unavailable titles and ships book when they become available.

HASKELL HOUSE PUBLISHERS

P.O. Box 420
Brooklyn, New York 11219
Telephone: 718-435-7878

ADDRESS FOR ORDERS:

Same as above.

PREPAYMENT:

Not required.

DISCOUNT POLICY:

No discount to libraries.

RETURN POLICY:

Only defective books are returnable. Permission to return is required.

SHIPPING AND BILLING POLICY:

Libraries are charged shipping. Invoices are sent with shipments only.

BACK ORDER POLICY:

Publisher will back order until the book is available or until the library cancels the order.

HAWORTH PRESS, INC.

---

12 West 32nd Street
New York, New York 10001
Telephone: 212-279-1200

ADDRESS FOR ORDERS:

Same as above.
Telephone: 800-342-9678

PREPAYMENT:

Prepayment is required on all journal subscriptions. Libraries can be billed for books and back issues with a purchase order.

DISCOUNT POLICY:

No discount to libraries.

RETURN POLICY:

Returns, in salable condition and accompanied by the original invoice, are accepted for return up to nine months from the invoice date. Written permission must be obtained from: Haworth Press, Inc./75 Griswold Street/ Binghampton, NY 13904. Address for returns: Haworth Press, Inc./16-22 Alice Street/Binghampton, NY 13904.

SHIPPING AND BILLING POLICY:

Postage and handling are included in all subscription rates. Postage and handling for books is $2.00 for the first book and $0.50 for each additional book. Invoices are sent with shipments unless the library specifies otherwise.

BACK ORDER POLICY:

Publisher automatically back orders unavailable items unless library instructs otherwise.

SPECIAL PLANS:

Standing orders are available for supplements.

OTHER:

Journal back volumes are now available on microform. Interested libraries should write to the Griswold Street address for more information.

HAYDEN BOOKS see HOWARD W. SAMS & COMPANY

HEALING ARTS PRESS see INNER TRADITIONS

HEALING TAO CENTER see CHARLES E. TUTTLE COMPANY, INC.

HEART OF THE LAKES PUBLISHING

2989 Lodi Road
P.O. Box 299
Interlaken, New York 14847-0299
Telephone: 607-532-4997

ADDRESS FOR ORDERS:

Same as above.

DISTRIBUTION/IMPRINTS:

Empire State Books (Imprint)

PREPAYMENT:

Not required, but always welcome.

DISCOUNT POLICY:

No discount on small orders. 10% to 40% discount on large orders depending on type and quantity of books ordered. Shipping is added to discounted orders.

RETURN POLICY:

Returns, within 90 days, are accepted only for defective books. Advance permission is not required.

SHIPPING AND BILLING POLICY:

Publisher pays shipping charges, via Library Rate or UPS (its choice). Invoices are sent with shipments unless the library specifies otherwise.

BACK ORDER POLICY:

Publisher keeps back/advance orders on file and ships when available unless the library specifies otherwise.

D. C. HEATH AND COMPANY

125 Spring Street
Lexington, Massachusetts 02173
Telephone: 617-862-6650

ADDRESS FOR ORDERS:

D. C. Heath and Company
Distribution Center
2700 N. Richardt Avenue
Indianapolis, Indiana 46219

DISTRIBUTION/IMPRINTS:

Division: Lexington Books

PREPAYMENT:

Not required.

DISCOUNT POLICY:

No discount to libraries.

RETURN POLICY:

Returns in salable condition are accepted within one year. Written permission is not required. Send returns to Indianapolis address. Video tapes are not returnable.

SHIPPING AND BILLING POLICY:

Libraries are charged actual shipping plus $2.00 handling. Invoices are sent separately.

BACK ORDER POLICY:

Publisher back orders unavailable titles and ships book when they become available unless the library instructs otherwise.

SPECIAL PLANS:

A standing order plan for seven subject categories is offered for Lexington Books. Interested libraries should contact Dorethes Bouchee (617-860-1208) for details.

HEINEMANN EDUCATIONAL BOOKS, INC.

70 Court Street
Portsmouth, New Hampshire 03801
Telephone: 603-431-7894

ADDRESS FOR ORDERS:

Same as above.

DISTRIBUTION/IMPRINTS:

Subsidiary: Baynton Cook

PREPAYMENT:

Not required with official purchase
order.

DISCOUNT POLICY:

10% discount to libraries.

RETURN POLICY:

Returns in salable condition and still
in print are accepted within one year of
original invoice date. Written
permission is required form Portsmouth
address. Invoice information and reason
for return must accompany returns.
Address for returns: Heinemann
Educational Books/80 Northfield
Ave/Edison, NJ 08818.

SHIPPING AND BILLING POLICY:

Libraries are charged shipping based on
weight for billed orders; prepaid orders
are charged $1.50 shipping. Invoices are
sent separately.

BACK ORDER POLICY:

Publisher back orders unavailable titles
and ships book when they become
available.

SPECIAL PLANS:

Publisher offers an Agency Plan.
Interested libraries should contact
publisher for more information.

W. S. HEINMAN, INC.

1780 Broadway, Suite 1004

New York, New York 10019
Telephone: 212-757-7628

ADDRESS FOR ORDERS:

Same as above.

DISTRIBUTION/IMPRINTS:

Publisher is subsidiary of E. J. Brill
Publishing Company.

PREPAYMENT:

Not required.

DISCOUNT POLICY:

No discount to libraries.

RETURN POLICY:

Only books damaged in transit or
defective books are returnable within 30
days of purchase. Written permission is
required.

SHIPPING AND BILLING POLICY:

Libraries are charged shipping (UPS) on
all orders. Invoices are sent with
shipments unless the library specifies
otherwise.

BACK ORDER POLICY:

Publisher informs library of order
status on the invoice and back orders
unavailable titles unless the library
instructs otherwise.

SPECIAL PLANS:

Publisher offers standing orders for
series and serials.

HELMS PUBLISHING see WESTERN MARINE ENTERPRISES

HEMISPHERE PUBLISHING CORPORATION see TAYLOR & FRANCIS GROUP

HERALD PRESS

616 Walnut Avenue
Scottdale, Pennsylvania 15683-1999
Telephone: 412-887-8500

ADDRESS FOR ORDERS:

Same as above.

DISTRIBUTION/IMPRINTS:

Distributes Kindred Press publications.

PREPAYMENT:

Prepayment is required for orders of less
than $5.00.

DISCOUNT POLICY:

20% discount to libraries regardless of
quantity.

RETURN POLICY:

Books are accepted for return within one
year. Written permission is required.
Requests must include invoice number and
date. Out-of-print books and damaged
books are not returnable nor are videos,
cassettes, and records.

SHIPPING AND BILLING POLICY:

Actual shipping costs (FOB Scottdale)
are added to all orders. $1.00 service
charge is added if publisher is required
to fill out library vouchers or
documents. Invoices are sent with
shipments only.

BACK ORDER POLICY:

Titles not currently available are
reported and back ordered unless library
instructs otherwise.

SPECIAL PLANS:

An approval plan for new titles is
available.

HERITAGE ASSOCIATES see JOHNSON BOOKS

HERITAGE PRESS see AVIATION BOOK COMPANY

HI WILLOW RESEARCH see LIBRARIES
UNLIMITED

HIGH NOON BOOKS see ACADEMIC THERAPY
PUBLICATIONS

JOHN HILL see LAMBERT GANN PUBLISHING
COMPANY

LAWRENCE HILL & COMPANY, iNC.

520 Riverside Avenue
Westport, Connecticut 06880
Telephone: 203-226-9392
          203-226-5980

ADDRESS FOR ORDERS:

Same as above.

DISTRIBUTION/IMPRINTS:

Distributed by: Chicago Review Press/814
N. Franklin St./Chicago, IL 60610.
Telephone: 312-337-0747.

PREPAYMENT:

Prepayment is required for single orders
only.

DISCOUNT POLICY:

20% discount to libraries.

RETURN POLICY:

Books in salable condition may be
returned after six months. Prior written
permission is required. Books should be
returned to the distributor.

SHIPPING AND BILLING POLICY:

Libraries are charged shipping. Invoices
are sent with shipments unless the
library specifies otherwise.

BACK ORDER POLICY:

Books will be back ordered if desired.

SPECIAL PLANS:

An approval plan is available at a 10% discount.

HIMALAYAN PUBLISHERS

RR 1, Box 405
Honesdale, Pennsylvania 18431
Telephone: 717-253-5551
         800-433-5472

ADDRESS FOR ORDERS:

Same as above.

PREPAYMENT:

Prepayment is required on first order.

DISCOUNT POLICY:

2-4 items: 20%
5-9 items: 40%
10-49 items: 41%
50-99 items: 43%
over 100:   45%

RETURN POLICY:

Returns in good condition are accepted within one year. All returns must include the original invoice number and date. Written authorization is required.

SHIPPING AND BILLING POLICY:

Libraries are charged shipping. Pro forma invoice is sent at time of order.

BACK ORDER POLICY:

Back orders are shipped when available.

HISTORIC DENVER, INC. see RENAISSANCE HOUSE PUBLISHERS

HIVE PUBLISHING COMPANY

---

214 Alpha Bldg.
Easton, Pennsylvania 18042
Telephone: 215-258-6663

ADDRESS FOR ORDERS:

P.O. Box 1004
Easton, PA 18042
Telephone: 215-258-6663
         215-252-5544 (FAX)

DISTRIBUTION/IMPRINTS:

Hive Management History Series (Imprint)
Books on the Square (Subsidiary)

PREPAYMENT:

Prepayment is required for orders under $25.

DISCOUNT POLICY:

No discount to libraries.

RETURN POLICY:

Returns are accepted within 45 days. Written permission is required. Returns by post should be sent to P.O. Box address; UPS returns should be sent to Alpha Bldg.

SHIPPING AND BILLING POLICY:

Shipping charges (Library Rate or UPS) are added to all invoices. Invoices are sent as the library specifies.

BACK ORDER POLICY:

Library is notified 30 days in advance of a title's availability.

SPECIAL PLANS:

10% discount is offered on standing orders.

HOGARTH PRESS see RANDOM HOUSE, INC.

HOLIDAY HOUSE, INC.

---

18 E. 53rd Street
New York, New York 10022
Telephone: 212-688-0085

ADDRESS FOR ORDERS:

Same as above.

PREPAYMENT:

Not required.

DISCOUNT POLICY:

1-9 single or assorted titles: 10%
10-49:   20%
over 50:   35%

RETURN POLICY:

Returns are accepted within one year under label provided by publisher. Written permission is required.

SHIPPING AND BILLING POLICY:

Libraries are charged shipping. Invoices are sent separately after shipments.

BACK ORDER POLICY:

Orders for unavailable books are cancelled unless library requests otherwise.

HOLLYM CORP. see CHARLES E. TUTTLE COMPANY, INC.

HOLT, RINEHART AND WINSTON PUBLISHERS

---

111 Fifth Avenue
New York, New York 10003
Telephone: 212-614-3333

ADDRESS FOR ORDERS:

Holt, Rinehart, and Winston Inc.
Order Fulfillment Department, 4th Floor
6277 Sea Harbor Drive
Orlando, Florida 32821

DISTRIBUTION/IMPRINT:

The Dryden Press (imprint)
Holt, Rinehart, and Winston (imprint)
Saunders College (imprint)

PREPAYMENT:

Not required.

RETURN POLICY:

No prior authorization is required on return of active titles. Returns of

damaged and defective books and books shipped in error must be authorized by publisher's Customer Relations Department. For all questions concerning returns and orders, the name and telephone number of Customer Relations correspondent is listed on the invoice/packing slip with each order.

SHIPPING AND BILLING POLICY:

Libraries pay postage. Shipments through postal service are insured at library's expense. Invoice are mailed after shipments. Packing lists go with shipments.

BACK ORDER POLICY:

Titles currently unavailable are back ordered unless library specifies cancellation.

HOOVER INSTITUTION PRESS

HHMB Rm. 22
Stanford University
Stanford, California 94305
Telephone: 415-723-3373

ADDRESS FOR ORDERS:

Same as above.

PREPAYMENT:

Not required.

DISCOUNT POLICY:

No discount to libraries except for standing orders described below.

RETURN POLICY:

Returns are accepted three months to one year from purchase date. Books must be in resalable condition and accompanied by a complete packing list and original invoice number and date. Returns of books declared out of print must be made within 90 days of declaration date. No prior authorization is required. Unacceptable returns will be shipped back to purchaser at purchaser's expense.

SHIPPING AND BILLING POLICY:

Invoices are sent with shipments unless the library specifies otherwise.

SPECIAL PLANS:

Standing orders from libraries are available. 15% discount is available for publication and bibliographical series. 20% discount is available for the Yearbook on International Communist Affairs.

OTHER:

Libraries are encouraged to order from wholesalers, but may order direct as well.

HOUGHTON MIFFLIN COMPANY

One Beacon Street
Boston, Massachusetts 02108
Telephone: 617-725-5000

ADDRESS FOR ORDERS:

Houghton Mifflin Company
Wayside Road
Burlington, MA 01803

DISTRIBUTION/IMPRINT:

Ticknor & Fields
Clarion Books

PREPAYMENT:

Not required.

DISCOUNT POLICY:

Library discount schedule for trade publications, including cloth and paperbound books, Peterson Field Guide to Bird Songs and Peterson Field Guide to Western Bird Songs, filmstrips, records or cassettes, and all editions of the American Heritage Dictionary, is as follows:

1 to 4 items	no discount
5 to 24 items	33 1/3 %
25 or more items	33 1/3 % postpaid

RETURN POLICY:

No written permission is required. Books may be returned at any time if they are still in print and in salable condition. The address for returns is the same as for orders.

SHIPPING AND BILLING POLICY:

Postage is either paid by publisher or charged to libraries. Shipments are not insured unless requested. Libraries pay insurance charges. Invoices are sent separately. Packing slips are enclosed with shipments.

BACK ORDER POLICY:

Titles not currently available are back ordered and reported unless otherwise instructed by library.

SPECIAL ORDER PLAN:

New Book Acquisitions Plan for Public Libraries is an advance copy plan to public library systems for trade titles. Each new title, in any or all the categories selected by a library, will automatically be forwarded prior to publication to subscribing library at a flat discount of 35% postpaid or 40% f.o.b. from the list price. Categories available are: Adult Fiction Only, Adult Fiction and Nonfiction, Children's, Paperback Adult, and Paperback Children.

Complete processing and catalog card kits services are available. Libraries have full return privileges on all titles. Additional new or backlist trade titles can be purchased at special library discount.

New Book Acquisitions Plan for School Libraries is designed for school libraries. The categories to choose are: Grades K-6, Junior High or Middle School, Senior High School, Paperback K-6, Paperback Junior High, and Paperback Senior High. Discount rate, return privilege, complete processing and catalog kits services are the same as New Acquisitions Plan for Public Libraries.

Under Special Purchase Order Plan, libraries agree to purchase during any 12-month period a minimum of 250 Houghton Mifflin Trade Division books. Subscribing libraries are permitted to combine orders for new and backlist, adult and children's publications. Discount applies to paperback books, and clothbound books, as well as to Houghton Mifflin children's picture books (flats) in the reinforced binding. A minimum of 10 books per order, either single or assorted titles, is required to earn the Plan discount. Participating libraries may choose either 35% postpaid or 40% f.o.b. discount. Agreement may be terminated by either party at any time upon written notice. All books are fully returnable, and any damaged or imperfect books may be returned for replacement or full credit.

HOWARD UNIVERSITY PRESS

2900 Van Ness Street, NW
Washington, DC 20008
Telephone: 202-686-6696

ADDRESS FOR ORDERS:

Same as above.

PREPAYMENT:

Not required for library orders with a purchase order number.

DISCOUNT POLICY:

Libraries receive a 20% discount on standing orders and 15% discount on all other orders.

RETURN POLICY:

Publisher does not require prior permission to return. Invoice number must be supplied with return. Period of eligibility is for the life of the book. The address for returns is: Howard University Press, Returns Department, 2200 Girard Avenue, Baltimore, MD 20782.

SHIPPING AND BILLING POLICY:

Publisher pays shipping charges on prepaid orders; library pay transportation for billed orders. There is no handling or billing charge. Invoices are sent with shipments unless library instructs to do otherwise.

BACK ORDER POLICY:

Publisher holds orders for unavailable titles unless library cancels the order.

SPECIAL ORDER PLAN:

Publisher has a standing order plan. The discount for standing orders is 20%. Titles are shipped as soon as they are available. Libraries are free to cancel at any time. Books received on standing orders can be returned.

HOWELL BOOK HOUSE, INC.

---

230 Park Avenue
New York, New York 10169
Telephone: 212-986-4488

ADDRESS FOR ORDERS:

Same as above.

DISTRIBUTION/IMPRINTS:

Distributes the publications of Tetra Press.

PREPAYMENT:

Not required.

DISCOUNT POLICY:

1-5 books:	no discount
6-14 books:	10%
15-24 books:	15%
25 or more:	20%

RETURN POLICY:

Full credit for returns will be issued for books in salable condition or if defective. Returns must not be made less than three months or more than one year from invoice date. Written permission is not required. Address for returns: Maple-Vail Fulfillment/York County Industrial Park, M-100/York, PA 17405.

SHIPPING AND BILLING POLICY:

Libraries are charged postage, at Library Rate, on billed orders; publisher pays postage on prepaid orders. Invoices are sent separately after shipments unless the library specifies otherwise.

BACK ORDER POLICY:

Titles are placed on back order and shipped when available.

HUDSON HILLS PRESS, INC.

---

230 Fifth Avenue, Suite 1308
New York, New York 10001-7704
Telephone:

ADDRESS FOR ORDERS:

Same as above.

DISTRIBUTION/IMPRINTS:

Distributed by: Rizzoli International Publications/597 Fifth Avenue/New York, NY 10017.

PREPAYMENT:

Not required, but prepaid orders are filled directly by publisher. On prepaid orders, libraries should add 5% of the total retail price (minimum $1.50 per order) as handling charge.

DISCOUNT POLICY:

Refer to policies of Rizzoli for this and other policies.

HULTON EDUCATIONAL PUBLICATIONS see DUFOUR EDITIONS, INC.

HUMAN KINETICS PUBLISHERS, INC.

P.O. Box 5076
Champaign, Illinois 61820
Telephone: 217-351-5076

ADDRESS FOR ORDERS:

Same as above.
Telephone: 800-DIAL-HKP (in US)
          800-334-3665 (in IL)

DISTRIBUTION/IMPRINTS:

Imprints: Human Kinetics Books; Leisure Press; Life Enhancement Publications.

Divisions: YMCA Program Store; American Coaching Effectiveness Program.

PREPAYMENT:

Not required with purchase order.

DISCOUNT POLICY:

No discount to libraries.

RETURN POLICY:

Returns in salable condition are accepted within one year. Written permission is not required. Address for returns: 1607 N. Market St/Champaign, Illinois 61820. Videotapes are not returnable.

SHIPPING AND BILLING POLICY:

Libraries are charged shipping. Invoices are sent with shipments unless the library specifies otherwise.

BACK ORDER POLICY:

Publisher back orders unavailable titles and ships book when they become available.

SPECIAL PLANS:

Standing orders can be accommodated.

HUMAN RESOURCE DEVELOPMENT PRESS (HRD)

---

22 Amherst Road
Amherst, Massachusetts 01002
Telephone: 413-253-3488

ADDRESS FOR ORDERS:

Same as above.

DISTRIBUTION/IMPRINTS:

Division: HRD Software

PREPAYMENT:

Prepayment is required on orders under $10.00.

DISCOUNT POLICY:

10 or more copies: 20% discount

RETURN POLICY:

Returns are accepted within 30 days. Permission, in writing or by telephone, is required. Computer software is non-returnable.

SHIPPING AND BILLING POLICY:

Libraries are charged shipping on billed orders; prepaid orders are shipped free. Invoices are sent with shipments unless ship to and bill to addresses are different.

BACK ORDER POLICY:

Publisher back orders unavailable titles and ships books when they become available.

HUMAN SCIENCES BOOKS see INDEPENDENT
PUBLISHERS GROUP

HUMAN SCIENCES PRESS, INC.

72 Fifth Avenue
New York, New York 10011
Telephone: 212-243-6000

ADDRESS FOR ORDERS:

Same as above.
Telephone: 800-444-8626

DISTRIBUTION/IMPRINTS:

Behavioral Publications (older imprint)
Insight Books (imprint)

PREPAYMENT:

Not required. Purchase orders are
acceptable.

DISCOUNT POLICY:

No discount on library orders.

RETURN POLICY:

Returns accepted within 30 days. Library
should write or call customer service
department for a return label. Items
purchased from catalogs as "discount
books" are non-returnable.

SHIPPING AND BILLING POLICY:

Shipping and handling charges depend
upon the size of the order and are added
to invoices. Publisher pays shipping and
handling on pre-paid orders. Invoices
are sent separately after shipments.

BACK ORDER POLICY:

Out-of-stock and not-yet-published items
are automatically back ordered unless
the purchase order specifies otherwise.

SPECIAL PLANS:

Standing orders, at a 20% discount, are
accepted for books in the following
series: Frontiers in Aging Series;
Depressive Illness Series. Each book in
the series is shipped automatically upon
publication on 30-day approval.

THE HUMANA PRESS, INC.

Crescent Manor
P.O. Box 2148
Clifton, New Jersey 07003
Telephone: 201-773-4389

ADDRESS FOR ORDERS:

Same as above.

PREPAYMENT:

Not required.

DISCOUNT POLICY:

No discount is available for libraries.

RETURN POLICY:

Returns are accepted within one year.
Prior written permission is required;
publisher supplies instructions and a
return label.

SHIPPING AND BILLING POLICY:

Shipping charges and nominal handling
charges are added to invoices. There are
no shipping charges for pre-paid orders.
Invoices are sent with shipments unless
the library specifies otherwise.

BACK ORDER POLICY:

Publisher will hold orders and notify
the library when book is or will be
available.

HUMANICS LEARNING PUBLICATIONS see
HUMANICS LIMITED

HUMANICS LIMITED

1389 Peachtree Street, N.E., Suite 370
Atlanta, Georgia 30309
Telephone: 404-874-2176
          800-874-8844

ADDRESS FOR ORDERS:

P.O. Box 7447
Atlanta, Georgia 30309

DISTRIBUTION/IMPRINTS:

Divisions: Humanics Learning
Publications; Humanics New Age
Publications.

PREPAYMENT:

All orders under $50.00 must be prepaid.

DISCOUNT POLICY:

10% discount to libraries, if discount
is mentioned in order.

RETURN POLICY:

Returns still in print are accepted for
credit only within one year. Written
permission is required. 15% restocking
fee on all returns. Invoice information
must accompany returns which should be
sent with postage prepaid to: Humanics
Limited/775 DeKalb Industrial Way/
Decatur, Georgia 30032.

SHIPPING AND BILLING POLICY:

Libraries are charged shipping plus
handling of 10% on net total of order on
all orders. Invoices are sent separately
and as specified by library.

BACK ORDER POLICY:

Publisher back orders unavailable titles
and ships books when they become
available, usually within 12 weeks.

HUMANICS NEW AGE PUBLICATIONS see
HUMANICS LIMITED

HUMANITIES PRESS INTERNATIONAL, INC.

171 First Avenue
Atlantic Highlands, New Jersey 07716-
1289
Telephone: 201-872-1441
800-221-3845

ADDRESS FOR ORDERS:

Same as above.

DISTRIBUTION/IMPRINTS:

Distributes: Aris & Phillips (UK);
Ashfield Press (UK); Athlone Press (UK);
Bibliopolis (Italy); Editions Rodopi
(Holland); John Donald (UK); Liverpool
University Press (UK); Lund Humphries
(UK); Macmillan (UK); Philip Allan (UK);
Wilfrid Laurier (Canada); Zed Books (UK).

PREPAYMENT:

Not required.

DISCOUNT POLICY:

10% discount to libraries.

RETURN POLICY:

Returns in salable condition and
accompanied by invoice number, date, and
purchase order number, are accepted
within one year. Claims for damaged or
incorrect books must be made within 10
days of receipt.

SHIPPING AND BILLING POLICY:

Libraries are charged shipping on all
orders. Invoices are sent separately
after shipments.

BACK ORDER POLICY:

Publisher back orders unavailable titles
for a period specified by the library.

SPECIAL PLANS:

Standing orders are available for all
series at a 10% discount.

HUNTER HOUSE, INC., PUBLISHERS

P.O. Box 847
Claremont, California 91711-0847
Telephone: 714-624-2277

ADDRESS FOR ORDERS:

c/o Publishers Services
P.O. Box 2510
Novato, California 94948
Telephone: 415-883-3140

DISTRIBUTION/IMPRINTS:

Distributes: Light Wave Press; Momenta
Publishing; Sufi Publishing; Sufi Message
Series.

Imprint: Broad Way Books.

PREPAYMENT:

Prepayment is required for all orders.

DISCOUNT POLICY:

One copy: no discount
2-4 copies: 10%
5 or more: 20%

RETURN POLICY:

Returns in resalable condition and accompanied by invoice number and date are accepted for credit within one year. Written permission is required. Returns should be sent to: Publishers Services/ 11A Commercial Blvd/Novato, CA 94947.

SHIPPING AND BILLING POLICY:

Libraries are charged actual shipping. Invoices are sent as library prefers.

BACK ORDER POLICY:

Publisher will back order indefinitely at the stated discount, although the price itself may change.

HUNTINGTON LIBRARY, ART COLLECTIONS AND BOTANICAL GARDENS

Publications Department
1151 Oxford Road
San Marino, California 91108
Telephone: 818-405-2172

ADDRESS FOR ORDERS:

Same as above.

PREPAYMENT:

Not required.

DISCOUNT POLICY:

10% discount to libraries.

RETURN POLICY:

Books, in salable condition, may be returned. Written requests for return must be made within six months of receipt.

SHIPPING AND BILLING POLICY:

Libraries are charged shipping at Library Rate. Invoices are sent with shipments unless the library specifies otherwise.

BACK ORDER POLICY:

A standing order is available at a 33 1/3% discount.

HYPERION PRESS, INC.

---

47 Riverside Avenue
Westport, Connecticut 06880
Telephone: 203-226-1091

ADDRESS FOR ORDERS:

Same as above.

PREPAYMENT:

Not required.

DISCOUNT POLICY:

No discount to libraries.

RETURN POLICY:

Returns are accepted within one year. Prior permission is required.

SHIPPING AND BILLING POLICY:

Libraries are charged actual shipping plus $1.00 handling. Invoices are sent with shipments unless the library specifies otherwise.

BACK ORDER POLICY:

Back orders are held for one year.

IAEA see UNIPUB

IBRD/WORLD BANK see JOHNS HOPKINS UNIVERSITY PRESS

IBS PRESS see BORGO PRESS

ICS PRESS

Institute for Contemporary Studies
243 Kearny Street
San Francisco, California 94108
Telephone: 415-981-5353

ADDRESS FOR ORDERS:

Same as above.

PREPAYMENT:

Not required.

DISCOUNT POLICY:

10% discount to libraries.

RETURN POLICY:

Written permission is required for
returns.

SHIPPING AND BILLING POLICY:

Libraries are charged shipping on all
orders. Invoices are always sent with
shipments.

BACK ORDER POLICY:

Publisher back orders unavailable books
unless instructed otherwise.

SPECIAL PLANS:

A standing order plan for all new
publications is available at a 10%
discount. Full return privileges apply,
and orders can be cancelled at any time.

ICUS BOOKS see PARAGON HOUSE PUBLISHERS

IHRDC see INTERNATIONAL HUMAN RESOURCES
DEVELOPMENT CORP

IDEALS

Box 391
State College, Pennsylvania 16801
Telephone: 814-237-4805

ADDRESS FOR ORDERS:

Same as above.

PREPAYMENT:

Not required.

DISCOUNT POLICY:

No discount to libraries.

RETURN POLICY:

Returns are accepted within 30 days.
Prior written permission is required.

SHIPPING AND BILLING POLICY:

Libraries pay shipping charges which
vary with weight. Invoices are sent
separately unless the library specifies
otherwise.

BACK ORDER POLICY:

Libraries are notified immediately of
back orders which are sent when
available unless the order is cancelled.

ILLUMINATI

P.O. Box 67E07
Los Angeles, California 90067
Telephone: 213-396-5102

ADDRESS FOR ORDERS:

Same as above.

DISTRIBUTION/IMPRINTS:

tadbooks (imprint); TallTales (imprint);
Regular Joe's Books (imprint);
PictoGrams (imprint).

PREPAYMENT:

Prepayment is required.

DISCOUNT POLICY:

20% discount on all orders.

RETURN POLICY:

Publisher is willing to follow
"industry standards". Time limit for
returns: one year?

SHIPPING AND BILLING POLICY:

Libraries are charged $1.00 shipping per
order. Invoices are sent with shipments
unless the library specifies otherwise.

BACK ORDER POLICY:

Publisher ships available books and
back-orders others indefinitely unless
asked not to do so.

IMAGENES PRESS see CHARLES E. TUTTLE
COMPANY, INC.

INDIANA UNIVERSITY PRESS

10th & Morton Streets
Bloomington, Indiana 47405
Telephone: 812-335-6804

ADDRESS FOR ORDERS:

Same as above.

DISTRIBUTION/IMPRINTS:

Distributes: Cleveland Museum of Art.

Imprint: Midland Books.

PREPAYMENT:

Not required with an established account.

DISCOUNT POLICY:

No discount to libraries.

RETURN POLICY:

Returns in salable condition and
accompanied by the invoice number are
accepted within one year of invoice
date. Written permission is not
required. Address for returns: I.U.

Press Warehouse/Dimension Mill/10th &
Morton Streets/Bloomington, IN 47405.

SHIPPING AND BILLING POLICY:

Libraries are charged shipping. Invoices
are sent per library's request.

BACK ORDER POLICY:

Publisher back orders unavailable titles
unless library requests that order be
cancelled.

INDUSTRIAL PRESS, INC.

---

200 Madison Avenue
New York, New York 10016
Telephone: 212-889-6330

ADDRESS FOR ORDERS:

Same as above.

PREPAYMENT:

Not required with purchase order.

DISCOUNT POLICY:

10% discount to libraries.

RETURN POLICY:

Returns are accepted within one year.
Written permission is required. Address
for returns: Industrial Press/P.O. Box
C-772/Brooklyn, NY 11205.

SHIPPING AND BILLING POLICY:

Libraries are charged shipping on billed
orders. Invoices are sent separately.

INFORM

---

381 Park Avenue South
New York, New York 10016
Telephone: 212-689-4040

ADDRESS FOR ORDERS:

Same as above.

PREPAYMENT:

Prepayment is required on all orders.

DISCOUNT POLICY:

No discount to libraries.

RETURN POLICY:

Returns in salable condition and accompanied by a copy of the original invoice are accepted within 10 days.

SHIPPING AND BILLING POLICY:

Libraries are charged shipping/handling of $2.50.

BACK ORDER POLICY:

Publisher back orders unavailable titles and ships books when they become available.

INFOSOURCE PUBLICATIONS INC. see ART DIRECTION BOOK COMPANY

INNER TRADITIONS

One Park Street
Rochester, Vermont 05767
Telephone: 802-767-3174

ADDRESS FOR ORDERS:

Harper & Row
Order Service Dept.
Keystone Industrial Park
Scranton, PA 18512

DISTRIBUTION/IMPRINTS:

Distributed by Harper & Row.

Destiny Books (Imprint)
Healing Arts Press (Imprint)
Park Street Press (Imprint)
Lindisfarne Press (Subsidiary)

PREPAYMENT:

Not required.

DISCOUNT POLICY:

20% discount on any quantity.

RETURN POLICY:

Returns except of limited editions are accepted within one year. Permission is not required. Address for returns: Key Distribution Center Bldg #1/Reeves St/ Dunmore, PA 18512.

SHIPPING AND BILLING POLICY:

Libraries are charged shipping. Invoices are sent according to library's instructions.

BACK ORDER POLICY:

Back orders are accepted; libraries should specify time limit.

INSIGHT BOOKS see HUMAN SCIENCE PRESS, INC.

INSTITUTE FOR BUSINESS PLANNING see PRENTICE-HALL

INSTITUTE FOR CONTEMPORARY STUDIES see ICS PRESS

INSTITUTE FOR INTERNATIONAL ECONOMICS

11 Dupont Circle, NW
Washington, D.C. 20036
Telephone: 202-328-9000

ADDRESS FOR ORDERS:

Same as above.

PREPAYMENT:

Not required.

DISCOUNT POLICY:

No discount to libraries.

RETURN POLICY:

Returns in salable condition,
accompanied by a packing slip noting
titles, invoice numbers, quantities, and
dates of purchase, and sent with postage
prepaid are accepted within one year.
Claims for defective, damaged, or
incorrect titles must be made within 20
days of receipt. Old editions are not
returnable after 90 days of the
publication of a new edition. Address
for returns: IIE, c/o TASCO/9 Jay Gould
Ct/Waldorf, MD 20601.

SHIPPING AND BILLING POLICY:

Libraries are charged shipping and
handling of $1.50 for the first book and
$0.75 for each additional book. Invoices
are sent with shipments.

BACK ORDER POLICY:

Publisher back orders unavailable titles
indefinitely.

SPECIAL PLANS:

A standing order plan is available at a
20% discount for all Institute
publications (about 8-10 titles per
year) or all volumes in the Policy
Analyses in International Economics
Series (about 4-6 titles per year).

INSTITUTE OF INTERNATIONAL EDUCATION

Publications Service
809 U. N. Plaza
New York, New York 10017
Telephone: 212-984-5412

ADDRESS FOR ORDERS:

Same as above.

PREPAYMENT:

Prepayment is required on all orders
under $14.95.

DISCOUNT POLICY:

No specific discount for libraries.

RETURN POLICY:

Returns, in salable condition, are
accepted. Written permission is
required.

SHIPPING AND BILLING POLICY:

Book Rate shipping is included in the
price; shipment by other means is extra
(First Class: $4.00 for the first book
and $2.00 for each additional book).
Invoices are sent with shipments unless
the library specifies otherwise.

BACK ORDER POLICY:

Back orders are not placed.

SPECIAL PLANS:

The following annuals are available on
standing order at 15% discount: Academic
Year Abroad; Vacation Study Abroad;
Study in the United Kingdom and Ireland;
Open Doors.

INSTITUTE OF MEDIEVAL MUSIC, LTD.

P.O. Box 295
Henryville, Pennsylvania 18332-0295
Telephone: 717-629-1278

ADDRESS FOR ORDERS:

Between April 17 and November 10, order
from the above US address; between
November 10 and April 16, order from:
Institut fur Mittelalterliche
Musikforschung
Melchtalstr. 11
CH-4102 Binningen
Switzerland
Telephone: 61 47 80 78

PREPAYMENT:

Not required for the most part.

DISCOUNT POLICY:

No discount to libraries.

RETURN POLICY:

Returns are accepted; time limits vary.
Returns should be sent to the US
address.

SHIPPING AND BILLING POLICY:

Actual shipping charges are added to
invoices. Invoices are customarily sent
with shipments. Official prices are in
DM, but publisher will invoice in the
currency of the library's country.

BACK ORDER POLICY:

Back orders are held until cancelled. Publisher prefers that correspondence be in either French or German.

SPECIAL PLANS:

Standing orders are available.

OTHER:

Publisher has a Canadian affiliate which is in the process of publishing its own books: Institute of Medieval Music/1270 Lampman Crescent/Ottawa K2C 1P8.

INSTITUTE OF MODERN LANGUAGES see NATIONAL TEXTBOOK COMPANY

INSTRUCTIONAL AIDS see CAREER PUBLISHING, INC.

INTER-UNIVERSITY SEMINAR ON ARMED FORCES AND SOCIETY see SEVEN LOCKS PRESS

INTERNATIONAL ATOMIC ENERGY AGENCY see UNIPUB

INTERNATIONAL EXHIBITIONS FOUNDATION see CHARLES E. TUTTLE COMPANY, INC.

INTERNATIONAL HELICOPTER FINANCIAL SERVICES see AVIATION BOOK COMPANY

INTERNATIONAL HUMAN RESOURCES DEVELOPMENT CORP (IHRDC PRESS)

---

137 Newbury Street
Boston, Massachusetts 02116
Telephone: 617-536-0202

ADDRESS FOR ORDERS:

Same as above.

PREPAYMENT:

Not required.

DISCOUNT POLICY:

10% discount to university and educational libraries only.

RETURN POLICY:

Returns in salable condition, still in print, and accompanied by a copy of the original invoice are accepted within one year from invoice date. Prior permission is required. Address for returns: c/o PSSC/231 Industrial Park/Fitchburg, MA 02140.

SHIPPING AND BILLING POLICY:

Libraries are charged actual shipping costs. Invoices are sent separately.

BACK ORDER POLICY:

Publisher back orders all out-of-stock titles unless library requests otherwise.

OTHER:

Requests for catalogs and other information are encouraged. Publisher is willing to work with libraries that require special treatment.

INTERNATIONAL LABOR OFFICE see UNIFO PUBLISHERS, LTD.

INTERNATIONAL LIBRARY BOOK PUBLISHERS, INC.

7315 Wisconsin Avenue, Suite 229E
Bethesda, Maryland 20814
Telephone: 301-961-8850

ADDRESS FOR ORDERS:

Same as above.

PREPAYMENT:

Not required.

RETURN POLICY:

Returns are accepted within 30 days if shrink-wrap has not been broken. Written permission is required. There is a $25.00 reshelving charge.

SHIPPING AND BILLING POLICY:

Libraries are charged shipping/handling of $5.00 for the first book plus $3.00 for each additional book except on prepaid orders which are shipped free. Invoices are sent with shipments unless the library specifies otherwise.

BACK ORDER POLICY:

Publisher back orders unavailable titles and ships books when they become available.

SPECIAL PLANS:

Standing orders are available at 10% discount.

INTERNATIONAL MARINE PUBLISHING COMPANY

P.O. Box 220
Camden, Maine 04843
Telephone: 207-236-4837
          800-637-9240 (in US)

ADDRESS FOR ORDERS:

Same as above.

DISTRIBUTION/IMPRINTS:

Distributes publications of: Fernhurst; DeGraff; Pisces; Woodenboat.

Subsidiary: Seven Seas Press

PREPAYMENT:

Prepayment not required if order exceeds $200.00. Appropriate credit must be established.

DISCOUNT POLICY:

20% discount on IMPC publications. For distributed publishers:

0 - $19.99:	no discount
$20-$39.99:	5%
$40-$69.99:	10%
$70-$99.99:	15%
over $100:	20%

RETURN POLICY:

Books in resalable condition may be returned without permission within one year. Sale Locker items and VHS tapes are not returnable. Address for returns: International Marine Publishing Company/ Rockland Industrial Park/5 Gordon Dr/ Rockland, ME 04841.

SHIPPING AND BILLING POLICY:

The following schedule of shipping charges applies to all orders:

Orders of less than $10.00:	$2.00
$10.00-$29.99:	$3.00
$30.00-$50.00:	$4.00
over $50.00:	$5.00

Invoices are generally sent after shipments; however, special arrangements are possible.

BACK ORDER POLICY:

Back orders are shipped as soon as material becomes available.

SPECIAL PLANS:

A standing order plan is offered at 33-40% discount depending upon quantity.

INTERNATIONAL MONETARY FUND see UNIFO PUBLISHERS, LTD.

INTERNATIONAL UNIVERSITIES PRESS, INC.

---

59 Boston Post Road
P.O. Box 1524
Madison, Connecticut 06443-1524
Telephone: 203-245-4000

ADDRESS FOR ORDERS:

Same as above.

DISTRIBUTION/IMPRINTS:

Sphinx Press (Sister company)

PREPAYMENT:

Not required with purchase order.

DISCOUNT POLICY:

10% discount to libraries on books and annuals.

RETURN POLICY:

Publisher must approve requests for return.

SHIPPING AND BILLING POLICY:

Invoices for orders of 5 or fewer books will have postage and handling charges of $2.75 for the first book and $1.50 for each additional book added. Invoices are sent with shipments.

BACK ORDER POLICY:

Back orders are accepted for unavailable titles.

SPECIAL PLANS:

A standing order plans are available for each of 14 series or annuals.

INTERPRINT see ISHIYAKU EUROAMERICA, INC. PUBLISHERS

INTERSTATE PRINTERS AND PUBLISHERS, INC.

P.O. Box 50
Danville, Illinois 61834-0050
Telephone: 217-446-0500
          (outside Il) 800-843-4774

ADDRESS FOR ORDERS:

Same as above.

PREPAYMENT:

Not required unless the item ordered is priced at $5 or less.

DISCOUNT POLICY:

Single copy orders   None
10 or more copies (same title)   20%

RETURN POLICY:

Written permission is required for returns except for defective books or in the case of a wrong shipment. There is a 90-day time limit. Address for returns: Interstate Printers and Publishers, Inc., c/o C & H Shipping and Handling, 211 East Harrison, Danville, Il 61832

SHIPPING AND BILLING POLICY:

Libraries pay shipping and handling charges. Invoices are sent with the shipment if the shipment and billing addresses are the same.

BACK ORDER POLICY:

Orders for titles not currently available are reported and back ordered unless the library instructs otherwise.

IOWA STATE UNIVERSITY PRESS

2121 South State Avenue
Ames, Iowa 50010
Telephone: 515-292-0140

ADDRESS FOR ORDERS:

Same as above.

PREPAYMENT:

Not required with an official purchase order.

DISCOUNT POLICY:

10% discount to libraries.

RETURN POLICY:

Returns, in salable condition and accompanied by invoice, price, discount, and quantity, are accepted within one year. Written permission is required.

SHIPPING AND BILLING POLICY:

Libraries are charged actual postage at Library Rate on all orders. Invoices are sent with shipments.

BACK ORDER POLICY:

Back orders are kept and cancelled if the date given in the purchase order has expired.

IRIS PRESS see ST. LUKES PRESS

IRISH-AMERICAN BOOK SOCIETY see DEVIN-ADAIR PUBLISHERS

RICHARD D. IRWIN, INC.

1818 Ridge Road
Homewood, Illinois 60430
Telephone: 312-798-6000

ADDRESS FOR ORDERS:

Same as above.
Telephone: 312-957-5800

DISTRIBUTION/IMPRINTS:

Imprints: Irwin; Dorsey Press; Dow Jones-Irwin.

Subsidiary: Business Publications, Inc.

PREPAYMENT:

Not required with valid purchase order.

DISCOUNT POLICY:

10% discount on text titles (Irwin, Business Publications, Inc., and Dorsey Press); 20% on trade titles (Dow Jones-Irwin).

RETURN POLICY:

Returns in salable condition are accepted within 18 months for credit only. Written permission is required. Invoice information must accompany returns. Address for returns: Richard D. Irwin, Inc/10 E. 168th St/South Holland, IL 60473.

SHIPPING AND BILLING POLICY:

Libraries are charged shipping on all orders. Invoices are sent separately at the same time the books are shipped.

BACK ORDER POLICY:

Publisher automatically back orders unavailable titles and notifies library of availability date.

SPECIAL PLANS:

Standing orders are accepted at the same discounts, etc. as above and may be cancelled by telephone or in writing at any time.

OTHER:

Publisher encourages libraries to order from wholesalers.

ISHIYAKU EUROAMERICA, INC. PUBLISHERS

11559 Rock Island Court
Maryland Heights, Missouri 63043
Telephone: 314-432-1933

ADDRESS FOR ORDERS:

Same as above.

DISTRIBUTION/IMPRINTS:

Distributes: Piccin Medical Books; Interprint.

PREPAYMENT:

Not required.

DISCOUNT POLICY:

10% discount for new library clients; 15% for established clients.

RETURN POLICY:

Returns in salable condition and accompanied by invoice or invoice copy are accepted within 15 days.

SHIPPING AND BILLING POLICY:

Libraries are charged shipping on billed orders; prepaid orders are shipped free. Invoices are sent after the order is received.

BACK ORDER POLICY:

Books are back ordered and held until library cancels.

ISLAND PRESS

P.O. Box 7
Covelo, California 95428
Telephone: 707-983-6432
          707-983-6414

ADDRESS FOR ORDERS:

Same as above.

PREPAYMENT:

Not required.

DISCOUNT POLICY:

10% discount to libraries on request
only.

RETURN POLICY:

Returns are accepted within one year of
receipt. Written permission is required.

SHIPPING AND BILLING POLICY:

Libraries are charged shipping plus
handling ($2.75 for the first book and
$1.25 for each additional book or $2.00
over actual postage for orders of five
or more books) on all orders. Invoices
are sent with shipments unless the
library specifies otherwise.

BACK ORDER POLICY:

Back orders are placed, and library is
notified.

SPECIAL PLANS:

Interested libraries should contact
publisher about arrangements for
standing orders.

JAHAN BOOK COMPANY see THREE CONTINENTS
PRESS, INC.

JAI PRESS, INC.

---

55 Old Post Road #2
P.O. Box 1678
Greenwich, Connecticut 06836
Telephone: 203-661-7602

ADDRESS FOR ORDERS:

Same as above.

PREPAYMENT:

Not required.

DISCOUNT POLICY:

No discount to libraries.

RETURN POLICY:

Prior written approval must be granted
before returns will be accepted.

SHIPPING AND BILLING POLICY:

Libraries are charged shipping. Invoices
are always sent with shipments.

BACK ORDER POLICY:

Back orders are placed.

SPECIAL PLANS:

Publisher offers standing orders for all
serial titles either individually or as
a group. Interested libraries should
contact publisher.

JALMAR PRESS

---

45 Hitching Post Drive, Bldg. 2
Rolling Hills Estates, CA 90274-4297
Telephone: 213-547-1240

ADDRESS FOR ORDERS:

Same as above.
Telephone: 800-662-9662

DISTRIBUTION/IMPRINTS:

Distributes the publications of: B.L.
Winch & Associates; Sorrento Press; Self-
Esteem Seminars; Oak Tree Press; Equal
Partners, Inc.; Oakmore House.

B. L. Winch & Associates (Division)

PREPAYMENT:

Not required.

DISCOUNT POLICY:

No discount to libraries.

RETURN POLICY:

Books may be returned for full credit within 30 days of receipt. Written permission is required.

SHIPPING AND BILLING POLICY:

Libraries are charged shipping cost of 10% ($2.00 minimum) on all orders. Invoices are sent separately after shipments unless the library specifies otherwise.

BACK ORDER POLICY:

Titles that are temporarily out of stock are carried on back order for 6 months.

JAVELIN see STERLING PUBLISHING COMPANY, INC.

THOMAS JEFFERSON MEMORIAL FOUNDATION see UNIVERSITY PRESS OF VIRGINIA

JESUIT HISTORICAL PRESS see LOYOLA UNIVERSITY PRESS

JEWISH PUBLICATION SOCIETY

1930 Chestnut, 21st Floor
Philadelphia, Pennsylvania 19103-4599
Telephone: 215-564-5925

ADDRESS FOR ORDERS:

Same as above.

PREPAYMENT:

Not required.

DISCOUNT POLICY:

20% discount to libraries.

RETURN POLICY:

Returns from trade accounts are accepted for full credit after three months and before one year from date of purchase provided books are returned in salable condition. Requests for permission to return must be made in advance, and the invoice number covering the purchase must be included with the request. No returns are allowed for workbooks. Address for returns: Jewish Publication Society/c/o Haddon Craftsmen/Winfield Avenue & Kane St./Scranton, PA 18505.

SHIPPING AND BILLING POLICY:

Libraries are charged shipping. Invoices are sent separately after shipments.

BACK ORDER POLICY:

Titles not currently available are back-ordered and books are shipped when available unless the library specifies otherwise.

SPECIAL PLANS:

Standing orders are offered.

JOHNS HOPKINS UNIVERSITY PRESS

Baltimore, Maryland 21211
Telephone: 301-228-6900

ADDRESS FOR ORDERS:

Same as above.

DISTRIBUTION/IMPRINT:

Resources for the Future, Inc.
IBRD/World Bank

PREPAYMENT:

Not required.

DISCOUNT POLICY:

Publisher does not offer discounts to libraries.

RETURN POLICY:

Written permission is not required for returns. There is a time limit of 18 months, and the title must be a current edition and in salable condition. Early English Manuscript Series are not returnable. Invoice numbers must accompany returns. The address for returns is: Johns Hopkins University

Press, 2200 Giard Avenue, Baltimore, MD
21211.

SHIPPING AND BILLING POLICY:

Libraries pay postage. Invoices are sent
separately after shipments.

BACK ORDER POLICY:

Titles not currently available are
reported and back ordered.

SPECIAL ORDER PLAN:

Publisher offers a standing order plan
for series under the following terms:

Automatic shipment of all new titles in
advance of publication date.

A 10% discount on all automatic
shipments, with invoices mailed
separately. All library orders other
than standing orders are filled at list
price.

Full return privileges within 18 months
of invoice date provided that the books
are clean, in salable condition, and
invoice number is given. Early English
Manuscripts in Facsimile are the only
exceptions: a 25% discount applies to
these, and they are not returnable.

Libraries may exclude selected subject
categories.

JOHNSON BOOKS

1880 S. 57th Court
Boulder, Colorado 80301
Telephone: 303-443-1576

ADDRESS FOR ORDERS:

Same as above.

DISTRIBUTION/IMPRINTS:

Distributes: Wayfinder Press; Stone Wall
Press; Meridian Hill Publications; Denver
Center Theatre Co; Heritage Associates.

Imprint: Spring Creek Press (for
flyfishing titles)

PREPAYMENT:

Not required.

DISCOUNT POLICY:

No discount to libraries.

RETURN POLICY:

Returns, in salable condition, are
accepted within one year when
accompanied by invoice number. Moon
calendar is not returnable.

SHIPPING AND BILLING POLICY:

Libraries are charged shipping plus a
minimum of $1.00 handling on all orders.
Invoices are sent with shipments unless
the library specifies otherwise.

BACK ORDER POLICY:

Back orders are placed unless library
instructs otherwise.

JOSSEY-BASS, INC., PUBLISHERS

350 Sansome Street
San Francisco, California 94104-1310
Telephone: 415-433-1740

ADDRESS FOR ORDERS:

Same as above.
Customer Service: 415-433-1767

PREPAYMENT:

Not required.

DISCOUNT POLICY:

No discount to libraries.

RETURN POLICY:

Returns of books in mint condition are
accepted within one year of invoice
date. Prior written permission is
required.

SHIPPING AND BILLING POLICY:

Shipping costs plus roughly 1/2% of
invoice total for handling/billing are
added to invoices on billed orders;
publisher pays shipping on prepaid
orders. Invoices are sent with shipments
unless the library specifies otherwise.

BACK ORDER POLICY:

Publisher will back order for up to six

months unless the purchase order instructs otherwise.

SPECIAL PLANS:

Standing orders are available for the following series: Jossey-Bass Behavioral Science Series; Jossey-Bass Management Series; Jossey-Bass Series in Higher Education; Jossey-Bass Series in Education; Jossey-Bass Public Administration Series; or the Jossey-Bass Health Series. Interested libraries should submit a standing order purchase order. Books will be shipped and billed as published with postage/handling added to the invoice. Returns are accepted as above.

JOY STREET PRESS see LITTLE, BROWN AND COMPANY

JUDSON PRESS

P.O Box 851
Valley Forge, Pennsylvania 19482-0851
Telephone: 215-768-2122

ADDRESS FOR ORDERS:

Same as above.

PREPAYMENT:

Not required for established account.

DISCOUNT POLICY:

All book orders from libraries receive a 25% discount with certain exceptions (e.g., hymnals) receiving less discount.

RETURN POLICY:

Written permission is required for returns. There is a time limit of one year from the date of invoice. Invoice number must be shown on all returns. The address for returns is the same as for orders.

SHIPPING AND BILLING POLICY:

Libraries pay postage. Invoices are sent separately after shipments. Minimum amount of order is $5 net, excluding shipping.

BACK ORDER POLICY:

Publisher back orders and reports titles that are not currently available.

KAR-BEN COPIES, INC.

6800 Tildenwood Lane
Rockville, Maryland 20852
Telephone: 301-984-8733
          800-4-KARBEN

ADDRESS FOR ORDERS:

Same as above.

PREPAYMENT:

Prepayment is required for orders under $35.00.

DISCOUNT POLICY:

12+ assorted titles: 10%
25+ assorted titles: 25%

RETURN POLICY:

No returns are accepted.

SHIPPING AND BILLING POLICY:

Libraries are charged shipping and handling of from $2.00 - $4.00 for orders of up to $100.00 and 5% on orders over $100.00. Invoices are sent with shipments only.

BACK ORDER POLICY:

Back orders are accepted.

SPECIAL PLANS:

A standing order plan is in the works.

WILLIAM KAUFMANN, INC.

---

95 First Street
Los Altos, California 94022
Telephone: 415-948-5810

ADDRESS FOR ORDERS:

Same as above.
Telephone: 415-965-4081

DISTRIBUTION/IMPRINTS:

Distributes: Tioga Publishing Company.

PREPAYMENT:

Not required.

DISCOUNT POLICY:

No discount to libraries.

RETURN POLICY:

Returns are accepted within one year.
Written permission is not required.

SHIPPING AND BILLING POLICY:

Libraries are charged shipping on billed
orders; prepaid orders are shipped free.
Invoices are sent with shipments unless
the library specifies otherwise.

BACK ORDER POLICY:

Back orders are held until cancelled.

KAV PUBLISHING see TRILLIUM PRESS, INC.

KAZAN BOOKS see VOLCANO PRESS, INC.

KEATS PUBLISHING, INC.

---

27 Pine Street
P.O. Box 876
New Canaan, CT 06840
Telephone: 203-966-8721

ADDRESS FOR ORDERS:

Same as above.

DISTRIBUTION/IMPRINTS:

Pine Grove Pamphlets (Imprint)

PREPAYMENT:

Orders under $15.00 net should be
prepaid.

DISCOUNT POLICY:

20% discount to libraries.

RETURN POLICY:

Books are returnable, for credit only,
up to one year from invoice date. Prior
permission is required. Return addresses
are provided when permission is given.

SHIPPING AND BILLING POLICY:

Libraries are charged shipping at
Library Rate unless the library requests
otherwise. Invoices are sent with
shipments unless the library specifies
otherwise or unless billing address is
different from shipping address.

BACK ORDER POLICY:

Publisher will back order all
unavailable items unless instructed
otherwise.

SPECIAL PLANS:

Interested libraries should contact
publisher about special plans.

AUGUSTUS M. KELLEY PUBLISHERS

---

300 Fairfield Road
Fairfield, New Jersey 07006
Telephone: (212) 685-7202

ADDRESS FOR ORDERS:

Same as above.

PREPAYMENT:

Not required

DISCOUNT POLICY:

No discount to libraries.

RETURN POLICY:

Returns are accepted within six months
of invoice date; prior written return
authorization is required.

SHIPPING AND BILLING POLICY:

Libraries pay actual postage or freight plus $0.75 handling. Invoices are sent with shipments unless the library requests otherwise.

BACK ORDER POLICY:

Titles are back-ordered for one year from order date unless the library requests otherwise.

KENDALL GREEN PUBLICATIONS see GALLAUDET UNIVERSITY PRESS

KENDALL-HUNT PUBLISHING COMPANY see WILLIAM C. BROWN, PUBLISHERS

KENNEBEC RIVER PRESS see HARPSWELL PRESS

KENNIKAT PRESS see ASSOCIATED FACULTY PRESS, INC.

KENT STATE UNIVERSITY PRESS

Kent, Ohio 44242
Telephone: 216-672-7913

ADDRESS FOR ORDERS:

Kent State University Press
c/o C.U.P. Services
P.O. Box 6525
Ithaca, New York 14851

PREPAYMENT:

Not required.

DISCOUNT POLICY:

There is no discount for library orders.

RETURN POLICY:

No book returns are accepted prior to 90 days, nor beyond one year from purchase date. Full credit will be issued if

invoice information is provided. Address returns to: Kent State University Press, 740 Cascadilla Street, Ithaca, NY 14850.

SHIPPING AND BILLING POLICY:

Libraries pay postage; amount determined by weight and destination. Invoices are included in the package.

BACK ORDER POLICY:

Titles not currently available are back ordered unless library instructs otherwise.

SPECIAL ORDER PLAN:

Publisher accepts standing orders for all of its titles, or series, as indicated by library.

KINDRED PRESS PUBLICATIONS see HERALD PRESS

JESSICA KINGSLEY PUBLISHERS see UNIPUB

KLOCK & KLOCK PUBLISHERS, INC. see RANDOM HOUSE, INC.

KNIGHTS PRESS

P.O. Box 454
Pound Ridge, New York 10576
Telephone: 203-322-7829

ADDRESS FOR ORDERS:

Same as above.

PREPAYMENT:

Not required, but an additional 2% discount is offered on prepaid orders.

DISCOUNT POLICY:

25% discount to libraries for orders of any size.

RETURN POLICY:

Books may be returned within one year of
invoice date for full credit if they are
in salable condition and, if possible,
accompanied by the invoice number.
Damaged books are replaced immediately.
Returns of up to 12 books can be sent to
publisher's address; otherwise, returns
should be sent to: Alex M. Yudkins
Associates/147 McKinley Ave./P.O. Box
6361/Bridgeport, CT 06606.

SHIPPING AND BILLING POLICY:

Libraries are charged shipping on all
orders. Invoices are sent with shipments
unless the library specifies otherwise.

SPECIAL PLANS:

Publisher offers a standing order plan
with any book returnable for full credit
within 10 days of receipt. Standing
orders should be started or stopped by a
signed letter on official letterhead.

OTHER:

Publisher produces only gay fiction of
the highest literary quality and is
discussing the production of hard-cover
library editions. Libraries are
encouraged to order direct.

_____

KNOPF see RANDOM HOUSE, INC.
_____

KNOPF BOOKS FOR YOUNG READERS see RANDOM
HOUSE, INC.
_____

KNOWLEDGE INDUSTRY PUBLICATIONS, INC.
_____

701 Westchester Avenue
White Plains, New York 10604
Telephone: 914-328-9157

ADDRESS FOR ORDERS:

Same as above.

PREPAYMENT:

Not required.

DISCOUNT POLICY:

Discount schedule (single titles):

1 to 4 copies	None
5 to 14 copies	10%
15 copies or more	20%

RETURN POLICY:

Libraries may return books within 10 days
of receipt with letter explaining the
reason for return. Knowledge Industry
Publications Studies are not returnable.
The address for returns is the same as
for orders.

SHIPPING AND BILLING POLICY:

Libraries pay postage/handling charges.
The amount is $3.00 per book. Invoices
are enclosed with books unless requested
otherwise.

BACK ORDER POLICY:

Publisher back orders titles that are not
currently available.

_____

KODANSHA INTERNATIONAL see HARPER AND
ROW, PUBLISHERS, INC.
_____

KOLOWALU see UNIVERSITY OF HAWAII PRESS
_____

KRAUS REPRINT COMPANY
_____

Route 100
Millwood, New York 10546
Telephone: 914-762-2200
Fax: 914-762-1195

ADDRESS FOR ORDERS:

Same as above.

PREPAYMENT:

Not required.

DISCOUNT POLICY:

There is no discount for library orders.

RETURN POLICY:

All sales are considered final. Returns will only be accepted for defective material. Prior authorization is required. All communications should be made within 30 days of receipt of material.

SHIPPING AND BILLING POLICY:

Orders for titles in stock are shipped within 10 working days. Invoices are sent separately after shipments.

BACK ORDER POLICY:

Publisher reports and back orders titles that are currently not available.

KREGEL PUBLICATIONS

---

733 Wealthy Street SE
Grand Rapids, Michigan 49506
Telephone: 616-451-4775

ADDRESS FOR ORDERS:

P.O. Box 2607
Grand Rapids, Michigan 49501
Telephone: 800-253-5465

DISTRIBUTION/IMPRINTS:

Imprint: Klock & Klock Publishers, Inc.

Division: Grand Rapids International Publishers

Distributes: Publicaciones Portavoz Evangelico

PREPAYMENT:

Not required.

DISCOUNT POLICY:

20% discount to libraries.

RETURN POLICY:

Returns, in salable condition and still in print, are accepted without permission if accompanied by invoice number, purchase date, and discount. Return to Wealthy St. address.

SHIPPING AND BILLING POLICY:

Libraries are charged shipping on all orders. Invoices are sent with shipments unless the library specifies otherwise.

BACK ORDER POLICY:

Publisher back orders new titles and titles that are temporarily out of print.

KRIEGER PUBLISHING COMPANY, INC.

P.O. Box 9542
Melbourne, Florida 32902
Telephone: 407-724-9542

ADDRESS FOR ORDERS:

Same as above.

PREPAYMENT:

Not required if library has an established account.

DISCOUNT POLICY:

Publisher allows discount to trade only.

RETURN POLICY:

Publisher requests libraries to write for return authorization before sending books. Shipping labels will be sent on approved returns. No returns are generally accepted on billing over 90 days. All returns must be in clean, salable condition.

SHIPPING AND BILLING POLICY:

Libraries pay postage. A packing slip is enclosed with the shipment. The original invoice and copy are affixed to outside of carton.

BACK ORDER POLICY:

Titles not currently available are reported and back ordered if they will be available in the near future.

KUMARIAN PRESS, INC.

---

630 Oakwood Avenue, Suite 119
West Hartford, Connecticut 06110-1505
Telephone: 203-524-0214

ADDRESS FOR ORDERS:

Same as above.

DISTRIBUTION/IMPRINTS:

Distributes the publications of the
International Center for Public
Enterprises in Developing Countries
(ICPE, Yugoslavia).

Library of Management for Development
(Imprint).

PREPAYMENT:

Not required.

DISCOUNT POLICY:

No discount to libraries.

RETURN POLICY:

Books, in clean and salable condition
and accompanied by invoice date and
number, are accepted for return. Prior
authorization is required, and requests
for return must be made within 90 days
of the invoice date. Defective books may
be returned within 10 days for
replacement or full credit. Damaged
books may be returned for replacement
only. Claims for short shipments must be
made within two weeks of invoice date.

SHIPPING AND BILLING POLICY:

Libraries are charged shipping (Fourth
Class Book Rate, Library Rate, or UPS).
Invoices are sent with shipments unless
the library specifies otherwise.

BACK ORDER POLICY:

Unavailable titles will be back ordered.

SPECIAL PLANS:

Interested libraries should contact
publisher about special plans.

OTHER:

Libraries with growing international
development studies programs will want
to consider the publisher's backlist.

KUNDALINI RESEARCH INSTITUTE see BORGO
PRESS

THE LABYRINTH PRESS

2814 Chapel Hill Road
Durham, North Carolina 27707
Telephone: 919-493-5051

ADDRESS FOR ORDERS:

Same as above.

PREPAYMENT:

Prepayment required for libraries without
established account.

DISCOUNT POLICY:

There is no discount for libraries.

RETURN POLICY:

Libraries must request written
permission before shipping returns.
Returned books must be in resalable
condition and sent to: Richard Owen
Roberts, Booksellers, Box 21, Wheaton, IL
60189.

SHIPPING AND BILLING POLICY:

Libraries pay shipping cost. There is a
minimum charge of $2 for orders of less
than $20. Invoices are enclosed with
shipments.

BACK ORDER POLICY:

Titles not available are back ordered and
shipped upon publication.

DAVID S. LAKE PUBLISHERS

19 Davis Drive
Belmont, California 94002

ADDRESS FOR ORDERS:

Same as above.

DISTRIBUTION/IMPRINTS:

Divisions: Fearon Teacher Aids; Fearon Education.

Imprint: Lake Books.

PREPAYMENT:

Not required.

DISCOUNT POLICY:

No discount to libraries, except on Fearon Education titles which are 25% off list (same as price shown in catalog).

RETURN POLICY:

Returns in salable condition, accompanied by invoice information and shipped with postage prepaid are accepted within one year. Written or verbal permission is required. Address for returns: 6 Davis Drive/ Belmont, CA 94002.

SHIPPING AND BILLING POLICY:

Libraries are charged shipping at 10% on billed orders; prepaid orders are shipped free at Fourth Class Rate. Invoices are sent with shipments unless the library specifies otherwise.

BACK ORDER POLICY:

Publisher back orders unavailable titles and ships and bills books when they become available.

LAMBERT GANN PUBLISHING COMPANY

Box 0
Pomeroy, Washington 99347
Telephone: 509-843-1094

ADDRESS FOR ORDERS:

Same as above.

DISTRIBUTION/IMPRINTS:

Distributes: Ed Dobson Traders Press; John Hill.

PREPAYMENT:

Not required.

DISCOUNT POLICY:

20% discount to libraries.

RETURN POLICY:

Returns are usually not accepted if the shrink-wrap is broken.

SHIPPING AND BILLING POLICY:

Libraries are charged shipping and handling of $3.00 for the first book and $1.00 for each additional book on all orders. Invoices are sent with shipments unless the library specifies otherwise.

BACK ORDER POLICY:

Publisher holds orders and telephones library when books are available to see if they are still wanted.

LANGE see APPLETON AND LANGE PUBLISHING COMPANY

LARK see STERLING PUBLISHING COMPANY, INC.

LARKSDALE

1706 Seamist
Houston, Texas 77008-3106
Telephone: 713-861-6214

ADDRESS FOR ORDERS:

Same as above.

DISTRIBUTION/IMPRINTS:

Distributes the publications of: Harle House; Linolean Press; Post Oak Press; Lindahl Books.

PREPAYMENT:

Not required.

DISCOUNT POLICY:

1 book: no discount
2 or more: 20%
large orders: publisher will quote

RETURN POLICY:

No returns are accepted.

SHIPPING AND BILLING POLICY:

Libraries are charged actual postage.
Invoices are sent separately after
shipments unless the library specifies
otherwise.

BACK ORDER POLICY:

Publisher back orders all books not yet
published or out of stock and notifies
library.

LAW JOURNAL SEMINARS PRESS

---

111 Eighth Avenue, Suite 900
New York, New York 10011
Telephone: 212-741-8300
            800-888-8300

ADDRESS FOR ORDERS:

Same as above.
Telephone: 800-888-8300
            212-463-5566

PREPAYMENT:

Not required except for course books.

DISCOUNT POLICY:

10% discount on prepaid orders.

10-49 copies: 20%
50-99:   25%
100 or more: 33 1/3%

RETURN POLICY:

Returns, in salable condition, are
accepted within 30-60 days. Written
permission is not required. Address for
returns: Law Journal Press/c/o Mercedes
Distribution Center/160 Imlay St/
Brooklyn, NY 11231.

SHIPPING AND BILLING POLICY:

Libraries are charged shipping on billed
orders; prepaid orders are shipped free.
Invoices are sent with shipments.

BACK ORDER POLICY:

Back orders are placed for any title
still in print.

SPECIAL PLANS:

Standing orders are available for
updates to looseleaf services which are
shipped and billed when published. All
orders for looseleaf services include
updates unless the library specifies
otherwise.

LAWRENCEVILLE PRESS see DELMAR
PUBLISHERS, INC.

LAWSON-GOULD see ALFRED PUBLISHING
COMPANY, INC.

LEA AND FEBIGER

---

600 South Washington Square
Philadelphia, Pennsylvania 19106
Telephone: 215-WA-2-1330

ADDRESS FOR ORDERS:

Same as above.

PREPAYMENT:

Not required.

DISCOUNT POLICY:

No discount.

RETURN POLICY:

Written permission is not required for
returns. Book returns are limited to 30
days. Any books may be returned for
credit within the specified time.
Returned books must be in salable
condition. The address for returns is
the same as for orders.

SHIPPING AND BILLING POLICY:

Publisher pays postage on prepaid orders.
Invoices are sent with shipments.

BACK ORDER POLICY:

Titles not currently available are reported and back ordered unless library requests otherwise.

LEARNING LINE

P.O. Box 1200
Palo Alto, California 94302
Telephone: 415-424-1400
                or
395 Portage Avenue
Palo Alto, California 94306

ADDRESS FOR ORDERS:

Same as above.

PREPAYMENT:

Not required.

DISCOUNT POLICY:

Catalog prices reflect the publisher's discount; no further discount is given.

RETURN POLICY:

Returns in salable condition are accepted within one year. Written permission is preferred. Address for returns: 1415 Pittman Street/ Sparks, New York 89431.

SHIPPING AND BILLING POLICY:

Libraries are charged shipping at 10% of the total order. Invoices are sent separately after shipments unless the library specifies otherwise.

BACK ORDER POLICY:

Publisher back orders unavailable titles and ships books when they become available unless the library cancels.

LEARNING RESOURCES NETWORK (LERN)

1554 Hayes Drive
Manhattan, Kansas 66502
Telephone: 913-539-5376

ADDRESS FOR ORDERS:

Same as above.

PREPAYMENT:

Not required with a purchase order.

DISCOUNT POLICY:

No discount to libraries.

RETURN POLICY:

Returns are accepted within 30 days of receipt.

SHIPPING AND BILLING POLICY:

Libraries are charged shipping on all orders. Invoices are sent with shipments unless the library specifies otherwise.

BACK ORDER POLICY:

Items on back order are usually available within 30 days.

LEATHER STOCKING BOOKS see MEDIA PRODUCTIONS & MARKETING INC.

LEETE'S ISLAND see INDEPENDENT PUBLISHERS GROUP

LEHIGH UNIVERSITY PRESS see ASSOCIATED UNIVERSITY PRESSES

LEISURE PRESS see HUMAN KINETICS PUBLISHERS, INC.

HAL LEONARD PUBLISHING CORPORATION

8112 West Bluemound Road
Milwaukee, Wisconsin 53213
Telephone: 414-774-3630

ADDRESS FOR ORDERS:

Same as above.

DISTRIBUTION/IMPRINTS:

Distributes the publications of: G. Schirmer; G. Ricordi; Associated Music Publishers; Faber Music Ltd.; Edward B. Marks Music; MCA Music; Berklee Press; Beacon Music; Editions Salabert.

PREPAYMENT:

Not required; publisher will ship on open account.

DISCOUNT POLICY:

No discount to libraries.

RETURN POLICY:

Returns are not accepted.

SHIPPING AND BILLING POLICY:

Libraries pay shipping on all orders. Orders on open account will be charged actual shipping; prepaid orders should include $1.50 for each book ordered. Invoices are sent separately.

BACK ORDER POLICY:

Back orders will be shipped automatically as materials become available.

LERNER PUBLICATIONS COMPANY

---

241 1st Avenue North
Minneapolis, Minnesota 55401
Telephone: 612-332-3344
           800-328-4929

ADDRESS FOR ORDERS:

Same as above.

DISTRIBUTION/IMPRINTS:

Division: First Avenue Editions.

PREPAYMENT:

Not required.

DISCOUNT POLICY:

No discount to libraries.

RETURN POLICY:

Returns, in salable condition and accompanied by invoice number on the boxes, are accepted within one year. Prior permission, preferably by telephone, is required.

SHIPPING AND BILLING POLICY:

Libraries are charged shipping/handling on billed orders; publisher pays shipping/handling (Fourth Class Book Rate) on prepaid orders. Invoices are sent separately, but a copy can be sent with shipments as well at library's request.

BACK ORDER POLICY:

Back orders are placed for all material currently unavailable unless the library instructs otherwise and will remain on back order until cancelled, preferably by telephone.

LEWIS PUBLISHERS, INC.

---

121 S. Main Street
P.O. Drawer 519
Chelsea, Michigan 48118
Telephone: 800-525-7894 (outside MI)
           313-475-8610 (collect in MI)

ADDRESS FOR ORDERS:

Same as above.

DISTRIBUTION/IMPRINTS:

Publisher distributes its own publication in the U.S. John Wiley & Sons is the distributor for foreign orders.

C.K. Smoley & Sons (Division)

PREPAYMENT:

Not required, but publisher advises prepayment on orders of less than $20.00 or if the library wishes to save shipping charges.

DISCOUNT POLICY:

Public and university libraries receive a 10% discount. No discount is offered to corporate or government agency libraries.

RETURN POLICY:

Returns of books, in clean, resalable
condition, are accepted within one year
of invoice date. Publisher prefers that
libraries obtain prior written
permission. Titles which are out-of-
print or "special deals" are non-
returnable.

SHIPPING AND BILLING POLICY:

Publisher pays shipping (at Special 4th
Class Book Rate) and handling on prepaid
orders. UPS on prepaid orders and all
shipping and handling charges on open
account orders are charged to the
library. Handling charges vary with each
order. Invoices are sent to the Bill To
address on the purchase order and will
accompany the shipment if the Ship To
address is the same. Publisher will try
to accommodate a library's special
requirements.

BACK ORDER POLICY:

Unless instructed otherwise, publisher
back orders all material currently
unavailable but expected to be available
and ships material as soon as it does
become available. Publisher attempts to
send regular updates when a book is
delayed.

SPECIAL PLANS:

A standing order program is offered for
Purdue Industrial Waste Conference
Proceedings.

LEXINGTON BOOKS see D. C. HEATH AND
COMPANY

LIBERTY CLASSICS see LIBERTY FUND, INC.

LIBERTY FUND, INC.

7440 N. Shadeland Avenue
Indianapolis, Indiana 46250
Telephone: 317-842-0880

ADDRESS FOR ORDERS:

Same as above.

DISTRIBUTION/IMPRINTS:

Imprints: Liberty Press; Liberty
Classics.

PREPAYMENT:

Not required, but free shipping with
prepaid orders.

DISCOUNT POLICY:

10% discount to libraries.

RETURN POLICY:

Returns in salable condition, accompanied
by invoice number, and sent with postage
prepaid are accepted within 90 days.
Defective books must be so marked and
defects clearly indicated. Prior
permission is required.

SHIPPING AND BILLING POLICY:

Libraries are charged shipping on billed
orders; prepaid orders are shipped free.
Invoices are sent separately after
shipments, but library specifications
are honored.

BACK ORDER POLICY:

All back orders are filled promptly when
books are available.

LIBERTY HOUSE see TAB BOOKS

LIBERTY PRESS see LIBERTY FUND, INC.

LIBRA PUBLISHERS, INC.

3089C Clairemont Drive, Suite 383
San Diego, California 92117
Telephone: 619-581-9449

ADDRESS FOR ORDERS:

Same as above.

PREPAYMENT:

Not required, but preferred.

DISCOUNT POLICY:

No discount to libraries.

RETURN POLICY:

Returns, in salable condition, are accepted for full credit or refund within 3 months. Written permission is required.

SHIPPING AND BILLING POLICY:

Prepaid orders are shipped free; library pays shipping on billed orders. Invoices are sent with shipments unless the library specifies otherwise.

BACK ORDER POLICY:

Publisher will notify library when a book will be available.

LIBRARIES UNLIMITED

P.O. Box 3988
Englewood, Colorado 80155-3988
Telephone: 303-770-1220

ADDRESS FOR ORDERS:

Same as above.
Telephone: 800-237-6124

DISTRIBUTION/IMPRINTS:

Distributes the publications of: Cutter Tables, Inc.; Hi Willow Research; Source Document Management Service; NAVA - Audiovisual Equipment Directory.

Ukrainian Academic Press (Division)

PREPAYMENT:

Not required for libraries.

DISCOUNT POLICY:

No discounts except for special offers.

RETURN POLICY:

Returns of books in salable condition accepted for six months and must be accompanied by a copy of the invoice. Prior permission is not required for libraries. Return address: Libraries Unlimited Warehouse/4897 Moline St./Denver, CO 80239.

SHIPPING AND BILLING POLICY:

Publisher pays shipping and handling on prepaid orders. Shipping and handling added to billed orders. Handling charges are: $0.75 (1-2 books); $1.50 (3-5 books); $2.00 (6-9 books); $2.50 (10-14 books); $3.00 (15-20 books); $4.00 (over 20 books). Invoices are sent separately unless the library specifies otherwise.

BACK ORDER POLICY:

Invoices indicate expected date of availability for back orders. The book is shipped when it is published. Libraries may request that titles not be back ordered.

SPECIAL PLANS:

All standing orders (for annuals or series) receive a 10% discount. All blanket orders, selective or not, receive a 20% discount. Blanket orders can be tailored for the individual library and can be cancelled at any time. Each book is shipped as soon as it is published with the above return privileges.

OTHER:

Libraries may order direct or through wholesalers. Publisher would appreciate any comments about its books.

LIBRARY OF MANAGEMENT FOR DEVELOPMENT see KUMARIAN PRESS, INC.

LIBRARY OF VICTORIAN CULTURE see AMERICAN LIFE BOOKS

LIBRARY PROFESSIONAL PUBLICATIONS see SHOE STRING PRESS, INC.

LIBRARYWORKS see NEAL-SCHUMAN PUBLISHERS, INC.

LIFE ENHANCEMENT PUBLICATIONS see HUMAN
KINETICS PUBLISHERS, INC.

LIGHT WAVE PRESS see HUNTER HOUSE, INC.
PUBLISHERS

LIGHTNING TREE

P.O. Box 1837
Santa Fe, New Mexico 87504
Telephone: 505-983-7434

ADDRESS FOR ORDERS:

Same as above.

PREPAYMENT:

Not required.

DISCOUNT POLICY:

No discount to libraries for single-copy
orders; titles may be assorted for
quantity discounts:

2-4 copies: 20%
5-49:   40%
50-99:   41%
100-249:   42%
250-499:   43%

RETURN POLICY:

Returns, in salable condition, are
accepted within 90 days from invoice
date. Written permission is not
required.

SHIPPING AND BILLING POLICY:

Libraries are charged shipping except on
prepaid orders of two or more books.
Invoices are sent with shipments; there
is a $0.50 charge for separate billing
to another address.

BACK ORDER POLICY:

Library is notified of back orders which
are kept on file until books are
available.

LIGUORI PUBLICATIONS

One Liguori Drive
Liguori, Missouri 63057
Telephone: 314-464-2500

ADDRESS FOR ORDERS:

Same as above.
Telephone: 800-325-9521

PREPAYMENT:

Not required, but publisher pays shipping
on prepaid orders.

DISCOUNT POLICY:

10-24 copies: 10%
25-49:   12%
50-99:   15%
100 or more: 20%
500 single title: 30%

RETURN POLICY:

Returns are accepted within one year.
Written permission is required. Out-of-
print titles are non-returnable.

SHIPPING AND BILLING POLICY:

Libraries are charged shipping plus
handling ($0.50 on orders up to $5.00;
$0.75 up to $10.00; $1.00 up to $25.00;
$1.25 over $25.00) on billed orders;
prepaid orders are shipped free.
Invoices are sent separately after
shipments.

BACK ORDER POLICY:

Publisher back orders unavailable titles
and ships books when they become
available.

LINDAHL BOOKS see LARKSDALE

LINDEN PRESS see SIMON & SCHUSTER, INC.

LINDISFARNE PRESS see INNER TRADITIONS

LINNET see SHOE STRING PRESS, INC.

LINOLEAN PRESS see LARKSDALE

LION PUBLISHING

1705 Hubbard Avenue
Batavia, Illinois 60510
Telephone: 312-879-0707

ADDRESS FOR ORDERS:

Same as above.
Telephone: 800-447-5466

PREPAYMENT:

Not required.

DISCOUNT POLICY:

No discount to libraries except by
arrangement for large-quantity orders and
occasional special offers.

RETURN POLICY:

Returns are accepted within one year.
Written permission is required.

SHIPPING AND BILLING POLICY:

Libraries are charged shipping. Invoices
are sent with shipments unless the
library specifies otherwise.

BACK ORDER POLICY:

Back orders are recorded and shipped
when available.

ALAN R. LISS, INC.

41 East 11th Street
New York, New York 10003
Telephone: 212-475-7700

ADDRESS FOR ORDERS:

Same as above.

PREPAYMENT:

Not required.

DISCOUNT POLICY:

Publisher does not grant discounts to
libraries.

RETURN POLICY:

Books are sold on a firm order basis
only. Requests to return incorrectly
shipped, defective or damaged books must
be in writing, and cite relevant invoice
and order numbers. Return requests
should be sent to the above address.

SHIPPING AND BILLING POLICY:

Orders accompanied by payment are shipped
post-paid. Publisher charges postage and
handling on all billed orders. The
amount of postage and handling charges
are based on actual weight and number of
books in order. Invoices are sent in the
manner requested by library.

BACK ORDER POLICY:

Publisher will hold an order for books
not currently in stock and process as
titles become available, unless terms of
order do not allow for back ordering.

SPECIAL ORDER PLAN:

Publisher accepts Continuation Orders for
any of publisher's series and serials.
Books are billed and shipped upon
publication, and there is no special
discount. A continuation order can be
started by sending an official purchase
order to Book Department. Such an order
can be cancelled at any time. Return
privileges are the same as for regular
orders. Publisher does not have a
standing order plan organized by
subjects.

OTHER INFORMATION:

Telephone orders are accepted. Journal
titles are available on a calendar year
subscription basis. Journal orders are
not cancellable.

LITERATURE EAST AND WEST see THREE
CONTINENTS PRESS, INC.

LITTLE, BROWN AND COMPANY

34 Beacon Street
Boston, Massachusetts 02108
Telephone: 617-227-0730

ADDRESS FOR ORDERS:

Order Department
Little, Brown and Company
200 West Street
Waltham, Massachusetts 02151
Telephone: 617-890-0250

DISTRIBUTION/IMPRINTS:

Distributes: Oxmoor House; Atlantic
Monthly Press Books; Time-Life Books;
AARP Books (American Association of
Retired Persons).

Imprints: Joy Street Books (for
children); New York Graphic Society
Books.

PREPAYMENT:

Libraries will be invoiced; in some
cases, a library must prepay the first
order until an account is set up.

DISCOUNT POLICY:

Library/Institutional discount is 20% of
the invoice price. Orders should request
the discount.

RETURN POLICY:

Returns, accompanied by a copy of the
invoice, may be sent to: Returns Dept/
Little, Brown and Company/200 West St/
Waltham, MA 02151.

SHIPPING AND BILLING POLICY:

Libraries are charged shipping which
varies with method. Invoices are usually
sent with shipments.

BACK ORDER POLICY:

A back order for an out-of-stock item
will be placed for up to four months; if
an item becomes available after four
months, the library will be notified and
asked to reorder.

SPECIAL PLANS:

Greenaway Plan offers publications of
Little, Brown (adult and children's
books), Atlantic Monthly Press, Oxmoor
House, and AARP to libraries with
budgets of $60,000 and at least four
branches at a 75% discount

New York Graphic Society Books on
Approval Plan is available to member
libraries at a 40% discount. For further
information, libraries should contact
Marketing Coordinator/Little, Brown &
Company/34 Beacon St/Boston, MA 02108.

LITTLE SIMON see SIMON & SCHUSTER, INC.

LITTLEFIELD, ADAMS AND COMPANY

81 Adams Drive
Totowa, New Jersey 07512
Telephone: 201-256-8600

ADDRESS FOR ORDERS:

Same as above.

DISTRIBUTION/IMPRINTS:

Distributes J. M. Dent (London)

Divisions: Barnes and Noble Books; Rowman
& Littlefield.

PREPAYMENT:

Not required.

DISCOUNT POLICY:

No discount to libraries.

RETURN POLICY:

Returns are accepted within 9 months
from purchase. Written permission is
required for shipping labels.

SHIPPING AND BILLING POLICY:

Libraries are charged shipping. Invoices
are sent separately after shipments.

BACK ORDER POLICY:

Publisher back orders unavailable titles
and ships books when they become
available unless the library cancels.

LITURGICAL PRESS

St. John's Abbey
Collegeville, Minnesota 56321
Telephone: 612-363-2213

ADDRESS FOR ORDERS:

Same as above.

PREPAYMENT:

Prepayment is requested for orders under
$10.00.

DISCOUNT POLICY:

No special discount to libraries.

RETURN POLICY:

Returns, in salable condition, are
accepted for credit within 12 months
after invoice date. Written permission
is required, and requests should include
invoice number and date. Audio and video
cassettes are not returnable unless
defective in which case publisher will
send replacements.

SHIPPING AND BILLING POLICY:

Libraries are charged shipping according
to the following schedule: $1.50 on
orders up to $5.00; $2.00 on orders up
to $20.00; $3.50 on orders up to $50.00;
$5.00 on orders up to $75.00; $7.50 on
orders up to $100.00; 8% on orders over
$100.00. Invoices are sent with
shipments in the case of written orders
or separately in the case of telephone
orders unless the library specifies
otherwise.

BACK ORDER POLICY:

Back orders are noted on invoices, and
the books are shipped when available.

LIVERIGHT see W. W. NORTON AND COMPANY,
INC.

LLEWELLYN PUBLICATIONS

213 E. 4th Street
St. Paul, Minnesota 55101
Telephone: 612-291-1970

ADDRESS FOR ORDERS:

P.O. Box 64383
St. Paul, MN 55164
Telephone: 800-THE-MOON

DISTRIBUTION/IMPRINTS:

Distributes Weiser Publications.

PREPAYMENT:

First order from a library must be
prepaid; succeeding orders will be
billed.

DISCOUNT POLICY:

30% discount; no minimum order.

RETURN POLICY:

Returns, with covers not removed, are
accepted with prior written or verbal
approval. Returns to 4th St. address.

SHIPPING AND BILLING POLICY:

Prepaid orders are shipped free;
shipping is added to the invoice on
billed orders. Invoices are sent after
shipments only.

BACK ORDER POLICY:

Forthcoming titles, when back ordered,
receive an additional 5% discount.

LODESTAR BOOKS see E. P. DUTTON

LOMOND PUBLICATIONS, INC.

P.O. Box 88
Mt. Airy, Maryland 21771
Telephone: 301-875-5475
          800-443-6299

ADDRESS FOR ORDERS:

Same as above.

PREPAYMENT:

Not required for book orders but required for subscriptions.

DISCOUNT POLICY:

20% discount for orders of 6 or more copies of the same title.

RETURN POLICY:

Returns accompanied by original invoice number and sent with postage prepaid are accepted within one year from invoice date. Written permission is not required.

SHIPPING AND BILLING POLICY:

Libraries are charged shipping plus $1.50 handling on billed orders; prepaid orders are shipped free. Invoices are sent with shipments unless the library specifies otherwise.

BACK ORDER POLICY:

Publisher back orders all titles unless they are permanently out of stock.

LONE STAR BOOKS see GULF PUBLISHING COMPANY, BOOK DIVISION

LONELY PLANET PUBLICATIONS

Embarcadero West
112 Linden Street
Oakland, California 94607
Telephone: 415-893-8555
          800-322-7333 (outside CA)
          415-893-8563 (FAX)

ADDRESS FOR ORDERS:

Same as above.

PREPAYMENT:

Not required.

DISCOUNT POLICY:

1-4 copies: 35%
5-24 copies: 40%
25-49 copies: 43%

50+ copies: 45%

RETURN POLICY:

Returns of current editions in perfect, resalable condition and accompanied by invoice and discount information, are accepted and full credit will be issued against future purchases. Damaged or defective books will be replaced immediately. No prior permission is required.

SHIPPING AND BILLING POLICY:

Publisher pays shipping costs. Invoices are sent with shipments unless Bill To address is different from Ship To address or unless the library specifies otherwise.

BACK ORDER POLICY:

Titles are back ordered as requested.

LONGMAN INC

---

95 Church Street
White Plains, New York 10601
Telephone: 914-993-5000

ADDRESS FOR ORDERS:

Longman Inc.
Order Department
Jacob Way
Reading, MA 01867-9984

PREPAYMENT:

Not required.

DISCOUNT POLICY:

There is no discount to libraries.

RETURN POLICY:

No prior authorization is required if original invoice or packing list accompanies return. A 10% service charge will be applied if above information is not supplied. Books must be new, resalable, unmarked, and current edition, purchased within 15 months prior to date of return. Cassettes, video tapes, software and audiovisual material may not be returned. Damaged or defective copies must be returned within 60 days of receipt for replacement. The address for returns is: Longman Inc., 5851 Guion Road, Indianapolis, IN 46254.

LORD JOHN PRESS

19073 Los Alimos Street
Northridge, California 91326
Telephone: 818-363-6621

ADDRESS FOR ORDERS:

Same as above.

PREPAYMENT:

Not required.

DISCOUNT POLICY:

No discount to libraries.

RETURN POLICY:

Returns are accepted within one year.
Written permission is required.

SHIPPING AND BILLING POLICY:

Libraries are charged shipping (Book
Rate or Library Rate as appropriate).
Invoices are sent with shipments.

BACK ORDER POLICY:

Publisher maintains a back order file.

LORRIMER SCREENPLAYS see FABER & FABER,
INC.

LOUISIANA STATE UNIVERSITY PRESS

Baton Rouge, Louisiana 70893
Telephone: 504-388-6294

ADDRESS FOR ORDERS:

Same as above.
Telephone: 504-388-8271

PREPAYMENT:

Not required.

DISCOUNT POLICY:

Libraries with standing orders receive a
20% discount; libraries without standing
orders receive a 10% discount.

RETURN POLICY:

Permission to return books is not
required; however, books returned for
credit must be clean, salable copies of
current editions. Defective books must
be so marked and defects clearly
indicated. All postage and handling
charges on returns must be paid by
library. Address for returns is:
Louisiana State University Press,
Warehouse-Printing Building, 3555 River
Road, Baton Rouge, LA 70893.

SHIPPING AND BILLING POLICY:

Publisher charges actual shipping cost to
libraries on both prepaid and billed
orders. There is no handling or billing
charge.

BACK ORDER POLICY:

Unless library specifies otherwise,
publisher back orders not-yet-published
and temporarily out-of-stock titles and
ships as soon as they are available.
Publisher sends a copy of invoice
indicating that book has been back
ordered and stating due date.

SPECIAL ORDER PLAN:

Publisher has a standing order plan in
which libraries can place an order for
all new books, books in series, or on
certain subjects. Discount for standing
orders is 20%.

LOYOLA UNIVERSITY PRESS

3441 N. Ashland Avenue
Chicago, Illinois 60657
Telephone: 312-281-1818

ADDRESS FOR ORDERS:

Same as above.
Telephone: 800-621-1008

DISTRIBUTION/IMPRINTS:

Distributes the publications of:
Gregorian University Press; Oriental

Institute Press; Jesuit Historical Press;
Biblical Institute Press.

PREPAYMENT:

Not required.

DISCOUNT POLICY:

20% discount to libraries.

RETURN POLICY:

Returns are accepted within one year of
purchase. Books must be returned in
salable condition, with shipping charges
prepaid, and with a copy of the invoice
included.

SHIPPING AND BILLING POLICY:

Libraries are charged shipping on all
orders. Invoices are sent separately.

BACK ORDER POLICY:

Unavailable titles are automatically
back ordered and shipped when available.

LYON ARBORETUM see UNIVERSITY OF HAWAII
PRESS

MCA MUSIC see HAL LEONARD PUBLISHING
CORPORATION

MEPC see ELSEVIER SCIENCE PUBLISHING
COMPANY, INC.

MIT PRESS

---

55 Hayward Street
Cambridge, Massachusetts 02142
Telephone: 617-253-2884 (orders)
          800-356-0343 (orders)
          617-253-5251 (Customer
   Service)

ADDRESS FOR ORDERS:

Same as above.

DISTRIBUTION/IMPRINTS:

Distributes Zone Books.
Bradford Books (imprint)
Architectural History Foundation Books
(imprint).

PREPAYMENT:

Not required.

DISCOUNT POLICY:

No discount to public or corporate
libraries; 10% discount to academic
libraries.

RETURN POLICY:

Returns in clean and salable condition
are accepted within one year of invoice
date. Returns of incorrect titles and
defective books must be made within 30
days of receipt and accompanied by
invoice numbers. No advance
authorization is required. Address for
returns: The MIT Press/c/o UNISERV,
Inc./525 Great Road (Rte.
119)/Littleton, MA 01460.

SHIPPING AND BILLING POLICY:

Libraries are charged shipping. Invoices
are sent with shipments unless the
library specifies otherwise.

BACK ORDER POLICY:

Publisher will back order any item
automatically unless the library
requests otherwise. On prepaid orders,
books will be back ordered unless
library requests a refund.

SPECIAL PLANS:

Library standing order plan is
available.

OTHER:

Publisher recommends that public
libraries order through wholesalers for
a discount.

MACDONALD see FRANKLIN WATTS, INC.

MCDOUGAL, LITTELL AND COMPANY

P.O. Box 1667
Evanston, Illinois 60204
Telephone: 312-869-2300

ADDRESS FOR ORDERS:

Same as above.
Telephone: 800-225-3809

PREPAYMENT:

Not required.

DISCOUNT POLICY:

No special discount to libraries.

RETURN POLICY:

Returns in resalable condition are
accepted within ten months. Prior
authorization is required; requests
should include invoice number, account
number, date of invoice, title, and
quantity.

SHIPPING AND BILLING POLICY:

Libraries are charged shipping on all
orders. Invoices are sent separately.

BACK ORDER POLICY:

All out-of-stock items will be back
ordered and shipped when available.

OTHER:

Libraries needing more information
should contact Product Information at
800-323-5435.

MARGARET K. MCELDERRY BOOKS see MACMILLAN
PUBLISHING COMPANY, INC.

MCFARLAND & COMPANY, INC, PUBLISHERS

Box 611, Highway 88
Jefferson, North Carolina 28640
Telephone: 919-246-4460

ADDRESS FOR ORDERS:

Same as above.

PREPAYMENT:

Not required.

DISCOUNT POLICY:

No discount to libraries.

RETURN POLICY:

Returns, in salable condition and still
in print, are accepted within one year
of invoice date. Written permission is
required.

SHIPPING AND BILLING POLICY:

Libraries are charged shipping of $1.50
for the first book and $0.75 for each
additional book. For orders over $100,
shipping is 4% of net; 3% of net for
orders over $200; and 2% for orders over
$500. Invoices are sent with shipments
unless the library's purchase order
specifies otherwise.

BACK ORDER POLICY:

Titles not currently available are back
ordered or cancelled according to
library's instructions.

MCGRAW-HILL BOOK COMPANY

---

11 West 19 Street
Third Floor
New York, New York 10011
Telephone: 212-337-5021

ADDRESS FOR ORDERS:

Same as above.

DISTRIBUTION/IMPRINTS:

Publisher distributes: Ashton Tate and
McGraw-Hill Book Company products.

PREPAYMENT:

Not required.

DISCOUNT POLICY:

10% or 20% (depending on discount class)
discount to college and public
libraries; special libraries receive a
20% discount for 6 or more copies of a
single title.

RETURN POLICY:

Returns in good condition of out-of-print titles are accepted within six months; titles still in print have no time limit. Written permission is not required. Invoice information must accompany returns which should be sent to the Returns Department at the distribution center serving the library's area.

SHIPPING AND BILLING POLICY:

Libraries are charged actual shipping. Invoices are sent with shipments.

BACK ORDER POLICY:

Publisher back orders unavailable titles and ships books when they become available.

SPECIAL PLANS:

Publisher offers a Library Service Plan which allows the library to receive automatically upon publication all books published in specified subject areas at special discount rates. The plan has two options: Automatic Plan and Non-Automatic Plan, the difference being that for the latter, libraries select books prior to publication from the publisher's seasonal catalog. Either option requires that libraries select a minimum of one major category or three sub-categories.

DAVID MCKAY COMPANY, INC.

---

201 East 50th Street
New York, New York 10022
Telephone:

ADDRESS FOR ORDERS:

Random House, Inc.
400 Hahn Road
Westminster, Maryland 21157
Telephone: 800-638-6460

DISTRIBUTION/IMPRINTS:

Distributed by Random House, Inc.

PREPAYMENT:

To this and other policies, the policies of Random House pertain.

MACMILLAN PUBLISHING COMPANY, INC.

---

866 Third Avenue
New York, New York 10022
Telephone: 212-935-2000

ADDRESS FOR ORDERS:

Macmillan Professional and Library Services, Distribution Center, Riverside, NJ 08075

DISTRIBUTION/IMPRINT:

Atheneum Publishers
Charles Scribner's Sons
Rawson Associates
Collier Books
The Free Press
Schirmer Books
Bradbury Press
Margaret K. McElderry Books
Aladdin Books
Audel Books

PREPAYMENT:

Not required.

DISCOUNT POLICY:

General library books, trade books, publisher's library edition, Macmillan and Collier paperbacks:

1 to 4 copies	0%
5 to 19 copies	25%
20 or more copies	40%

Professional, technical, and college textbooks:

1 and 2 copies	0%
3 or more copies	10%

School textbooks: 25%

Special reference books: 0%

RETURN POLICY:

Books returns are unlimited. No prior permission is required; however, original invoice upon which the books were billed must be included with returns in order to receive proper credit. Address for returns is the same as for orders.

SHIPPING AND BILLING POLICY:

Libraries pay postage. The amount of postage depends on weight and destination for general titles. On reference sets, there is a standard shipping and handling charge for each specific set. Invoices are sent separately after shipments. If library has special instructions, they must be shown on purchase order.

BACK ORDER POLICY:

Titles not currently available are either back ordered or cancelled as library requests.

SPECIAL ORDER PLAN:

Under Macmillan Service Order Program for Public Libraries, Macmillan offers three programs: Adult Program, Young Adult Program, and Juvenile Program. Libraries receive shipments of new publications before general release. Macmillan pays shipping and handling charges for books sent under the service order program. Libraries receive a 42% discount.

MCPHERSON & COMPANY

81 Cornell Street
P.O. Box 1126
Kingston, New York 12401
Telephone: 914-331-5807

ADDRESS FOR ORDERS:

Same as above.

DISTRIBUTION/IMPRINTS:

Distributes: Tanam Press; Edinburgh Review (magazine).

Imprints: Documentext; Treacle Press; McPherson & Company.

PREPAYMENT:

Not required.

DISCOUNT POLICY:

20% discount to libraries for orders of more than $75.00 list price.

RETURN POLICY:

Returns are not accepted from libraries except in the case of damaged or defective books which must be returned immediately for replacement.

SHIPPING AND BILLING POLICY:

Publisher pays shipping charges within the U.S. Invoices are sent with shipments unless the library specifies otherwise.

BACK ORDER POLICY:

Publisher will back order for a time limit specified by the library.

MADRIGAL PUBLISHING COMPANY see STACKPOLE BOOKS

MAIN STREET PRESS

William Case House
Pittstown, New Jersey 08867
Telephone: 201-735-9424

ADDRESS FOR ORDERS:

Same as above.

PREPAYMENT:

Prepayment required for single-copy orders.

DISCOUNT POLICY:

30% discount on all orders.

RETURN POLICY:

In-print Books, in salable condition and accompanied by invoice numbers, are accepted for return. Prior permission is required. Address for returns: Main Street Press/80 Northfield Avenue/Bldg. 424, Raritan Center/Edison, New Jersey 08818.

SHIPPING AND BILLING POLICY:

Libraries are charged shipping Library Rate plus handling of approximately $1.75 per copy. Invoices are sent separately unless the library specifies otherwise.

BACK ORDER POLICY:

Publisher back orders automatically and informs the library when titles will be available.

OTHER:

Publisher fills direct orders within 48 hours if titles are in stock.

MARINERS MUSEUM see UNIVERSITY PRESS OF VIRGINIA

MARKET DATA RETRIEVAL

---

16 Progress Drive
Shelton, Connecticut 06484
Telephone: 800-243-5538
         203-926-4800

ADDRESS FOR ORDERS:

Same as above.

PREPAYMENT:

Prepayment is required only for private libraries who do not have established accounts.

DISCOUNT POLICY:

There is no library discount.

RETURN POLICY:

Normally written permission is required. Returns are limited to 60 days. The address for returns is the same as for orders.

SHIPPING AND BILLING POLICY:

Shipping costs are added to the bill. The amount of handling charge is dependent on size of the order. Invoices are sent separately after shipments in all cases.

BACK ORDER POLICY:

Publisher back orders unavailable titles and fills orders when they become available.

MARKETSCOPE see WESTERN MARINE ENTERPRISES

MARKHAM PRESS FUND see BAYLOR UNIVERSITY PRESS

EDWARD B. MARKS MUSIC see HAL LEONARD PUBLISHING CORPORATION

MARLBORO PRESS

P.O. Box 157
Marlboro, Vermont 05344
Telephone: 802-257-0781

ADDRESS FOR ORDERS:

Same as above.

PREPAYMENT:

Not required.

DISCOUNT POLICY:

10% discount to libraries.

RETURN POLICY:

Only damaged or defective books, accompanied by invoice number and date of purchase order, may be returned. The time limit for returns is three months from date of purchase.

SHIPPING AND BILLING POLICY:

Libraries are charged shipping. Invoices are sent with shipments unless the library specifies otherwise.

MASTERWORKS OF MODERN JEWISH WRITING see MARKUS WIENER PUBLISHING, INC.

MEADOWBROOK, INC.

18318 Minnetonka Boulevard
Deephaven, Minnesota 55391
Telephone: 612-473-5400

ADDRESS FOR ORDERS:

Same as above.
Telephone: 800-338-2232

PREPAYMENT:

Not required with purchase order.

DISCOUNT POLICY:

6-29 books: 20%
20-99:   40%

Mixed titles are allowed.

RETURN POLICY:

Returns are accepted within 2 weeks.
Written permission is required.

SHIPPING AND BILLING POLICY:

Libraries are charged shipping of $1.25
for the first book and $0.50 for each
additional book. Invoices are sent
separately after shipments only.

BACK ORDER POLICY:

Publisher automatically back orders
unavailable titles unless the library
instructs otherwise.

MECKLER BOOKS see MECKLER CORPORATION

MECKLER CORPORATION

---

11 Ferry Lane West
Westport, Connecticut 06880
Telephone: 203-226-6967

ADDRESS FOR ORDERS:

Same as above.

DISTRIBUTION/IMPRINTS:

Imprint: Meckler Books

PREPAYMENT:

Orders under $50.00 should be prepaid if
library does not have an account with
publisher.

DISCOUNT POLICY:

10% discount to libraries.

RETURN POLICY:

Returns are accepted within 12 months.
Written permission is required. Annuals
are not returnable.

SHIPPING AND BILLING POLICY:

Libraries are charged shipping on bill
orders; prepaid orders are shipped free.
Invoices are sent with shipments unless
the library specifies otherwise.

BACK ORDER POLICY:

Back orders are held until filled or
cancelled.

SPECIAL PLANS:

Standing order plan is available.

MED-PSYCH BOOKS see MEDIA PRODUCTIONS &
MARKETING INC.

MEDIA MARKETING GROUP

P.O. Box 611
DeKalb, Illinois 60115
Telephone: 815-895-6842

ADDRESS FOR ORDERS:

Same as above.

DISTRIBUTION/IMPRINTS:

Divisions: Gabriel Micrographics;
Minnesota Scholarly Press.

PREPAYMENT:

Not required.

DISCOUNT POLICY:

No discount to libraries.

RETURN POLICY:

Returns are accepted within 3 months.
Written permission is required.

SHIPPING AND BILLING POLICY:

Libraries are charged shipping on all orders plus $3.00 handling. Invoices are sent with shipments unless the library specifies otherwise.

MEDIA PRODUCTIONS & MARKETING, INC.

2440 'O' Street, Suite 202
Lincoln, Nebraska 68510-1125
Telephone: 402-474-2676

ADDRESS FOR ORDERS:

Same as above.

DISTRIBUTION/IMPRINTS:

Distributes the publications of: Pine Mountain Press; Med-Psych Books; Leather Stocking Books.

Media Publishing (Imprint)
Midgard Press (Subsidiary - distributes some titles)

PREPAYMENT:

Not required.

DISCOUNT POLICY:

No discount to libraries.

RETURN POLICY:

Returns, in salable condition, are accepted within one year. Permission to return is not required.

SHIPPING AND BILLING POLICY:

Billed order are charged shipping (FOB Lincoln); prepaid orders are shipped free. There is a handling charge of $1.00. Invoices are sent with shipments unless the library specifies otherwise.

BACK ORDER POLICY:

Publisher notifies library of back order and ships when available.

MENASHA RIDGE BOOKS see SYRACUSE UNIVERSITY PRESS

MERCER UNIVERSITY PRESS

1400 Coleman Avenue
Macon, Georgia 31207
Telephone: 912-744-2880

ADDRESS FOR ORDERS:

Same as above.
Telephone: 800-342-0841, x2880 (in GA)
          800-637-2378, x2880 (in US)

PREPAYMENT:

Not required, but prepaid orders are shipped free.

DISCOUNT POLICY:

10% discount to libraries.

RETURN POLICY:

Returns in salable condition and with postage prepaid are accepted for credit within one year. Written permission is required from fulfillment department.

SHIPPING AND BILLING POLICY:

Libraries are charged actual shipping by whichever method they prefer; prepaid orders are shipped free. Invoices are sent separately after shipments and as library specifies.

BACK ORDER POLICY:

Publisher back orders unavailable titles and ships books when they become available; library may write to cancel orders.

SPECIAL PLANS:

Standing orders are available for particular series usually at a 40% discount. Interested libraries should contact the Marketing Department for details.

MERIDIAN HILL PUBLICATIONS see JOHNSON BOOKS

MERIWETHER PUBLISHING, LTD.

885 Elkton Drive
Colorado Springs, Colorado 80907
Telephone: 719-594-4422

ADDRESS FOR ORDERS:

Same as above.

DISTRIBUTION/IMPRINTS:

Contemporary Drama Service (Subsidiary)

PREPAYMENT:

Not required with purchase order.

DISCOUNT POLICY:

No discount to libraries.

RETURN POLICY:

Returns are accepted within 30 days or with special approval. Prior permission is required, and requests must include date of purchase and invoice number. Books must be returned with postage prepaid and in salable condition. Play preview copies are not returnable.

SHIPPING AND BILLING POLICY:

Libraries pay shipping (UPS) on all orders. Invoices are sent separately after shipments unless the library specifies otherwise.

BACK ORDER POLICY:

Back orders will be sent when available unless the library specifies a deadline.

SPECIAL PLANS:

Items sent on approval may be returned within 30 days. Shipping, including return postage, is free.

MERRIAM-WEBSTER INC.

47 Federal Street
P.O. Box 281
Springfield, Massachusetts 01102
Telephone: 413-734-3134
          800-828-1880
FAX: 413-731-5979

ADDRESS FOR ORDERS:

Same as above.

PREPAYMENT:

Required on orders for less than $25.

DISCOUNT POLICY:

Publisher allows the following discounts to libraries open to public use.

All titles combinable, with the exception of Webster's Third New International Dictionary:

1 to 24 copies	10%
25 to 49 copies	15%
50 to 99 copies	20%

Webster's Third New International Dictionary:

1 to 24 copies	10%
25 to 49 copies	20%

RETURN POLICY:

Publisher requests libraries to write for return authorization before sending returns. The address for returns is the same as for orders.

SHIPPING AND BILLING POLICY:

Libraries pay postage. There is no handling charge. Invoices are sent separately after shipments.

BACK ORDER POLICY:

Publisher reports and back orders titles not currently available.

MESORAH PUBLICATIONS, LTD.

1969 Coney Island Avenue
Brooklyn, New York 11223
Telephone: 718-339-1700

ADDRESS FOR ORDERS:

Same as above.
Telephone: 800-MESORAH (outside NY)

DISTRIBUTION/IMPRINTS:

Distributes: Artscroll Series which
includes Artscroll History Series,
Artscroll Youth Series; Artscroll Mesorah
Series, and Artscroll Tanach Series.

PREPAYMENT:

All library orders require prepayment.

DISCOUNT POLICY:

10% discount to libraries. For large
orders (24 or more copies of the same
title), libraries should contact
publisher.

RETURN POLICY:

Only damaged books may be returned.

SHIPPING AND BILLING POLICY:

Prepaid orders are shipped free.

BACK ORDER POLICY:

Publisher will back order only if books
can be shipped within 30 days;
otherwise, the order will be returned.

SPECIAL PLANS:

Libraries that belong to the Bible Study
Program or those that resell books
should contact the Director of Marketing
for special terms.

METAMORPHOUS PRESS, INC.

3249 NW 29th Avenue
Portland, Oregon 97210-0616
Telephone: 503-228-4972

ADDRESS FOR ORDERS:

P.O. Box 10616
Portland, Oregon 97210-0616

DISTRIBUTION/IMPRINTS:

Distributes: Future Pace; Syntony;
Southern Institute Press; Beynch Press;
Flint, Inc.

PREPAYMENT:

Prepayment is required for orders under
$50.00 or four books.

DISCOUNT POLICY:

20% discount to libraries as long as
payment is received within 60 days of
invoice date.

RETURN POLICY:

Returns in salable condition and
accompanied by the reason for return and
invoice copy are accepted without
permission. Return books to 29th St.
address.

SHIPPING AND BILLING POLICY:

Single book orders carry a flat $2.00
freight charge; additional books shipped
at $0.75 each. Invoices are sent with
shipments unless the library specifies
otherwise.

BACK ORDER POLICY:

Publisher will back order any book
expected to be available in the future.

METHUEN see ROUTLEDGE, CHAPMAN AND HALL,
INC.

METROPOLITAN PRESS see BINFORD & MORT
PUBLISHERS

MICROSOFT PRESS

16011 NE 36th Way
Box 97017
Redmond, Washington 98073-9717
Telephone: 206-882-8080

ADDRESS FOR ORDERS:

Harper & Row Publishers, Inc.
Keystone Industrial Park
Scranton, PA 18512
Telephone: 800-242-7737

DISTRIBUTION/IMPRINTS:

Distributed by Harper & Row.

Tempus (Imprint)

PREPAYMENT:

Libraries with established accounts with
Harper & Row will be billed; otherwise,
prepayment should accompany the order.

DISCOUNT POLICY:

1-9 copies: 20%
10-19 copies: 35%
20 or more: 40%

RETURN POLICY:

Active titles are eligible for return if
they are accompanied by the invoice
number, discount, and original order
date; otherwise, returns will be
credited at 40%. There is no time limit
for returns provided that books are in
salable condition and still in print.
Prior permission is not required.
Address for returns: Harper & Row
Publishers, Inc./Key Distribution
Center, Bldg #1/Dunmore, PA 18512.

SHIPPING AND BILLING POLICY:

Publisher pays shipping for both billed
and prepaid orders. Invoices are sent
separately from Harper & Row.

BACK ORDER POLICY:

Titles remain on back order until they
are released.

SPECIAL PLANS:

Contact publisher (at 206-882-8080) for
information about sales representatives.

MIDDLE ATLANTIC PRESS, INC.

---

848 Church Street
P.O. Box 945
Wilmington, Delaware 19899
Telephone: 302-654-9922

ADDRESS FOR ORDERS:

Same as above.

DISTRIBUTION/IMPRINTS:

Distributed by: National Book Network/
4720 A Boston Way/Lanham, MD 20706.
Telephone: 301-459-8696.

PREPAYMENT:

For this and other policies, libraries
should contact distributor.

MIDGARD PRESS see MEDIA PRODUCTION &
MARKETING INC.

MIDLAND BOOKS see INDIANA UNIVERSITY
PRESS

MINI PRINT CORP see SCARECROW PRESS, INC.

MINNESOTA SCHOLARLY PRESS see MEDIA
MARKETING GROUP

MISSISSIPPI RIVER PUBLISHING COMPANY see
PEACHTREE PUBLISHING

MISTY HILLS PRESS

5024 Turner Road
Sebastopol, California 95472
Telephone: 707-823-7437

ADDRESS FOR ORDERS:

Same as above.

PREPAYMENT:

Not required.

DISCOUNT POLICY:

No discount to libraries.

RETURN POLICY:

Returns are accepted within two weeks.

SHIPPING AND BILLING POLICY:

Publisher pays shipping to libraries. Invoices are sent with shipments unless the library specifies otherwise.

BACK ORDER POLICY:

Back orders are shipped when available.

MITCHELL PUBLISHING, INC.

---

915 River Street
Santa Cruz, California 95060
Telephone: 408-425-3851
         800-435-2665

ADDRESS FOR ORDERS:

Mitchell Publishing/Random House
400 Hahn Road
Westminster, Maryland 21157
Telephone: 800-638-6460

PREPAYMENT:

Not required for customers with established credit.

DISCOUNT POLICY:

All prices are net.

RETURN POLICY:

Returns, accompanied by ISBN, title, and invoice number, are accepted within 15 months of invoice date. Prior written authorization is required. Texts which are sold with software are not returnable. Address for returns: Returns Authorization Desk/Random House/400 Hahn Rd./Westminster, MD 21157.

SHIPPING AND BILLING POLICY:

Shipping is charged on both prepaid and billed orders. Invoices are sent separately.

BACK ORDER POLICY:

If a title is out-of-stock, it will be kept on back order for up to 90 days and shipped when available. If title is not yet published, it will be kept on back order for up to one year.

MODERN LANGUAGE ASSOCIATION OF AMERICA

---

10 Astor Place
New York, New York 10003
Telephone: 212-614-6383

ADDRESS FOR ORDERS:

Same as above.

DISTRIBUTION/IMPRINT:

Association of Departments of English
Association of Departments of
  Languages

PREPAYMENT:

Prepayment required for orders of less than $50, excluding postage and handling.

DISCOUNT POLICY:

There is no discount for libraries. MLA discounts only on copies purchased for resale.

RETURN POLICY:

No return is accepted except damaged books and books shipped in error. The address for returns is the same as for orders.

SHIPPING AND BILLING POLICY:

Publisher adds shipping charges to invoices. Libraries should include $1 for shipping when placing prepaid orders. The amount of shipping charge varies for orders over $50 depending on weight and class of shipment. Invoice is sent separately after shipment.

BACK ORDER POLICY:

MLA accepts requests for back orders and fills the order when available.

SPECIAL ORDER PLAN:

MLA accepts standing orders for publications in series, but offers no special terms (except that MLA will bill even if the price is less that $50.)

MODERN LIBRARY see RANDOM HOUSE, INC.

MOMENTA PUBLISHING see HUNTER HOUSE, INC., PUBLISHERS

MONAD PRESS see PATHFINDER PRESS

MONTANA MAGAZINE see FALCON PRESS PUBLISHING COMPANY

MONTHLY REVIEW PRESS

122 West 27th Street
New York, New York 10001
Telephone: 212-691-2555

ADDRESS FOR ORDERS:

Same as above.

DISTRIBUTION/IMPRINTS:

Publisher is the sole U.S. distributor of the books of the Latin American Bureau (England).

New Feminist Library (imprint)

PREPAYMENT:

Not required for customers with an account.

DISCOUNT POLICY:

10% discount on all library orders.

RETURN POLICY:

Returns, in resalable condition, are accepted from 90 days to one year from invoice date after original invoice has been paid. Prior written permission is required. Address for returns: Monthly Review Press/c/o Mercedes Distribution Center/62 Imlay St./Brooklyn, NY 11231.

SHIPPING AND BILLING POLICY:

Library pays shipping on all orders. Invoices are sent with shipments unless the library specifies otherwise.

BACK ORDER POLICY:

Publisher places unavailable titles on back order unless requested otherwise.

MOON PUBLICATIONS

722 Wall Street
Chico, California 95928
Telephone: 916-345-5473

ADDRESS FOR ORDERS:

Same as above.

PREPAYMENT:

Not required, but publisher will pay Book Rate shipping on prepaid orders.

DISCOUNT POLICY:

20% discount to libraries.

RETURN POLICY:

Returns in salable condition, accompanied by the invoice number, and shipped with postage prepaid are accepted within one year for credit.

SHIPPING AND BILLING POLICY:

Libraries are charged shipping on billed orders; publisher pays shipping on prepaid orders. Invoices are sent with shipments unless the library specifies otherwise.

BACK ORDER POLICY:

Publisher back orders unavailable titles and notifies library of back order status.

OTHER:

Publisher prefers that libraries order through a wholesaler.

MORAVIAN MUSIC FOUNDATION see ASSOCIATED UNIVERSITY PRESSES

MOREHOUSE-BARLOW COMPANY

78 Danbury Road
Wilton, Connecticut 06897
Telephone: 203-762-0721

ADDRESS FOR ORDERS:

Same as above.

DISTRIBUTION/IMPRINTS:

Distributes: Episcopal Radio-TV
Foundation publications.

PREPAYMENT:

Prepayment is required on orders under
$25.00.

DISCOUNT POLICY:

25% discount to libraries.

RETURN POLICY:

Returns in good condition are accepted
within one year and should be sent to
the Returns & Adjustments Department.

SHIPPING AND BILLING POLICY:

Libraries are charged actual postage
plus $1.50 handling on billed orders;
prepaid orders should add $1.00 for
Library Rate or $2.00 for UPS. Invoices
are sent separately after shipments.

BACK ORDER POLICY:

Publisher back orders unavailable titles;
no handling charge on back orders.

MORGAN-RAND PUBLICATIONS, INC.

2200 Sansom Street
Philadelphia, Pennsylvania 19103
Telephone: 215-557-8200

ADDRESS FOR ORDERS:

Same as above.
Telephone: 800-354-8673

PREPAYMENT:

Not required.

DISCOUNT POLICY:

No discount to libraries.

RETURN POLICY:

No returns are accepted.

SHIPPING AND BILLING POLICY:

Libraries are charged shipping which
varies for each title (from nothing to
$3.00). Invoices are sent with shipments
unless the library specifies otherwise.

BACK ORDER POLICY:

Back orders are placed upon request.

OTHER:

All orders are shipped within 24 hours.

FELIX MORROW see CHARLES E. TUTTLE
COMPANY, INC.

C. V. MOSBY COMPANY

11830 Westline Industrial Drive
St. Louis, Missouri 63146
Telephone: 314-872-8370

ADDRESS FOR ORDERS:

Same as above.
Telephone: 800-325-4177
          800-633-6699

DISTRIBUTION/IMPRINT:

Blackwell Scientific Publications
Year Book Medical Publishers
B. C. Decker

PREPAYMENT:

Prepayment is not a standard requirement,
but it is helpful. If a check for
payment in full accompanies the order,
publisher absorbs standard shipping and
handling charges normally added to
invoices for those orders not prepaid.

DISCOUNT POLICY:

Discount is 10% on the purchase of 10 books or more, if the books are billed and shipped at one time to one address.

RETURN POLICY:

Books being returned should be sent prepaid to C. V. Mosby Company, Highway 50 and CC, Linn, MO 65051. Written permission is not required if the books to be returned are new, unmarked, received in a resalable condition, and accompanied by a copy of the appropriate invoice. Books distributed by the Mosby Company are shipped on a 30-day examination basis.

SHIPPING AND BILLING POLICY:

On orders prepaid in full, publisher absorbs shipping and handling charges. On billed orders, shipping and handling charges are added. Two copies of the invoice are normally mailed directly to the billing address (if this is different from the ship-to address) and a packing list is included with the shipment.

BACK ORDER POLICY:

Titles temporarily out-of-stock or not-yet-published will be back ordered, and this fact indicated on the invoice, including estimated month of future shipment.

OTHER INFORMATION:

The Mosby Company does not have a standing order program with special discounts. However, all books are shipped on a 30-day examination basis to approved accounts, and full prepayment with orders will eliminate postage and handling charges.

A quarterly publication, EX LIBRIS, is available on a complimentary basis to those libraries wishing to receive it. It is a book release date calendar indicating publication date for new textbooks and references, as well as revised editions.

MOTOR PUBLICATIONS see DELMAR PUBLISHERS, INC.

MOUNTAIN PRESS PUBLISHING COMPANY

P.O. Box 2399
Missoula, Montana 59806
Telephone: 406-728-1900

ADDRESS FOR ORDERS:

Same as above.

PREPAYMENT:

Not required.

DISCOUNT POLICY:

No discount to libraries.

RETURN POLICY:

Returns are accepted at any time. Prior permission is not required.

SHIPPING AND BILLING POLICY:

Publisher pays shipping. Invoices are sent as specified by library.

BACK ORDER POLICY:

Publisher will back order forever.

THE MOUNTAINEERS BOOKS

---

306 Second Avenue West
Seattle, Washington 98119
Telephone: 206-285-2665
          800-553-4453

ADDRESS FOR ORDERS:

Same as above.

DISTRIBUTION/IMPRINTS:

Publisher's titles are distributed outside the US by: Douglas & McIntyre Ltd (Vancouver, BC); Cordee Publications (Leicester, England)

PREPAYMENT:

Not required.

DISCOUNT POLICY:

Discount schedule is:
1 copy: 20%
2-4 copies: 33 1/3%
5-24 copies: 40%
25-49 copies: 41%
50-99 copies: 42%

etc.

RETURN POLICY:

Returns are accepted within one year. Written permission is required. Invoice information must accompany returns or credit will be given at 55% discount. Flat posters are ineligible for return. Books damaged in shipment should be returned immediately for credit or replacement; defective books may be returned for replacement at any time.

SHIPPING AND BILLING POLICY:

Libraries are charged shipping except for prepaid orders which are shipped free. Invoices are mailed separately only.

BACK ORDER POLICY:

Publisher back orders unavailable titles and ships books when they become available.

SPECIAL PLANS:

No special library plans at this time, but publisher will consider special programs; interested libraries should contact the Marketing and Sales Manager.

MOYER BELL LIMITED

Colonial Hill
Mount Kisco, New York 10549
Telephone: 914-666-0084

ADDRESS FOR ORDERS:

Same as above.

DISTRIBUTION/IMPRINTS:

Trade books are distributed by Kampmann and Company; art catalogues should be ordered direct.

Moyer Bell distributes publications of: Serge Sabarsky Gallery; M. Knoedler & Co.; Gordon Fraser; Museum Boymans van Beuningen; Boston Children's Museum.

PREPAYMENT:

Not required.

DISCOUNT POLICY:

No discount to libraries.

RETURN POLICY:

Prior permission is not required, but returns must still be in print. Trade titles should be returned to Kampmann & Co.; distributed titles should be returned to: Moyer Bell Ltd/c/o Kraus Reprint/Route 100/Millwood, NY 10546.

SHIPPING AND BILLING POLICY:

Libraries are charged shipping on all orders. Invoices are sent separately after shipments unless the library specifies otherwise.

BACK ORDER POLICY:

Back orders are held for 90 days.

MULTI-VISION INC. see AVIATION BOOK COMPANY

MULTNOMAH PRESS

10209 S.E. Division Street
Portland, Oregon 97266
Telephone: 503-257-0526

ADDRESS FOR ORDERS:

Same as above.

PREPAYMENT:

Not required.

DISCOUNT POLICY:

Less than $25.00 : 20% if prepaid
5-24 assorted copies: 40%
25-49 assorted copies: 41%
50-99 assorted copies: 42%
etc.

2% discount on orders paid 30 days from shipping date.

RETURN POLICY:

Returns in salable condition, accompanied by invoice information, and sent with postage prepaid are accepted for as long as the title is in print. Written permission is not required. Damaged books must be returned within 30 days to receive credit; defective books should be returned as soon as the defect is discovered. Publisher will pay return postage for damaged or defective books.

SHIPPING AND BILLING POLICY:

Libraries are charged shipping on billed orders; publisher pays shipping on prepaid orders. Invoices are sent separately.

BACK ORDER POLICY:

Back orders remain on file until the book is available.

MULVEY BOOKS see INDEPENDENT PUBLISHERS GROUP

MUNCY MANUSCRIPTS, INC.

P.O. Box 1561
Grapevine, Texas 76051
Telephone: 817-329-0060

ADDRESS FOR ORDERS:

Texas Monthly Press
P.O. Box 1569
Austin, Texas
Telephone: 800-288-3288

PREPAYMENT:

Not required.

DISCOUNT POLICY:

1 copy: no discount
2-9:   20%
10 or more: 30%

RETURN POLICY:

Permission is not required. Address for returns: Texas Monthly Press/3800 Drosett Drive #H/Austin, TX 78744.

SHIPPING AND BILLING POLICY:

Libraries are charged actual shipping on all orders. Invoices are sent separately.

BACK ORDER POLICY:

Publisher back orders unavailable titles unless the library instructs otherwise.

SPECIAL PLANS:

Library Standing Order Plan is available at a maximum 40% discount.

MUSEUM BOYMANS VAN BEUNINGEN see MOYER BELL LIMITED

MUSEUM OF NEW MEXICO PRESS

P.O. Box 2087
Santa Fe, New Mexico 87503
Telephone: 505-827-6454

ADDRESS FOR ORDERS:

Same as above.

PREPAYMENT:

Not required.

DISCOUNT POLICY:

20% discount to libraries.

RETURN POLICY:

Returns are accepted within one year. Written permission is required.

SHIPPING AND BILLING POLICY:

Libraries are charged shipping. Invoices are sent with shipments unless the library specifies otherwise.

BACK ORDER POLICY:

Publisher back orders unavailable titles and ships books when they become available.

MUSTANG PUBLISHING COMPANY

P.O. Box 9327
New Haven, Connecticut 06533
Telephone: 203-624-5485

ADDRESS FOR ORDERS:

Same as above.

DISTRIBUTION/IMPRINTS:

Distributed by Kampmann & Co. (NY).

PREPAYMENT:

Prepayment is required for all orders under $100.00.

DISCOUNT POLICY:

1-5 copies: no discount
5 or more: 20%

RETURN POLICY:

Written permission from Kampmann & Co. is required.

SHIPPING AND BILLING POLICY:

Libraries are charged shipping and handling of $1.00 per book (for 1-4 books) and $0.50 per book over 5 books or actual UPS charge. Invoices are sent separately.

BACK ORDER POLICY:

Publisher back orders at library's request.

NTC BUSINESS BOOKS see NATIONAL TEXTBOOK COMPANY

NAIAD PRESS, INC.

P.O. Box 10543
Tallahassee, Florida 32302
Telephone: 904-539-9322

ADDRESS FOR ORDERS:

Same as above.

PREPAYMENT:

Not required.

DISCOUNT POLICY:

20% discount to libraries.

RETURN POLICY:

Publisher seldom allows returns. Cover and title pages of defective books may be returned within 30 days and a replacement requested. Address for returns: Rt. One/Box3319/Havana, Florida 32333.

SHIPPING AND BILLING POLICY:

Libraries are charged actual postage on all orders. Invoices are sent as specified by library.

BACK ORDER POLICY:

Publisher will back order automatically unless instructed otherwise.

SPECIAL PLANS:

A standing order for all new books as published is available at a 30% discount.

NATIONAL ACADEMY PRESS

2101 Constitution Avenue, NW
Washington, D.C. 20418
Telephone: 202-334-3318

ADDRESS FOR ORDERS:

Same as above.
Telephone: 202-334-3313

PREPAYMENT:

Not required with purchase order.

DISCOUNT POLICY:

10% college and university discount; 25% standing order discount.

RETURN POLICY:

Returns are accepted within one year of shipping date. Written permission is required from the Returns Department; no returns are accepted without an authorized return label. Publications-on-Demand are not returnable.

SHIPPING AND BILLING POLICY:

Libraries are charged shipping except on prepaid orders which are shipped free Invoices are sent with shipments.

SPECIAL PLANS:

A standing order plan for new publications is available. Libraries select to receive books from at least three of 22 subject categories; books are shipped automatically upon publication at 25% discount for established accounts. There are no return privileges.

Publisher back orders unavailable titles; out-of-print materials are available from University Microfilms International.

SPECIAL PLANS:

A standing order plan is available for all new NASW books; the requested number of copies is shipped automatically (provided that library has not cancelled or has an outstanding account of over 90 days) and invoiced at the regular price less 10% postage and handling. No returns are accepted.

NATIONAL ASSOCIATION OF SOCIAL WORKERS

7981 Eastern Avenue
Silver Spring, Maryland 20910
Telephone: 301-565-0333

ADDRESS FOR ORDERS:

Same as above.
Telephone: 800-638-8799

PREPAYMENT:

Prepayment is required on orders of less than $25.00.

DISCOUNT POLICY:

3-10 copies of the same title:	10%
11-25 single and assorted titles:	20%
26-50:	30%
over 51:	35%

RETURN POLICY:

Returns in salable condition, accompanied by original invoice, and sent with postage prepaid are accepted within 6 months of purchase. 50% of any order may be returned. Prior permission is not required.

SHIPPING AND BILLING POLICY:

Libraries are charged shipping on all orders: orders in excess of $100.00 will be billed actual shipping plus $5.00 handling; domestic orders under $100.00 will be charged 10% postage/handling (minimum of $0.50); Canadian orders are charged 15%. Invoices are sent with shipments as well as after; publisher will honor library's preference.

BACK ORDER POLICY:

NATIONAL BESTSELLER CORP. see INDEPENDENT PUBLISHERS GROUP

NATIONAL BRAILLE PRESS, INC.

---

88 St. Stephen Street
Boston, Massachusetts 02115
Telephone: 617-266-6160

ADDRESS FOR ORDERS:

Same as above.

DISTRIBUTION/IMPRINTS:

Distributes Braille reprints of various other publishers' books.

PREPAYMENT:

Prepayment is required on all orders.

DISCOUNT POLICY:

No discount to libraries; all publications are subsidized.

RETURN POLICY:

Returns are accepted within 4 weeks. Written permission is required.

SHIPPING AND BILLING POLICY:

All Braille publications are shipped "Free Matter for the Blind"; UPS is $3.00 extra per title.

BACK ORDER POLICY:

Publisher generally does not reprint titles that have been sold out.

Publisher holds orders for unavailable titles and ships when they become available.

NATIONAL COUNCIL OF TEACHERS OF ENGLISH

1111 Kenyon Road
Urbana, Illinois 61801
Telephone: 217-328-3870

ADDRESS FOR ORDERS:

Same as above.

PREPAYMENT:

Orders for less than $15 must be prepaid; orders over $50 must have a purchase order or be prepaid.

DISCOUNT POLICY:

There is no discount for libraries.

RETURN POLICY:

Items may not be returned without prior written authorization from the NCTE Book Order Department. Address to request for return permission is the same as for orders.

Requests for authorization to return materials must include the title, quantity, and the NCTE invoice number. The NCTE invoice number is an 8-digit number listed in the upper right hand corner on the packing list and invoice.

Returned books must be received in salable condition. It is library's responsibility to insure shipments to NCTE against damage in transit.

Upon receipt of the information requested above, NCTE will issue an authorization letter. A copy of the letter must be accompany the returned items.

SHIPPING AND BILLING POLICY:

There is no shipping charge for prepaid orders; publisher adds $1.25 for shipping and handling of the first book, and $.50 for each additional book, on billed orders. If bill-to and ship-to addresses are the same, invoice goes with shipment. If the addresses are different, or if library so requests, invoice is mailed separately to bill-to address.

BACK ORDER POLICY:

NATIONAL GEOGRAPHIC SOCIETY

Educational Services
Washington, D.C. 20036
Telephone: 800-368-2728

ADDRESS FOR ORDERS:

Same as above.

PREPAYMENT:

Not required.

DISCOUNT POLICY:

Catalog prices are net to libraries and schools.

RETURN POLICY:

No prior permission is required if returns are made within 30 days. The address for returns is the same as for orders.

SHIPPING AND BILLING POLICY:

Postage and handling charges are added to invoice. Invoices are sent either with shipments or separately as the library requests.

BACK ORDER POLICY:

Titles not currently available are either back ordered or cancelled.

SPECIAL ORDER PLAN:

Publisher sends new publications to libraries requesting standing orders. Libraries have 30 days to react to the shipment.

NATIONAL PUBLISHERS OF THE BLACK HILLS, INC.

---

47 Nepperhan Avenue
Elmsford, New York 10523
Telephone: 914-592-6006

ADDRESS FOR ORDERS:

National Publishers
321 Kansas City Street
Rapid City, SD 57701
Telephone: 800-843-8892

PREPAYMENT:

Not required.

DISCOUNT POLICY:

20% discount on orders of 16 or more
books.

RETURN POLICY:

Returns for credit of current editions
in mint condition are accepted within
six months, but extensions may be
granted upon request. There is a 15%
restock fee on returns over $200.00.
Written permission is required. Return
books to Rapid City address.

SHIPPING AND BILLING POLICY:

Libraries are charged actual shipping
plus 4% handling charge on all orders.
Invoices are sent with shipments.

BACK ORDER POLICY:

Back orders are filed, and books are
shipped when published.

NATIONAL REGISTER PUBLISHING COMPANY

3004 Glenview Road
Wilmette, Illinois 60091
Telephone: 312-256-6067

ADDRESS FOR ORDERS:

Same as above.
Telephone: 312-441-2211
          800-323-6772

PREPAYMENT:

Not required.

DISCOUNT POLICY:

10% discount for standing orders direct
from libraries.

RETURN POLICY:

Returns are accepted within 30 days, and
orders are cancelled at the library's
request. Prior permission is not
required. Address for returns: 2170
South Manheim Road/Des Plaines, Illinois
60018.

SHIPPING AND BILLING POLICY:

Libraries are charged shipping and
handling which vary with each title
(from $3.75 to $30.10). Invoices are
sent separately.

BACK ORDER POLICY:

Books not available at time of order
usually become available within 30 days.

NATIONAL TEXTBOOK COMPANY

4255 W. Touhy
Lincolnwood, Illinois 60646
Telephone: 312-679-5500
          800-323-4900

ADDRESS FOR ORDERS:

Same as above.

DISTRIBUTION/IMPRINTS:

Imprints: VGM Career Books; NTC Business
Books; Voluntad; Passport Books; Crain
Books; Institute of Modern Languages.

PREPAYMENT:

Prepayment is required on all orders
under $25.00.

DISCOUNT POLICY:

No discount to libraries.

RETURN POLICY:

Returns in resalable condition are
accepted within one year. Written
permission is required.

SHIPPING AND BILLING POLICY:

Libraries are charged shipping and
handling of 6-7% of invoice on billed
orders; prepaid orders are shipped free.
Invoices are sent separately.

BACK ORDER POLICY:

Publisher back orders unavailable titles and ships books when they become available unless the library instructs otherwise.

SPECIAL PLANS:

Standing orders at 20% discount are offered for the following: VGM Career Books; Occupational Outlook Handbook; World of Information; Debate Books; ACTFL Professional Books.

NATIONAL UNIVERSITY PUBLICATIONS see ASSOCIATED FACULTY PRESS, INC.

NATUREGRAPH PUBLISHERS, INC.

P.O. Box 1075
Happy Camp, California 96039
Telephone: 916-493-5353

ADDRESS FOR ORDERS:

Same as above.

PREPAYMENT:

Not required.

DISCOUNT POLICY:

1-4 copies: no discount
5-49:   25%
over 50:   40%

RETURN POLICY:

All titles are returnable if the library finds a book to be other than expected. Publisher has no policy for libraries since no book from them has ever been returned. Address for returns (UPS): 3543 Indian Creek Road/Happy Camp, CA 96039.

SHIPPING AND BILLING POLICY:

Actual postage is added to the invoice on billed orders; prepaid orders should include $1.00 for the first book and $0.20 for each additional book. Invoices are sent with shipments unless the library specifies otherwise.

BACK ORDER POLICY:

Publisher will back order and ship as soon as books are available.

NAUTILUS BOOKS see INDEPENDENT PUBLISHING GROUP

NAVAJO COMMUNITY COLLEGE PRESS see NORTHLAND PRESS

NEAL-SCHUMAN PUBLISHERS, INC.

---

23 Leonard Street
New York, New York 10013
Telephone: 212-925-8650

ADDRESS FOR ORDERS:

Same as above.

DISTRIBUTION/IMPRINT:

Libraryworks

PREPAYMENT:

Not required from public, academic and school libraries with established accounts.

DISCOUNT POLICY:

There is no discount for libraries.

RETURN POLICY:

Written permission is required. No returns will be accepted after six months from invoice date. All returns must be prepaid. Books must be in resalable condition. The address for returns is: M & B Fulfillment Service, 540 Barnum Avenue, Bridgeport, CT 06608.

SHIPPING AND BILLING POLICY:

Publisher charges shipping cost to libraries on billed orders. The amount of the charge varies with order. Invoices are sent with shipment unless otherwise specified by library.

BACK ORDER POLICY:

Publisher back orders until notified to cancel by library.

THOMAS NELSON, INC., PUBLISHERS

P.O. Box 141000
Nashville, Tennessee 37214-1000
Telephone: 615-889-9000
         800-251-4000

ADDRESS FOR ORDERS:

Same as above.

PREPAYMENT:

Not required.

DISCOUNT POLICY:

Libraries receive a 25% discount.

RETURN POLICY:

Books are returnable 90 days after purchase and up to one year from purchase date. Out-of-print titles and titles not on publisher's current list are non-returnable. Bibles are not returnable, but may be authorized for return if a replacement order of equal value is placed. No authorization to return is required. Returned books must be in salable condition. The address for returns is: Thomas Nelson Returns Center, 731-D Massman Drive, Nashville, TN 37210.

SHIPPING AND BILLING POLICY:

Libraries pay postage. There is no handling charge. Invoices are sent separately after shipments.

BACK ORDER POLICY:

Titles not currently available are reported and back ordered.

OTHER INFORMATION:

Publisher handles any order confirmations, payment voucher confirmations, or other documents which the library may wish the publisher to handle.

NETWORK PUBLICATIONS

A Division of ETR Associates
P.O. Box 1830
Santa Cruz, California 95061-1830
Telephone: 408-438-4060

ADDRESS FOR ORDERS:

Same as above.
Telephone: 408-438-4080

PREPAYMENT:

Not required; minimum order of $10.00.

DISCOUNT POLICY:

Negotiable discount based on quantity.

RETURN POLICY:

Returns in salable condition and accompanied by original invoice information are accepted within 30 days. Libraries must telephone Customer Service (408-438-4081) for a return authorization number. Address for returns: Network Publications/4 Carbonero Way/Scotts Valley, CA 95066.

SHIPPING AND BILLING POLICY:

Libraries are charged shipping of 15% for orders under $200.00. Invoices are sent with shipments unless bill-to and ship-to addresses are different.

BACK ORDER POLICY:

Publisher notifies library of back orders on the invoice, and books are shipped as soon as they are available.

NEW AMERICAN LIBRARY see E. P. DUTTON

NEW AMERICAS PRESS

P.O. Box 40874
San Francisco, California 94140
Telephone: 415-648-9110

ADDRESS FOR ORDERS:

Same as above.

DISTRIBUTION/IMPRINTS:

Solidarity Publications (Imprint -
   former corporate name)

PREPAYMENT:

Not required with institutional purchase
order.

DISCOUNT POLICY:

Less than $4.00 retail:	none
1-4 copies (over $4):	10%
over 5 copies (mixed titles):	20%

RETURN POLICY:

Books damaged in shipment may be
returned within 60 days of invoice date;
other books may be returned within one
year. Written permission is requested.
Upon receipt of books in salable
condition, publisher will issue either
credit or a cash refund at the library's
preference. Address for returns: New
Americas Press/3382 26th St./San
Francisco, CA 94110.

SHIPPING AND BILLING POLICY:

Libraries are charged shipping plus a
handling charge of around 7-10% ($1.00
minimum) or 15% for UPS on all orders.
Invoices are sent with shipments unless
the library specifies otherwise.

BACK ORDER POLICY:

Orders are held if the material is
expected within one year.

OTHER:

Libraries are encouraged to order direct
but may also use wholesalers.

NEW DIRECTION BOOKS see W. W. NORTON AND
COMPANY, INC.

NEW ERA BOOKS see PARAGON HOUSE
PUBLISHING

NEW FEMINIST LIBRARY see MONTHLY REVIEW
PRESS

NEW HORIZON PRESS

P.O. Box 669
Far Hills, New Jersey 07931
Telephone: 201-234-9546
         201-234-9566

ADDRESS FOR ORDERS:

Same as above.

DISTRIBUTION/IMPRINTS:

Publisher either distributes its own
books or is distributed by Bookfriends
(Wilkes Barre, PA).

PREPAYMENT:

Required for orders of $20.00 or less.

DISCOUNT POLICY:

1-2 books:	20%
3-6 books:	25%
7-20 books:	30%

RETURN POLICY:

Returns are accepted within 18 months.
Prior permission is not required.
Address for returns: Bookfriends/1
Passan Drive/Wilkes Barre, PA 18702.

SHIPPING AND BILLING POLICY:

Libraries are charged shipping on all
orders. Invoices are usually sent after
shipments.

BACK ORDER POLICY:

Orders are held for up to one year, and
books are shipped when available.

SPECIAL PLANS:

Publisher prefers that libraries order
direct but also deals with wholesalers.

NEW SOCIETY PUBLISHERS

4527 Springfield Avenue
Philadelphia, Pennsylvania 19143
Telephone: 215-382-6543

ADDRESS FOR ORDERS:

Same as above.

PREPAYMENT:

Not required.

DISCOUNT POLICY:

No discount to libraries.

RETURN POLICY:

Returns are accepted within one year. Written permission is not required. If books are damaged upon arrival, publisher must be notified within 10 days.

SHIPPING AND BILLING POLICY:

Libraries are charged shipping of $1.50 for the first book and $0.50 for each additional book on all orders. Invoices are sent with shipments unless the library specifies otherwise.

BACK ORDER POLICY:

Publisher back orders unavailable titles and ships books when they become available unless the library instructs otherwise.

NEW YORK GRAPHIC SOCIETY see LITTLE, BROWN AND COMPANY

NEW YORK INSTITUTE OF FINANCE see PRENTICE-HALL

NEW YORK UNIVERSITY PRESS see COLUMBIA UNIVERSITY PRESS

NEWBURY HOUSE PUBLISHERS see HARPER AND ROW, PUBLISHERS, INC.

NEWCASTLE PUBLISHING COMPANY see BORGO PRESS

NEWMARKET PRESS see HARPER AND ROW, PUBLISHERS, INC.

NICHOLSON PUBLICATIONS see SALEM HOUSE PUBLISHERS

NICK LYONS BOOKS

---

31 West 21st Street
New York, New York 10010
Telephone: 212-620-9580

ADDRESS FOR ORDERS:

Same as above.

PREPAYMENT:

Orders of 4 or fewer books must be prepaid.

DISCOUNT POLICY:

1-4 books: 10% prepaid
5 or more: 10% net 30 days

RETURN POLICY:

Returns in salable condition and still in print are accepted. Library should contact Customer Service before returning books.

SHIPPING AND BILLING POLICY:

Libraries are charged shipping on billed orders; prepaid orders are shipped free. Invoices are sent separately.

BACK ORDER POLICY:

Back orders are placed unless the library instructs otherwise.

NOLO PRESS

---

950 Parker Street
Berkeley, California 94710
Telephone: 415-549-1976

ADDRESS FOR ORDERS:

Same as above.
Telephone: 800-992-NOLO
         800-445-NOLO (in CA)

DISTRIBUTION/IMPRINTS:

Nolo Press also distributed by:
Publishers Group West; Book People.

PREPAYMENT:

Orders for fewer than 5 books require
prepayment.

DISCOUNT POLICY:

1-4 books: no discount
5 or more: 25% prepaid
              20% billed

RETURN POLICY:

Books that are unmarked and in salable
condition may be returned within 60 days
of receipt of invoice. Short shipments
or discrepancies must be claimed within
10 days of receipt of merchandise.

SHIPPING AND BILLING POLICY:

Publisher pays postage for orders of 1-4
books. Libraries are billed at library
rate for both prepaid and billed orders
of 5 or more books.

BACK ORDER POLICY:

Publisher back-orders one month before
publication date only.

NORTH CAROLINA GENEALOGICAL SOCIETY see
REPRINT COMPANY, PUBLISHERS

NORTH CAROLINA MUSEUM OF ART see
UNIVERSITY OF NORTH CAROLINA PRESS

NORTH LIGHT BOOKS see F & W PUBLICATIONS

NORTH-HOLLAND see ELSEVIER SCIENCE
PUBLISHING COMPANY, INC.

NORTHLAND PRESS

P.O. Box N
Flagstaff, Arizona 86002
Telephone: 602-774-5251

ADDRESS FOR ORDERS:

Same as above.

DISTRIBUTION/IMPRINTS:

Distributes publications of Navajo
Community College Press.

PREPAYMENT:

Not required.

DISCOUNT POLICY:

25% discount on all library orders.

RETURN POLICY:

Returns of books still in print and in
resalable condition accepted for one
year of purchase. Prior written
permission is required. Returns by UPS
may be sent to: Northland Press/2900
North Fort Valley Road/Flagstaff, AZ
86001.

SHIPPING AND BILLING POLICY:

Libraries are charged shipping on all
orders. Orders for less than $50.00 are
shipped by post at library rate; order
for more than $50.00 are shipped by UPS.
Invoices are sent separately after
shipments.

BACK ORDER POLICY:

Publisher will back order at library's
request.

SPECIAL PLANS:

Libraries with a standing order plan
receive a 25% discount; books
(approximately 16 per year) are billed
and shipped as they are released and are
subject to the return policies above.

NORTHWOODS PRESS see CONSERVATORY OF
AMERICAN LETTERS

W. W. NORTON AND COMPANY, INC.

500 Fifth Avenue
New York, New York 10110
Telephone: 212-354-5500

ADDRESS FOR ORDERS:

Same as above.
Telephone: 800-233-4830
FAX: 800-458-6515

DISTRIBUTION/IMPRINT:

Liveright
New Direction Books
Smithsonian Exposition Books
Thames and Hudson Inc.
Ecco Press
Dembner Books

PREPAYMENT:

Not required.

DISCOUNT POLICY:

A discount of 25% for trade books and a
20% discount for textbooks are allowed
for library orders.

RETURN POLICY:

Written permission is not required for
returns of defective books. The address
for returns is: W. W. Norton and Company,
c/o National Book Company, Keystone
Industrial Park, Scranton, PA 18512.

SHIPPING AND BILLING POLICY:

Libraries pay postage. There is no
handling charge. Invoices are included
within the shipment or are sent
separately, according to library's
instructions.

BACK ORDER POLICY:

Titles not currently available are either
reported and back ordered or cancelled,
according to library's instructions.

SPECIAL ORDER PLAN:

Four special order plans are available:

Norton Advance Copy Plan
Norton Music Standing Order Plan
New Directions Standing Order Plan
Thames and Hudson On Approval Plan

Contact publisher for details.

NORVIK PRESS see DUFOUR EDITIONS, INC.

NOYES & ANDREWS see NOYES PUBLICATIONS

NOYES & SOMERVILLE see NOYES PUBLICATIONS

NOYES DATA CORPORATION see NOYES
PUBLICATIONS

NOYES PUBLICATIONS

120 Mill Road
Park Ridge, New Jersey 07656
Telephone: 201-391-8484

ADDRESS FOR ORDERS:

Same as above.

DISTRIBUTION/IMPRINTS:

Subsidiaries: Noyes Data Corporation;
Noyes Publications; Noyes & Somerville;
Noyes & Andrews, Inc (50% owned).

PREPAYMENT:

Not required.

DISCOUNT POLICY:

10% discount to libraries.

RETURN POLICY:

Returns are accepted within one year.
Written permission is required.

SHIPPING AND BILLING POLICY:

Libraries are charged shipping and handling of $3.00 for the first book plus $1.00 for each additional book except on prepaid orders which are shipped free. Invoices are sent with shipments.

BACK ORDER POLICY:

Back orders are accepted.

OAK TREE PRESS see JALMAR PRESS

OAK TREE PUBLICATIONS, INC.

9601 Aero Drive #202
San Diego, California 92123
Telephone: 619-560-5163

ADDRESS FOR ORDERS:

Same as above.

DISTRIBUTION/IMPRINTS:

Value Communications, Inc. (Division)
A. S. Barnes (Imprint)
ValueTales (Imprint)

PREPAYMENT:

Required for orders of less than $50.00.

DISCOUNT POLICY:

1-4 books: no discount
5-24 books: 10% billed; 20% prepaid
25-49 books: 15% billed; 25% prepaid
50 or more: 20% billed; 30% prepaid

RETURN POLICY:

Returns, for credit against future orders only, are accepted from 90 days to one year after invoice date. Prior approval is required. Returns must be in salable condition and accompanied by invoice information and date. Address for returns: Oak Tree Pub., Inc./c/o Haddon Distribution Center/O'Neill Highway/Dunmore, PA 18512.

SHIPPING AND BILLING POLICY:

Publisher pays freight on all prepaid orders of $50.00 or more. Prepaid orders for less than $50.00 must include

shipping/handling charge of $1.50 for the first book and $0.75 for each additional book; for over 5 books, an additional $0.10 per book is charged. Other orders shipped at either Fourth Class Book Rate or by UPS (at library's request) and are billed based on weight. Invoices are sent separately.

BACK ORDER POLICY:

Back orders are shipped as soon as they are available.

OAKMORE HOUSE see JALMAR PRESS

OCEANA PUBLICATIONS, INC.

Dobbs Ferry, New York 10522
Telephone: 914-693-5944

ADDRESS FOR ORDERS:

Same as above.

PREPAYMENT:

Prepayment required from libraries with no regular account for orders under $50.

DISCOUNT POLICY:

Publisher allows no discount to libraries, except to those law libraries participating in Standing Order Legal Text plan. These libraries receive a 10% discount on all Oceana publications.

RETURN POLICY:

Publisher requires libraries to write for permission before shipping returns. This policy also applies to defective/damaged books or incorrect shipments. All sales are presumed to be final, but consideration may be given for special circumstances. The address for returns is the same as for orders.

SHIPPING AND BILLING POLICY:

Libraries pay postage and handling charges. Packing slip is enclosed in shipment. Invoice is enclosed in shipment or mailed separately according to library instructions.

BACK ORDER POLICY:

Titles not currently available are back ordered or cancelled according to library instructions.

SPECIAL ORDER PLAN:

Publisher has a Standing Order Legal Text plan. Each month participating libraries receive a packet of slips. If desired, library files the slip in its back order file, and the title is billed and shipped at 10% discount automatically when published. If the title is not desired, the slip is returned. Slips are sent out three to four months prior to publication.

_____

OCEANA VIEW see INDEPENDENT PUBLISHERS GROUP

_____

_____

OHIO STATE UNIVERSITY PRESS

_____

1050 Carmack Road
Columbus, Ohio 43210
Telephone: 614-292-6930

ADDRESS FOR ORDERS:

Same as above.

DISTRIBUTION/IMPRINTS:

Sandstone Books (Imprint)

PREPAYMENT:

Not required with library purchase order.

DISCOUNT POLICY:

No discount to libraries.

RETURN POLICY:

Returns, in resalable condition, are accepted after 90 days but before one year. Written or verbal permission from business manager is required. Logan Elm Press books are non-returnable unless damaged in shipment. Address for returns: OSU Press Warehouse/2578 Kenny Rd/Columbus, OH 43210.

SHIPPING AND BILLING POLICY:

Libraries are charged shipping on all orders; prepaid orders should include $2.00 shipping charge. Invoices are sent with shipments unless the library specifies otherwise.

BACK ORDER POLICY:

Back orders are noted on invoices.

SPECIAL PLANS:

A standing order to the Hawthorne Centenary Edition is available at 20% discount. Other standing orders can be negotiated. Interested libraries should contact the marketing manager.

OTHER:

All books are printed on acid-free paper.

_____

OHIO UNIVERSITY/SWALLOW PRESS

_____

Scott Quadrangel
Athens, Ohio 45701
Telephone: 614-593-1155

ADDRESS FOR ORDERS:

Ohio University Press/Swallow Press
CUP Services
P.O. Box 6525
Ithaca, NY 14851
Telephone: 800-666-2211

DISTRIBUTION/IMPRINT:

Swallow Press
Center for International Studies,
  Ohio University
Singapore University Press
Ravan Press
Gadjah Mada University Press

PREPAYMENT:

Not required.

DISCOUNT POLICY:

There is no discount for publications distributed by Ohio University Press.

RETURN POLICY:

Libraries may return books in resalable condition 90 days to one year from date of purchase. Invoice number must be cited for proper credit to be issued. Libraries pay shipping cost for returns.

SHIPPING AND BILLING POLICY:

Invoices are issued and sent by CUP Services and are included with shipments. Library pays postage and handling fee set by CUP Services. Remittances are to be sent to address shown on invoice.

BACK ORDER POLICY:

Titles not currently available are back ordered unless library requests otherwise.

SPECIAL ORDER PLAN:

Publisher ships one copy of each of all new publications at 20% discount for Ohio University Press or Swallow Press or both imprints. Exclusions are permitted. Catalog listings are available from Ohio University Press, Scott Quadrangle, Athens, OH 45701.

Libraries entering a standing order plan for OU or Swallow Press titles are allowed to select from publisher's back list at a 20% discount at the onset of the standing order. Terms of standing order is for one year.

DISCOUNT POLICY:

Libraries receive a 20% discount for standing orders only.

RETURN POLICY:

Returns are limited to 120 days. No permission is required. Books must be in clean, resalable condition. The address for returns is same as for orders.

SHIPPING AND BILLING POLICY:

All shipments are made via UPS. Invoices are enclosed with shipment unless library requests otherwise.

BACK ORDER POLICY:

Unavailable titles are back ordered and shipped when they become available.

OTHER INFORMATION:

Orbis Books focuses on liberation theology; peace and justice issues; contemporary theology; and missiology.

OLD CAPITOL MUSEUM see UNIVERSITY PRESS OF MISSISSIPPI

ONTARIO FILM INSTITUTE see ASSOCIATED UNIVERSITY PRESSES

OPTIMA PUBLICATIONS see AVIATION BOOK COMPANY

ORBIS BOOKS

Maryknoll, New York 10545
Telephone: 914-941-7590

ADDRESS FOR ORDERS:

Same as above.

PREPAYMENT:

Not required.

OREGON HISTORICAL SOCIETY PRESS

1230 SW Park Avenue
Portland, Oregon 97205
Telephone: 503-222-1741

ADDRESS FOR ORDERS:

Same as above.

PREPAYMENT:

Not required.

DISCOUNT POLICY:

20% discount to libraries.

RETURN POLICY:

Returns are accepted within one year. Prior permission is required. Mark returns to: Attn: Returns.

SHIPPING AND BILLING POLICY:

Libraries pay shipping on billed orders; publisher pays shipping on prepaid orders. Invoices are sent with shipments unless the library specifies otherwise.

BACK ORDER POLICY:

Standing orders are available for all publications or for particular series or subjects.

OREGON STATE UNIVERSITY PRESS

101 Waldo Hall
Oregon State University
Corvallis, Oregon 97331
Telephone: 503-754-3166

ADDRESS FOR ORDERS:

Same as above.

PREPAYMENT:

Not normally required, but unusually large orders (over 50 copies) from a library that had not ordered from publisher previously would be subject to Business Manager's approval.

DISCOUNT POLICY:

10% discount to libraries.

RETURN POLICY:

Returns, in salable condition, are accepted within one year. Written permission is required.

SHIPPING AND BILLING POLICY:

Libraries are charged shipping of $2.00 per order for prepaid orders or actual costs according to weight for billed orders. Invoices are sent with shipments unless the library specifies otherwise.

BACK ORDER POLICY:

Back orders are placed for titles in the process of being printed or reprinted.

SPECIAL PLANS:

Publisher offers standing orders for new titles as they are published and for the Yearbook of the Association of Pacific Coast Geographers.

ORGANIZATION FOR ECONOMIC COOPERATION AND DEVELOPMENT see UNIFO PUBLISHERS, LTD.

ORIENTAL INSTITUTE see UNIVERSITY OF CHICAGO PRESS

ORION BOOKS see CROWN PUBLISHERS, INC.

OSBORNE PUBLICATIONS see AVIATION BOOK COMPANY

OSLER HOUSE see ST. LUKES PRESS

OUTDOOR LIFE BOOKS see STACKPOLE BOOKS

OUTLET BOOK COMPANY see CROWN PUBLISHERS, INC.

PETER OWEN, LTD. see DUFOUR EDITIONS, INC.

RICHARD C. OWEN PUBLISHERS, INC.

Rockefeller Center Box 819
New York, New York 10185
Telephone: 212-864-7849

ADDRESS FOR ORDERS:

Same as above.

DISTRIBUTION/IMPRINTS:

Distributes: "Ready to Read" (Department of Education, Wellington, NZ); Whole Language Consultants (Winnipeg, Canada).

PREPAYMENT:

Not required.

DISCOUNT POLICY:

No discount to libraries.

RETURN POLICY:

Returns in unmarked or undamaged condition are accepted within one year. Written permission is required. Video tapes, audio tapes, and "Ready to Read" packages that have been opened are not returnable.

SHIPPING AND BILLING POLICY:

Libraries are charged shipping except on prepaid orders which are shipped free. Invoices are sent separately.

BACK ORDER POLICY:

Publisher back orders unavailable titles.

OX BOW PRESS

P.O. Box 4045
Woodbridge, Connecticut 06525
Telephone: 203-387-5900

ADDRESS FOR ORDERS:

Same as above.

PREPAYMENT:

Not required.

DISCOUNT POLICY:

No discount to libraries.

RETURN POLICY:

Returns in salable condition and still in print are accepted at any time. There is a 10% restocking fee on all returns. Prior permission is required.

SHIPPING AND BILLING POLICY:

Libraries are charged shipping except on prepaid orders which are shipped free. Invoices are sent with shipments unless the library specifies otherwise.

BACK ORDER POLICY:

Publisher back orders unavailable titles unless the library instructs otherwise.

OTHER:

Quote by publisher from Pliny's Natural History: "Were it not for books, human culture would pass into oblivion as quickly as man himself."

OXFORD UNIVERSITY PRESS

---

200 Madison Avenue
New York, New York 10016
Telephone: 212-679-7300

ADDRESS FOR ORDERS:

Oxford University Press
16-00 Pollitt Drive
Fair Lawn, NJ 07410

PREPAYMENT:

Not required.

DISCOUNT POLICY:

Oxford University Press offers a 10% discount for standing order plans.

RETURN POLICY:

No prior permission is required from libraries; however, invoice date and number must be indicated in return shipments. The address for returns is the same as for orders.

SHIPPING AND BILLING POLICY:

Libraries pay postage. There is no handling charge. Invoices are sent with shipments unless library has a special instruction.

BACK ORDER POLICY:

Titles currently unavailable are reported and back ordered unless otherwise instructed by library.

SPECIAL ORDER PLAN:

On a standing order plan, libraries may receive books in selected subject area(s) or in all subject areas. New books are sent upon publication. An invoice, itemized by author and title, will be sent with each shipment. Accounts are payable within 60 days.

Books may be returned for credit within one year of the purchase date. Prior authorization is not required, but the book must be unmarked and in resalable condition. Libraries receive a 10% discount on standing orders.

OXMOOR HOUSE see LITTLE, BROWN AND COMPANY

JEROME S. OZER, PUBLISHER

340 Tenafly Road
Englewood, New Jersey 07631
Telephone: 201-567-7040

ADDRESS FOR ORDERS:

Same as above.

DISTRIBUTION/IMPRINTS:

Distributes publications of Center for Migration Studies.

Film Review Publications (Imprint)

PREPAYMENT:

Not required.

DISCOUNT POLICY:

Net to libraries.

RETURN POLICY:

Books in salable condition are returnable for credit. Written permission is required.

SHIPPING AND BILLING POLICY:

Libraries are charged shipping at Library Rate or UPS. Invoices are sent with shipments unless the library specifies otherwise.

BACK ORDER POLICY:

Publisher accepts back orders.

SPECIAL PLANS:

Standing orders are accepted.

PBC INTERNATIONAL see RIZZOLI INTERNATIONAL PUBLICATIONS, INC.

PACESETTER PRESS see GULF PUBLISHING COMPANY BOOK DIVISION

PACIFIC BOOKS, PUBLISHERS

P.O. Box 558
Palo Alto, California 94302-0558
Telephone: 415-856-0550

ADDRESS FOR ORDERS:

Same as above.

PREPAYMENT:

Not required.

DISCOUNT POLICY:

10% discount to public and school libraries.

RETURN POLICY:

Returns are accepted within 90 days. Written permission is required.

SHIPPING AND BILLING POLICY:

Libraries are charged actual postage or freight on all orders. Invoices are sent with shipments unless the library specifies otherwise.

BACK ORDER POLICY:

Back orders are held until filled or cancelled by library.

PACIFIC FORUM see UNIVERSITY OF HAWAII PRESS

PACIFIC INFORMATION INC.

11684 Ventura Boulevard, Suite 295
Studio City, California 91604
Telephone: 818-797-7654

ADDRESS FOR ORDERS:

Same as above.

DISTRIBUTION/IMPRINTS:

Distributes the publications of the American Literary Association.

PREPAYMENT:

Not required.

DISCOUNT POLICY:

1 - 5 books:	10%
6 - 20 books:	20%
21 or more:	40%

RETURN POLICY:

Books in salable condition and accompanied by a copy of the original invoice may be returned for full credit not less than 90 days or more than 12 months from invoice date. Prior authorization is required.

SHIPPING AND BILLING POLICY:

Libraries pay shipping and handling charges of $2.40 for the first book and $0.50 for each additional book. UPS and air mail are extra. No shipping/handling charges for prepaid orders. Invoices are sent with shipments only.

BACK ORDER POLICY:

Publisher maintains a back order file.

SPECIAL PLANS:

Publisher's software directory is available on standing order.

PACIFIC PRESS PUBLISHING ASSOCIATION

P.O. Box 7000
Boise, Idaho 83707
Telephone: 208-465-2500

ADDRESS FOR ORDERS:

Same as above.

PREPAYMENT:

Prepayment is required.

DISCOUNT POLICY:

40% discount to libraries.

RETURN POLICY:

Returns are accepted within one year. Written permission is required.

SHIPPING AND BILLING POLICY:

Libraries are charged shipping plus a handling charge of 10% of the invoice amount on all orders.

BACK ORDER POLICY:

Books placed on back order are shipped when available.

SPECIAL PLANS:

Libraries interested in standing orders should contact publisher.

PACIFIC SEARCH PRESS see WESTERN MARINE ENTERPRISES

PALADIN PRESS

P.O. Box 1307
Boulder, Colorado 80306
Telephone: (303) 443-7250

ADDRESS FOR ORDERS:

Same as above.

PREPAYMENT:

Prepayment is required.

DISCOUNT POLICY:

20% discount to libraries.

RETURN POLICY:

Returns are accepted without prior permission for one year. Video tapes are non-returnable.

SHIPPING AND BILLING POLICY:

Shipping charged at 4% of order amount after discount. Invoices are sent with shipments unless library requests otherwise.

BACK ORDER POLICY:

Back orders are shipped when available and cancelled only upon request.

RETURN POLICY:

Returns accompanied by a copy of the invoice are accepted within one year from date of purchase. Written permission is requested. Address for returns: Paragon House Publishers/c/o J. Williams Distribution/40F Cotters Lane/ East Brunswick, NJ 08816.

SHIPPING AND BILLING POLICY:

Libraries are charged shipping by whatever method they specify. Invoices are sent separately after shipments for all orders.

BACK ORDER POLICY:

Publisher informs library of back order status and expected release date of books which are shipped as soon as they are released unless the library instructs otherwise.

PANDORA'S BOOKS see BORGO PRESS

PANTHEON see RANDOM HOUSE, INC.

PARK STREET PRESS see INNER TRADITIONS

PAPERWEIGHT PRESS see CHARLES E. TUTTLE COMPANY, INC.

PASSPORT BOOKS see NATIONAL TEXTBOOK COMPANY

PARAGON HOUSE PUBLISHING

PATH PRESS see INDEPENDENT PUBLISHERS GROUP

---

90 Fifth Avenue
New York, New York 10011
Telephone: 212-620-2820

ADDRESS FOR ORDERS:

Same as above.

DISTRIBUTION/IMPRINTS:

Imprints: Tesoro Books; Athena Books; ICUS Books; New ERA Books; PWPA Books; Washington Institute Books.

PREPAYMENT:

Not required.

DISCOUNT POLICY:

20% discount to libraries.

PATHFINDER PRESS

---

410 West Street
New York, New York 10014
Telephone: 212-741-0690

ADDRESS FOR ORDERS:

Same as above.

DISTRIBUTION/IMPRINTS:

Distributes: Monad Press, an imprint of the Anchor Foundation.

PREPAYMENT:

Not required.

DISCOUNT POLICY:

No discount to libraries.

RETURN POLICY:

Returns are accepted at any time without permission. Address for returns: 165 Charles St/New York, NY 10014.

SHIPPING AND BILLING POLICY:

Libraries are charged shipping on all orders. Invoices are sent with shipments.

BACK ORDER POLICY:

Publisher back orders upon request.

SPECIAL PLANS:

Standing orders for any of publisher's series are available.

PATRIOT PRESS see DEVIN-ADAIR PUBLISHERS

PAULIST PRESS

997 MacArthur Blvd.
Mahwah, New Jersey 07430
Telephone: 201-825-7300

ADDRESS FOR ORDERS:

Same as above.

PREPAYMENT:

Orders for less than $10 must be prepaid.

DISCOUNT POLICY:

Publisher allows a 20% discount on all library orders.

RETURN POLICY:

No return is accepted from libraries.

SHIPPING AND BILLING POLICY:

Libraries pay shipping charge. The amount of shipping charge is $1 for orders of $1 to $9.99; and $0.50 for each additional order of $10. Invoice is sent with shipment.

BACK ORDER POLICY:

Orders for unavailable titles are returned with note to reorder.

PAUPER'S PRESS see BORGO PRESS

PEABODY MUSEUM PUBLICATIONS

11 Divinity Avenue
Cambridge, Massachusetts 02138
Telephone: 617-495-3938

ADDRESS FOR ORDERS:

Harvard University Press
79 Graden Street
Cambridge, MA 02138
Telephone: 617-495-2480

DISTRIBUTION/IMPRINTS:

Distributed by Harvard University Press.

PREPAYMENT:

Not required.

DISCOUNT POLICY:

10% discount to libraries.

RETURN POLICY:

Books in salable condition may be returned within one year of invoice date. Incorrect titles and defective books may be returned for replacement or credit within 60 days if accompanied by a copy of the invoice. Claims for short shipments or non-delivery must be made to Customer Service (Harvard U.P.) within 75 days of invoice date. Address for returns: Harvard University Press/c/o Uniserv, Inc./525 Great Neck Road (Route 119)/P.O. Box 1034/Littleton, MA 01460.

SHIPPING AND BILLING POLICY:

Invoices are sent with shipments.

SPECIAL PLANS:

Standing orders are available for all series; a blanket order plan for all titles is also available.

PEACHTREE PUBLISHERS, LTD.

---

494 Armour Circle, NE
Atlanta, Georgia 30324
Telephone: 404-876-8761

ADDRESS FOR ORDERS:

Same as above.

DISTRIBUTION/IMPRINTS:

Distributes the publications of: Mississippi River Publishing Co.; Chambers and Ashers (one title); Southern Homes Magazine (one title).

PREPAYMENT:

Not required.

DISCOUNT POLICY:

1-3 copies: no discount
over 4:   20%

RETURN POLICY:

Returns are accepted within a reasonable period of time. Returns should be accompanied by invoice number and date for full credit. No written permission is required.

SHIPPING AND BILLING POLICY:

Libraries are charged shipping (UPS unless otherwise instructed) on both prepaid and billed orders. Invoices are sent separately unless the library specifies otherwise.

BACK ORDER POLICY:

Back orders are held unless publisher receives specific instructions to the contrary.

F. E. PEACOCK PUBLISHERS, INC.

---

115 N. Prospect Avenue
Itasca, Illinois 60143
Telephone: 312-773-1155

ADDRESS FOR ORDERS:

Same as above.

PREPAYMENT:

Prepayment is required for customers without an account.

DISCOUNT POLICY:

No discount to libraries.

RETURN POLICY:

Returns, in salable condition and accompanied by the invoice, are accepted within one year. Libraries should call or write for authorization. Address for returns: Publishers Storage & Shipping/(F.E. Peacock Publishers, Inc.)/288 Airport Industrial Drive/ Ypsilanti, MI 48197.

SHIPPING AND BILLING POLICY:

Libraries are charged shipping (UPS) on all orders. $3.50 are charged for telephone orders to publisher's warehouse. Invoices are sent after shipments only.

BACK ORDER POLICY:

Publisher notifies the library that a book is out of stock and back orders unless the library instructs otherwise.

PEANUT BUTTER PUBLISHING

---

329 2nd Avenue West
Seattle, Washington 98119
Telephone: 206-281-5965

ADDRESS FOR ORDERS:

Peanut Butter Publishing
c/o H.D.L. Publishing
702 Randolph Avenue
Costa Mesa, CA 92626

DISTRIBUTION/IMPRINTS:

Distributed by H.D.L. Publishing.

PREPAYMENT:

Prepayment is not required, but shipping is free on prepaid orders.

DISCOUNT POLICY:

1-4 copies:	20%
5 or more:	33%

RETURN POLICY:

Written permission is required for returns. Returns should be sent to H.D.L. Publishing.

SHIPPING AND BILLING POLICY:

Libraries are charged actual freight except on prepaid orders for which publisher pays shipping. Invoices are sent separately unless the library specifies otherwise.

BACK ORDER POLICY:

Orders are held until items are available.

PELICAN PUBLISHING COMPANY

1101 Monroe Street
Gretna, Louisiana 70053
Telephone: 504-368-1175

ADDRESS FOR ORDERS:

Pelican Publishing Company
P.O. Box 189
Gretna, LA 70054
Telephone: 800-843-4558 (in LA)
          800-843-1724 (outside LA)

PREPAYMENT:

Prepayment is required if publisher does not have on file a signed and approved credit application.

DISCOUNT POLICY:

1 copy:	no discount
2 or more:	20%

RETURN POLICY:

With prior permission and with the invoice number supplied, any book may be returned for credit after 90 days and before one year from invoice date.

Videos and giftware are not returnable. Return books to Monroe Street address.

SHIPPING AND BILLING POLICY:

Libraries are charged shipping. Invoices are sent with shipments unless the library specifies otherwise.

BACK ORDER POLICY:

Publisher will back order any item that is out of stock unless the library instructs otherwise.

SPECIAL PLANS:

Standing orders are available with the same policies as regular orders.

PELION PRESS see ROSEN PUBLISHING GROUP, INC.

PEMBROKE PRESS see INDEPENDENT PUBLISHERS GROUP

PENDRAGON PRESS

RR 1, Box 159, Ferry Road
Stuyvesant, New York 12173-9720
Telephone: 518-828-3008

ADDRESS FOR ORDERS:

Same as above.

PREPAYMENT:

Not required.

DISCOUNT POLICY:

10% discount on standing orders only.

RETURN POLICY:

Returns are accepted for credit within one year. Written permission is required.

SHIPPING AND BILLING POLICY:

Libraries are charged shipping (Library Rate) plus $1.00 handling except on prepaid orders which are shipped free. Invoices are sent with shipments unless the library specifies otherwise.

BACK ORDER POLICY:

Publisher back orders unavailable titles and ships books when they become available.

SPECIAL PLANS:

Standing orders are available at a 10% discount. Postage/handling are free and returns are unquestioned.

PENGUIN see VIKING PENGUIN INC.

PENKEVILLE PUBLISHING COMPANY

P.O. Box 212
Greenwood, Florida 32443
Telephone: 904-569-2811

ADDRESS FOR ORDERS:

Same as above.

PREPAYMENT:

Not required.

DISCOUNT POLICY:

No discount to libraries.

RETURN POLICY:

Returns are accepted within three months. No prior permission is required.

SHIPPING AND BILLING POLICY:

Libraries are charged postage. Invoices are sent with shipments unless the library specifies otherwise.

BACK ORDER POLICY:

Publishers back orders unavailable titles and queries library when items are available.

SPECIAL PLANS:

Publisher accepts standing orders and will ship and bill upon publication.

PENNSYLVANIA STATE UNIVERSITY PRESS

215 Wagner Bldg.
University Park, Pennsylvania 16802
Telephone: 814-865-1327

ADDRESS FOR ORDERS:

Same as above.

DISTRIBUTION/IMPRINTS:

Distributes publications of: College Art Association; American Academy in Rome.

PREPAYMENT:

Not required.

DISCOUNT POLICY:

No discount to libraries.

RETURN POLICY:

Returns are accepted within one year of invoice date. Prior written permission is required.

SHIPPING AND BILLING POLICY:

Libraries are charged shipping on both billed and prepaid orders. Invoices are sent with shipments unless the library specifies otherwise.

BACK ORDER POLICY:

Books not yet published or out of stock are back ordered and shipped and billed when published or reprinted.

SPECIAL PLANS:

Standing orders are available for series. No special discount is offered.

OTHER:

Publisher prefers that libraries order from wholesalers.

PERGAMON PRESS, INC.

Maxwell House, Fairview Park
Elmsford, New York 10523
Telephone: 914-592-7700
FAX: 914-592-3625

ADDRESS FOR BOOK ORDERS:

Same as above.

PREPAYMENT:

Not required from libraries with
established accounts. Prepayment is
required for orders of under $50 from
other libraries.

DISCOUNT POLICY:

There is no discount except to
participants to Library Standing Order or
Library Selection Order Plans. See
Special Order Plans.

RETURN POLICY:

Books are returnable without permission
if defective or if received on approval,
but return must be accompanied by a copy
of invoice or invoice number. Other
returns must be authorized in writing by
publisher. The address for returns is
the same as for orders.

SHIPPING AND BILLING POLICY:

Publisher charges shipping, handling, and
insurance based on net value of invoice.
Packing slips are always enclosed with
shipments as are invoices except in case
of drop shipment or if requested
otherwise by library.

BACK ORDER POLICY:

All book orders are kept on file and
automatically filled when title becomes
available.

SPECIAL ORDER PLANS:

Library Standing Order Plan: Library
automatically receives indicated number
of copies of each newly published title
in subject areas designated by library.
Participants receive a 15% discount, in
addition to automatic benefit of any
prepublication prices, on all their
orders from publisher.

Library Selective Order Plan: Library
receives periodic New Book bulletin and
announcements of titles scheduled for
publication in subject areas designated

by library. Books are only shipped in
response to orders placed with publisher
and carry a 12.5% discount.

With either of the above plans, library
may open a deposit account and receive an
additional 10% discount on all its book
purchases.

PERIGEE BOOKS see PUTNAM PUBLISHING GROUP

PERKINS PUBLICATIONS see INDEPENDENT
PUBLISHING GROUP

PERMANENT PRESS see SECOND CHANCE PRESS

PERSEVERANCE PRESS see CAPRA PRESS

PETERSON'S GUIDES, INC.

166 Bunn Drive
P.O. Box 2123
Princeton, New Jersey 08543-2123
Telephone: 609-924-5338
          800-338-3282

ADDRESS FOR ORDERS:

Same as above.

PREPAYMENT:

Orders under $15.00 must be prepaid.

DISCOUNT POLICY:

1-4 volumes: 10%
5-49 volumes: 15%
50 or more: 20%

RETURN POLICY:

Requests for replacement of or credit
for misshipments, defective books, or
damaged books will be honored if the
request is made within 30 days of
receipt. Returns must be accompanied by
an itemized statement of titles being
returned, invoice numbers, discounts,
and the reason for return. Return

shipping must be prepaid. All software
must be returned via UPS. Credit memos
will be issued unless a refund request
is received in writing. Address for
returns: Peterson's Guides, Inc./Eight-A
Corporate Center/2 Corporate Drive/
Cranbury, New Jersey 08512.

SHIPPING AND BILLING POLICY:

Libraries are charged shipping (Fourth
Class or UPS) on all orders. Invoices
are sent with shipments unless
the billing address is different from
the shipping address.

BACK ORDER POLICY:

Back orders are held until a book is
available unless the library specifies
otherwise.

SPECIAL PLANS:

Annual and bi-annual standing order plan
is available at a 20% discount.

PETROCELLI BOOKS, INC.

Research Park, 251 Wall Street
Princeton, New Jersey 08540
Telephone: 609-924-5851

ADDRESS FOR ORDERS:

Same as above.

DISTRIBUTION/IMPRINTS:

Distributed by TAB Books/P.O. Box 40/
Blue Ridge Summit, PA.

PREPAYMENT:

Not required.

DISCOUNT POLICY:

Discount is determined by distributor.

RETURN POLICY:

Returns are accepted within one year.
Written permission is required.

SHIPPING AND BILLING POLICY:

Libraries are charged actual shipping.
Invoices are sent with shipments unless
the library specifies otherwise.

BACK ORDER POLICY:

Publisher back orders unavailable titles
and ships books when they become
available.

PHAIDON PRESS see SALEM HOUSE PUBLISHERS

PHAROS BOOKS see ST. MARTIN'S PRESS

PHILOMEL BOOKS see PUTNAM PUBLISHING
GROUP

PHILOSOPHICAL LIBRARY, INC.

200 West 57th Street
New York, New York 10019
Telephone: 212-265-6050

ADDRESS FOR ORDERS:

Same as above.

PREPAYMENT:

Not required for orders over $20.

DISCOUNT POLICY:

No discount except for orders of ten or
more books.

RETURN POLICY:

Written permission must be obtained
before mailing returns. Book returns are
limited to six months. There are no
special non-refundable titles.
Publishers issues credit only; there are
no cash refunds.

SHIPPING AND BILLING POLICY:

Invoices are enclosed in packages.
Libraries pay postage and handling
charges. The minimum shipping and
handling charge is $0.95.

BACK ORDER POLICY:

Publisher holds orders until books are ready unless library gives contrary instructions.

SPECIAL ORDER PLAN:

Publisher accepts standing orders from libraries. Books are sent, as published, with invoice. Ordinary returns and discount policies apply for standing orders.

PHOENIX MILITARIA see STACKPOLE BOOKS

PHOTOGRAPHIC ARTS CENTER, LTD.

127 East 59th Street #201
New York, New York 10022
Telephone: 212-838-8640
          212-873-7065 (FAX)

ADDRESS FOR ORDERS:

Same as above.

DISTRIBUTION/IMPRINTS:

Division: Consultant Press.

PREPAYMENT:

Not required.

DISCOUNT POLICY:

15% discount on prepaid orders only.

RETURN POLICY:

All books are sold with a ten-day "no questions asked" return privilege. Address for returns: PAC - Suite 8B/302 West 86th St/New York, NY 10024.

SHIPPING AND BILLING POLICY:

Libraries are charged shipping except on prepaid orders which are shipped free. Invoices are sent with shipments unless the library specifies otherwise.

BACK ORDER POLICY:

Publisher accepts back orders.

SPECIAL PLANS:

Standing orders are accepted for serial publications.

PICCIN MEDICAL BOOKS see ISHIYAKU EUROAMERICA, INC., PUBLISHERS

PICKWICK PUBLICATIONS

4137 Timberlane Drive
Allison Park, Pennsylvania 15101-2932
Telephone: 412-487-2159

ADDRESS FOR ORDERS:

Same as above.

PREPAYMENT:

Not required.

DISCOUNT POLICY:

No discount except for standing orders.

RETURN POLICY:

Publisher accepts returns, for replacement only, of damaged or defective books. Prior authorization is required. All returns must include invoice numbers.

SHIPPING AND BILLING POLICY:

Libraries pay shipping and handling charge ($0.15 per book plus jiffy bag). Invoices are sent with shipments unless the library specifies otherwise.

BACK ORDER POLICY:

Publisher will back order books until they become available unless library requests otherwise.

SPECIAL PLANS:

Standing orders available at 10% discount.

PICTOGRAMS see ILLUMINATI

PICTURE BOOK STUDIO

10 Central Street
Saxonville, Massachusetts 01701
Telephone: 800-462-1252
          617-655-9696

ADDRESS FOR ORDERS:

Same as above.

PREPAYMENT:

Not required.

DISCOUNT POLICY:

Discount to libraries for any combination
of books ordered simultaneously is as
follows:
    1-9:   10%
    10-29:   20%
    30-49:   30%
    50 or more: 40%

SHIPPING AND BILLING POLICY:

Libraries are charged shipping by
whatever means they request. Invoices
are sent with shipments, but copies can
be mailed separately.

BACK ORDER POLICY:

Publisher back orders for as long a
period as the library requests.

SPECIAL PLANS:

Publisher offers a standing order plan
for Bologna Annuals. Publisher also
offers a Library Preview Service by
which a library receives a sample
package (with reviews, card kits, free
shipping both ways, and 20% discount on
books that are kept) of approximately 35
of publisher's most popular books.

PIERIAN PRESS, INC.

5000 Washtenaw Avenue
Ann Arbor, Michigan 48104
Telephone: 313-434-5530

ADDRESS FOR ORDERS:

Pierian Press, Inc.

P.O. Box 1808
Ann Arbor, Michigan 48106
Telephone: 1-800-678-2435

DISTRIBUTION/IMPRINT:

Greenfield Books (imprint)

PREPAYMENT:

Not required.

DISCOUNT POLICY:

There is no discount for library orders.

RETURN POLICY:

Libraries may return books with
explanation; no advance permission is
required. The address for returns is the
same as for orders.

SHIPPING AND BILLING POLICY:

There is no postage charge for prepaid
orders; libraries pay shipping charge for
billed orders. Invoices are enclosed
with books unless requested otherwise.

BACK ORDER POLICY:

Orders for unavailable titles are
returned to library with suggested time
for reorder.

OTHER INFORMATION:

All titles are available to libraries on
a 30 day approval. Publisher offers
personal periodical subscription rate
(lower than institutional rates) for
individual librarians.

PILGRIM PRESS

132 West 31st Street
New York, New York 10001
Telephone: 212-239-8700

ADDRESS FOR ORDERS:

Pilgrim Press
c/o Publishers Distribution Center
P.O. Box C831
Rutherford, NJ 07070
Telephone: 201-939-6064

DISTRIBUTION/IMPRINTS:

United Church Press (Division imprint)

PREPAYMENT:

Not required.

DISCOUNT POLICY:

10% discount on all orders.

RETURN POLICY:

Returns, in mint condition and shipped postpaid, are accepted after 90 days and within one year of invoice date. Books that have been out-of-print for six months are non-returnable. Credit for returns will be given at the full purchase price when complete invoice and discount information is supplied; otherwise, books will be credited at 46%. Prior permission must be obtained. Address for returns: The Pilgrim Press/c/o Publishers Distribution Center/25 Branca Rd./East Rutherford, NJ 07073.

SHIPPING AND BILLING POLICY:

Libraries are charged actual postage at library rate for both billed and prepaid orders. Invoices are sent with shipments unless the library specifies otherwise.

BACK ORDER POLICY:

Titles not currently available are kept on back order unless library specifies otherwise.

PILOT BOOKS

103 Cooper Street
Babylon, New York 11702
Telephone: 516-422-2225

ADDRESS FOR ORDERS:

Same as above.

PREPAYMENT:

Not required.

DISCOUNT POLICY:

No discount to libraries.

RETURN POLICY:

Returns are accepted from libraries within 120 days. No prior permission is required.

SHIPPING AND BILLING POLICY:

Libraries pay shipping plus $1.50 handling on order of less than 3 books. Publisher pays all charges on orders for more than 2 books. Invoices are sent with shipments unless the library specifies otherwise.

SPECIAL PLANS:

Standing orders are accepted.

OTHER:

Publisher processes and ships orders within 48 hours; its publications are handled by the leading library wholesalers.

PILOT PUBLICATIONS see AVIATION BOOK COMPANY

PINE GROVE PAMPHLETS see KEATS PUBLISHING, INC.

PINE MOUNTAIN PRESS see MEDIA PRODUCTIONS & MARKETING INC.

PINEAPPLE PRESS, INC.

P.O. Drawer 16008
Sarasota, Florida 34239
Telephone: 813-952-1085

ADDRESS FOR ORDERS:

Same as above.

PREPAYMENT:

Not required.

DISCOUNT POLICY:

10% discount for orders of four or more copies.

RETURN POLICY:

Returns are accepted within 12 months. Written permission is not required. Address for returns: 1962 Main St/Sarasota, FL 34230.

SHIPPING AND BILLING POLICY:

Libraries are charged shipping on billed orders; publisher pays shipping on prepaid orders. Invoices are sent with shipments unless the library specifies otherwise.

BACK ORDER POLICY:

Library is notified if books will be delayed more than sixty days; otherwise, orders are filled as stock is available.

OTHER:

Direct orders are filled within 24 hours of receipt.

PIONEER PRESS see WARREN H. GREEN, INC.

PISCES see INTERNATIONAL MARINE PUBLISHING COMPANY

PLEIADES RECORDS see SOUTHERN ILLINOIS UNIVERSITY PRESS

PLURIBUS PRESS

---

160 E. Illinois
Chicago, Illinois 60611
Telephone: 312-467-0424

ADDRESS FOR ORDERS:

Same as above.

DISTRIBUTION/IMPRINTS:

Precept Press (Imprint)
Teach'em, Inc (Imprint)

PREPAYMENT:

Prepayment is required for orders under $25.00

DISCOUNT POLICY:

No discount to libraries on direct orders.

RETURN POLICY:

Returns for refund are accepted within 30 days.

SHIPPING AND BILLING POLICY:

Libraries pay shipping/handling of $3.00 for each prepaid order; billed orders include an additional $3.00 invoicing charge. Invoices are sent with shipments.

BACK ORDER POLICY:

Books on back order are shipped when available.

POETRY WALES PRESS see DUFOUR EDITIONS, INC.

POLYGON BOOKS see DUFOUR EDITIONS, INC.

POPULAR PRESS

Bowling Green State University
Bowling Green, Ohio 43403
Telephone: 419-372-7865

ADDRESS FOR ORDERS:

Same as above.

PREPAYMENT:

Not required.

DISCOUNT POLICY:

No discount to libraries.

RETURN POLICY:

Books must be returned within one year and in good condition. Prior written permission is required.

SHIPPING AND BILLING POLICY:

Libraries are charged shipping plus handling charges of $1.00 for the first book and $0.50 for each additional book up to $5.00. Invoices are sent with shipments unless the library specifies otherwise.

BACK ORDER POLICY:

Publisher will back order.

POST OAK PRESS see LARKSDALE

POST-APOLLO PRESS see THREE CONTINENTS PRESS, INC.

POWER see FLEMING H. REVELL COMPANY

PRACTICING LAW INSTITUTE

---

810 Seventh Avenue
New York, New York 10019
Telephone: 212-765-5700

ADDRESS FOR ORDERS:

Same as above.

PREPAYMENT:

Not required, but with prepayment, libraries do not pay shipping and handling charge.

DISCOUNT POLICY:

Publisher extends a 10% discount on video and audio cassette programs, and books, with the exception of Legal Notes & Viewpoints Quarterly, when ordered directly from the publishers. To receive the discount, attach the appropriate order form to library's purchase order or

letterhead, stating that library is entitled to the 10% discount.

RETURN POLICY:

Books may be returned within 30 days of receipt provided they are in salable condition. Invoice must be included. Written permission is not necessary. Audio and video cassettes are not returnable. The address for returns is: Bookcrafters Distribution Center, 615 E. Industrial Park, Chelsea, MI 48118.

SHIPPING AND BILLING POLICY:

Publisher pays postage and handling charge for prepaid orders. There is a minimum shipping and handling charge of $4.

BACK ORDER POLICY:

Publisher accepts library's requests for back orders.

SPECIAL ORDER PLAN:

Publisher offers standing orders, with special discounts.

PRAEGER PUBLISHERS see GREENWOOD PRESS, INC.

PRAXIS PUBLICATIONS, INC.

P.O. Box 9869
Madison, Wisconsin 53715
Telephone: 608-244-5633

ADDRESS FOR ORDERS:

Same as above.

PREPAYMENT:

Not required with purchase order.

DISCOUNT POLICY:

10%-40% variable discount based on quantity ordered.

RETURN POLICY:

Returns of undamaged books are accepted within one year. Written permission is required. Address for returns: 416 Memphis Avenue/Madison, WI 53714.

SHIPPING AND BILLING POLICY:

Libraries are charged shipping and handling charge of normally $2.50 per book, but less on volume orders. Invoices are sent according to the library's request.

BACK ORDER POLICY:

Publisher back orders when appropriate.

SPECIAL PLANS:

A standing order plan is available.

PRECEPT PRESS see PLURIBUS PRESS

PRENTICE-HALL

Englewood Cliffs, New Jersey 07632
Telephone: 201-592-2000

ADDRESS FOR ORDERS:

Prentice-Hall
200 Old Tappan Road
Old Tappan, NJ 07675

DISTRIBUTION/IMPRINT:

Appleton-Century-Crofts
Arco Publishing
Center for Applied Research in
    Education (CARE)
Executive Reports Corporation
Institute for Business Planning
New York Institute of Finance
Prentice-Hall International
Prentice-Hall of Canada
Reston Publishing Co
Rewards Paperbacks
Spectrum Books

PREPAYMENT:

Not required.

DISCOUNT POLICY:

Short discount books (Reference, Technical, Professional books, with one of the following letter codes: sk, sf, u, d, p, e, m, h, tq, cq, n, c, w.)

1 to 4 books	no discount
5 or more books	20%
Profile members, no minimum	20%

Long discount books (Children's, Trade & Popular books, with one of the following codes: t, j).

1 to 9 books	no discount
10 to 24 books	20%
25 to 99 books	30%
100 or more books	35%
Profile members, no minimum	40%

All categories may be combined to earn quantity discounts. Certain standing order plans will receive higher discounts.

RETURN POLICY:

Publisher does not require permission to return; however, all returns must be accompanied by a copy of invoice in order to receive credit. Collect returns will be refused. Pre-processed books are not returnable. The address for returns is: Prentice-Hall, Book Returns Department, West Nyack, NY 10994.

SHIPPING AND BILLING POLICY:

Libraries pay shipping charges, based upon the total weight of the shipment. Books will be sent Library Rate unless library instructs otherwise. Invoices are sent with the shipment unless directions are provided to the contrary.

BACK ORDER POLICY:

Titles currently unavailable are either back ordered or cancelled as library requests. If a title is out-of-print in paperback, cloth may be substituted at paperback price. If a title is out-of-print in cloth, a paperback may be substituted at the paperback price. Library may cancel this substitution policy by requesting such in writing.

PROFILE LIBRARY PLAN:

There are three options open to libraries under Prentice-Hall's Profile Library Plan:

Pre-selection plan--Using library's profile as a guide, the library receives a quarterly checklist of all publications from those publishers and imprints affiliated with Prentice-Hall. Books which fit into the library's profile are noted. Along with this checklist, the library will receive BOOK NEWS, a quarterly catalog which contains annotations for every title on the list. The librarian can then make changes if he wishes. Upon return of the checklist, books will be shipped on approval.

Automatic plan--This allows titles to be shipped to the library upon in-stock in the categories library chooses. The library can receive books on approval immediately upon in-stock (and at least 8 weeks in advance of the publication date.)

Combination plan--This plan allows a library to pre-select through the checklist and BOOK NEWS in certain categories, and get certain obvious categories of books automatically as they are published.

Return privileges are guaranteed, and profile library plan member libraries are entitled to preferred discount schedule regardless of quantity ordered.

PRENTICE-HALL BOOKS FOR YOUNG READERS see PRENTICE-HALL

PRENTICE-HALL INTERNATIONAL see PRENTICE-HALL

PRESSWORKS PUBLISHING, INC.

P.O. Box 12606
Dallas, Texas 75225
Telephone: 214-369-3113

ADDRESS FOR ORDERS:

Same as above.

PREPAYMENT:

Not required.

DISCOUNT POLICY:

10% discount to libraries.

RETURN POLICY:

Returns in good condition are accepted within nine months without permission. Address for returns: as above, or 6140 Deloache/Dallas, TX 75225.

SHIPPING AND BILLING POLICY:

Shipping (Fourth Class or UPS) and handling are charged on all orders. Invoices are sent with shipments unless the library specifies otherwise.

BACK ORDER POLICY:

Publisher will back order unless instructed otherwise.

PRIMA PUBLISHING see ST. MARTIN'S PRESS

PRINCETON ARCHITECTURAL PRESS

2 Research Way, Forrestal Center
Princeton, New Jersey 08540
Telephone: 609-987-2424

ADDRESS FOR ORDERS:

Same as above.
Telephone: 800-458-1131 (orders only)

PREPAYMENT:

Not required.

DISCOUNT POLICY:

No discount to libraries.

RETURN POLICY:

Returns in good condition are accepted up to 6 months of shipping date. There is a 5% restocking fee. Written permission is required. Address for returns: Mid-Atlantic Book Service, Inc/ 5 Lawrence St/Bloomfield, NJ 07003.

SHIPPING AND BILLING POLICY:

Libraries pay shipping plus a handling charge of the greater of $0.50 or 15% of shipping charge. Invoices are sent separately only.

BACK ORDER POLICY:

Publisher back orders and notifies the library of the expected date of publication.

PRINCETON BOOK COMPANY, PUBLISHERS

P.O. Box 57
Pennington, New Jersey 08534-0057
Telephone: 609-737-8177

ADDRESS FOR ORDERS:

Same as above.

DISTRIBUTION/IMPRINTS:

Distributes: Dance Books Limited; Dance
Notation Bureau; Dalcroze Society;
English Folk Dance & Song Society.

Imprint: Dance Horizons

PREPAYMENT:

Not required, but prepaid orders are
shipped free.

DISCOUNT POLICY:

No discount to libraries.

RETURN POLICY:

Returns in unmarked and undamaged
condition are accepted within one year
of the order date. Prior written
permission is required. Address for
returns: Princeton Book Company,
Publishers/12 W. Delaware Ave/
Pennington, NJ 08534.

SHIPPING AND BILLING POLICY:

Libraries are charged actual shipping on
billed orders; prepaid orders are
shipped free. Invoices are sent
separately.

BACK ORDER POLICY:

Back orders can be held for as long as
the library specifies.

SPECIAL PLANS:

A standing order for all new titles is
available; interested libraries should
contact the Marketing Director.

PRINCETON UNIVERSITY PRESS

3175 Princeton Pike
Lawrenceville, New Jersey 08648
Telephone: 800-777-ISBN

ADDRESS FOR ORDERS:

Same as above.

PREPAYMENT:

Not required.

DISCOUNT POLICY:

Libraries pay list prices regardless of
number of copies ordered.

RETURN POLICY:

No prior written permission is necessary,
if the book was purchased within the past
year, and if the return is accompanied by
a copy of the invoice under which the
book was originally billed. Out-of-print
titles and books in non-salable
conditions are not returnable. The
address for returns is the same as for
orders.

SHIPPING AND BILLING POLICY:

Libraries pay postage. The amount of
handling charge is usually 3% of the net
amount of the order. Invoices are either
sent with shipment or separately as
library requests.

BACK ORDER POLICY:

Titles not currently available are either
back ordered or cancelled as library
requests.

PRO-ED, INC.

5341 Industrial Oaks Boulevard
Austin, Texas 78735
Telephone: 512-892-3142

ADDRESS FOR ORDERS:

Same as above.

PREPAYMENT:

Not required.

DISCOUNT POLICY:

No discount to libraries.

RETURN POLICY:

Returns are accepted up to 6 months from date of purchase. Written permission is required.

SHIPPING AND BILLING POLICY:

Prepaid orders are shipped free; others are charged 10% shipping/handling. Invoices are sent separately.

BACK ORDER POLICY:

Back orders are accepted.

PROCEDURAL ASPECTS OF INTERNATIONAL LAW INSTITUTE see UNIVERSITY PRESS OF VIRGINIA

PRODUCTIVITY PRESS

P.O. Box 3007
Cambridge, Massachusetts 02140
Telephone: 617-497-5146

ADDRESS FOR ORDERS:

Same as above.

DISTRIBUTION/IMPRINTS:

In addition to distributing its own books, publisher has Golden-Lee Distributors as its contracted distributor.

PREPAYMENT:

Not required within the U.S.

DISCOUNT POLICY:

20% discount on all orders.

RETURN POLICY:

Returns, in salable condition, accepted within 6 months of purchase. Prior permission is not required. Address for returns: Productivity Press/2067 Massachusetts Avenue/Cambridge, MA 02140.

SHIPPING AND BILLING POLICY:

Libraries pay shipping as well as handling charges of $3.00 for the first book and $1.00 for each additional book.

Invoices are sent with shipments unless the library specifies otherwise.

BACK ORDER POLICY:

Back orders are shipped as soon as they are available.

SPECIAL PLANS:

Special order plans can be negotiated.

PROFESSIONAL PUBLICATIONS, INC.

1250 Fifth Avenue
Belmont, California 94002
Telephone: 415-593-9119
          415-592-4519 (FAX)

ADDRESS FOR ORDERS:

Same as above.

PREPAYMENT:

Prepayment required for all library orders.

DISCOUNT POLICY:

25% discount on orders for up to ten books and 40% on orders for more than ten books.

RETURN POLICY:

Returns are accepted at any time and must be accompanied by an invoice copy and explanation. Written permission is not required. All cassette tapes are non-returnable. Address for returns: 288 Airport Industrial Dr/Ypsilanti, MI 48197.

SHIPPING AND BILLING POLICY:

Shipping is free on prepaid orders.

BACK ORDER POLICY:

Publisher will notify library of items on back order.

SPECIAL PLANS:

Publisher has no special plans but is willing to work with library in order to make ordering materials as convenient as possible.

order. Invoices are sent with shipments unless the library specifies otherwise.

PROSPECT PRESS see GORSUCH SCARISBRICK, PUBLISHERS

BACK ORDER POLICY:

Back orders are accepted.

PROSPERITY PRESS see ARTHUR H. CLARK COMPANY

PUBLISHING HORIZONS, INC.

PUBLICATIONS IN MORMON STUDIES see UNIVERSITY OF UTAH PRESS

2950 North High Street
P.O. Box 02190
Columbus, Ohio 43202
Telephone: 614-261-6565

PUBLICATIONS IN THE AMERICAN WEST see UNIVERSITY OF UTAH PRESS

ADDRESS FOR ORDERS:

Same as above.

PREPAYMENT:

Not required.

PUBLISHING CENTER FOR CULTURAL RESOURCES

DISCOUNT POLICY:

No discount to libraries.

625 Broadway
New York, New York 10012-2662
Telephone: 212-260-2010

RETURN POLICY:

Returns, with written permission, are accepted within 12 months from invoice date.

ADDRESS FOR ORDERS:

Same as above.

SHIPPING AND BILLING POLICY:

DISTRIBUTION/IMPRINTS:

Distributes some publications of: New York Public Library; reports of the Research Division of the National Endowment for the Arts; Design Arts Program; New York Landmarks Conservancy.

Prepaid orders are shipped free; others pay a minimum $2.00 postage/handling charge. Invoices are sent with shipments unless the library specifies otherwise.

BACK ORDER POLICY:

PREPAYMENT:

Not required.

If a book is due within one year, publisher will either hold order after notifying the library or follow library's instructions.

DISCOUNT POLICY:

No discount to libraries.

SPECIAL PLANS:

RETURN POLICY:

Returns are accepted within one year. Written permission is required.

Interested libraries should contact publisher in order to work out possible plans.

SHIPPING AND BILLING POLICY:

Libraries are charged shipping of $1.00 per book to a maximum of $5.00 per

PUDOC see VIKING PENGUIN INC.

PURDUE UNIVERSITY PRESS

South Campus Courts-D
West Lafayette, Indiana 47907
Telephone: 317-494-2035

ADDRESS FOR ORDERS:

Same as above except phone: 317-494-2040

PREPAYMENT:

Not required.

DISCOUNT POLICY:

No discount for libraries.

RETURN POLICY:

Returns of unsoiled, salable copies are
allowed within a period of no fewer than
90 days and no more than one year from
purchase date. The address for returns
is the same as for orders.

SHIPPING AND BILLING POLICY:

Publisher pays postage and handling
charges for prepaid orders: libraries pay
them for billed orders. The amount of
handling charges is $0.75 for the first
book; $1.10 for two books; and $0.40 per
book plus $0.30 handling fee for 3 or
more books. Invoices are sent with
shipments unless library requests
otherwise.

BACK ORDER POLICY:

Publisher back orders titles currently
unavailable. Reports will be sent only
when the publication date is not near.

SPECIAL ORDER PLAN:

One copy of each new book or books on a
specific subject area will be sent to
libraries at a discount of 20% as soon as
the book is received from the bindery.
Books may be returned within 30 days if
not needed for full credit.

PURNELL REFERENCE BOOKS see RAINTREE
PUBLISHING

G. P. PUTNAM'S SONS see PUTNAM PUBLISHING
GROUP

THE PUTNAM PUBLISHING GROUP

200 Madison Avenue
New York, New York 10016
Telephone: 212-951-8511

ADDRESS FOR ORDERS:

Same as above, or

The Putnam Publishing Group
1 Grosset Drive
Kirkwood, NY 13795
Telephone: 1-800-847-5515
   in New York: 609-775-1740

DISTRIBUTION/IMPRINT:

Grosset and Dunlap, Inc.
Coward-McCann
Philomel Books
G.P. Putnam's Sons
Perigee Books

PREPAYMENT:

Prepayment or library's purchase order
accepted.

DISCOUNT POLICY:

Guaranteed library bindings are net.

20% discount on all trade and pb books.

40% discount available for Library
Approval Plan members. For further
information, call 212-951-8511.

Library card kits are available at a
price of $.95 per kit.

RETURN POLICY:

Publisher requests libraries to write for
return permission. Return labels are
sent to libraries with authorization. To
replace newly-shipped damaged books, call
Returns Department at 1-800-631-8571.

SHIPPING AND BILLING POLICY:

All books are shipped f.o.b. publisher's
warehouse in Kirkwood, NY. Appropriate
shipping charges will be added to bill.
Invoices are sent separately.

BACK ORDER POLICY:

Titles not available are not automatically back ordered unless library is an established account or makes specific request.

SPECIAL ORDER PLAN:

Publisher offers Library Approval Plan. For further information, call 212-951-8511.

QED INFORMATION SCIENCES, INC.

170 Linden Street
Wellesley, Massachusetts 02181
Telephone: 617-237-5656

ADDRESS FOR ORDERS:

P.O. Box 181
Wellesley, MA 02181
Telephone: 800-343-4848

PREPAYMENT:

Not required with purchase order.

DISCOUNT POLICY:

No discount to libraries.

RETURN POLICY:

Returns are accepted within 30 days. Written permission is required except for books on approval. Address for returns: Publishers Storage & Shipping/ 231 Industrial Park/Fitchburg, MA 01420.

SHIPPING AND BILLING POLICY:

Libraries are charged shipping and handling of $2.50 for the first book and $0.50 for each additional book. Invoices are sent with shipments and to the billing address.

BACK ORDER POLICY:

Back orders are filled as books are received unless the library instructs otherwise.

SPECIAL PLANS:

A standing order plan for a minimum of one copy of each new title offers 20% discount (which applies to all firm orders as well as long as the plan is in

effect). The plan may be cancelled by written notice 30 days in advance.

QED PRESS

155 Cypress Street
Fort Bragg, California 95437
Telephone: 707-964-9520

ADDRESS FOR ORDERS:

Same as above.

PREPAYMENT:

All accounts are 30 days payable.

DISCOUNT POLICY:

2-5 copies:	20%
6-10:	30%
11-49:	35%
50 or more:	40%

RETURN POLICY:

Returns in salable condition are accepted within 6 months. Written permission is not required.

SHIPPING AND BILLING POLICY:

Libraries are charged shipping and handling on billed orders of $2.00 for the first book plus $1.00 for the second book and $0.50 for each additional book; prepaid orders are shipped free. Invoices are sent with shipments, but publisher can accommodate alternate requests.

SPECIAL PLANS:

Publisher's standing order plan is available upon request; the plan offers 20% discount, shipment within 30 days of publication via UPS, and billing as above. The plan may be cancelled by 30 days advance written notice.

OTHER:

There are two other publishing companies in the U.S. with similar names: Q.E.D. Press of Ann Arbor; QED Information Sciences, Inc.

QUANTUM EDITIONS see GORSUCH SCARISBRICK, PUBLISHERS

QUEST BOOKS see THEOSOPHICAL PUBLISHING HOUSE

QUINTESSENCE PUBLISHING COMPANY, INC.

---

870 Oak Creek Drive
Lombard, Illinois 60148-6405
Telephone: 312-620-4443

ADDRESS FOR ORDERS:

Same as above.
Telephone: 800-621-0387 (in US)
           800-826-2958 (in IL)

PREPAYMENT:

first-time orders must be prepaid; after the first order, terms are net 30 days.

DISCOUNT POLICY:

10% discount to libraries.

RETURN POLICY:

Returns are accepted within 30 days. Written permission must first be obtained from the Customer Service Manager.

SHIPPING AND BILLING POLICY:

Shipping is free for prepaid orders; library pays shipping on billed orders. Invoices are sent after shipments.

BACK ORDER POLICY:

Standing orders are accepted.

QUORUM BOOKS see GREENWOOD PRESS, INC.

R & E PUBLISHERS

P.O. Box 2008
Saratoga, California 95070
Telephone: 408-866-6303

ADDRESS FOR ORDERS:

Same as above.

PREPAYMENT:

Not required.

DISCOUNT POLICY:

No discount for library orders.

RETURN POLICY:

Returns, with written permission, are accepted within 3 months. Address for returns: R & E/936 Industrial Ave/ Palo Alto, CA 94303.

SHIPPING AND BILLING POLICY:

Libraries are charged shipping plus handling ($1.50 for the first book and $0.25 for each additional book). Invoices are sent with shipments unless the library specifies otherwise.

BACK ORDER POLICY:

Back orders are noted on the invoice and filled later.

RGR PUBLICATIONS see AVIATION BOOK COMPANY

RAINBOW BOOKS

P.O. Box 1069
Moore Haven, Florida 33471
Telephone: 813-946-0293

ADDRESS FOR ORDERS:

Same as above.

PREPAYMENT:

Not required.

DISCOUNT POLICY:

20% discount to libraries that order
direct.

RETURN POLICY:

Books may be returned within 60 days, if
defective, by simply mailing them, with
a copy of the original invoice and note
of explanation, to: Rainbow Books, Order
Dept. Postal Address: POB 1069; UPS
address: 2299 Riverside Dr.

SHIPPING AND BILLING POLICY:

Publisher charges a minimum of $2.00
shipping and handling; other costs are
based on weight. Invoices are sent with
shipments and affixed to the outside of
packages.

BACK ORDER POLICY:

Publisher will advise if a title is
temporarily out of stock and when it
will be available. Shipments can usually
be made in 60 days.

SPECIAL PLANS:

A standing order plan for new
publications is available. Return
shipping is paid by the library.

RAINTREE CHILDREN'S BOOKS see RAINTREE
PUBLISHING

RAINTREE PUBLISHING

---

310 West Wisconsin Avenue
Milwaukee, Wisconsin 53203
Telephone: 414-273-0873
          800-558-7264

ADDRESS FOR ORDERS:

Same as above.

DISTRIBUTION/IMPRINT:

Raintree Children's Books
Purnell Reference Books
George Philip Raintree

PREPAYMENT:

Not required.

DISCOUNT POLICY:

Libraries receive a 25% discount off
list price.

RETURN POLICY:

Libraries must obtain approval by phone
or letter before sending returns.
Damaged and stamped books are not
returnable. Only exception is books
received damaged or defective being
returned for replacement. Credit
approved will be applied to account
balance or future purchases. Refunds
will be issued upon request. The address
for returns is: Raintree Publishers
Distribution Center, 5855 N. 94th
Street, Milwaukee, WI 53225.

SHIPPING AND BILLING POLICY:

Libraries pay shipping and handling
charges. The amount of shipping charge
is 5% of total dollar amount excluding
taxes. A $5 shipping and handling charge
for orders of $75 or less. Invoices are
sent to bill-to address specified by the
library. A packing slip accompanies the
shipment.

BACK ORDER POLICY:

Publisher back orders unavailable titles
and fulfills when they become available.
The maximum delay is two months.

ON APPROVAL PLAN:

Orders can be sent on approval for 30,
45, and 60 days. Publisher sends out a
notice after this period asking if
library wishes to return or be billed for
the materials.

OTHER INFORMATION:

Publisher can arrange immediate shipments
and delayed billings of up to three
months.

RANDOM HOUSE, INC.

---

201 East 50th Street
New York, New York 10022
Telephone: 212-751-2600

ADDRESS FOR ORDERS:

Random House, Inc.
400 Hahn Road

Westminster, Maryland 21157
Telephone: 800-638-6460 (except MD & AK)
          800-492-0782 (in MD)

DISTRIBUTION/IMPRINTS:

Distributes: Reader's Digest Books;
Shambhala Publications; Sierra Club
Books; Warner Books (hardcover).

Divisions: Random House; Knopf; Pantheon;
Villard; Vintage; Modern Library; Times
Books; Schocken Books; Fodor's; Chatto &
Windus; Hogarth Press; Jonathan Cape;
Bodley Head; Happy House; Ballantine
Books; Del Rey; Fawcett; Columbine;
Random House Books for Young Readers;
Knopf Books for Young Readers; Beginner
Books.

PREPAYMENT:

Not required.

DISCOUNT POLICY:

For orders over $50.00, 25% discount is
given to libraries for adult and juvenile
trade titles except where "no educational
discount" is noted. Freight-pass-through
allowance of $0.50 for books over $10.00
is not included when discounts are
calculated.

RETURN POLICY:

Returns in resalable condition and
accompanied by invoice information and
reason for return are accepted within
one year of purchase. Written permission
is not required. Address for returns:
Returns Dept/400 Bennett Cerf Dr/
Westminster, MD 21157.

SHIPPING AND BILLING POLICY:

Prices are FOB shipping point; postage
and handling of approximately 6% ($2.00
minimum) will be charged. Invoices are
sent with shipments unless the library
specifies otherwise.

BACK ORDER POLICY:

Out-of-stock items are back ordered for
60 days; items not-yet-published are
back ordered for one year.

SPECIAL PLANS:

A Greenaway Plan is available;
interested libraries should contact
Random House Library Marketing/201 E.
50th St/New York, NY 10022.

RAVEN ARTS PRESS see DUFOUR EDITIONS,
INC.

RAVEN PRESS

1185 Avenue of the Americas
New York, New York 10036
Telephone: 212-930-9500

ADDRESS FOR ORDERS:

Same as above.

PREPAYMENT:

Not required.

DISCOUNT POLICY:

No discount.

RETURN POLICY:

No return is permitted after two years
from invoice date. Permission to return
from publisher is not required. Invoice
number and date in parcel are required to
speed handling and issuance of credit.
Returns must arrive at publisher 's
warehouse in perfect and resalable
condition to receive credit. All return
costs must be assumed by the library.

Returns must not be sent to Raven Press.
The address for returns is: Raven Press
Warehouse, c/o IBS, 35 Hayward Avenue,
Carteret. New Jersey 07008.

SHIPPING AND BILLING POLICY:

If orders are prepaid, publisher absorbs
shipping and handling costs. Publisher
charges shipping plus $2 handling fee per
order when billing is needed. Invoice is
enclosed with shipment unless bill-to
address is different from the ship-to
address or if the library specifies a
separate mailing.

BACK ORDER POLICY:

Publisher back orders all unavailable
titles unless the library specifies no
back order.

SPECIAL ORDER PLAN:

Libraries may place a continuation order
with the publisher for a particular
series, e.g., "Advances in Neurology."

Each volume in the series is shipped as soon as it is published. There is no special discount for standing orders.

RAWSON ASSOCIATES see MACMILLAN PUBLISHING COMPANY, INC.

READER'S DIGEST BOOKS see RANDOM HOUSE, INC.

READING RAINBOW GAZETTE, INC.

648 Broadway, Suite 402
New York, New York 10012
Telephone: 212-529-1133

ADDRESS FOR ORDERS:

Same as above.

DISTRIBUTION/IMPRINTS:

Reading Rainbow Library (8 paperback volumes) is distributed by Checkerboard Press; Pooh Sticker Books (94 paperback volumes) are distributed by E. P. Dutton.

PREPAYMENT:

Prepayment is required for orders under $25.00.

DISCOUNT POLICY:

Quantity discounts are available.

RETURN POLICY:

Returns are not accepted.

SHIPPING AND BILLING POLICY:

Libraries are charged shipping on billed orders; prices include shipping/handling for prepaid orders. Invoices are sent separately.

BACK ORDER POLICY:

Publisher will notify library if there will be a delay of more than 30 days.

REBEL PUBLISHING see CHIDVILAS

RED DUST, INC.

P.O. Box 630, Gracie Station
New York, New York 10028
Telephone: 212-348-4388

ADDRESS FOR ORDERS:

Same as above.

PREPAYMENT:

Not required.

DISCOUNT POLICY:

20% discount to libraries.

RETURN POLICY:

Returns in good condition are accepted within one year. Written permission is required. Address for returns: 1148 5th Ave/New York, NY 10128.

SHIPPING AND BILLING POLICY:

Libraries are charged shipping. Invoices are sent with shipments unless the library specifies otherwise.

BACK ORDER POLICY:

All books are available.

REGAL BOOKS

Post Office Box 6850
Oxnard, California 93031
Telephone: 805-644-9721

ADDRESS FOR ORDERS:

Same as above.

DISTRIBUTION/IMPRINT:

Vision House

PREPAYMENT:

Not required.

DISCOUNT POLICY:

There is no discount for libraries. However, if a library wishes to place quantity orders, special arrangements may be made with the Sales Department.

RETURN POLICY:

Publisher requests libraries to write for return authorization. Libraries may return books within one year at a 50% discount. Special discount items sold prior to going out-of-print and for giveaway purposes are not returnable. To insure the proper discount, enclose a copy of the invoice with the item being returned. The address for returns is: Regal Books/GL Publications, 2300 Knoll Drive, Ventura, California 93003.

SHIPPING AND BILLING POLICY:

Libraries pay shipping charges. The amount of charge is the actual cost of shipping, or a flat 10%. Invoices are sent after shipments.

BACK ORDER POLICY:

Unavailable titles are back ordered until they become available.

REGIONAL PUBLISHING COMPANY see GENEALOGICAL PUBLISHING COMPANY

REGULAR JOE'S BOOKS see ILLUMINATI

RELIGIOUS ETHICS, INC. see GEORGETOWN UNIVERSITY PRESS

RENAISSANCE HOUSE PUBLISHERS

P.O. Box 177
Frederick, Colorado 80530
Telephone: 303-833-2030

ADDRESS FOR ORDERS:

Same as above.
Telephone: 800-521-9221

DISTRIBUTION/IMPRINTS:

Distributes publications of Historic Denver, Inc.

PREPAYMENT:

Not required.

DISCOUNT POLICY:

0 - 4 copies (mixed titles): no disc.
5 ore more: 20%

RETURN POLICY:

Returns in salable condition are accepted within one year. Claims for damaged books or short shipments must be made immediately.

SHIPPING AND BILLING POLICY:

Libraries are charged shipping on all orders. Invoices are sent with shipments unless the library specifies otherwise.

BACK ORDER POLICY:

Books not available are placed on back order.

SPECIAL PLANS:

Publisher will set up an individual approval plan for libraries that order on a regular basis.

OTHER:

Libraries may order direct or through wholesalers. Publisher is attempting to increase its visibility among major public libraries.

REPRINT COMPANY, PUBLISHERS

P.O. Box 5401
601 Hillcrest Offices
Spartanburg, South Carolina 19304
Telephone: 803-582-0732

ADDRESS FOR ORDERS:

Same as above.

DISTRIBUTION/IMPRINTS:

Distributes the publications of: The South Carolina Historical Society (Charleston); The North Carolina Genealogical Society (Raleigh); The R. J. Taylor, Jr. Foundation (Atlanta)

PREPAYMENT:

Not required.

DISCOUNT POLICY:

No discount to libraries except for special offers.

RETURN POLICY:

Any book may be returned within thirty days. Written permission is required.

SHIPPING AND BILLING POLICY:

Libraries are charged postage and handling of $1.75 for the first book and $0.25 for each additional book. Invoices are sent with shipments unless the library specifies otherwise.

BACK ORDER POLICY:

Back order files are maintained, and library is notified when a title is being reprinted at which time the library may choose to order or not.

SPECIAL PLANS:

50% discount for standing orders to the special microfiche program of the South Carolina Historical Society.

RESOURCE PUBLICATIONS, INC.

---

160 E. Virginia Street, Suite 290
San Jose, California 95112-5848
Telephone: 408-286-8505

ADDRESS FOR ORDERS:

Same as above.

PREPAYMENT:

Not required.

DISCOUNT POLICY:

Less than $25.00:	no discount
$25.00-$99.99	10%
over $100.00	20%

RETURN POLICY:

Only books received on approval or which are defective may be returned. Library should write for permission to return.

SHIPPING AND BILLING POLICY:

Publisher pays shipping on prepaid orders; library pays shipping and handling ($1.50 minimum) on billed orders. Invoices are sent with shipments unless the library specifies otherwise.

BACK ORDER POLICY:

Back orders are kept on file, and the library is notified of scheduled date of availability.

SPECIAL PLANS:

Publisher will accept "on approval" orders when those orders are clearly so marked.

RESOURCES FOR THE FUTURE, INC. see JOHNS HOPKINS UNIVERSITY PRESS

RESTON see APPLETON AND LANGE PUBLISHING COMPANY

RESTON PUBLISHING COMPANY see PRENTICE-HALL

RETAIL REPORTING BUREAU see FAIRCHILD BOOKS & VISUALS/PROFESSIONAL BOOKS

FLEMING H. REVELL COMPANY

---

184 Central Avenue
Old Tappan, New Jersey 07675
Telephone: 201-768-8060

ADDRESS FOR ORDERS:

Same as above.
Telephone: 201-768-8060
          800-631-1970

DISTRIBUTION/IMPRINT:

Chosen
Power
Spire

PREPAYMENT:

Prepayment requested.

DISCOUNT POLICY:

Libraries receive a 25% discount.

RETURN POLICY:

Books may be returned within one year.
Mass market titles are not returnable.

SHIPPING AND BILLING POLICY:

Libraries pay postage and handling
charges. The amount of handling charge
is 6% of discounted total cost. Invoices
are sent separately after shipments.

BACK ORDER POLICY:

Unavailable titles are back ordered and
shipped when available, unless library
requests otherwise.

REWARDS PAPERBACKS see PRENTICE-HALL

RICE UNIVERSITY PRESS see TEXAS A & M
UNIVERSITY PRESS

LYNNE RIENNER PUBLISHERS, INC.

---

948 North Street, Suite 8
Boulder, Colorado 80302
Telephone: 303-444-6684

ADDRESS FOR ORDERS:

Same as above.

PREPAYMENT:

Not required.

DISCOUNT POLICY:

No discount for libraries.

RETURN POLICY:

Written authorization is required.
Address for returns: Lynne Rienner
Publishers/Longwood Publishing Group/61A
Emory St/Sanford, ME 04073.

SHIPPING AND BILLING POLICY:

Libraries pay shipping (either Library
Rate or UPS) plus handling of $2.00 for
the first book and $1.00 for each
additional book on all orders. Invoices
are sent with shipments unless the
library specifies otherwise.

BACK ORDER POLICY:

Back orders are accepted; cancellation
dates from libraries would be helpful.

SPECIAL PLANS:

Standing orders are available for each
new publication; standing orders for
series are not recommended.

DAN RIVER PRESS see CONSERVATORY OF
AMERICAN LETTERS

RIZZOLI INTERNATIONAL PUBLICATIONS, INC.

---

597 Fifth Avenue
New York, New York 10017
Telephone: 212-223-0100

ADDRESS FOR ORDERS:

Same as above.

DISTRIBUTION/IMPRINTS:

Distributes: Eridanos Press; Hudson Hills
Press; PBC International; Timken
Publishers; Vendome Press.

Imprints: Electa; Skira.

PREPAYMENT:

Not required once an account is
established.

DISCOUNT POLICY:

10% discount to libraries.

RETURN POLICY:

No returns are accepted except for
damaged books. Libraries should
telephone publisher if there are
problems.

SHIPPING AND BILLING POLICY:

3% of net should be added for shipping
on prepaid orders; billed orders will
include charge for actual postage.
Invoices are sent separately prior to
shipments.

BACK ORDER POLICY:

Publisher will keep items on back order
for up to five years unless the library
instructs otherwise.

SPECIAL PLANS:

Publisher offers two plans: Greenaway
Plan includes receipt before publication
date of one copy of every new title
published or distributed by Rizzoli at a
40% discount, non-returnable, but
subject to library's restrictions on
price, cloth/paper, etc. Plan is
seasonal and renewable at the start of
the fall and spring.

Approval Plan includes receipt before
publication date of every new title
published or distributed by Rizzoli at a
33 1/3% discount, returnable within 30
days, and subject to library's
restrictions of price, cloth/paper, etc.
Plan is renewable annually.

ROCKEFELLER UNIVERSITY PRESS

1230 York Avenue
New York, New York 10021
Telephone: 212-570-8568

ADDRESS FOR ORDERS:

Rockefeller University Press
P.O. Box 5483
Church Street Station
New York, New York 10249

Telephone: 212-570-8572

PREPAYMENT:

Not required for book orders.

DISCOUNT POLICY:

No discount to libraries.

RETURN POLICY:

Returns in salable condition and sent
with postage prepaid are accepted within
3 months. Prior permission is required
from Order Service at the York Avenue
address. Journals are non-returnable.

SHIPPING AND BILLING POLICY:

Libraries are charged shipping except on
prepaid orders which are shipped free.
Invoices are sent with shipments unless
the library specifies otherwise.

ROCKPORT PUBLICATIONS see F & W
PUBLICATIONS

RODALE PRESS, INC.

33 East Minor Street
Emmaus, Pennsylvania 18098
Telephone: 215-967-5171

ADDRESS FOR ORDERS:

Same as above.

PREPAYMENT:

Not required.

DISCOUNT POLICY:

Libraries receive a 20 % discount on all
orders.

RETURN POLICY:

Publisher requests that libraries write
for return permission before sending
returns. Books may be returned for
credit any time as long as they are still
in print. The address for returns is:
Rodale Press Mail Distribution Center,
400 South 10th Street, Emmaus,
Pennsylvania 18098.

SHIPPING AND BILLING POLICY:

Libraries pay postage. There is no handling charge. Invoices are sent separately after shipments.

BACK ORDER POLICY:

Publisher back orders currently unavailable titles unless there is a specific instructions from the library.

SPECIAL ORDER PLAN:

Libraries may select the new titles they would like to purchase and receive a 55 % discount for non-returnable or 40 % for returnable items. They may cancel at any time. Libraries may choose cloth or paper.

RONIN PUBLISHING

Box 1035
Berkeley, California 94701
Telephone: 415-540-6278

ADDRESS FOR ORDERS:

Same as above.

PREPAYMENT:

Prepayment is required for orders of fewer than 5 copies.

DISCOUNT POLICY:

5 copies: 25%
over 5:   40%

RETURN POLICY:

Returns are accepted within 9 months. Written permission is required. Address for returns: 11A Commercial Blvd/Novato, California 94947.

SHIPPING AND BILLING POLICY:

Libraries are charged actual shipping costs.

BACK ORDER POLICY:

Orders are held for up to six months.

ROSEN PUBLISHING GROUP, INC.

29 E. 21st Street
New York, New York 10010
Telephone: 212-777-3017

ADDRESS FOR ORDERS:

Same as above.
Telephone: 800-237-9932

DISTRIBUTION/IMPRINTS:

Pelion Press (Imprint)

PREPAYMENT:

Not required.

DISCOUNT POLICY:

No discount to libraries.

RETURN POLICY:

Returns are accepted within six months of shipping date. Written permission is required.

SHIPPING AND BILLING POLICY:

Libraries are charged shipping plus handling ($1.25 for the first book and $0.30 for each additional book). Invoices are sent with shipments unless the library specifies otherwise.

BACK ORDER POLICY:

Books on back order are shipped as soon as they are available; if books have been on back order for a long time, they are not invoiced until shipped.

ROSS BOOKS

P.O. Box 4340
Berkeley, California 94704
Telephone: 415-841-2474
        800-367-0930 (in US)
        800-537-3338 (in CA)

ADDRESS FOR ORDERS:

Same as above.

PREPAYMENT:

Not required.

DISCOUNT POLICY:

20% discount on library orders of 5 or more copies.

RETURN POLICY:

Books may be returned within one year, with prior permission, provided that books are in salable condition. Address for returns: Ross Books/1735 Martin Luther King Jr Way/Berkeley, CA 94709.

SHIPPING AND BILLING POLICY:

Libraries are charged shipping. Invoices are sent with shipments unless the library specifies otherwise.

SPECIAL PLANS:

Publisher will be happy to negotiate special plans with libraries.

FRED B. ROTHMAN AND COMPANY

10368 West Centennial Road
Littleton, Colorado 80127
Telephone: 303-979-5657

ADDRESS FOR ORDERS:

Same as above.

PREPAYMENT:

Not required.

DISCOUNT POLICY:

Orders of 10 or more copies receive a special discount. There is no discount for orders of fewer than 10 copies.

RETURN POLICY:

Written permission is not required for returns. Time limit is six months to one year. The address for returns is the same as for orders.

SHIPPING AND BILLING POLICY:

Libraries pay postage and insurance. Invoices are sent separately after

shipment unless library requests otherwise.

BACK ORDER POLICY:

Titles not currently available are reported and back ordered unless library requests otherwise.

SPECIAL ORDER PLAN:

Publisher has a standing order plan whereby libraries can order either all publications, all reprints, or all original publications. Publisher grants a 10% discount and full return privileges. Shipping and handling is the same as for other orders. The standing order plan can be started and cancelled simply by writing a letter.

ROTOVISION see WATSON-GUPTILL
PUBLICATIONS

ROUNDTABLE PUBLISHING, INC.

---

933 Pico Boulevard
Santa Monica, California 90405
Telephone: 213-450-9777

ADDRESS FOR ORDERS:

Same as above.
Telephone (for orders only):
        800-222-5322
        800-826-7611 (in CA)

PREPAYMENT:

Not required.

DISCOUNT POLICY:

10% discount and one free book of publisher's choice are given for every book ordered.

RETURN POLICY:

No returns are accepted from libraries.

SHIPPING AND BILLING POLICY:

Libraries are charged shipping at Library Rate. Invoices are sent with shipments unless the library specifies otherwise.

BACK ORDER POLICY:

Orders are held and the books are shipped when available.

OTHER:

Publisher ships within two days of receipt of a purchase order.

ROUTLEDGE & KEGAN PAUL see ROUTLEDGE, CHAPMAN AND HALL, INC.

ROUTLEDGE, CHAPMAN AND HALL, INC.

---

29 West 35th Street
New York, New York 10001
Telephone: 212-244-3336

ADDRESS FOR ORDERS:

Same as above.

DISTRIBUTION/IMPRINT:

Methuen
Routledge
Tavistock
Croom Helm
Routledge & Kegan Paul
Theatre Arts
Ark Paperbacks
Kegan Paul International

PREPAYMENT:

Not required if placed on official purchase order or letterhead.

DISCOUNT POLICY:

Trade books:

    1 to 4 books   none
    5 or more books   10%

Academic, scholarly, professional, reference, and scientific books: no discount, except for standing order accounts.

RETURN POLICY:

No prior permission is necessary. Returned books must be in print and in resalable condition. Invoice reference required for full credit. The return address is: Routledge, Chapman & Hall, 80

Northfield Avenue, Building 424, Edison, NJ 08817.

SHIPPING AND BILLING POLICY:

Libraries pay postage. Invoices are sent with shipment unless otherwise specified. Terms are net 30 days.

BACK ORDER POLICY:

All unfilled orders are automatically back ordered unless library instructs otherwise.

SPECIAL ORDER PLAN:

Publisher accepts Standing Orders and offers additional discounts to libraries. Write Sales Manager for complete information.

ROWMAN & LITTLEFIELD see LITTLEFIELD, ADAMS AND COMPANY

ROXBURY PUBLISHING COMPANY

P.O. Box 491044
Los Angeles, California 90049
Telephone: 213-458-3493

ADDRESS FOR ORDERS:

Same as above.

DISTRIBUTION/IMPRINTS:

Distributes Techniques of Writing Memos, Letters, and Reports by Courtland L. Bovee (Banner Books).

PREPAYMENT:

Not required.

DISCOUNT POLICY:

1 copy: no discount
5 or more: 20%

RETURN POLICY:

Books, in unmarked, resalable condition, are accepted for return within one year.

SHIPPING AND BILLING POLICY:

Libraries are charged shipping. Invoices are sent with shipments.

BACK ORDER POLICY:

All titles are available.

RUNNING PRESS BOOK PUBLISHERS

125 S. 22nd Street
Philadelphia, Pennsylvania 19103
Telephone: 215-567-5080

ADDRESS FOR ORDERS:

Same as above.
Telephone: 800-428-1111 (outside PA)

DISTRIBUTION/IMPRINTS:

Imprint: Courage Books.

PREPAYMENT:

Not required.

DISCOUNT POLICY:

10% discount on 2 or more books (assorted titles).

RETURN POLICY:

Returns are accepted within one year. Authorization from Customer Service Department is required. All Courage Books are non-returnable. Address for returns: Running Press Warehouse/3201 Reed St/Philadelphia, PA 19146.

SHIPPING AND BILLING POLICY:

Libraries are charged shipping on all orders. Invoices are sent separately.

BACK ORDER POLICY:

Publisher back orders unavailable titles and notifies library; orders for out-of-print titles are cancelled.

SPECIAL PLANS:

A standing order is available for publisher's Best of Journalism series. A Greenaway Plan is also available which offers one copy of every Running Press and Courage Books title at a 50%

discount, non-returnable. Invoicing is once per season.

RUTGERS UNIVERSITY PRESS

109 Church Street
New Brunswick, New Jersey 08901
Telephone: 201-932-7037

ADDRESS FOR ORDERS:

Rutgers University Press Distribution Center
P.O. Box 4869
Hampton Station
Baltimore, MD 21211
Telephone: 301-338-6947

PREPAYMENT:

Not required with purchase order.

DISCOUNT POLICY:

No discount to libraries.

RETURN POLICY:

No returns are accepted except for damaged books.

SHIPPING AND BILLING POLICY:

Libraries are charged shipping (usually at Library Rate) on all orders. Invoices are usually sent after shipments unless the library specifies otherwise.

BACK ORDER POLICY:

Back orders are held for one year.

SPECIAL PLANS:

Publisher offers 40% discount on all standing orders.

OTHER:

Libraries may order direct, but publisher works mainly with wholesalers.

SAE see SOCIETY OF AUTOMOTIVE ENGINEERS

SRA see SCIENCE RESEARCH ASSOCIATES, INC.

ST PUBLICATIONS (SIGNS OF THE TIMES)

407 Gilbert Avenue
Cincinnati, Ohio 45202
Telephone: 513-421-2050

ADDRESS FOR ORDERS:

Same as above.

PREPAYMENT:

Prepayment is required on all orders.

DISCOUNT POLICY:

No discount to libraries.

RETURN POLICY:

Within 15 days of receipt, books may be returned for any reason with no permission required. Current editions in resalable condition will usually be accepted within 3 months.

SHIPPING AND BILLING POLICY:

Shipping and handling charges are assessed on all orders as follows: $2.00 for the first book and $0.50 for each additional book.

BACK ORDER POLICY:

Items will be placed on back order and shipped when available.

SACRED HEARTS KID'S CLUB see TABOR PUBLISHING

ST. JAMES PRESS, INC.

233 East Ontario Street
Chicago, Illinois 60611
Telephone: 312-329-0806

ADDRESS FOR ORDERS:

Same as above.

DISTRIBUTION/IMPRINTS:

Distributes the publications of Longman (UK) and Macmillan (UK).

PREPAYMENT:

Not required.

DISCOUNT POLICY:

No discount to libraries except for standing orders and a 2.5% discount for prepaid orders.

RETURN POLICY:

Returns, in good condition, are accepted within three months of invoice date. Prior permission is not required.

SHIPPING AND BILLING POLICY:

Publisher pays shipping and handling on prepaid orders; others are charged postage plus handling charges of from $0.40 down to $0.15 depending on the number of books. Invoices are sent with shipments unless the library specifies otherwise.

BACK ORDER POLICY:

Publisher will back order any books not yet published and will hold until publication or cancellation.

SPECIAL PLANS:

10% discount offered for any standing order.

ST. LUKES PRESS

1407 Union Avenue
Suite 401
Memphis, Tennessee 38104
Telephone: 901-357-5441

ADDRESS FOR ORDERS:

Same as above.
Telephone: 800-524-5554, wait for tone and dial 4617 (touch tone phones only).

DISTRIBUTION/IMPRINTS:

Distributes: Iris Press; Osler House; Shelby House.

PREPAYMENT:

Not required.

DISCOUNT POLICY:

Discount to libraries is 10% on 10 or more volumes (mixed or single title).

RETURN POLICY:

Returns are accepted within 30 days. Written permission is requested. Fine art books and limited editions are not returnable.

SHIPPING AND BILLING POLICY:

Libraries are charged shipping via UPS unless otherwise requested. Invoices are sent with shipments unless the library specifies otherwise.

BACK ORDER POLICY:

Publisher will ask library to confirm orders held over 30 days.

SPECIAL PLANS:

Publisher offers an approval plan and a standing order plan at a 10% discount. Libraries may cancel anytime with a 14 day notice.

ST. MARTIN'S PRESS

---

175 Fifth Avenue
New York, New York 10010
Telephone: 212-674-5151
        800-221-7945

ADDRESS FOR ORDERS:

Same as above.

DISTRIBUTION/IMPRINT:

Jeremy Tarcher, Inc.
Prima Publishing
Universe Books

Pharos Books
Academy Editions
Audio Renaissance Tapes
Tor Books

PREPAYMENT:

Not required.

DISCOUNT POLICY:

Publisher's discount rate varies depending on the type of material:

Trade cloth	10%
Trade paper	10%
College cloth	20%
College paper	20%
Reference	10%
Mass market	10%

RETURN POLICY:

Books can be returned without prior permission if they are in print and in salable condition. Return of a college book is limited to one year from invoice date. All returns must be prepaid; no collect shipments will be accepted. The address for returns of trade and college books is: St. Martin's Press, c/o Haddon Craftsmen Inc., O'Neill Highway, Dunmore, PA 18512. The address for returns of mass market books is: Compusort Systems, Inc., c/o WPS, 275 Secaucus Road, Secaucus, NJ 07094.

SHIPPING AND BILLING POLICY:

All shipping costs are paid by the library. If bill-to and ship-to addresses are the same, invoice goes with shipment; otherwise it goes separately.

BACK ORDER POLICY:

Not-yet-published titles are held until release of the book. Back orders are held for 90 days.

SAINT MARY'S PRESS

Terrace Heights
Winona, Minnesota 55987
Telephone: 507-452-9090
        800-533-8095

ADDRESS FOR ORDERS:

Same as above.

PREPAYMENT:

Not required.

DISCOUNT POLICY:

10-19 books:	10%
20 or more:	20%

RETURN POLICY:

Returns in unmarked and undamaged condition are accepted within one year. Written permission is required.

SHIPPING AND BILLING POLICY:

Prepaid orders are shipped free; library pays shipping on billed orders. Invoices are ususaly sent separately after shipments unless the library specifies otherwise.

BACK ORDER POLICY:

Back orders for future publications are accepted.

ST. WILLIBROAD'S PRESS see BORGO PRESS

SALEM HOUSE PUBLISHERS

---

462 Boston Street
Topsfield, Massachusetts 01983
Telephone: 617-887-2440
          800-624-8947

ADDRESS FOR ORDERS:

Same as above.
Telephone: 617-887-8199

DISTRIBUTION/IMPRINTS:

Distributes the publications of: Angus & Robertson; Sirius Quality Paperbacks; Bay Book; British Tourist Authority; Automobile Association of Britain; Nicholson Publications; Phaidon Press.

PREPAYMENT:

Not required.

DISCOUNT POLICY:

20% discount to libraries.

RETURN POLICY:

Returns, accompanied by invoice numbers, are accepted after three months from invoice date for as long as the book is in print. Prior permission is not required. Out-of-print books are not returnable. Address for returns: Salem House Publishers/c/o Returns Department/Mercedes Distribution Center, Inc/160 Imlay St/Brooklyn, NY 11231.

SHIPPING AND BILLING POLICY:

Prepaid orders are shipped free; actual shipping charges are added to billed orders. Invoices are sent with USPS shipments and separately with UPS shipments.

BACK ORDER POLICY:

Back orders are cancelled after 6 months unless publisher receives a special order.

SPECIAL PLANS:

Publisher will provide standing orders to those libraries that request them.

SALESMAN'S GUIDE, INC.

1140 Broadway
New York, New York 10001
Telephone: 212-684-2985
          800-223-1797

ADDRESS FOR ORDERS:

Same as above.

PREPAYMENT:

Not required.

DISCOUNT POLICY:

No discount to libraries.

RETURN POLICY:

Verbal permission to return is acceptable within 60 days.

SHIPPING AND BILLING POLICY:

Publisher pays shipping on prepaid orders; library pays shipping on billed

orders. Invoices are sent with
shipments.

SPECIAL PLANS:

Library standing orders are accepted
with a purchase order.

HOWARD W. SAMS & COMPANY

4300 W. 62nd Street
Indianapolis, Indiana 46268
Telephone: 317-298-5400

ADDRESS FOR ORDERS:

Same as above.
Telephone: 800-428-7267

DISTRIBUTION/IMPRINTS:

Hayden Books (Imprint)

PREPAYMENT:

Not required.

DISCOUNT POLICY:

25% discount to libraries.

RETURN POLICY:

Written permission is requested for
returns.

SHIPPING AND BILLING POLICY:

Libraries are charged shipping plus
handling ($2.50). Invoices are sent with
shipments unless the library specifies
otherwise.

BACK ORDER POLICY:

Back orders are shipped automatically
when stock is received.

SAN JACINTO PUBLISHING COMPANY see TEXAS
A & M UNIVERSITY PRESS

PORTER SARGENT PUBLISHERS, INC.

11 Beacon Street
Boston, Massachusetts 02108
Telephone: 617-523-1670

ADDRESS FOR ORDERS:

Same as above.

PREPAYMENT:

Not required.

DISCOUNT POLICY:

10% discount to libraries.

RETURN POLICY:

Reference books may be returned within 3
months. Written permission is required.

SHIPPING AND BILLING POLICY:

Actual shipping charges are added to
invoices. Invoices are sent with
shipments unless ship-to and bill-to
addresses are different.

BACK ORDER POLICY:

Publisher will back order if library so
requests.

SPECIAL PLANS:

Standing orders are accepted for
publisher's reference books. Orders
should specify title, quantity,
beginning edition, and binding (cloth or
paper). Standing orders must be
cancelled in writing.

SAUNDERS COLLEGE see HOLT, RINEHART AND
WINSTON PUBLISHERS

W. B. SAUNDERS COMPANY

The Curtis Center
Independence Square West
Philadelphia, Pennsylvania 19106
Telephone: 215-238-7800

ADDRESS FOR ORDERS:

Harcourt Brace Jovanovich

Orlando, Florida 32887
Telephone: 305-345-2000

DISTRIBUTION/IMPRINTS:

Publisher imprints: Bailliere Tindall;
Grune & Stratton .

PREPAYMENT:

Not required.

DISCOUNT POLICY:

Single copy price less 10%.

RETURN POLICY:

No prior authorization required. A
packing slip must be enclosed with
returns. Time limit for acceptance of
returns is within 60 days after a new
edition is published. Returns should be
sent to: 151 Benigno Blvd/ Bellmawr, New
Jersey 08031.

SHIPPING AND BILLING POLICY:

Shipping is charged unless the order is
prepaid. Invoices will only be sent with
shipments.

BACK ORDER POLICY:

Back orders are held indefinitely.

SCALA BOOKS see HARPER AND ROW,
PUBLISHERS, INC.

SCARECROW PRESS, INC.

---

52 Liberty Street
Metuchen, New Jersey 08840
Telephone: 201-548-8600
        800-537-7107

ADDRESS FOR ORDERS:

Scarecrow Press, Inc.
P.O. Box 4167
Metuchen, New Jersey 08840

DISTRIBUTION/IMPRINT:

Mini Print Corp (division)

PREPAYMENT:

Not required.

DISCOUNT POLICY:

List prices are net to libraries.

RETURN POLICY:

Publisher requires written permission for
returns. Books must be returned within
six months of transaction. Publisher has
no non-returnable titles. The address
for returns is the same as for orders.

SHIPPING AND BILLING POLICY:

Libraries pay postage and handling
charges. Invoices are sent with
shipments unless library requests
otherwise.

BACK ORDER POLICY:

Titles currently unavailable are reported
and back ordered.

SPECIAL ORDER PLAN:

Under Scarecrow Press Standing Order
Plan, the publisher sends monthly all new
publications and bills at a 15 %
discount. Any book may be returned for
full credit; no permission is required.
Additional copies of any book may be
purchased at a 15 % discount, with no
charge of postage. Libraries may cancel
the Plan at any time without penalty.

In addition to the above-mentioned
standard policy, the publisher accepts
adjusted plans to meet specific
requirements of any library, extending
the same 15 % discount. Variations can
be in coverage, time and date of
shipment, payment, returns, etc.

G. SCHIRMER see HAL LEONARD PUBLISHING
CORPORATION

SCHIRMER BOOKS see MACMILLAN PUBLISHING
COMPANY, INC.

SCHOCKEN BOOKS see RANDOM HOUSE, INC.

SCHOLARLY RESOURCES, INC.

104 Greenhill Avenue
Wilmington, Delaware 19805-1897
Telephone: 302-654-7713
         800-772-8937

ADDRESS FOR ORDERS:

Same as above.

PREPAYMENT:

Not required.

DISCOUNT POLICY:

None on library orders.

RETURN POLICY:

Publisher requires prior written
permission for returns. The address for
returns is the same as for orders.

SHIPPING AND BILLING POLICY:

Publisher pays shipping charge and bills
libraries. Invoices are sent separately
after shipments unless library requests
otherwise.

BACK ORDER POLICY:

Titles not currently available are either
back ordered or cancelled, as library
requests.

SPECIAL ORDER PLAN:

Standing orders are accepted for a number
of annual series. When a library places
a standing order, successive annual
volumes are shipped to the library
immediately upon publication. Library
may cancel a standing order at any time.

Scholars Press Customer Services
P.O. Box 6525
Ithaca, NY 14851
Telephone: (607) 277-2211

PREPAYMENT:

Not required with approved credit.

DISCOUNT POLICY:

1-4 books: 25%
5 or more books: 40%

RETURN POLICY:

Returns accepted within one year.
Returns must be in salable condition
and accompanied by original invoice.
Prior permission is not required.
Address for returns: Scholars Press
Customer Services/c/o C.U.P.
Services/740 Cascadilla Street/Ithaca,
NY 14850.

SHIPPING AND BILLING POLICY:

Libraries pay shipping of $2.50 per
order regardless of amount of order.
Invoices sent with shipments unless the
library specifies otherwise.

BACK ORDER POLICY:

Back orders held and shipped upon
receipt.

STANDING ORDER PLANS:

Three plans are available: Religious
Studies; Classics; Combined Religious
Studies and Classics. 33% discount is
offered to subscribers. Books are
shipped monthly with extended quarterly
billing.

OTHER INFORMATION:

Publisher specializes in highly
technical works in religion, biblical
studies, Judaic studies, and classics.

SCHOLARS PRESS

P.O. Box 1608
Decatur, Georgia 30031
Telephone: (404) 636-4757

ADDRESS FOR ORDERS:

SCHOLARS' FACSIMILES & REPRINTS

P.O. Box 344
Delmar, New York 12054
Telephone:

ADDRESS FOR ORDERS:

Same as above.

DISTRIBUTION/IMPRINTS:

Caravan Books (Imprint)

PREPAYMENT:

Not required.

DISCOUNT POLICY:

No discount except for standing orders.

RETURN POLICY:

Defective copies only can be returned for replacement.

SHIPPING AND BILLING POLICY:

Libraries are charged shipping plus approximately $3.50 handling. Invoices are sent with shipments.

BACK ORDER POLICY:

Back orders are held and books shipped upon publication.

SPECIAL PLANS:

Standing orders available at 20% discount.

SCHOLIUM INTERNATIONAL, INC.

---

99 Seaview Boulevard
Port Washington, New York 11050-4610
Telephone: 516-484-3290

ADDRESS FOR ORDERS:

Same as above.

DISTRIBUTION/IMPRINTS:

Publisher distributes:
    Selected science, technology, and
        computer science titles of
        Macmillan Education Ltd. (UK);
    Intercept Ltd.;
    IFS Publications Ltd.;
    Royal Society of Chemistry (UK);
    Royal Society of London, Viewpoint
        Publications;
    Dechema Chemistry Data Series
        (West Germany).

PREPAYMENT:

Not required.

DISCOUNT POLICY:

10% discount applicable to libraries except for Dechema titles which are net.

RETURN POLICY:

Publisher will replace at no charge defective or damaged books or accept for full credit returns of books which were not ordered or supplied in error. Books supplied as ordered are not returnable.

SHIPPING AND BILLING POLICY:

Libraries are charged actual shipping. Invoices are usually sent with shipments.

BACK ORDER POLICY:

Publisher will hold orders on back order and supply books when available unless library instructs otherwise.

SCIENCE RESEARCH ASSOCIATES, INC.

---

155 North Wacker Drive
Chicago, Illinois 60606
Telephone: 312-984-2000

ADDRESS FOR ORDERS:

Same as above.

PREPAYMENT:

Not required.

DISCOUNT POLICY:

Libraries receive school prices as listed in catalog.

RETURN POLICY:

Enclose a statement providing billing and shipping address, invoice number, and reason for return, or enclose a copy of invoice and reason for return. Shipments must be sent prepaid and insured. Materials returned for credit must be in clean, salable, unused condition and in sets of packages as sold. Materials must have been purchased within the past 12 months. The address for returns is: SRA Returned Materials Section, Science

Research Associates, 777 Mark Street, Wood Dale, IL 60191.

SHIPPING AND BILLING POLICY:

F.o.b. shipping point, SRA prepays and adds to invoice. Packing slip is included with shipment. Invoice is sent separately. Terms are net 30 days.

BACK ORDER POLICY:

Titles not currently available are back ordered unless library specifies otherwise.

SCIENTIFIC AMERICAN BOOKS see W. H. FREEMAN AND COMPANY

CHARLES SCRIBNER'S SONS see MACMILLAN PUBLISHING COMPANY, INC.

SCRIPTURE PRESS PUBLICATIONS, INC.

1825 College Avenue
Wheaton, Illinois 60187
Telephone: 312-668-6000

ADDRESS FOR ORDERS:

Same as above.
Telephone: 800-323-9409

DISTRIBUTION/IMPRINTS:

Victor Books (Division)

PREPAYMENT:

Not required.

DISCOUNT POLICY:

25% discount to libraries.

RETURN POLICY:

Books on publisher's current list may be returned. No prior permission is required.

SHIPPING AND BILLING POLICY:

Libraries are charged postage on all orders. Invoices are sent separately.

BACK ORDER POLICY:

Back orders are shipped with postage prepaid.

SPECIAL PLANS:

VictorMatic Plan is available for all new Victor Books at a 45% discount and full return privileges.

SEA CHALLENGERS see WESTERN MARINE ENTERPRISES

SECOND CHANCE PRESS

RD2 Noyac Road
Sag Harbor, New York 11963
Telephone: 516-725-1101

ADDRESS FOR ORDERS:

Same as above.

DISTRIBUTION/IMPRINT:

The Permanent Press (imprint)

PREPAYMENT:

Not required.

DISCOUNT POLICY:

No discount to libraries.

RETURN POLICY:

Libraries must obtain written permission before returning books. A 25% penalty on all returns. No returns accepted after one year. Credit balance held against future orders. No refunds. Single copy is not returnable.

SHIPPING AND BILLING POLICY:

Libraries pay shipping and handling charge. The amount is $2 for the first book, $.25 for each additional book.

BACK ORDER POLICY:

Publisher back orders and fills
temporarily out-of-stock titles.

SELF-COUNSEL PRESS see TAB BOOKS

SELF-ESTEEM SEMINARS see JALMAR PRESS

SELF-REALIZATION FELLOWSHIP

3880 San Rafael Avenue
Los Angeles, California 90065
Telephone: 213-225-2474

ADDRESS FOR ORDERS:

Same as above.

PREPAYMENT:

Not required.

DISCOUNT POLICY:

1 unit: 25% (plus shipping)
2-5 units: 30% (plus shipping)
over 5:   40% (with free shipping)

RETURN POLICY:

All books in salable condition may be
returned at any time for full credit
without permission.

SHIPPING AND BILLING POLICY:

Free shipping via least expensive way is
offered on prepaid orders and on orders
of 6 or more units. Invoices are sent
with shipments unless the library
specifies otherwise.

BACK ORDER POLICY:

Publisher will back order at customer's
request.

SEPHARDIC HOUSE see SEPHER-HERMON PRESS,
INC.

SEPHER-HERMON PRESS, INC.

1265 46th Street
Brooklyn, New York 11219
Telephone: 718-972-9010

ADDRESS FOR ORDERS:

Same as above.

DISTRIBUTION/IMPRINTS:

Distributes: Jewish Chronicle
Publications (London); Bar-Ilan
University Press (Israel); Sephardic
House (NY).

PREPAYMENT:

Prepayment is required for orders of less
than $25.00.

DISCOUNT POLICY:

10-15% discount depending on size of
order; academic publications are net.

RETURN POLICY:

Returns are accepted within one year.
Written permission is required. Non-
trade publications specially obtained
for a client are not returnable.

SHIPPING AND BILLING POLICY:

Libraries are charged shipping and
handling of from $0.50 to $2.00
depending on the size of the shipment
except on prepaid orders. Invoices are
sent with shipments unless the library
specifies otherwise.

BACK ORDER POLICY:

Publisher back orders unless otherwise
instructed.

SPECIAL PLANS:

Standing orders are accepted.

SERVANT PUBLICATIONS

P.O. BOX 8617
840 Airport Boulevard
Ann Arbor, Michigan 48107
Telephone: 313-761-8505

ADDRESS FOR ORDERS:

Same as above.

PREPAYMENT:

Not required.

DISCOUNT POLICY:

20% discount for orders over $100.00

RETURN POLICY:

Prior permission is not required.

SHIPPING AND BILLING POLICY:

Billed order are charged actual postage
or UPS charge. Invoices are sent with
shipments, but duplicate invoices can be
sent separately if necessary.

BACK ORDER POLICY:

Publisher places back orders and
notifies customer after 30 days if not
available.

SEVEN LOCKS PRESS

P.O. Box 27
Cabin John, Maryland 20818
Telephone: 301-320-2130

ADDRESS FOR ORDERS:

Same as above.

DISTRIBUTION/IMPRINTS:

Distributes publications of the Inter-
University Seminar on Armed Forces and
Society.

Isadore Stephanus Sons (subsidiary)

PREPAYMENT:

Prepayment preferred on single-copy
orders.

DISCOUNT POLICY:

None.

RETURN POLICY:

25% of an order may be returned within
one year. Prior written permission is
required. Address for returns: 7307
MacArthur Blvd, Ste. 213/Bethesda, MD
20816.

SHIPPING AND BILLING POLICY:

Libraries are charged shipping. Invoices
are sent with shipments unless the
library specifies otherwise.

BACK ORDER POLICY:

Back orders are shipped when available.

SHAMBHALA PUBLICATIONS see RANDOM HOUSE,
INC.

SHAMELESS HUSSY PRESS

Box 5540
Berkeley, California 94705
Telephone: 415-547-1062

ADDRESS FOR ORDERS:

Same as above.

DISTRIBUTION/IMPRINTS:

Distributed by Inland and Bookpeople.

PREPAYMENT:

Not required.

DISCOUNT POLICY:

20% discount is offered.

RETURN POLICY:

Written permission is required.

SHIPPING AND BILLING POLICY:

Libraries are charged shipping plus
$1.00 handling on all orders. Invoices
are sent with shipments.

BACK ORDER POLICY:

Orders are held and filled as books are reprinted.

SPECIAL PLANS:

Publisher will consider special plans.

SHARON PUBLICATIONS

1086 Teaneck Road
Teaneck, New Jersey 07666
Telephone: 201-833-1800

ADDRESS FOR ORDERS:

Same as above.

DISTRIBUTION/IMPRINTS:

New American Library (NAL) distributes Sharon Star Books.

PREPAYMENT:

Prepayment is required for orders of $50.00 retail or less.

DISCOUNT POLICY:

25% discount to libraries.

RETURN POLICY:

Returns are accepted within one year. Libraries should obtain a return label from the Sales Department (201-833-1800).

SHIPPING AND BILLING POLICY:

Libraries are charged shipping (FOB New Jersey - USPS or UPS depending upon library's requirements). Invoices are sent with smaller shipments; for larger orders, invoices are sent separately within 10 days of shipping.

BACK ORDER POLICY:

Publisher holds orders unless or until library instructs otherwise.

M. E. SHARPE, INC.

---

80 Business Park Drive
Armonk, New York 10504
Telephone: 914-273-1800

ADDRESS FOR ORDERS:

Same as above.

DISTRIBUTION/IMPRINTS:

Distributes publications of: Australian National University; Contemporary China Center.

PREPAYMENT:

Not required.

DISCOUNT POLICY:

No discount to libraries.

RETURN POLICY:

Returns, in salable condition, are accepted up to six months of invoice date. Prior written permission is required.

SHIPPING AND BILLING POLICY:

Libraries are charged postage/handling charges of $2.00 (1-3 books) or $4.00 (4 or more books). Special arrangements such as UPS or first class mail are extra. Invoices are sent separately.

BACK ORDER POLICY:

Publisher will back-order at library's request.

SPECIAL PLANS:

Standing order plans for specific subject areas are available.

SHELBY HOUSE see ST. LUKES PRESS

SHENGOLD PUBLISHERS, INC.

---

23 West 45th Street
New York, New York 10036
Telephone: 212-944-2555

ADDRESS FOR ORDERS:

Same as above.

PREPAYMENT:

Prepayment is required for orders under $35.00.

DISCOUNT POLICY:

20% discount for two or more books.

RETURN POLICY:

Returns are accepted within 45 days. Written permission is required.

SHIPPING AND BILLING POLICY:

Libraries are charged shipping plus $0.50 handling per book. Invoices are sent with shipments.

BACK ORDER POLICY:

Publisher will back order up to 3 months.

SHEPHERD-WALWYN, LTD. see DUFOUR EDITIONS, INC.

SHERIDAN HOUSE

---

145 Palisade Street
Dobbs Ferry, New York 10522
Telephone: 914-693-2410

ADDRESS FOR ORDERS:

Same as above.

DISTRIBUTION/IMPRINTS:

Sheridan Medical Books (Division)

PREPAYMENT:

Not required, but appreciated for small orders.

DISCOUNT POLICY:

No discount to libraries.

RETURN POLICY:

Returns are accepted within 6 weeks after receipt. Permission is required.

SHIPPING AND BILLING POLICY:

Libraries are shipping except on prepaid orders which are shipped free. Invoices are sent as requested.

BACK ORDER POLICY:

Publisher will back order unless the order is cancelled.

SHERIDAN MEDICAL BOOKS see SHERIDAN HOUSE

SHOE STRING PRESS, INC.

---

925 Sherman Avenue
P.O. Box 4327
Hamden, Connecticut 06514
Telephone: 203-248-6307

ADDRESS FOR ORDERS:

Same as above.

DISTRIBUTION/IMPRINTS:

Distributes: Tompson & Butler (Grantham, NH).

Imprints: Archon Books; Library Professional Publications; Linnet.

PREPAYMENT:

Not required.

DISCOUNT POLICY:

No discount to libraries.

RETURN POLICY:

Returns are accepted within one year. Written permission is required.

SHIPPING AND BILLING POLICY:

Libraries are charged shipping and handling of $1.15 for the first book and $0.35 for each additional book on all orders. Invoices are sent with shipments unless the library specifies otherwise.

BACK ORDER POLICY:

Publisher back orders unavailable titles for one year unless the library instructs otherwise.

SIDEWINDER PRESS see BORGO PRESS

SIERRA CLUB BOOKS see RANDOM HOUSE, INC.

ELISABETH SIFTON BOOKS see VIKING PENGUIN INC.

SIMON & SCHUSTER, INC.

Gulf & Wstern Plaza
New York, New York 10023
Telephone: 212-373-8828

ADDRESS FOR ORDERS:

Simon & Schuster, Inc.
Order Department
200 Old Tappan Road
Old Tappan, NJ 07675

DISTRIBUTION/IMPRINT:

Simon & Schuster
The Linden Press
Fireside
Wanderer
Little Simon
Simon & Schuster Books for Young Readers
Prentice Hall Books for Young Readers

PREPAYMENT:

Not required.

DISCOUNT POLICY:

Library discount schedule for assorted books is as follows:

1 to 9 books	0%
10 to 24 books	25%
25 to 49 books	30%
50 to 99 books	33%
100 to 249 books	35%
250 or more books	40%

RETURN POLICY:

Publisher requests libraries to write to Customer Services Department (at the above address) for return permission. Books must be in salable condition. Customer Service Department sends return labels and instructions. When the publisher receives notification from the warehouse that the books have been received, a credit is issued to the library.

SHIPPING AND BILLING POLICY:

Libraries pay postage. There is no handling or billing charge. Invoices are sent separately after shipments. Packing slips are enclosed in shipments.

BACK ORDER POLICY:

Titles currently unavailable are either cancelled or back ordered according to library instructions.

SPECIAL ORDER PLAN:

Publisher offers a Greenaway standing order plan to libraries having an annual budget of $50,000 or having 10 branch libraries. Books are sent on a non-returnable basis well in advance of publication at a discount of 70% f.o.b. shipping point. Available options are:

Simon & Schuster cloth books
Simon & Schuster original paperback
Juvenile cloth
Juvenile original paperbacks
Cloth distribution lines
Paperback distribution lines

SIMON & SCHUSTER BOOKS FOR YOUNG READERS see SIMON & SCHUSTER

SINAUER ASSOCIATES, INC.

Sunderland, Massachusetts 01375-0407
Telephone: 413-665-3722

ADDRESS FOR ORDERS:

Same as above.

PREPAYMENT:

Not required.

DISCOUNT POLICY:

No discount for libraries.

RETURN POLICY:

Written permission is required for returns in resalable condition within one year of invoice date. Cash refunds available upon request. Invoice information must accompany returns which are shipped prepaid. A 10% penalty will be assessed on incorrect returns. Returns address is: Publishers Storage & Shipping Corporation/ 231 Industrial Park/ Fitchburg, MA 01420.

SHIPPING AND BILLING POLICY:

Shipping charges are paid by publisher on all North America orders. There is a $3.00 charge for RUSH orders telephoned to the warehouse. Invoices are sent with the shipments if total is known; otherwise, they are sent separately.

BACK ORDER POLICY:

Items are placed on back order and the library is offered the option to cancel.

_____

SIRIUS QUALITY PAPERBACKS see SALEM HOUSE PUBLISHERS

_____

SKYLINE PRESS see INDEPENDENT PUBLISHERS GROUP

_____

SKYPRINTS CORP see AVIATION BOOK COMPANY

_____

SLAVICA PUBLISHERS, INC.

P.O. Box 14388
Columbus, Ohio 43214-0388
Telephone: 614-268-4002

ADDRESS FOR ORDERS:

Same as above.

DISTRIBUTION:

Distributes Yale Russian and East European Publications.

PREPAYMENT:

Not required unless library has failed to pay past invoices on time.

DISCOUNT POLICY:

10% discount on a single book or journal; 20% on two or more.

RETURN POLICY:

Returns are accepted within six months. Prior written permission is required.

SHIPPING AND BILLING POLICY:

Libraries are charged actual postage on billed orders; prepaid orders have a flat $2.00 charge. Invoice are sent with shipments unless otherwise requested.

BACK ORDER POLICY:

Back orders are placed for items that are out-of-stock or to be reprinted and shipped when available.

STANDING ORDER PLANS:

Standing order plan available at usual discounts and shipping charges.

_____

SLEEPY HOLLOW PRESS see INDEPENDENT PUBLISHERS GROUP

_____

SMART LUCK see COMMUNICATION CREATIVITY

_____

SMITHSONIAN EXPOSITION BOOKS see W. W. NORTON AND COMPANY, INC.

_____

SMITHSONIAN INSTITUTION PRESS
_____

955 L'Enfant Plaza, Room 2100

Washington, D.C. 20560
Telephone: 202-287-3738

ADDRESS FOR ORDERS:

Smithsonian Press
Customer Service
P.O. Box 900
Blue Ridge Summit, PA 17214
Telephone: 717-794-2148

DISTRIBUTION/IMPRINTS:

Distributes the publications of: Freer
Gallery of Art; National Archives.

PREPAYMENT:

Not required.

DISCOUNT POLICY:

No discount to libraries.

RETURN POLICY:

Returns are accepted within one year.
Written permission is required.
Posters are not returnable. Address for
returns: c/o TAB Books/13347 Blue Ridge
Ave/Blue Ridge Summit, PA 17214.

SHIPPING AND BILLING POLICY:

Libraries are charged shipping. Invoices
are sent with shipments unless the
library specifies otherwise.

BACK ORDER POLICY:

Publisher will back order titles and
notify library. Books will be kept on
back order until they are shipped or the
order is cancelled.

SNOW LION PUBLICATIONS, INC.

---

110 N. Geneva
P.O. Box 6483
Ithaca, New York 14851
Telephone: 607-273-8506

ADDRESS FOR ORDERS:

Same as above.

PREPAYMENT:

Not required.

DISCOUNT POLICY:

No discount to libraries.

RETURN POLICY:

Books in original condition may be
returned at any time without permission.
Address for returns: 408 E. State St/PO
Box 6483/Ithaca, NY 14851.

SHIPPING AND BILLING POLICY:

Libraries are charged shipping plus
$1.00 handling on large orders. Invoices
are sent separately unless the library
specifies otherwise.

BACK ORDER POLICY:

Back orders are placed automatically,
the library is notified, and the books
are shipped and billed when available.

SPECIAL PLANS:

Standing orders are accepted.

SOCIETY OF AUTOMOTIVE ENGINEERS (SAE)

---

400 Commonwealth Drive
Warrendale, Pennsylvania 15096
Telephone: 412-776-4841

ADDRESS FOR ORDERS:

Same as above.
Telephone: 412-776-4970

DISTRIBUTION/IMPRINTS:

Publisher distributes: Mechanical
Engineering Publications (MEP), England;
Coordinating Research Council (CRC).

PREPAYMENT:

Not required.

DISCOUNT POLICY:

No discounts offered.

RETURN POLICY:

Returns accepted only for incorrect or
damaged shipments, within six months for

overseas orders and three months for
domestic.

SHIPPING AND BILLING POLICY:

Publisher pays for third class shipping
charges and will ship by any method
requested, at library's expense.
Invoices are sent with shipments.
Handling charges are assessed on invoice
totals as follows:

Up to $14.99:	$4.00
$15-29.99:	$4.50
$30-49.99:	$5.50
$50-74.99:	$6.50
$75-99.99:	$7.50
$100-149.99:	$8.50
$150-199.99:	$10.00
$200+:	$11.00

SPECIAL PLANS:

Standing order plans available for
various categories of publications.
Material is available upon request.
Deposit accounts offer 20% discount from
list prices.

OTHER:

When ordering a paper, libraries should
indicate the paper number and, where
applicable, the SP or P number of the
book in which the paper appears.

SOLDIER CREEK PRESS

P.O. Drawer U
Lake Crystal, Minnesota 56055
Telephone: 612-873-6620
          507-726-2985 (evenings)

ADDRESS FOR ORDERS:

Same as above.

PREPAYMENT:

Not required.

DISCOUNT POLICY:

20% discount if 10 or more copies of any
one title are ordered.

RETURN POLICY:

Returns With a letter of explanation are
accepted within one year. Written
permission is not required.

SHIPPING AND BILLING POLICY:

Libraries are charged shipping of $2.00
per book except on prepaid orders which
are shipped free. Invoices are sent with
shipments unless the library specifies
otherwise.

BACK ORDER POLICY:

Publisher will hold orders.

SOLIDARITY PUBLICATIONS see NEW AMERICAS
PRESS

SORRENTO PRESS see JALMAR PRESS

SOURCE DOCUMENT MANAGEMENT SERVICE see
LIBRARIES UNLIMITED

SOUTH CAROLINA HISTORICAL SOCIETY see
REPRINT COMPANY, PUBLISHERS

SOUTH-WESTERN PUBLISHING COMPANY

5101 Madison Road
Cincinnati, Ohio 45227
Telephone: 800-543-8444

ADDRESS FOR ORDERS:

Same as above.

PREPAYMENT:

Prepayment is required for orders
totalling less than $25 unless an open
account has been established previously.
Include a $3 charge to cover handling and
transportation. Check or money order
should be submitted with the order.

DISCOUNT POLICY:

South-Western sells materials to
libraries at the following discount:

    1 to 5 copies   list price

  6 to 10 copies   10%
  11 or more copies   20%

The above prices apply in the U.S. and
territories served by the publisher's own
offices.

RETURN POLICY:

South-Western will accept 100% returns of
its textbooks and materials without prior
authorization* provided the materials are
returned within 18 months of the invoice
date, accompanied by a copy of the
original invoice, are returned postpaid
to the office from which they were
purchased, are in salable condition.
South-Western must be notified of any
damaged or defective materials within 60
days of date of shipment. *All returns
from libraries outside the U.S. must have
prior authorization.

SHIPPING AND BILLING POLICY:

Libraries pay shipping charges. Books
are accompanied by packing slips.
Invoices are sent separately after
shipments. Terms are 30 days net from
date of sale.

RETURN POLICY:

No written permission is required. Books
of non-current editions are not
returnable. Libraries must return books
within 18 months from invoice date,
giving invoice number, price, and
discount for each title returned. Books
received after 18 months deadline will be
returned to sender or destroyed. Books
without complete information will be
credited at 50% of list. The address
for returns is the same as for orders.
If sending return by UPS, address it to:
Southern Illinois University Press,
McLafferty Road, Carbondale, Illinois
62901.

SHIPPING AND BILLING POLICY:

Libraries pay shipping charges. There is
no handling or billing charge. Invoices
are sent either separately or with
shipments as library requests.

BACK ORDER POLICY:

Titles not currently available are either
back ordered or cancelled as library
requests.

SOUTHERN BOOKS COMPANY see GENEALOGICAL
PUBLISHING COMPANY

SOUTHERN ILLINOIS UNIVERSITY PRESS

P.O. Box 3697
Carbondale, Illinois 62902-3697
Telephone: 618-453-2281

ADDRESS FOR ORDERS:

Same as above.

DISTRIBUTION/IMPRINT:

Arcturus Books (imprint)
Pleiades Records (imprint)

PREPAYMENT:

Not required.

DISCOUNT POLICY:

Libraries receive a 10% discount on
standing orders only.

SOUTHERN INSTITUTE PRESS see METAMORPHOUS
PRESS, INC.

SOUTHERN METHODIST UNIVERSITY PRESS see
TEXAS A & M UNIVERSITY PRESS

SPECTRUM BOOKS see PRENTICE-HALL

SPHINX PRESS see INTERNATIONAL UNIVERSITY
PRESS, INC.

SPIRE see FLEMING H. REVELL COMPANY

SPOKEN LANGUAGE SERVICES, INC.

P.O. Box 783

Ithaca, New York 14851
Telephone: 607-257-0500

ADDRESS FOR ORDERS:

Same as above.

PREPAYMENT:

Prepayment is required unless an account
has been established.

DISCOUNT POLICY:

10% discount to libraries.

RETURN POLICY:

Returns are accepted within 6 months.
Permission is required. Audio cassettes
are not returnable. Address for returns:
107 Hanshaw Road/Ithaca, NY 14850.

SHIPPING AND BILLING POLICY:

Libraries are charged shipping. Invoices
are sent with prepaid shipments and
separately otherwise.

BACK ORDER POLICY:

Publisher back orders temporarily-out-
of-stock items only.

OTHER:

Publisher requests that libraries use
correct ISBN's on orders.

SPOKESMAN PRESS see DUFOUR EDITIONS, INC.

SPRING PUBLICATIONS, INC

P.O. Box 222069
Dallas, Texas 75222
Telephone: 214-943-4093

ADDRESS FOR ORDERS:

Same as above.

DISTRIBUTION/IMPRINTS:

Distributes: Dallas Institute
Publications.

PREPAYMENT:

Prepayment is required on single title
orders.

DISCOUNT POLICY:

There is a 15% discount on any size
order.

RETURN POLICY:

Returns are accepted within one year of
purchase date. Written permission is
required. Invoice information must
accompany resalable returns which should
be sent with postage prepaid.
Return address for UPS: Spring
Publications/408 North Bishop
#108/Dallas, TX 75208.

SHIPPING AND BILLING POLICY:

Libraries are charged shipping except on
prepaid orders in which case charges are
waived. Invoices are sent with shipments
unless the library specifies otherwise.

BACK ORDER POLICY:

Publisher notifies library of back
orders and gives an approximate
availability date.

SPECIAL PLANS:

Standing order plan available for
publisher's journal title.

SPRINGER-VERLAG NEW YORK, INC.

---

175 Fifth Avenue
New York, New York 10010
Telephone: 212-673-2660

ADDRESS FOR ORDERS:

Same as above.

PREPAYMENT:

Not required.

DISCOUNT POLICY:

There is no discount for library orders
unless the ordering library is a member
of any publisher's special plans.

RETURN POLICY:

No returns are accepted without expressed permission of the publisher. Books must be in resalable condition. All return requests must indicate invoice number to facilitate processing. Where this information is not supplied, the publisher imposes a penalty of 10%. No returns will be accepted after 12 months from the date of invoice. The address for returns is: Springer-Verlag New York, 44 Hartz Way, Secaucus, NJ 07094.

SHIPPING AND BILLING POLICY:

Libraries pay postage. Invoices are sent before the shipment arrives.

BACK ORDER POLICY:

Titles not currently available are reported and back ordered, unless library requests otherwise.

SPECIAL ORDER PLAN:

There are two means by which a library may obtain a discount from the publisher.

The Library Approval Plan enables a library to obtain a 15% discount on all recently published titles except for main handbooks for which a 10% discount is available. To enroll in this plan, a library must agree to accept upon publication all titles within a major subject area, for example, medicine. A library may limit the type of publication by restricting the individualized profile to only monographs. All titles are received on approval and any titles may be returned for full credit. Books should not be returned after one year. Another means by which a library can receive a 10% discount on major handbooks is via Library Prepayment Plan. In addition a 15% discount is supplied to any series ordered on a standing order basis. The plan allows a library to prepay the established cost of any one of major handbooks--the Beilstein, Gmelin or Landolt-Boernstein. The library will receive each new volume automatically upon publication. Thirty days before the termination date of prepayment period a new prepayment quote will be sent to the library.

SPRINGHOUSE PUBLISHING COMPANY

1111 Bethlehem Pike
Springhouse, Pennsylvania 19477
Telephone: 215-646-8700

ADDRESS FOR ORDERS:

Same as above.

DISTRIBUTION/IMPRINTS:

Publications are available through the following medical wholesalers: J. A. Majors; Login Brothers; Matthews Book Co.; Rittenhouse. NACS members can order specific titles from NACSCORP/528 E. Lorain St/Oberlin, OH 44074.

PREPAYMENT:

Not required.

DISCOUNT POLICY:

Libraries should contact local sales representatives for information on discounts and order plans.

RETURN POLICY:

Returns in salable condition and still in print are accepted. Returns must be sent with postage prepaid and accompanied by original invoice for full credit. Address for returns: Springhouse Publishing Co/705 E. Union/ West Chester, PA 19382.

OTHER:

Libraries should contact local sales representatives for more information.

SPIRITUAL COMMUNITY PUBLICATIONS see BORGO PRESS

STACKPOLE BOOKS

P.O. Box 1831
Cameron and Kelker Streets
Harrisburg, Pennsylvania 17105
Telephone: 800-732-3669
        717-234-5091

ADDRESS FOR ORDERS:

Same as above.

DISTRIBUTION/IMPRINT:

Outdoor Life Books
Asprey
Blue J Publishers

Madrigal Publishing Company
Phoenix Militaria
Billart Publishing

PREPAYMENT:

Not required.

DISCOUNT POLICY:

Library discount schedule is as follows.
This is for assorted titles and hardcover
and paperback books may be combined for
quantity discount.

1 to 4 books	20%
5 to 24 books	40%
25 to 99 books	43%
100 or more	46%

RETURN POLICY:

Publisher accepts returns of damaged
books in shipment for replacement. The
address for returns is the same as for
orders.

SHIPPING AND BILLING POLICY:

Libraries pay shipping charges. Invoices
are included with shipments. There is no
handling charge or billing charge.

BACK ORDER POLICY:

Titles not available are automatically
back ordered unless library instructs
otherwise.

STAR PUBLICATIONS see TRILLIUM PRESS,
INC.

STAR PUBLISHING COMPANY

---

940 Emmett Avenue
Belmont, California 94002
Telephone: 415-591-3505

ADDRESS FOR ORDERS:

Star Publishing Co.
P.O. Box 68
Belmont, CA 94002-0068

PREPAYMENT:

Not required.

DISCOUNT POLICY:

20% discount to libraries.

RETURN POLICY:

Returns are accepted within 90 days.
Prior written permission is required.

SHIPPING AND BILLING POLICY:

Publisher pays shipping on prepaid
orders; others billed for actual
postage. Invoices are sent separately
unless the library specifies otherwise.

BACK ORDER POLICY:

Back orders are held and the library is
notified of availability.

STARMONT HOUSE see BORGO PRESS

STARRHILL PRESS

P.O. Box 32342
Washington, D.C. 20007

ADDRESS FOR ORDERS:

Same as above.

PREPAYMENT:

Not required.

DISCOUNT POLICY:

No discount on single copies; 50%
discount on a minimum order of 12 copies.

RETURN POLICY:

No returns are accepted.

SHIPPING AND BILLING POLICY:

Libraries are charged shipping (UPS)
except on prepaid orders which are
shipped free. Invoices are sent with
shipments.

BACK ORDER POLICY:

All books are available.

STECK-VAUGHN COMPANY

3520 Executive Center Drive
Austin, Texas 78731
Telephone: 512-343-8227

ADDRESS FOR ORDERS:

Same as above.
Telephone: 800-531-5015
          800-252-9317 (in Texas)

PREPAYMENT:

Orders totaling less than $50 should be accompanied by payment in full. Cash payments should include state tax (if applicable) and an 8% shipping/handling charge.

DISCOUNT POLICY:

Prices listed in the catalog reflect educational discount; there is no further discount.

RETURN POLICY:

Current edition of books in salable condition may be returned for exchange or credit within 30 days of purchase. Prior approval from the credit department is required. Transportation charges must be paid by the library and the books sent insured. To receive proper credit, a letter of explanation and packing slip are requested in the shipment.

SHIPPING AND BILLING POLICY:

Steck-Vaughn will determine the fastest and most economical shipping method. Shipping charges will be added to the invoice.

BACK ORDER POLICY:

Titles not available are reported and back ordered or cancelled according to library's instruction.

STERLING PUBLISHING COMPANY, INC

Two Park Avenue
New York, New York 10016
Telephone: 212-532-7160

ADDRESS FOR ORDERS:

Same as above.

DISTRIBUTION/IMPRINTS:

Publisher distributes: Aquarian Press; Blandford Press; David & Charles; Davis Publications; Dawnwood Press; BBC; Guinness Superlatives; Summerhill Publications; Athletic Institute; Javelin; Patrick Stephens; Lark; Arms & Armour; Cassell; Thorsons; Turnstone Press; Sun Design.

PREPAYMENT:

Required for orders under $40.00.

DISCOUNT POLICY:

20% discount to libraries.

RETURN POLICY:

Permission is required within 30 days of receipt. Non-returnable items are the Guinness Book of World Records, prepaid books, and annual catalogs. Address for returns: Sterling Publications/ Shipping and Receiving/ 900 Magnolia Avenue/ Elizabeth, New Jersey 07201.

SHIPPING AND BILLING POLICY:

Libraries are charged actual shipping. Invoices are sent with shipments unless the library specifies otherwise.

BACK ORDER POLICY:

Publisher back orders unavailable titles and ships books when they become available unless the library instructs otherwise.

PATRICK STEPHENS see STERLING PUBLISHING COMPANY, INC.

STEWART, TABORI & CHANG, INC.

---

740 Broadway
New York, New York 10003

Telephone: 212-460-5000

ADDRESS FOR ORDERS:

Workman Publishing
1 West 39 Street
New York, New York 10018
Telephone: 212-398-9160
         800-722-7202

DISTRIBUTION/IMPRINTS:

Distributed by Workman Publishing.

PREPAYMENT:

Not required.

DISCOUNT POLICY:

45% discount to libraries for any
quantity (net 30 days; non-returnable).

RETURN POLICY:

Titles are returnable only through
wholesalers. Titles ordered direct are
non-returnable.

SHIPPING AND BILLING POLICY:

Libraries are charged shipping on all
orders. Invoices are sent separately.

STILLPOINT PUBLISHING see E. P. DUTTON

STONE WALL PRESS, INC.

1241 30th Street NW
Washington, D.C. 20007
Telephone: 202-333-1860

ADDRESS FOR ORDERS:

Same as above.

DISTRIBUTION/IMPRINTS:

Distributed by Johnson Books (Boulder,
CO), but publisher will accept small
orders direct.

PREPAYMENT:

Prepayment is required for direct orders.

DISCOUNT POLICY:

20% discount is offered.

RETURN POLICY:

No returns are accepted for direct
orders.

SHIPPING AND BILLING POLICY:

Publisher pays shipping (at Library
Rate) on prepaid orders.

STRAVON EDUCATIONAL PRESS

845 Third Avenue
New York, New York 10022
Telephone: 212-371-2880

ADDRESS FOR ORDERS:

Same as above.

DISTRIBUTION:

None.

PREPAYMENT:

Not required.

DISCOUNT POLICY:

No discount to libraries.

RETURN POLICY:

All books are returnable within six
months. Prior written permission is
required.

SHIPPING AND BILLING POLICY:

Actual postage or UPS charges are added
to both prepaid and billed orders.
Invoices are sent with shipments unless
requested otherwise.

BACK ORDER POLICY:

Library is notified when a book is
available and should re-order at that
time.

SUFI PUBLISHING see HUNTER HOUSE, INC., PUBLISHERS

SUMMA PUBLICATIONS, INC.

P.O. Box 20725
Birmingham, Alabama 35216
Telephone: 205-822-0463

ADDRESS FOR ORDERS:

Same as above.

PREPAYMENT:

Not required.

DISCOUNT POLICY:

30% discount on orders over $500.00

RETURN POLICY:

Returns are permitted within 6 months of invoice date only if books are damaged or if the incorrect volume was shipped.

SHIPPING AND BILLING POLICY:

Libraries are charged shipping/handling of $1.75 for the first book and $0.75 for each additional book. Invoices are sent with shipments unless the library specifies otherwise.

BACK ORDER POLICY:

Back orders are placed, and the books are shipped when available.

SPECIAL PLANS:

Standing order plan is offered at a 20% discount.

SUMMERHILL PUBLICATIONS see STERLING PUBLISHING COMPANY, INC.

SUMMIT PRESS see ARTHUR H. CLARK COMPANY

SUN DANCE PRESS see BORGO PRESS

SUN DESIGN see STERLING PUBLISHING COMPANY, INC.

SUN TRACKS see UNIVERSITY OF ARIZONA PRESS

SUNDIAL see SUNSTONE PRESS

SUNSTONE PRESS

P.O. Box 2321
Santa Fe, New Mexico 87504-2321
Telephone: 505-988-4418

ADDRESS FOR ORDERS:

Same as above.

DISTRIBUTION/IMPRINTS:

Distributes Sundial imprint.

PREPAYMENT:

Not required.

DISCOUNT POLICY:

20% discount given to libraries.

RETURN POLICY:

Books returned must be unmarked and have no labels or stickers. Returns are accepted within 90 days.

SHIPPING AND BILLING POLICY:

Libraries are charged shipping. Invoices are sent with shipments.

BACK ORDER POLICY:

Back orders are accepted.

STANDING ORDER PLANS:

Standing order plan is available - books
are shipped when published, at the usual
discount.

SURREY BOOKS

500 North Michigan Avenue, #1940
Chicago, Illinois 60611
Telephone: 312-661-0050

ADDRESS FOR ORDERS:

Same as above.

PREPAYMENT:

Prepayment required for orders under 5
copies.

DISCOUNT POLICY:

1-4 copies: no discount
5-24 copies: 20%
over 25:   40%

RETURN POLICY:

Written permission is required on
returns of more than 5 copies. Books in
salable condition are accepted within
one year of the date of shipment.

SHIPPING AND BILLING POLICY:

Shipping charges on all orders are $1.50
on first book and $0.50 for each
additional book. Invoices are sent with
shipments unless a separate bill-to
address is requested.

BACK ORDER POLICY:

Orders are placed on back order and
shipped when available.

SUSQUEHANNA UNIVERSITY PRESS see
ASSOCIATED UNIVERSITY PRESSES

SWALLOW PRESS see OHIO UNIVERSITY/SWALLOW
PRESS

SYNTONY see METAMORPHOUS PRESS, INC.

SYRACUSE UNIVERSITY PRESS

1600 Jamesville Avenue
Syracuse, New York 13244-5160
Telephone: 315-423-2596

ADDRESS FOR ORDERS:

Same as above.

DISTRIBUTION/IMPRINTS:

Distributes publications of: American
University of Beirut; Union College
Press; Shiloah Institute (Tel-Aviv
University, Israel); Foreign and
Comparative Studies (Syracuse
University).

PREPAYMENT:

Not required.

DISCOUNT POLICY:

10% discount given to libraries.

RETURN POLICY:

Requests for returns must specify date
and number of invoice. Books may be
returned no earlier than three months
and no later than twelve months from
date of invoice. Books returned must be
in salable condition. Prior permission
is requested, but not required.

SHIPPING AND BILLING POLICY:

Shipping costs plus handling charge of
$.50 per book to a maximum of $2.00 per
invoice charged on both billed and
prepaid orders. Invoices are sent with
shipments unless otherwise requested.

BACK ORDER POLICY:

Publisher back orders and notifies
customer.

T. J. PUBLISHERS, INC.

817 Silver Spring Avenue, Suite 206
Silver Spring, Maryland 20910
Telephone: 301-585-4440

ADDRESS FOR ORDERS:

Same as above.

PREPAYMENT:

Prepayment is required on first orders
only.

DISCOUNT POLICY:

1-4 copies: 10%
5-25:   15%
26-49:   20%
50-99:   25%
100-149:   30%
over 150:   40%

RETURN POLICY:

Returns, in salable condition and
accompanied by the invoice number and
date, are accepted within 9 months of
invoice date. There is a 10% return
charge except for defective materials.
Written permission is required.
Videotapes are not returnable.

SHIPPING AND BILLING POLICY:

Libraries are charged shipping. Invoices
are sent separately.

BACK ORDER POLICY:

Titles will be back ordered until
received in stock unless the library
specifies otherwise.

TBW BOOKS, INC.

36 Old Mill Road
Falmouth, Maine 04105
Telephone: 207-781-3002

ADDRESS FOR ORDERS:

Same as above.

DISTRIBUTION/IMPRINT:

Kennebec River Press (distribution)

PREPAYMENT:

Not required, but would certainly find it
more convenient.

DISCOUNT POLICY:

Publisher offers a 20% discount for
library orders.

RETURN POLICY:

Libraries are asked to let the publisher
know that they wish to return book(s) and
request a shipping label. Returns are
limited to 90 days. The address for
returns is the same as for orders.

SHIPPING AND BILLING POLICY:

There is no shipping charge for prepaid
orders. Publisher charges shipping costs
to libraries for billed orders. The
amount depends on weight and size of the
books. Invoices are sent with shipment,
unless otherwise requested by library.

BACK ORDER POLICY:

Publisher notifies libraries when books
become available.

SPECIAL ORDER PLAN:

Publisher accepts standing orders from
libraries.

TCA PRODUCTIONS see AVIATION BOOK COMPANY

TPR see TAB BOOKS

TAB BOOKS

Blue Ridge Summit, Pennsylvania 17294-
    0850
Telephone: 717-794-2191

ADDRESS FOR ORDERS:

Same as above.
Telephone: 800-233-1128

DISTRIBUTION/IMPRINTS:

Distributes: Petrocelli Books, Inc.;
Self-Counsel Press.

Liberty House (Imprint)
Aero (Imprint)
Detail & Scale (Imprint)
TPR (Division)

PREPAYMENT:

Not required.

DISCOUNT POLICY:

Trade paperback

1-4 copies: 20%
5 or more: 40%

Trade Hardcover & Reference ("R" Class)

1-4 copies: 15%
5 or more: 25%

RETURN POLICY:

Books, in resalable condition, may be
returned after 120 days and before one
year from invoice date without prior
authorization. No original invoice or
discount information is needed. Returns
will be credited at the average discount
for each account as calculated once
every three months for purchases during
the previous 12-month period. Books
declared out of print may be returned
within 90 days of notice. Defective
books must be returned immediately for
replacement.

SHIPPING AND BILLING POLICY:

Books are shipped FOB Blue Ridge Summit,
and charges are added to invoices for
all orders. Invoices are sent with
shipments and will be sent separately
after shipments only if bill-to and
ship-to addresses are different.

BACK ORDER POLICY:

Back orders are handled as requested.
Items placed on back order will be
shipped as soon as they are available or
once monthly.

SPECIAL PLANS:

Standing orders receive a 40% discount
on paperbacks, 25% discount on
hardcovers, and 25% on class "R"
publications. All shipments are made on
a fully returnable basis. Standing orders
can be cancelled upon 30 days written
notice.

TABOR PUBLISHING

25115 Avenue Stanford
Suite 130
Valencia, California 91355 79
Telephone: 800-527-4747

ADDRESS FOR ORDERS:

Tabor Publishing (DLM)
One DLM Park
Allen, Texas 75002

DISTRIBUTION/IMPRINTS:

Publisher imprints: Sacred Hearts Kids'
Club; Hanna-Barbera; DeSales Program.

PREPAYMENT:

All orders under $25.00 must be prepaid,
including 8% shipping and handling and
appropriate sales tax.

DISCOUNT POLICY:

No discount offered.

RETURN POLICY:

Written permission is required for
returns in salable condition within 90
days of purchase. Invoice information
must be included along with the reason
for return. Shipments are to be sent
according to publisher's instructions at
library's expense.

SHIPPING AND BILLING POLICY:

Orders are sent by UPS unless a special
delivery service is requested. All
orders are subject to shipping charges.
Invoices are sent with shipments unless
otherwise specified.

BACK ORDER POLICY:

Items are placed on back order and
shipped when available.

TAFT GROUP

5130 MacArthur Blvd, NW
Washington, D.C. 20016
Telephone: 202-966-7086

ADDRESS FOR ORDERS:

Same as above.

PREPAYMENT:

Prepayment is required on all orders of less than $55.00.

DISCOUNT POLICY:

No specific discount to libraries.

RETURN POLICY:

Books in new condition may be returned within 60 days for refund or credit. Written permission is not required. Upon cancellation of subscription to newsletters, refunds will be given on remaining issues.

SHIPPING AND BILLING POLICY:

Shipping charges vary with each item as indicated in publisher's catalog; prepaid orders are shipped free. Invoices are sent with shipments unless the library specifies otherwise.

BACK ORDER POLICY:

All customers are notified in writing of items that are out of stock and are given the option to cancel the order or wait for shipment.

SPECIAL PLANS:

Standing orders are available for items on subscription at 5% discount.

TAI CHI FOUNDATION see CHARLES E. TUTTLE COMPANY, INC.

TALLTALES see ILLUMINATI

TANAM PRESS see MCPHERSON & COMPANY

TANNER LECTURES ON HUMAN VALUE see UNIVERSITY OF UTAH PRESS

JEREMY TARCHER, INC. see ST. MARTIN'S PRESS

TAVISTOCK see ROUTLEDGE, CHAPMAN AND HALL, INC.

R. J. TAYLOR, JR. FOUNDATION see REPRINT COMPANY, PUBLISHERS

TAYLOR & FRANCIS, INC.

---

242 Cherry Street
Philadelphia, Pennsylvania 19106-1906
Telephone: 215-238-0939

ADDRESS FOR ORDERS:

Same as above.
Telephone: 800-821-8312

DISTRIBUTION/IMPRINTS:

Publisher distributes: British Medical Association; Browcom Group Ltd.; Cassell Tycooly; Adam Hilger; British Institute of Physics; Japan Inter Press; Open University Press; Sell's Publications Ltd.; Editions Renyi Multilingual Matters; Swets Publishing .

Publisher imprints: Falmer Press; Crane Russak and Company; International Publications Service.

PREPAYMENT:

Not required with purchase order number.

DISCOUNT POLICY:

No discount for libraries.

RETURN POLICY:

Prior permission must be obtained for returns in resalable condition. Requests must cite the invoice number and reason for return. Returns will be accepted 90 days to one year from date of invoice on overstock and must include a copy of the invoice and the Return Authorization Number. Dated materials must be returned within 60 days of purchase. Transportation charges will not be credited, unless return is for damaged or misshipped items. Returns received without prior written approval and/or with incomplete invoice information will be processed with a 10% penalty.

SHIPPING AND BILLING POLICY:

Shipping/handling charges are applied to all orders as follows: $1.75 for first book, .50 for each additional book; 4% of order over $50.00. Packing slips are sent with shipments; invoices are sent separately.

BACK ORDER POLICY:

Unavailable materials are placed on back order indefinitely; however, library cancellation deadlines are adhered to.

SPECIAL PLANS:

Standing order plans are available for yearbooks, directories, and books in series only.

TAYLOR PUBLISHING COMPANY

1550 Mockingbird Lane
Dallas, Texas 75235
Telephone: 214-637-2800

ADDRESS FOR ORDERS:

Same as above
Telephone: 214-637-2800, ext. 589

DISTRIBUTION:

Distributes: Algonquin Books of Chapel Hill; Breitenbush Books; Menasha Ridge Books.

PREPAYMENT:

Prepayment is required for orders under $50.00.

DISCOUNT POLICY:

25% discount on all trade titles.

RETURN POLICY:

Returns are accepted not before six months and not later than two years from invoice date. Prior authorization is not required. Address for returns: Taylor

Publishing Company, 1525 Hinton St., Dallas, TX 75235.

SHIPPING AND BILLING POLICY:

Shipping is prepaid and added to the invoice unless otherwise requested. Invoices are sent separately after shipments only.

BACK ORDER POLICY:

Back orders are shipped automatically when available.

TEACH'EM, INC. see PLURIBUS PRESS

TEACHERS COLLEGE PRESS

1234 Amsterdam Avenue
New York, New York 10027
Telephone: 212-678-3929

ADDRESS FOR ORDERS:

Teachers College Press
P.O. Box 939
Wolfeboro, NH 03894

DISCOUNT POLICY:

There is no discount for library orders.

RETURN POLICY:

Returns must be authorized in writing and are allowed only within 12 months of invoice date. In order to receive authorization, invoice number and date must be furnished. Books must be prepaid and received in salable condition. Unauthorized returns in salable condition will be credited at the net invoice amount less 50%.

SHIPPING AND BILLING POLICY:

Libraries pay postage. Charges for insurance, special delivery, airmail, etc., are additional. A minimum shipping charge of $1.75 applies to all orders. Invoices are sent with shipments if shipping and billing address are the same. Otherwise, invoices are sent to billing address.

BACK ORDER POLICY:

Titles currently unavailable are reported
and back ordered.

TECHNOMIC PUBLISHING COMPANY, INC.

---

851 New Holland Avenue
Box 3535
Lancaster, Pennsylvania 17604
Telephone: 717-291-5609

ADDRESS FOR ORDERS:

Same as above.

PREPAYMENT:

Prepayment is required for orders of less
than $30.00 and orders from outside the
U.S.

DISCOUNT POLICY:

5-9 copies: 15%, etc.

RETURN POLICY:

Returns are accepted on stock orders or
textbook adoptions of five or more
copies.

SHIPPING AND BILLING POLICY:

No charge on prepaid orders. Shipping
charge is added to billed orders.
Invoices are sent with shipments unless
billing and shipping addresses are
different.

BACK ORDER POLICY:

Publisher holds orders until
publications are available unless
requested to do otherwise.

OTHER INFORMATION:

Publisher has acquired the entire
inventory of Ann Arbor Science titles.

TEMPLE UNIVERSITY PRESS

Broad and Oxford Street
Room 305 USB
Philadelphia, Pennsylvania 19122
Telephone: 215-787-8787

ADDRESS FOR ORDERS:

Temple University Press
Order Department
Broad and Oxford Street
Philadelphia, PA 19122

PREPAYMENT:

Prepayment is required except for
established accounts or where prepayment
is prohibited by state or local
restrictions.

DISCOUNT POLICY:

Libraries receive no discount.

RETURN POLICY:

Libraries must receive publisher's
permission before returning books. A
copy of original invoice must be
enclosed. Address for returns is:
Temple University Press Warehouse,
Traylor Building, Broad Street and Lehigh
Avenue, 7th Floor, Philadelphia, PA
19122.

SHIPPING AND BILLING POLICY:

Libraries pay shipping charges. Invoices
are sent with shipments.

BACK ORDER POLICY:

Not-yet-published and out-of-stock titles
are automatically back ordered unless
otherwise stated in order. Library
receives acknowledgement indicating back
order status.

TEN SPEED PRESS

Box 7123
Berkeley, California 94707
Telephone: 415-845-8414
          415-524-1801
          415-524-1052 (FAX)

ADDRESS FOR ORDERS:

Same as above.

DISTRIBUTION/IMPRINTS:

Celestial Arts (Subsidiary)

PREPAYMENT:

Required for small amounts (under ten copies).

DISCOUNT POLICY:

Libraries with established credit are given trade discounts.

RETURN POLICY:

Returns accepted within one year of purchase. Prior permission is not required. Address for returns: 1303 Ninth St.,/Berkeley, CA 94710.

SHIPPING AND BILLING POLICY:

Libraries are charged shipping. Invoices are sent with shipments.

BACK ORDER POLICY:

Publisher back-orders new books.

TESORO BOOKS see PARAGON HOUSE PUBLISHING

TETRA PRESS see HOWELL BOOK HOUSE, INC.

TEXAS A & M UNIVERSITY PRESS

Drawer C
College Station, Texas 77843
Telephone: 409-845-1436

ADDRESS FOR ORDERS:

Same as above.

DISTRIBUTION/IMPRINTS:

Distributes the publications of: Texas Christian University Press; Southern Methodist University Press; Texas State Historical Association; Rice University Press; San Jacinto Publishing Company.

PREPAYMENT:

Not required.

DISCOUNT POLICY:

20% discount to libraries.

RETURN POLICY:

Books may be returned with a written explanation of the reason for return. Damaged books may be returned within one year; time limits for others depend upon circumstances.

SHIPPING AND BILLING POLICY:

Libraries are charged shipping on all orders. Invoices are sent with shipments unless the library specifies otherwise.

BACK ORDER POLICY:

Back orders are logged in the computer file at time of receipt; invoices accompany books when shipped.

SPECIAL PLANS:

Standing orders, at a 20% discount, may be placed for all books on publisher's list or all books in selected subjects.

TEXAS CHRISTIAN UNIVERSITY PRESS see TEXAS A & M UNIVERSITY PRESS

TEXAS STATE HISTORICAL ASSOCIATION see TEXAS A & M UNIVERSITY PRESS

THAMES AND HUDSON INC. see W. W. NORTON AND COMPANY, INC.

THEATRE ARTS see ROUTLEDGE, CHAPMAN AND HALL, INC.

THEATRE COMMUNICATIONS GROUP

355 Lexington Avenue
New York, New York 10017
Telephone: 212-697-5230

ADDRESS FOR ORDERS:

Same as above.

Attn: Order Dept.

PREPAYMENT:

Prepayment is required on orders under $15.00.

DISCOUNT POLICY:

1-4 books: 10% discount
5 or more: 20% discount

RETURN POLICY:

Written permission is not necessary. Books returned must still be in print, and a packing slip indicating titles, quantities, invoice dates and numbers must accompany the returns which should be sent with postage prepaid.

SHIPPING AND BILLING POLICY:

Actual shipping costs are invoiced for orders of over $15.00; for orders under $15.00 the following charges are added: orders of $2.00-$7.00 add $1.50; orders of $7.01-$15.00 add $2.00. Invoices are sent separately.

BACK ORDER POLICY:

Orders for titles not yet published or temporarily out of stock will be back ordered unless the library indicates otherwise.

THEOSOPHICAL PUBLISHING HOUSE

---

306 W. Geneva Road
Wheaton, Illinois 60187
Telephone: 800-654-9430

ADDRESS FOR ORDERS:

Same as above.

DISTRIBUTION/IMPRINTS:

Quest Books (Trade paperback imprint)
The Quest (Quarterly metaphysical magazine)

PREPAYMENT:

Not required with established credit.

DISCOUNT POLICY:

1-4 books: 20%

5-24:   40%

RETURN POLICY:

Written permission to return is required; requests should include invoice number and date.

SHIPPING AND BILLING POLICY:

Publisher pays shipping on orders of 5 or more books and charges freight only on lesser orders. Invoices are sent with shipments.

BACK ORDER POLICY:

Publisher will notify library of back orders.

CHARLES C. THOMAS, PUBLISHER

P.O. Box 19265
2600 South First Street
Springfield, Illinois 62794-9265
Telephone: 217-789-8980

ADDRESS FOR ORDERS:

Same as above.

PREPAYMENT:

Prepayment is required only on pro-forma accounts.

DISCOUNT POLICY:

10% discount to libraries.

RETURN POLICY:

Returns in salable condition are accepted within 6 months from invoice date. Written permission is required. Out-of-print titles or old editions and printings are not returnable.

SHIPPING AND BILLING POLICY:

Libraries are charged shipping of $2.25 minimum or 3% (UPS, etc. are extra) except on prepaid orders which are shipped free. Invoices are sent with shipments unless the library specifies otherwise.

BACK ORDER POLICY:

Publisher back orders upon request.

SPECIAL PLANS:

A publisher standing order is available upon request.

THREE CONTINENTS PRESS, INC.

1636 Connecticut Avenue, N.W.
Suite 501
Washington, D.C. 20009
Telephone: 202-332-3885
            202-332-3886

ADDRESS FOR ORDERS:

Same as above.

DISTRIBUTION/IMPRINTS:

Publisher distributes: Graham Brash (Singapore); Outrigger (New Zealand); Forest Books (London); Post-Apollo Press (California); Jahan Book Co. (California); Literature East & West (Texas).

PREPAYMENT:

Not required.

DISCOUNT POLICY:

No discount on single-book orders; 20% on orders of 2 or more books.

RETURN POLICY:

Written permission is required for return of books in mint condition for credit only (no cash refund). A 25% restocking fee is deducted unless the return is due to publisher error. Books no longer distributed by publisher are considered non-returnable.

SHIPPING AND BILLING POLICY:

Exact shipping costs are charged on all orders. Invoices are sent with shipments unless otherwise requested.

BACK ORDER POLICY:

Books are back ordered, and routine notices of availability citing PO number and date expected are sent.

SPECIAL PLANS:

Standing order plans are available for new titles at a 20% discount. Standing order plans may be selective; publisher can accommodate special requests.

TICKNOR & FIELDS see HOUGHTON MIFFLIN COMPANY

TIDEWATER PUBLISHERS see CORNELL MARITIME PRESS, INC.

TIMBER PRESS

9999 SW Wilshire
Portland, Oregon 97225
Telephone: 503-292-0745
            800-327-5680

ADDRESS FOR ORDERS:

Same as above.

DISTRIBUTION/IMPRINTS:

Affiliations: Dioscorides Press; Amadeus Press; Areopagitica Press.

PREPAYMENT:

Not required.

DISCOUNT POLICY:

No discount to libraries.

RETURN POLICY:

Returns are accepted within one year. Written permission is required.

SHIPPING AND BILLING POLICY:

Libraries are charged shipping (UPS) of $3.00 for the first book and $2.00 for each additional book. Invoices are sent with shipments unless the library specifies otherwise.

BACK ORDER POLICY:

Publisher back orders unless library instructs otherwise.

SPECIAL PLANS:

A standing order is available for
Horticultural Reviews and Plant Breeding
Reviews at a 15% discount.

TIME-LIFE BOOKS see LITTLE, BROWN AND
COMPANY

TIMES ATLAS OF WORLD HISTORY see HAMMOND
INCORPORATED

TIMES BOOKS see RANDOM HOUSE, INC.

TIOGA PUBLISHING COMPANY see WILLIAM
KAUFMANN, INC.

TOMBOUCTOU BOOKS see CITY LIGHTS BOOKS

TOMPSON & BUTLER see SHOE STRING PRESS,
INC.

TOOTHPASTE PRESS see COFFEE HOUSE PRESS

TOR BOOKS see ST. MARTIN'S PRESS

TOTLINE BOOKS see WARREN PUBLISHING
HOUSE, INC.

TRANSNATIONAL PUBLISHERS, INC.

P.O. Box 7282
Ardsley-on-Hudson, New York 10503
Telephone: 914-693-0089

ADDRESS FOR ORDERS:

Same as above.

PREPAYMENT:

Prepayment is not required, but prepaid
orders are shipped free of charge.

DISCOUNT POLICY:

No discount to libraries.

RETURN POLICY:

Books can be returned up to one year of
order date. Credit will be issued for
books returned in salable condition.
Written permission is required. Address
for returns: 22 Myrtle Avenue/Dobbs
Ferry, NY 10522.

SHIPPING AND BILLING POLICY:

Libraries are charged shipping/handling
of $2.40 for the first paperback, $3.20
for the first hardback ($3.90 for two
hardbacks, etc.). Invoices are usually
sent with shipments unless the library
specifies otherwise.

BACK ORDER POLICY:

Publisher holds orders and ships when
book is available.

SPECIAL PLANS:

Standing orders are available for series.

TREACLE PRESS see MCPHERSON & COMPANY

TRILLIUM PRESS, INC.

P.O. Box 209
Monroe, New York 10950
Telephone: 914-783-2999

ADDRESS FOR ORDERS:

Same as above.

DISTRIBUTION/IMPRINTS:

Distributes: Cloud 10 Publications; Star
Publications; KAV Publishing.

PREPAYMENT:

Not required.

DISCOUNT POLICY:

No discount to libraries.

RETURN POLICY:

Returns, in salable condition and with postage prepaid, are accepted within one week of receipt. Written permission is required. Address for returns: Trillium Press - Returns/247 High St/Box 209/ Monroe, NY 10950.

SHIPPING AND BILLING POLICY:

Libraries are charged shipping of $2.50 on orders up to $25.00 and 10% on orders over $25.00. Invoices are sent separately unless the library specifies otherwise.

BACK ORDER POLICY:

Back orders are placed, the library is notified, and the books are shipped and billed when available.

OTHER:

Orders are handled the same day they are received.

TRINITY UNIVERSITY PRESS

---

715 Stadium Drive
P.O. Box 97
San Antonio, Texas 78284
Telephone: 512-736-7619

ADDRESS FOR ORDERS:

Same as above.

PREPAYMENT:

Not required, but prepaid orders are shipped free.

DISCOUNT POLICY:

1-2 books: 25% discount
3 or more: 40%

RETURN POLICY:

Returns are accepted within one year. Written permission is required except in cases of publisher's error.

SHIPPING AND BILLING POLICY:

Libraries are charged shipping and handling of $0.50 for 1-2 books, $0.75 for 3-6 books, $1.00 for 6-10 books, and $1.25 for over 10 books except on prepaid orders which are shipped free. Invoices are sent with shipments unless the library specifies otherwise.

BACK ORDER POLICY:

Publisher back orders unavailable titles and ships books when they become available.

SPECIAL PLANS:

Standing orders are available.

TROLL ASSOCIATES

---

100 Corporate Drive
Mahwah, New Jersey 07430
Telephone: 800-526-5289

ADDRESS FOR ORDERS:

Same as above.

PREPAYMENT:

Not required.

DISCOUNT POLICY:

Library pays net price as shown in catalog for library editions. Publisher allows a 25% discount on orders of 50 or more assorted copies of paperback editions.

RETURN POLICY:

Libraries must write for permission, indicating publisher's invoice number, if they wish to return materials. Returns are limited to one year from date of purchase. The address for returns is the same as for orders.

SHIPPING AND BILLING POLICY:

Publisher charges a 5% shipping charge on all orders. This policy applies to both prepaid and billed orders. Publisher sends invoice separately after shipment unless library requests otherwise.

BACK ORDER POLICY:

Publisher back orders unavailable titles up to 90 days. Orders are cancelled after 90 days.

TUNDRA BOOKS OF NORTHERN NEW YORK

P.O. Box 1030
Plattsburgh, New York 12901

ADDRESS FOR ORDERS:

University of Toronto Press
340 Nagel Drive
Buffalo, New York 14225
Telephone: 716-683-4547

DISTRIBUTION/IMPRINTS:

University of Toronto Press distributes publisher's books.

PREPAYMENT:

Prepayment required on first order only, and is not necessary after an account has been established.

DISCOUNT POLICY:

Assorted or single titles:

1-4 copies: 25%
5-9 copies: 30%
10+ copies: 35%

Regional Library systems--Assorted or single titles:

All copies: 40%

RETURN POLICY:

Returns are accepted within one year. Written permission is required for returns of more than 100 books. Invoice information must accompany returns or a 5% penalty will be applied. Defective books must be so labeled.

SHIPPING AND BILLING POLICY:

Libraries are charged average shipping as follows: $2.00 for first book; $0.50 for each additional book. Invoices are sent with shipments unless the library specifies otherwise.

BACK ORDER POLICY:

Books are held on back order until the cancellation date specified by the library.

SPECIAL PLANS:

Publisher offers standing order plans which can be requested in writing.

TURNSTONE PRESS see STERLING PUBLISHING COMPANY, INC.

TURTLE ISLAND FOUNDATION see CITY LIGHTS BOOKS

TUSKEGEE AIRMEN INC. see AVIATION BOOK COMPANY

CHARLES E. TUTTLE COMPANY, INC.

---

28 South Main Street
P.O. Box 410
Rutland, Vermont 05701-0410
Telephone: 802-773-8930

ADDRESS FOR ORDERS:

Same as above.

DISTRIBUTION/IMPRINTS:

Distributes: John Weatherhill, Inc (Tokyo); Shufunotomo Co. (Tokyo); Academy Books; International Exhibitions Foundation; Tai Chi Foundation; Personally Oriented Ltd (Japan); Kosei Pub Co (Tokyo); CFW Publications (Hong Kong); Imagenes Press; Asia Society (NY); Seoul International; Hollym Corp (Seoul); Paperweight Press; Hong Kong Publishing Co; Dragon Publishing Co; Howard Publishing Co (Hong Kong); Travel Publishing Asia Lts (Hong Kong); Felix Morrow; Healing Tao Center (NY).

PREPAYMENT:

Not required.

DISCOUNT POLICY:

25% discount to libraries.

RETURN POLICY:

Returns are accepted within one year.
Address for returns: Charles E. Tuttle
Co/28 South Main St/Rutland, VT 05701.

SHIPPING AND BILLING POLICY:

Libraries are charged shipping on all
orders. Invoices are sent with shipments
unless the library specifies otherwise.

BACK ORDER POLICY:

Publisher back orders unavailable titles
for one year unless the library
instructs otherwise.

TWAYNE PUBLISHERS see G. K. HALL &
COMPANY

TWIN PEAKS PRESS

P. O. Box 129
Vancouver, Washington 98666
Telephone: 206-694-2462

ADDRESS FOR ORDERS:

Same as above.

PREPAYMENT:

Not required.

DISCOUNT POLICY:

No discount to libraries.

RETURN POLICY:

Publisher requires written permission on
all returns.

SHIPPING AND BILLING POLICY:

Shipping charges are added to invoices.
Invoices are sent with shipments unless
the library specifies otherwise.

TYNDALE HOUSE PUBLISHERS

---

336 Gundersen Drive
Wheaton, Illinois 60187
Telephone: 312-668-8300
           800-323-9400

ADDRESS FOR ORDERS:

Tyndale House Publishers
P.O. Box 80
Wheaton, Illinois 60187

PREPAYMENT:

Publisher prefers to receive payment with
orders.

DISCOUNT POLICY:

Book discount (excluding Bibles):

1-4 copies	25%
5-99 copies	40%
100-499 copies	43%
500-999 copies	44%
500 or more of one title	50%

Bible & Bible portions
(Assorted bindings & editions):

1-4 copies	25%
5-99 copies	40%
100-249 copies	41%
250-299 copies	42%
2500 or more	50%

RETURN POLICY:

No permission is necessary. Returned
materials must be clean, salable and free
of marks or labels. Only titles that are
listed on the current order form may be
returned for credit. Titles not listed
are out-of-print and are not returnable.
Titles coded on the order form with a dot
are scheduled out-of-print and are
likewise not returnable. Current order
forms are available upon request.
Incorrect titles received or materials
damaged in shipment must be reported
immediately and returned within 30 days.
A return packing slip must be enclosed
with each return shipment, giving
quantities, titles, and reason for
return. All returns must be sent post
paid to: Tyndale House Publishing
Returns, 351 Executive Drive, Carol
Streem, Illinois 60188.

SHIPPING AND BILLING POLICY:

Libraries pay shipping charges. There is
no handling charge. Invoices are sent
separately to the bill-to address.
Packing slips are enclosed with
shipments.

BACK ORDER POLICY:

Titles not currently available are either back ordered or cancelled as library requests.

OTHER INFORMATION:

Publisher specializes in scholarly books in the arts and humanities. All books are printed on acid-free paper. Libraries may order direct or through wholesalers.

UAHC PRESS see UNION OF AMERICAN HEBREW CONGREGATIONS

UMI RESEARCH PRESS

300 N. Zeeb Road
Ann Arbor, Michigan 48106
Phone: (313) 761-4700

ADDRESS FOR ORDERS:

Same as above.

PREPAYMENT:

Not required.

DISCOUNT POLICY:

10% discount on standing orders.

RETURN POLICY:

Books may be returned in undamaged and resalable condition within 90 days of purchase. Invoice or invoice number should be returned with books.
Address for returns: UMI Research Press/Attn: Customer Service/300 N. Zeeb Road/Ann Arbor, MI 48106.

SHIPPING AND BILLING POLICY:

Shipping and handling charged at $1.50 for the first copy and $.50 for each additional copy. Invoices are sent separately after shipment, but special requests are honored.

BACK ORDER POLICY:

Orders for out-of-stock items are automatically placed on back order unless otherwise specified.

STANDING ORDER PLANS:

Standing orders for established series are available at 10% discount.

UNESCO see UNIPUB

UNGAR see HARPER AND ROW, PUBLISHERS, INC.

UNICORN PRESS, INC.

P.O. Box 3307
Greensboro, North Carolina 27402
Telephone: 919-288-0822

ADDRESS FOR ORDERS:

Same as above.

PREPAYMENT:

Not required.

DISCOUNT POLICY:

10% discount to libraries.

RETURN POLICY:

No time limit on returns. Prior permission for a mailing label is requested.

SHIPPING AND BILLING POLICY:

Libraries are charged actual shipping. Invoices are sent with shipments unless the library specifies otherwise.

BACK ORDER POLICY:

Publisher accepts back orders.

OTHER:

All of publisher's books are sewn into signatures with real linen thread and printed on acid-free paper. Genuine

cloth is used as is genuine Red Label
Davey Board.

UNIFO PUBLISHERS, LTD.

P.O. Box 3858
Sarasota, Florida 34230-3858
Telephone: 813-953-7900

ADDRESS FOR ORDERS:

Same as above.

DISTRIBUTION:

Distributes the publications of: United
Nations; International Labor Office;
World Bank; International Monetary Fund;
Organization for Economic Co-operation
and Development; United Nations
University.

PREPAYMENT:

Not required.

DISCOUNT POLICY:

No discount to libraries.

RETURN POLICY:

Full credit (no cash refunds) allowed on
books returned within 90 days. Prior
written permission is required.

SHIPPING AND BILLING POLICY:

Shipping and handling billed at 2 1/2%
of invoiced amount. No shipping and
handling on prepaid orders.

BACK ORDER POLICY:

Back orders are held and library is
notified.

STANDING ORDER PLANS:

Standing order plan is available.
Special discount offered subject to
total volume and method of payment.

OTHER INFORMATION:

90% of business is direct with
libraries. Publisher provides libraries
with a consolidated supply source for
international documentation.

UNION COLLEGE PRESS see SYRACUSE
UNIVERSITY PRESS

UNION OF AMERICAN HEBREW CONGREGATIONS

---

838 Fifth Avenue
New York, New York 10021
Telephone: 212-249-0100

ADDRESS FOR ORDERS:

Same as above.

DISTRIBUTION:

None.

PREPAYMENT:

Required on all orders under $10.00;
required unless the library has
established an account.

DISCOUNT POLICY:

15% discount for library orders.

RETURN POLICY:

Returns are accepted within six months.
Write to Sylvia Goldenbach, UAHC Press,
838 Fifth Avenue for permission to
return. Address for returns: UAHC Press,
c/o Mercedes Distribution Center, 160
Imlay Street, Brooklyn, NY 11231.

SHIPPING AND BILLING POLICY:

$1.25 postage and handling for first
book plus $.50 for each additional
book billed to libraries on both prepaid
and billed orders. Invoices sent with
shipment unless billing address is
different from shipping address.

BACK ORDER POLICY:

Back orders are not accepted.

OTHER INFORMATION:

"Largest publisher of Reform Jewish
books in North America"; in business
since 1873.

UNIPUB

4611-F Assembly Drive
Lanham, Maryland 20706-4391
Telephone: 301-459-7666
         800-274-4888 (in U.S.)
         800-233-0504 (in Canada)

ADDRESS FOR ORDERS:

Same as above.

DISTRIBUTION/IMPRINT:

FAO-Food and Agriculture Organization of
   the United Nations
GATT-General Agreement on Tariffs and
   Trade
IAEA-International Atomic Energy Agency
JKP-Jessica Kingsley Publishers
PUDOC-Centre for Agricultural Publishing
   and Documentation
UNESCO-United Nations Educational,
Scientific, and Cultural Organization
Who's Who
Verlag Josef Margraf

PREPAYMENT:

Libraries with no account must make
prepayment. Add 5% or minimum of $2.50
to the list price in the U.S.

DISCOUNT POLICY:

There is no discount for libraries.

RETURN POLICY:

UNIPUB will not accept any returns
without prior written authorization.
Libraries are requested to include
library's account number and the invoice
number in return requests. Returns will
not be accepted unless publisher's Return
Authorization Label is used.

Libraries are requested to notify UNIPUB
of any damaged publications within two
weeks of receipt of the material.

SHIPPING AND BILLING POLICY:

The amount of shipping charge is 5% or
minimum of $2.50 in the U.S., and 8% or
$4.00 outside. Invoices are sent with
shipment unless otherwise requested by
library.

BACK ORDER POLICY:

Titles not currently available are back
ordered unless advised to the contrary by
library.

UNITED CHURCH PRESS see PILGRIM PRESS

UNITED NATIONS see UNIFO PUBLISHERS, LTD.

UNITED NATIONS EDUCATIONAL, SCIENTIFIC,
AND CULTURAL ORGANIZATION see UNIPUB

UNITED NATIONS UNIVERSITY see UNIFO
PUBLISHERS, LTD.

UNITED STATES GAMES SYSTEMS, INC.

179 Ludlow Street
Stamford, Connecticut 06902
Telephone: 203-353-8400

ADDRESS FOR ORDERS:

Same as above.

DISTRIBUTION/IMPRINTS:

Best of Cards (Division)
Kingsbridge (Subsidiary)
Sovereign (Subsidiary)

PREPAYMENT:

Not required.

DISCOUNT POLICY:

20% discount to libraries.

RETURN POLICY:

Returns are accepted within 30 days.
Prior written permission is required.

SHIPPING AND BILLING POLICY:

Libraries are charged actual shipping
costs (usually UPS). Invoices are sent
separately.

BACK ORDER POLICY:

Libraries should re-order on estimated date of availability.

UNIVERSE BOOKS

381 Park Avenue South
New York, New York 10016
Telephone: 212-685-7400

ADDRESS FOR ORDERS:

St. Martin's Press
175 Fifth Avenue
New York, New York 1001
Telephone: 800-325-5525 (outside NYC)
              674-5151 (in NYC)

PREPAYMENT:

This and other policies follow those of St. Martin's Press.

UNIVERSITY ASSOCIATES

8517 Production Avenue
San Diego, California 92121
Telephone: 619-578-5900

ADDRESS FOR ORDERS:

Same as above.

PREPAYMENT:

Prepayment is required for orders under $75.00.

DISCOUNT POLICY:

No discount to libraries.

RETURN POLICY:

Returns are accepted within six months provided that the invoice has been paid within 60 days; if not, no return privileges apply. No films, videotapes or one part of a multi-part product are returnable. Written permission is required. Invoice information must accompany returns which should be sent via a traceable means with postage

prepaid and authorization labels attached.

SHIPPING AND BILLING POLICY:

Libraries are charged shipping as follows:

        Up to $75: $3.50
        $75.01-150: $7.00
        $150.01-300: $16.00

Invoices are mailed to bill-to address or as designated on purchase order.

BACK ORDER POLICY:

Publisher back orders unavailable titles and ships books when they become available unless the library instructs otherwise.

UNIVERSITY OF ALABAMA PRESS

Post Office Box 2877
Tuscaloosa, Alabama 35487-2877
Telephone: 205-348-5180

ADDRESS FOR ORDERS:

Same as above.

DISTRIBUTION/IMPRINT:

American Dialect Society
Alabama Review

PREPAYMENT:

Not required.

DISCOUNT POLICY:

Libraries receive a 10% discount on standing orders and orders placed through sales representatives for all publications.

RETURN POLICY:

Written permission is not required for returns from libraries. Books must be returned within one year except for defective books which may be returned at any time. The address for returns is: University of Alabama Press, Central Receiving, New Warehouse, Tuscaloosa, Alabama 35487.

SHIPPING AND BILLING POLICY:

Libraries pay postage. The actual amount of postage is the only charge. Invoices are sent with shipments unless library instructs otherwise.

BACK ORDER POLICY:

Titles not currently available are reported and back ordered unless requested otherwise by library.

SPECIAL ORDER PLAN:

Publisher permits a 10% discount on standing orders for all books. Books are shipped as published. Publisher is able to set up any sort of individual plan that best suits the needs of the library.

UNIVERSITY OF ALASKA PRESS

Signers' Hall
University of Alaska
Fairbanks, Alaska 99775-1580
Telephone: 907-474-6389

ADDRESS FOR ORDERS:

Same as above.

DISTRIBUTION:

Press distributes publications of some other University of Alaska departments, but not exclusively.

PREPAYMENT:

Not required.

DISCOUNT POLICY:

10% discount to libraries.

RETURN POLICY:

Full credit for returns with full invoice information, in salable condition, with shipping charges prepaid, and returned not earlier than 90 days or later than one year after invoice date. Prior written permission is required.

SHIPPING AND BILLING POLICY:

Libraries are charged actual postage at library rate. Invoices are sent with shipments unless otherwise requested.

BACK ORDER POLICY:

Libraries are notified of back orders which are shipped when available.

STANDING ORDER PLANS:

Standing orders receive 15% discount.

OTHER INFORMATION:

Publishing emphasis is on scholarly and nonfiction works related to Alaska, the circumpolar north, and the North Pacific Rim.

UNIVERSITY OF ARIZONA PRESS

1230 North Park Avenue, #102
Tucson, Arizona 85719
Telephone: 602-621-1441

ADDRESS FOR ORDERS:

Same as above.
Telephone: 602-882-3065
         800-426-3797

DISTRIBUTION/IMPRINT:

Anthropolo gical Papers of the
    University of Arizona
Monographs of the Association
    for Asian Studies
Sun Tracks

PREPAYMENT:

Not required.

DISCOUNT POLICY:

A 15% discount is allowed to academic and other non-profit libraries on standing orders.

RETURN POLICY:

Permission to return books must be requested in writing within one year of invoice date, stating titles and quantities to be returned. For full credit, books must be returned to the Press and arrive in undamaged and salable condition.

Returns due to the publisher's error must be made within 30 days, and the publisher will pay postage; otherwise, the library pays shipping costs of returns. The address for returns is: 250 E. Valencia Road, Tucson, AZ 85706.

SHIPPING AND BILLING POLICY:

Libraries pay postage. There is no handling charge or billing charge.

BACK ORDER POLICY:

Titles not currently available are reported and back ordered, unless library requests cancellation of the order.

SPECIAL ORDER PLAN:

Standing orders are accepted for :(1) all books published by the press; (2) any and all series publications; and (3) by broad, general category of books.

UNIVERSITY OF CALIFORNIA PRESS

2120 Berkeley Way
Berkeley, California 94720
Telephone: 800-822-6657
         650-295-9492 (MCI)
         415-643-7127 (FAX)

ADDRESS FOR ORDERS:

Same as above.

PREPAYMENT:

Required unless the library has an open account.

DISCOUNT POLICY:

10% discount to libraries.

RETURN POLICY:

Returns are accepted from three months to one year from date of purchase. Returns must be in salable condition and shipping must be prepaid. Full credit is allowed if returns are accompanied by original invoice number, date, and discount received; otherwise, 50% discount off list price is allowed. Returns should be insured. Claims for damaged books must be made within 30 days of invoice date. Defective books must be accompanied by an indication of the defect and returned under separate cover. Prior permission is not required for defective copies. Address for returns: University of California Press/1095 Essex Street/Richmond, CA 94801.

SHIPPING AND BILLING POLICY:

Shipping charged on all orders: $1.50 for first book, $0.50 for each additional book. Invoices are sent after shipments, but special instructions will be followed if possible.

BACK ORDER POLICY:

Publisher retains orders unless instructed otherwise and ships when available.

STANDING ORDER PLANS:

Standing orders are available for specific series.

UNIVERSITY OF CHICAGO PRESS

5801 S. Ellis
Chicago, Illinois 60637
Telephone: 312-702-7747

ADDRESS FOR ORDERS:

University of Chicago Press
11030 S. Langley
Chicago, Illinois 60628-3893
Telephone: 800-621-2736

DISTRIBUTION/IMPRINTS:

Publisher distributes:
    Art Institute of Chicago Musem
        Studies
    Metropolitan Museum Journal
    Bulletin of the Atomic Scientists
    Oriental Institute (books published
        before 1977)
    Center for the Study of Language and
        Information
    Works of Gioacchino Rossini
        (Fondazione Rossini)
    Glenbow Museum

PREPAYMENT:

Not required.

DISCOUNT POLICY:

No discount for libraries except for standing orders.

RETURN POLICY:

Returns, in clean and salable condition and accompanied by invoice number, date, and packing list, are accepted within 18 months of invoice date. Unsalable returns will be returned to library at library's expense. Returns should be sent to the S. Langley address.

SHIPPING AND BILLING POLICY:

Publisher charges shipping, at least expensive trackable means (UPS or motor freight) unless a waiver of liability is on file. Invoices are always sent separately.

BACK ORDER POLICY:

Books will be back ordered as specified by the library.

SPECIAL PLANS:

Standing order plan available at 20% discount.

OTHER:

Publisher encourages libraries to order from wholesalers.

UNIVERSITY OF DELAWARE PRESS see ASSOCIATED UNIVERSITY PRESSES

UNIVERSITY OF EDINBURGH PRESS see COLUMBIA UNIVERSITY PRESS

UNIVERSITY OF FLORIDA PRESS see UNIVERSITY PRESSES OF FLORIDA

UNIVERSITY OF GEORGIA PRESS

Terrell Hall
Athens, Georgia 30602
Telephone: 404-542-2830

ADDRESS FOR ORDERS:

Same as above.
Telephone: 404-542-0066

PREPAYMENT:

Not required.

DISCOUNT POLICY:

No discount to libraries.

RETURN POLICY:

Returns in salable condition, in print, and sent with postage prepaid are accepted for full credit within one year. Prior permission is required.

SHIPPING AND BILLING POLICY:

Libraries are charged actual shipping on billed orders; prepaid orders should include $1.00 for the first book and $0.50 for each additional book. Invoices are sent with shipments unless the library specifies otherwise.

BACK ORDER POLICY:

Publisher back orders unavailable titles unless the library instructs otherwise.

SPECIAL PLANS:

A standing order is available which allows libraries to receive one copy of each new book at a 10% discount.

UNIVERSITY OF HAWAII PRESS

2840 Kolowalu Street
Honolulu, Hawaii 96822
Telephone: 808-948-8697

ADDRESS FOR ORDERS:

Same as above.

DISTRIBUTION/IMPRINTS:

Distributes the publications of many University of Hawaii related organizations, such as the Water Research Center, Pacific Forum, and the Lyon Arboretum as well as presses as the Philippines Press.

Imprints: University of Hawaii Press; East-West Center; Kolowalu.

PREPAYMENT:

Not required with purchase order.

DISCOUNT POLICY:

20% discount to Hawaiian libraries only.

RETURN POLICY:

Returns are accepted within one year. Written permission from the Business Office is required. Address for returns: University of Hawaii Warehouse/1330 Lower Campus Road/Honolulu, HI 96822.

SHIPPING AND BILLING POLICY:

Libraries are charged actual shipping. Invoices are sent with shipments unless the library specifies otherwise.

BACK ORDER POLICY:

Publisher back orders unavailable titles and ships books when they become available.

SPECIAL PLANS:

A standing order plan is available; interested libraries should write to the UH Press Marketing Department.

OTHER:

Orders for the mainland USA are shipped from a New York warehouse.

UNIVERSITY OF IDAHO PRESS

P.O. Box 3368, University Station
Moscow, Idaho 83843
Telephone: 208-885-6245

ADDRESS FOR ORDERS:

Same as above.

PREPAYMENT:

Not required.

DISCOUNT POLICY:

20% discount to libraries.

RETURN POLICY:

Returns, in salable condition and with reference to the original invoice and date, are accepted for full credit no sooner than 90 days and not more than one year. Prior written permission is required.

SHIPPING AND BILLING POLICY:

Libraries pay shipping. Invoices are sent with shipments unless the library specifies otherwise.

BACK ORDER POLICY:

Items are automatically back ordered, and the library is notified of the expected shipping date. No bill is sent until the items are shipped.

SPECIAL PLANS:

Publisher offers a standing order plan at a 20% discount.

UNIVERSITY OF ILLINOIS PRESS

---

54 East Gregory Drive
Champaign, Illinois 61820
Telephone: 217-333-0950

ADDRESS FOR ORDERS:

University of Illinois Press
c/o CUP Services
P.O. Box 6525
Ithaca, NY 14851
Telephone: 800-666-2211

DISTRIBUTION/IMPRINTS:

Distributes: Vanderbilt University Press; British Film Institute.

PREPAYMENT:

Not required with purchase order.

DISCOUNT POLICY:

No scheduled discount to libraries.

RETURN POLICY:

Returns in salable condition and still in print are accepted at any time. Written permission is not required. Address for returns: University of Illinois Press/c/o CUP Services/740 Cascadilla St/Ithaca, NY 14850.

SHIPPING AND BILLING POLICY:

Libraries are charged shipping (FOB shipping point); prepaid orders should add $1.95 shipping/handling per order. Invoices are sent separately unless the library specifies otherwise.

BACK ORDER POLICY:

Publisher back orders unavailable titles.

SPECIAL PLANS:

Standing orders may be set up for series or for at least one copy of every new title.

UNIVERSITY OF IOWA PRESS

---

119 West Park Road
Iowa City, Iowa 52242
Telephone: 319-335-2000

ADDRESS FOR ORDERS:

University of Iowa Press
Publications Order Dept., GSB
Iowa City, Iowa 52242
Telephone: 319-335-8777

PREPAYMENT:

Not required.

DISCOUNT POLICY:

No discount to libraries.

RETURN POLICY:

Returns of books in good condition accepted within one year. Written permission is required, and requests should include invoice numbers and totals. Return to Publications Order Dept. address.

SHIPPING AND BILLING POLICY:

Libraries are charged shipping (UPS) of $2.00 for the first book and $0.50 for each additional book. Invoices are usually sent with shipments unless the library specifies otherwise.

BACK ORDER POLICY:

Publisher will keep back orders for up to 90 days, or longer upon request.

UNIVERSITY OF MASSACHUSETTS PRESS

P.O. Box 429
Amherst, Massachusetts 01004
Telephone: 413-545-2217

ADDRESS FOR ORDERS:

Same as above.

PREPAYMENT:

Prepayment is required on orders of two titles or fewer (add $1.50 for postage and handling). Libraries can be billed for orders of three or more titles.

DISCOUNT POLICY:

None.

RETURN POLICY:

Returns are accepted within one year of invoice date; prior written permission is required except for damaged or misshipped books. Address for returns: University of Massachusetts Press Warehouse, Main Library Receiving Dock, University of Massachusetts, Amherst, MA 01003.

SHIPPING AND BILLING POLICY:

Libraries are charged actual postage on billed orders; $1.50 postage and handling charged on prepaid orders. Invoices sent with shipments unless requested otherwise or unless billing address is different from shipping address.

BACK ORDER POLICY:

Publisher will back order unless the library requests otherwise.

STANDING ORDER PLANS:

15% discount is offered on library standing orders, on a returnable basis. Libraries only required to pay shipping charges.

OTHER INFORMATION:

Single copy orders are best handled as prepaid or through a wholesaler.

UNIVERSITY OF MINNESOTA PRESS

2037 University Avenue S.E.
Minneapolis, Minnesota 55414
Telephone: 612-624-2516

ADDRESS FOR ORDERS:

Same as above.
Telephone: 612-624-0005

PREPAYMENT:

Not required.

DISCOUNT POLICY:

No discount to libraries.

RETURN POLICY:

Returns, in clean, salable condition and
accompanied by invoice number and
quantity purchased, are accepted within
one year of invoice date. Old editions
and out-of-print titles are not
accepted. Written permission is
required. Address for returns:
University of Minnesota Press/c/o
Burgess Companies/7108 Ohms Lane/
Minneapolis, MN 55435.

SHIPPING AND BILLING POLICY:

Libraries are charged shipping on billed
orders; prepaid orders are shipped free.
Invoices are sent with shipments unless
the library specifies otherwise.

BACK ORDER POLICY:

Publisher back orders until the
cancellation date specified by the
customer.

SPECIAL PLANS:

Standing orders are accepted and can be
cancelled at any time.

UNIVERSITY OF MISSOURI PRESS

200 Lewis Hall
Columbia, Missouri 65211
Telephone: 314-882-7641

ADDRESS FOR ORDERS:

CUP Services
P.O. Box 6525
Ithaca, New York 14851
Telephone: 800-666-2211

DISTRIBUTION/IMPRINTS:

Distributed by CUP Services.

PREPAYMENT:

Not required.

DISCOUNT POLICY:

No discount to libraries except for
standing orders.

RETURN POLICY:

Prior permission is not required for
returns. Invoices should be included.
Out-of-print titles are non-returnable.
Address for returns: CUP Services/740
Cascadilla Street/Ithaca, NY 14850.

SHIPPING AND BILLING POLICY:

Libraries are charged actual shipping.
Invoices are sent separately.

SPECIAL PLANS:

20% discount is offered for standing
orders. Correspondence regarding
standing orders should be sent to the
Lewis Hall address.

UNIVERSITY OF NEBRASKA PRESS

901 North 17th Street
Lincoln, Nebraska 68588-0520
Telephone: 402-472-3581

ADDRESS FOR ORDERS:

Same as above.
Telephone: 402-472-3584

DISTRIBUTION/IMPRINTS:

Distributes selected titles of the
University of Alberta Press.

PREPAYMENT:

Not required.

DISCOUNT POLICY:

20% discount to libraries.

RETURN POLICY:

Returns, in clean, salable condition, are accepted no sooner than three months or more than one year from purchase. Full credit allowed if returns are accompanied by correct invoice numbers. Defective books must be so marked and defects clearly indicated. Prior permission is not required.

SHIPPING AND BILLING POLICY:

Libraries pay shipping which is based on weight and specified method of shipping. Invoices are sent separately unless the library specifies otherwise.

BACK ORDER POLICY:

Unless library specifies otherwise, publisher will place on back order both new and out-of-stock titles.

SPECIAL PLANS:

Standing order plan is available; interested libraries should contact publisher for details.

UNIVERSITY OF NEVADA PRESS

Reno, Nevada 89557-0076
Telephone: 702-784-6573

ADDRESS FOR ORDERS:

Same as above.

DISTRIBUTION/IMPRINTS:

Distributes the publications of: College of Agriculture Publications (UNR); Associated Faculty Press - University of Nevada Basque Studies Program, Occasional Papers Series.

PREPAYMENT:

Not required.

DISCOUNT POLICY:

20% discount to libraries.

RETURN POLICY:

Returns are accepted not sooner than 90 days after invoice date and not longer than one year. Books must be in clean, salable condition. Posters are not returnable.

SHIPPING AND BILLING POLICY:

Libraries are charged shipping on all orders. Invoices are sent with shipments unless the library specifies otherwise.

BACK ORDER POLICY:

Books not yet published or temporarily unavailable are placed on back order.

SPECIAL PLANS:

Standing orders are not accepted from libraries.

UNIVERSITY OF NEW MEXICO PRESS

Journalism Building
Albuquerque, New Mexico 87131
Telephone: 505-277-2346

ADDRESS FOR ORDERS:

Order Department
Same as above
Telephone: 505-277-7564

PREPAYMENT:

Not required.

DISCOUNT POLICY:

33 1/3% discount on any quantity to school, public, and academic libraries.

RETURN POLICY:

Returns in salable condition and accompanied by invoice number and date are accepted within 6 months of receipt. Prior permission is required. Send returns to Returns Department at the address above.

SHIPPING AND BILLING POLICY:

Libraries are charged actual shipping; prepaid orders should include $1.00 postage/handling for each book ordered. Invoices are sent with shipments unless the library specifies otherwise.

BACK ORDER POLICY:

Publisher back orders unavailable titles and ships books when they become available unless the library instructs otherwise.

SPECIAL PLANS:

Publisher offers a standing order plan at a 40% discount (which applies to any other order as well as long as the standing order is in effect) and return privileges within 30 days (at library's expense). Selections can be restricted by category, price, and binding.

UNIVERSITY OF NORTH CAROLINA PRESS

P.O. Box 2288
Chapel Hill, North Carolina 27515-2288
Telephone: 919-966-3561
          919-966-5722

ADDRESS FOR ORDERS:

Same as above.

DISTRIBUTION/IMPRINTS:

Distributes the publications of: North Carolina Museum of Art; Studies in Comparative Literature (UNC); Dental Laboratory Manuals (UNC); Studies in the Romance Languages (UNC); Studies in the Germanic Languages (UNC).

PREPAYMENT:

Not required.

DISCOUNT POLICY:

No discount to libraries except for special offers.

RETURN POLICY:

Permission to return is not required. Books must be clean, salable copies of titles listed in publisher's current complete catalog or Publishers Trade List Annual. Full credit is allowed only if the invoice number is supplied; otherwise, maximum discount applies. Address for returns: UNC Press Warehouse/ 100 Airport Drive/Chapel Hill, NC 27514.

SHIPPING AND BILLING POLICY:

Libraries are charged shipping on all orders. Invoices are sent with shipments unless the library specifies otherwise.

BACK ORDER POLICY:

Unless the library specifies otherwise, books not in stock at the time of order are automatically back ordered and released when stock arrives.

SPECIAL PLANS:

Publisher's standing order at 10% discount is available.

UNIVERSITY OF NORTH FLORIDA PRESS see UNIVERSITY PRESSES OF FLORIDA

UNIVERSITY OF PENNSYLVANIA PRESS, INC.

Blockley Hall
418 Service Drive
Philadelphia, Pennsylvania 19104-6097
Telephone: 215-898-6262

ADDRESS FOR ORDERS:

Same as above.

PREPAYMENT:

Prepayment of 1/2 of the total order must be made if library has no established account and order is 10 units or more.

DISCOUNT POLICY:

There is no discount for library orders, except on blanket standing orders.

RETURN POLICY:

Publisher accepts all books for full credit if returned within one year of purchase date. Books must be in clean, salable, unmarked condition. Specific invoice numbers for each title returned must be supplied. The address for returns is: University of Pennsylvania Press, 2200 Girard Avenue, Baltimore, MD 21211.

SHIPPING AND BILLING POLICY:

For billed orders, publisher adds shipping cost on invoice. Invoices are enclosed within shipment if requested.

BACK ORDER POLICY:

Titles are automatically back ordered
unless cancellation is specifically
requested.

SPECIAL ORDER PLAN:

On blanket standing order plan, libraries
receive each of all the new titles
published at a 20% discount.

UNIVERSITY OF PITTSBURGH PRESS

---

127 N. Bellefield Avenue
Pittsburgh, Pennsylvania 15260
Telephone: 412-624-4110

ADDRESS FOR ORDERS:

Harper & Row Publishers, Inc.
Keystone Industrial Park
Scranton, PA 18512

DISTRIBUTION/IMPRINTS:

Distributed by Harper & Row.

PREPAYMENT:

Not required.

DISCOUNT POLICY:

No discount to libraries except for
standing orders.

RETURN POLICY:

Returns of books in salable condition
accepted not before 90 days nor after
one year of invoice date. Full credit is
allowed for returns accompanied by full
invoice information and packing slip;
otherwise, 60% discount will be applied.
Out-of-print titles are non-returnable.
Address for returns: Harper & Row
Publishers, Inc./Key Distribution
Center/Building #1/Reeves
Street/Dunmore, PA 18512.

SHIPPING AND BILLING POLICY:

Libraries are charged shipping on all
orders. Invoices are sent
separately.

BACK ORDER POLICY:

Orders are placed on back order until
the books are available or until the
order is cancelled.

SPECIAL PLANS:

Standing orders are offered for various
series at a 20% discount. As each new
title is published, the library is
billed, and the book is shipped. Returns
are accepted according to the above
policies. Notification in writing is
necessary to cancel a standing order.

UNIVERSITY OF SOUTH CAROLINA PRESS

---

508 Assembly Street
Columbia, South Carolina 29208
Telephone: 803-777-5243

ADDRESS FOR ORDERS:

Same as above.

PREPAYMENT:

Prepayment is required only if no account
has been established.

DISCOUNT POLICY:

1 copy: no discount
2 or more: 20%

RETURN POLICY:

Returns in salable condition are granted
if the circumstances of a particular
request warrant such a decision.

SHIPPING AND BILLING POLICY:

Libraries are charged actual shipping on
billed orders; prepaid orders are
charged $1.50 for the first book and
$1.00 for each additional book. Invoices
are sent according to library
preference.

BACK ORDER POLICY:

Publisher back orders unavailable items
at library's request.

UNIVERSITY OF SOUTH FLORIDA PRESS see
UNIVERSITY PRESSES OF FLORIDA

UNIVERSITY OF TENNESSEE PRESS

293 Communications Building
Knoxville, Tennessee 37996-0325
Telephone: 615-974-3321

ADDRESS FOR ORDERS:

University of Tennessee Press
P.O. Box 250
Ithaca, New York 14850
Telephone: 800-666-2211

PREPAYMENT:

Not required.

DISCOUNT POLICY:

10% discount to libraries.

RETURN POLICY:

Books may be returned at any time
without prior permission as long as they
are still in print. Books must be in
new, resalable condition and accompanied
by a packing list showing quantities,
discounts, and invoice numbers. If no
invoice number is given, credit will be
issued at the maximum discount. Address
for returns: University of Tennessee
Press/740 Cascadilla St/Ithaca, NY
14850.

SHIPPING AND BILLING POLICY:

$1.50 shipping/handling is charged for
all orders. Invoices are sent
separately.

BACK ORDER POLICY:

A back order notice appears on the
packing slip accompanying other orders,
and the book is shipped as soon as it is
available. If the book is temporarily
out of stock and the paperback edition
is available, libraries are asked if
they would accept the paperback.

SPECIAL PLANS:

Standing order plans with the above
return privileges are available.

UNIVERSITY OF TEXAS PRESS

P.O. Box 7819
Austin, Texas 78713
Telephone: 512-471-4032

ADDRESS FOR ORDERS:

Same as above.
Telephone: 800-252-3206

PREPAYMENT:

Not required.

DISCOUNT POLICY:

No discount to libraries on regular
orders.

RETURN POLICY:

Publisher's permission is not required
unless return exceeds 25 copies of a
title or totals 250 or more books. Books
must be in salable condition,
accompanied by invoice number and date,
still in print and returned with postage
prepaid not less than 4 months after
invoice date. Address for returns:
University of Texas Press/2100 Comal
St/Austin, TX 78722.

SHIPPING AND BILLING POLICY:

Libraries are charged shipping. Invoices
are sent with shipments.

BACK ORDER POLICY:

Titles are back ordered unless the
library instructs otherwise.

SPECIAL PLANS:

Standing orders for all new titles or
for series are available to libraries at
15% discount.

UNIVERSITY OF UTAH ANTHROPOLOGICAL PAPERS
see UNIVERSITY OF UTAH PRESS

UNIVERSITY OF UTAH PRESS

101 University Services Building
Salt Lake City, Utah 84112
Telephone: 801-581-6771

ADDRESS FOR ORDERS:

Same as above.

DISTRIBUTION/IMPRINT:

Bonneville Books
Publications in the American West
The Tanner Lectures on Human Values
University of Utah Anthropological Papers
Utah Centennial Series
Publications in Mormon Studies
Ethics in a Changing World

PREPAYMENT:

Not required.

DISCOUNT POLICY:

Publisher allows a 30% discount on
standing orders.

RETURN POLICY:

Publisher permits return of books under
the following stipulations. Libraries
must request and receive publisher's
written permission before shipping
returns. A request must include
publisher's invoice number. A special
mailing label must be used in shipping
returns. No returns shall be requested
before 3 months or after 12 months from
the invoice date.

Full credit will be issued only if books
are in salable condition--clean,
unmarked, and free of labels. If book
arrives damaged, an adjustment in credit
will be indicated on the credit memo.
Libraries should not apply credit until
after receipt of publisher's credit memo.

The address for returns is the same as
for orders.

SHIPPING AND BILLING POLICY:

Libraries pay shipping charge. Invoice
is sent with shipment unless library
specifies otherwise.

BACK ORDER POLICY:

Publisher maintains back order file until
book becomes available. Orders are
filled automatically upon publication.

SPECIAL ORDER PLAN:

Publisher accepts standing orders and
offers a 30% discount.

UNIVERSITY OF WASHINGTON PRESS

P.O. Box 50096
Seattle, Washington 98105
Telephone: 206-543-4050

ADDRESS FOR ORDERS:

Same as above.
Telephone: 800-441-4115

PREPAYMENT:

Not required.

DISCOUNT POLICY:

No discount to libraries.

RETURN POLICY:

Returns of defective books only accepted
30 days from invoice date. A packing
list noting the original invoice number
must be enclosed. Prior permission is
not required.

SHIPPING AND BILLING POLICY:

Actual shipping costs are added to the
invoice. Invoices are sent with
shipments unless the library specifies
otherwise.

BACK ORDER POLICY:

Publisher will back order all material
that is not-yet-published or out-of-
stock unless library requests otherwise.

OTHER:

Publisher prefers that libraries order
through wholesalers.

UNIVERSITY OF WEST FLORIDA PRESS see
UNIVERSITY PRESSES OF FLORIDA

UNIVERSITY OF WISCONSIN PRESS

114 North Murray Street
Madison, Wisconsin 75715
Telephone: 608-262-8782

ADDRESS FOR ORDERS:

Same as above.

PREPAYMENT:

Not required.

DISCOUNT POLICY:

Libraries receive a 10% discount on
standing orders only.

RETURN POLICY:

Publisher does not require prior written
permission for library returns. Library
must give publisher's invoice numbers in
all claim forms.

SHIPPING AND BILLING POLICY:

Libraries pay postage. Invoices are sent
with shipment unless library requests
otherwise.

BACK ORDER POLICY:

Titles not currently available are
reported and back ordered.

SPECIAL ORDER PLAN:

One copy of each new publication is
shipped and billed when ready. Certain
subject categories, journals, books in
series, etc., may be omitted. Any book
received and deemed not to be of interest
to the library may be returned.

UNIVERSITY PRESS OF AMERICA

4720 Boston Way
Lanham, Maryland 20706
Telephone: (301) 459-3366

ADDRESS FOR ORDERS:

University Press of America
8705 Bollman Place
Savage, Maryland 20763

DISTRIBUTION:

Distributes the publications of:
American Enterprise Institute; Urban
Institute; Ethics and Public Policy
Council; Center for Strategic and
International Studies.

PREPAYMENT:

Publisher prefers that libraries open an
account.

DISCOUNT POLICY:

10% discount to libraries.

RETURN POLICY:

Books must be returned within one year.
Prior written permission is required.
Return books to address in Savage, MD.

SHIPPING AND BILLING POLICY:

Libraries are charged shipping for all
orders. Publisher prefers to ship UPS.
Invoices are sent separately.

BACK ORDER POLICY:

Back orders are noted on the invoice.

STANDING ORDER PLANS:

Standing orders offered for several
disciplines. Discounts vary,
but 10% for most (AEI is 30%).

OTHER INFORMATION:

Libraries may order direct or through
wholesalers. Telephone orders for up to
three titles are accepted.

UNIVERSITY PRESS OF KENTUCKY

663 S. Limestone Street
Lexington, Kentucky 40506-0336
Telephone: 606-257-2951

ADDRESS FOR ORDERS:

University Press of Kentucky
P.O. Box 6525
Ithaca, New York 14851
Telephone: 607-277-2211

DISTRIBUTION/IMPRINTS:

Distributed by CUP Services.

PREPAYMENT:

Not required.

DISCOUNT POLICY:

No discount to libraries.

RETURN POLICY:

Books are eligible for return as long as
they remain in print. Returns will be
credited at 48% of the price indicated
in the previous year's Publishers Trade
List Annual unless the library furnishes
discount and invoice date and number. No
prior permission is required. Out-of-
print books and books in unsalable
condition are not returnable. Address
for returns: CUP Services/740 Cascadilla
Street/Ithaca, NY 14850.

SHIPPING AND BILLING POLICY:

$2.50 is charged on prepaid orders;
delivery costs are added to invoices on
billed orders. Invoices are sent with
shipments.

BACK ORDER POLICY:

Publisher will back order if a
reprinting is in the works.

SPECIAL PLANS:

A standing order for all new titles is
available at a 10% discount. Interested
libraries should write to the Marketing
Manager at the Lexington address.

OTHER:

Publisher prefers that libraries order
through wholesalers.

UNIVERSITY PRESS OF MISSISSIPPI

3825 Ridgewood Road
Jackson, Mississippi 39211
Telephone: 601-982-6205

ADDRESS FOR ORDERS:

Same as above.

DISTRIBUTION/IMPRINTS:

Distributes: Old Capitol Museum (State
Historical Museum) titles.

Imprint: Muscadine Books.

PREPAYMENT:

Prepayment required for libraries without
an established account.

DISCOUNT POLICY:

10% discount on regular orders; 20% for
standing orders.

RETURN POLICY:

Returns in salable condition,
accompanied by invoice information, and
sent with postage prepaid are accepted
within one year. Written permission is
required. Out of print titles are not
returnable.

SHIPPING AND BILLING POLICY:

Libraries are charged actual shipping
for billed orders; prepaid orders should
include $2.00 for the first book and
$.75 for each additional book. Invoices
are sent with shipments unless the
library specifies otherwise.

BACK ORDER POLICY:

Publisher back orders unavailable
titles, notifies library, and ships and
bills books when they become available.

UNIVERSITY PRESS OF NEW ENGLAND

---

17 1/2 Lebanon Street
Hanover, New Hampshire 03755
Telephone: 603-646-3349
          603-646-3340

ADDRESS FOR ORDERS:

Same as above.

DISTRIBUTION/IMPRINTS:

Distributes: various issues of "Studies
in the History of Art" (National Gallery
of Art); Anthrozoos (quarterly journal of
the Delta Society).

PREPAYMENT:

Not required.

DISCOUNT POLICY:

No discount to libraries.

RETURN POLICY:

Books in salable condition and still in print are eligible for return, without permission, between 3 months and 1 year from invoice date. Returns must include invoice number and date and have postage prepaid. Defects should be clearly noted.

SHIPPING AND BILLING POLICY:

Libraries are charged shipping plus handling ($1.50 for the first book and $0.25 for each additional book) on all orders. Invoices are sent with shipments unless the library specifies otherwise.

BACK ORDER POLICY:

Publisher will back order at library's request.

SPECIAL PLANS:

Standing orders are accepted.

Publisher requires prior written permission for library returns. Books must be returned before one year from the date of purchase. Returned books must be unmarked and as new. Out-of-print books are not returnable. The address for returns is the same as for orders.

SHIPPING AND BILLING POLICY:

Libraries pay postage. Shipping and handling charges are included on the invoice. Invoices are sent separately.

BACK ORDER POLICY:

Titles currently unavailable are reported and back ordered.

SPECIAL ORDER PLAN:

Libraries may place a standing order for one or more series, or for all publications. Publisher keeps orders on file and ships new titles in the designated series as they become available.

UNIVERSITY PRESS OF VIRGINIA

Post Office Box 3608
University Station
Charlottesville, Virginia 22903
Telephone: 804-924-3468

ADDRESS FOR ORDERS:

Same as above.

DISTRIBUTION/IMPRINT:

American Antiquarian Society
Colonial Williamsburg
Colonial Society of Massachusetts
Winterthur Museum
Eleutherian-Mills Hagley Foundation
Bibliographical Society of America
Grolier Club
Procedural Aspects of International Law
  Institute
The Mariners Museum
Thomas Jefferson Memorial Foundation

PREPAYMENT:

Not required.

DISCOUNT POLICY:

Libraries receive a 10% discount on all orders.

RETURN POLICY:

UNIVERSITY PRESSES OF FLORIDA

---

15 Northwest 15th Street
Gainesville, Florida 32603
Telephone: 904-392-1351

ADDRESS FOR ORDERS:

Same as above.

DISTRIBUTION/IMPRINTS:

Imprints: Florida A&M University Press;
Florida Atlantic University Press;
Florida International University Press;
Florida State University Press;
University of Central Florida Press;
University of Florida Press; University
of North Florida Press; University of
South Florida Press; University of West
Florida.

PREPAYMENT:

Not required with purchase order.

DISCOUNT POLICY:

No special discount to libraries at present.

RETURN POLICY:

Returns in salable condition, accompanied by invoice number, and sent with postage prepaid are accepted within one year of invoice date. Written permission is required.

SHIPPING AND BILLING POLICY:

Libraries are charged shipping. Invoices are sent with shipments.

SPECIAL PLANS:

A standing order plan is available.

URBAN & SCHWARZENBERG

7 E. Redwood Street
Baltimore, Maryland 21202
Telephone: 301-539-2550

ADDRESS FOR ORDERS:

Same as above.

PREPAYMENT:

Not required with purchase order.

DISCOUNT POLICY:

No special discount to libraries.

RETURN POLICY:

Returns in salable condition and still in print are accepted at any time. Prior authorization is required.

SHIPPING AND BILLING POLICY:

Libraries are charged shipping except for prepaid orders which are shipped free. Invoices are sent as specified by the library.

BACK ORDER POLICY:

Publisher back orders unavailable titles and ships books when they become available.

URBAN INSTITUTE see UNIVERSITY PRESS OF AMERICA

UTAH GEOGRAPHIC SERIES see FALCON PRESS PUBLISHING COMPANY

UTAH STATE UNIVERSITY PRESS

Utah State University
Logan, Utah 84322-7800
Telephone: 801-750-1362

ADDRESS FOR ORDERS:

Same as above.

PREPAYMENT:

Not required.

DISCOUNT POLICY:

10% discount to libraries for any quantity.

RETURN POLICY:

Books, in salable condition, are accepted for return within one year. Written permission is required.

SHIPPING AND BILLING POLICY:

Libraries are charged $1.75 shipping for up to 4 books or actual postage for orders of more than 4 books. Invoices are sent with shipments unless the library specifies otherwise.

BACK ORDER POLICY:

Publisher will place back orders for unavailable titles and hold orders until books are available unless the library requests otherwise.

SPECIAL PLANS:

Standing orders are available for all titles. Interested libraries should contact publisher.

VCH PUBLISHERS, INC.

220 East 23rd Street, Suite 909
New York, New York 10010-4606
Telephone: 212-683-8333

ADDRESS FOR ORDERS:

VCH Publishers, Inc.
303 N.W. 12th Avenue
Deerfield Beach, Florida 33442-1788
Telephone: 800-422-8824

DISTRIBUTION/IMPRINTS:

Distributes: Gustav Fischer Verlag;
Wilhelm Ernst & Sohn; Physik-Verlag.

Imprints: Acta humaniora; Deutsche
Forschungsgemeinschaft; Edition Medizin.

PREPAYMENT:

Not required with purchase order.

DISCOUNT POLICY:

No discount to libraries.

RETURN POLICY:

Returns are accepted within 6 months.
Written permission is required from
Deerfield Beach.

SHIPPING AND BILLING POLICY:

Libraries are charged shipping except on
prepaid orders. Invoices are sent
separately.

BACK ORDER POLICY:

If a book is currently unavailable,
publisher will return the order and ask
library if it wishes to place a back
order.

OTHER:

Publisher produces a newsletter to
inform librarians of upcoming titles.

VGM CAREER BOOKS see NATIONAL TEXTBOOK
COMPANY

VACATION WORKBOOKS see F & W PUBLICATIONS

VALUE COMMUNICATIONS, INC. see OAK TREE
PUBLICATIONS

VALUE TALES see OAK TREE PUBLICATIONS

ALFRED VAN DER MARCK EDITIONS see HARPER
AND ROW, PUBLISHERS, INC.

VAN NOSTRAND REINHOLD COMPANY

---

115 Fifth Avenue
New York, New York 10002
Telephone: 212-254-3232

ADDRESS FOR ORDERS:

Van Nostrand Reinhold Company
7625 Empire Drive
Florence, KY 41042
Telephone: 606-525-6600

DISTRIBUTION/IMPRINTS:

Distributes the publications of:
Architectural Press.

AVI (Imprint)

PREPAYMENT:

Not required.

DISCOUNT POLICY:

10% standard discount to libraries.

RETURN POLICY:

Returns must be made within 60 days
after receipt. No written permission is
required. Out-of-print titles and run-
out titles are not returnable. Address
returns to: Returns Department/7625
Empire Drive/Florence, KY 41042.

SHIPPING AND BILLING POLICY:

Libraries are charged shipping on all
orders plus a handling charge of usually
7% of list price. Invoices are sent with
shipments.

BACK ORDER POLICY:

All unpublished titles are automatically back ordered unless the library instructs otherwise.

VANDERBILT UNIVERSITY PRESS see UNIVERSITY OF ILLINOIS PRESS

VANGUARD PRESS, INC.

---

424 Madison Avenue
New York, New York 10017
Telephone: 212-753-3906

ADDRESS FOR ORDERS:

Same as above.

DISTRIBUTION:

Columbia Publishing Company

PREPAYMENT:

Not required.

DISCOUNT POLICY:

Discount rate for library orders is 10% on all orders.

RETURN POLICY:

Written permission required. Book returns are limited to one year from invoice date. Limited editions are not returnable. Address for returns is: Vanguard Press Inc., c/o M & B Fulfillment Service, 27 Harrison Street, Bridgeport, CT 06604.

SHIPPING AND BILLING POLICY:

Libraries pay shipping charge. Publisher charges only the actual postage charge. Invoices are sent separately to the billing address.

BACK ORDER POLICY:

Publisher back orders unavailable titles for one year.

VENDOME PRESS see RIZZOLI INTERNATIONAL PUBLICATIONS

VESTAL PRESS, LTD.

P.O. Box 97
Vestal, New York 13851-0097
Telephone: 607-797-4872

ADDRESS FOR ORDERS:

Same as above.

DISTRIBUTION/IMPRINTS:

Distributes the publications of Bowers & Merena Galleries, Inc.

PREPAYMENT:

Not required.

DISCOUNT POLICY:

10% discount on three or more copies of any titles.

RETURN POLICY:

Returns are accepted within six months. Address for returns: 320 N. Jensen Road/ Vestal, NY 13851-0097.

SHIPPING AND BILLING POLICY:

Publisher pays shipping on library orders. Invoices are sent separately unless the library specifies otherwise.

BACK ORDER POLICY:

Back orders are kept on file until filled.

SPECIAL PLANS:

A standing order plan is available.

VICTOR BOOKS see SCRIPTURE PRESS PUBLICATIONS, INC.

VICTORIA & ALBERT MUSEUM see FABER & FABER, INC.

VIDEO PROFESSOR see CAREER PUBLISHING, INC.

VIKING see VIKING PENGUIN

VIKING KESTREL see VIKING PENGUIN

VIKING PENGUIN INC.

40 West 23rd Street
New York, New York 10010-5290
Telephone: 212-337-5200

SPECIAL NOTE AND ADDRESS FOR ORDERS:

Viking Penguin does not accept orders for fewer that 10 copies assorted. The address for orders is the same as above. Publisher no longer supplies proforma invoices for orders with a net value of less than $500.

DISTRIBUTION/IMPRINT:

Penguin
Puffin
Viking Kestrel
Viking
Stephen Greene Press
Frederick Warne
Elisabeth Sifton Books

PREPAYMENT:

Not required.

DISCOUNT POLICY:

Discount schedule for schools and libraries:

10 to 24 copies assorted	0%
25 or more copies assorted	20%

The above mentioned schedule applies to one purchase order only; i.e., multiple purchase orders cannot be combined for a better discount.

BACK ORDER POLICY:

Publisher will not back order back list titles which are out of stock at the time of library's order.

VILLAGE PRESS see AVIATION BOOK COMPANY

VILLARD see RANDOM HOUSE, INC.

VINTAGE see RANDOM HOUSE, INC.

VIRGINIA CENTER FOR THE CREATIVE ARTS see ASSOCIATED UNIVERSITY PRESSES

VISION HOUSE see REGAL BOOKS

VISUALS/PROFESSIONAL BOOKS see FAIRCHILD BOOKS AND VISUALS/PROFESSIONAL BOOKS

VOGEL AVIATION see AVIATION BOOK COMPANY

VOLCANO PRESS, INC.

P.O. Box 270
Volcano, California 95689
Telephone: 209-296-3445

ADDRESS FOR ORDERS:

Same as above.

DISTRIBUTION/IMPRINTS:

Distributed by Publishers Services, Inc.

Kazan Books (Imprint)

PREPAYMENT:

Not required.

DISCOUNT POLICY:

1 copy: 10%
2-9 copies: 35%
10 or more: 40%

RETURN POLICY:

Returns, in resalable condition, are
accepted for credit within one year of
invoice date. Written permission is
required.

SHIPPING AND BILLING POLICY:

Shipping plus handling ($2.00 for the
first book; $0.50 for each additional
book) is charged on billed orders.
Invoices are sent with shipments unless
the library specifies otherwise.

BACK ORDER POLICY:

Publisher will hold orders and ship
material as soon as it is available
unless the library cancels the order.

WALKER AND COMPANY

---

720 Fifth Avenue
New York, New York 10019
Telephone: 212-265-3632

ADDRESS FOR ORDERS:

Same as above.

PREPAYMENT:

Not required.

DISCOUNT POLICY:

Trade books:

1-4 assorted books: no discount
5-9:   20%
10 or more: 25%

Reinforced editions:

1-4:   no discount
5 or more: 10%

RETURN POLICY:

Returns are accepted as long as a book
is still in print. Prior permission is
not required. Address for returns:
Walker & Co./c/o Gateway Distribution/
950 North Shore Drive/Lake Bluff,
Illinois 60044.

SHIPPING AND BILLING POLICY:

Libraries are charged actual shipping.
Invoices are sent with shipments unless
the library specifies otherwise.

BACK ORDER POLICY:

Publisher will back order indefinitely
unless instructed otherwise.

SPECIAL PLANS:

Publisher offers standing order plans on
all titles at a 35% discount. Plans are
available for mysteries, westerns,
romances, adventures, children's books,
and large print inspirational titles.
Interested libraries should contact the
publisher.

OTHER:

Walker titles are generally available
from wholesalers, but publisher will
work with any library that wishes to
order direct.

FREDERICK WARNE see VIKING PENGUIN INC.

WARNER BOOKS see RANDOM HOUSE, INC.

WARREN PUBLISHING HOUSE, INC.

17909 Bothell Way S.E. #101
Bothell, Washington 98012
Telephone: 206-485-3335

ADDRESS FOR ORDERS:

Totline/Warren Publishing House, Inc.
P.O. Box 2255
Everett, Washington 98203
Telephone: 800-334-4769

DISTRIBUTION/IMPRINTS:

Totline Books (Imprint)

PREPAYMENT:

Not required with purchase order.

DISCOUNT POLICY:

10% discount on library orders.

RETURN POLICY:

Books, in salable condition and with postage prepaid, are accepted for return for up to one month. Return to Bothell, WA address.

SHIPPING AND BILLING POLICY:

Publisher pays shipping on prepaid orders; library pays shipping (from $1.00 to $4.00 for orders up to $100.00; 5% for orders over $100.00) on billed orders. Invoices are sent separately after shipments unless the library specifies otherwise.

BACK ORDER POLICY:

Books that are back ordered are sent and billed separately.

WASHINGTON INSTITUTE BOOKS see PARAGON HOUSE PUBLISHING

WATER RESEARCH CENTER see UNIVERSITY OF HAWAII PRESS

WATER ROW BOOKS, INC.

P.O. Box 438
Sudbury, Massachusetts 01776
Telephone: 617-443-8910

ADDRESS FOR ORDERS:

Same as above.

DISTRIBUTION/IMPRINTS:

Weinberg Books (Division)
Water Row Press (Imprint)

PREPAYMENT:

Not required.

DISCOUNT POLICY:

1 copy: net price
2+ copies: 20% discount

RETURN POLICY:

Written permission is required within 90 days of invoice date for returns.

SHIPPING AND BILLING POLICY:

Shipping costs are charged on all orders. Invoices are sent with shipments unless otherwise requested.

BACK ORDER POLICY:

Items can be placed on back order.

WATERFRONT BOOKS

---

98 Brookes Avenue
Burlington, Vermont 05401
Attn: Sherrill N. Musty, Publisher
Telephone: 802-658-7477

ADDRESS FOR ORDERS:

Same as above.
Telephone: 800-456-7500, ext. 2000

DISTRIBUTION/IMPRINTS:

Publications of Waterfront Books are distributed by Bookpeople, Children's Small Press Collection, Gryphon House, Publisher's Group West, QualityBooks, and Inland Book Company.

PREPAYMENT:

Not required but preferred.

DISCOUNT POLICY:

0-4 books: no discount
5-100 books: 20%
more than 100:   25%

RETURN POLICY:

Prior written permission is required. Publisher reserves the right to deny unjustified requests.

SHIPPING AND BILLING POLICY:

Libraries pay shipping (UPS) on all orders. Invoices are sent with shipments unless the library specifies otherwise.

BACK ORDER POLICY:

Publisher has no back order policy due to lack of necessity.

WATOSH PUBLISHING see AVIATION BOOK COMPANY

WATSON-GUPTILL PUBLICATIONS

1515 Broadway
New York, New York 10036
Telephone: 212-764-7300

ADDRESS FOR ORDERS:

Watson-Guptill Publications
1695 Oak Street
Lakewood, NJ 08701
Telephone: 201-363-4511

DISTRIBUTION/IMPRINT:

AMPHOTO (American Photographic
    Books Publishing Co.)
Billboard Books
Whitney Library of Design

PREPAYMENT:

Not required.

DISCOUNT POLICY:

Library discount schedule is as follows:

1 to 4 copies	20%
5 to 24 copies	25%
25 or more	30%

Paperbound and clothbound books may be combined for discount.

RETURN POLICY:

Publisher requests libraries to write to Oak Street address for permission before shipping returns. Books may be returned after 90 days and within one year of purchase date. Requests must include: title, quantity, invoice number, and invoice date. If returns is made without invoice information, it will be credited

at 30% discount. The address for returns is the same as for orders.

SHIPPING AND BILLING POLICY:

Libraries pay postage. Packing slips are enclosed in shipments. Invoices are mailed separately. Terms are 30 days net.

BACK ORDER POLICY:

Titles currently unavailable are automatically back ordered unless library instructs otherwise.

SPECIAL ORDER PLAN:

Under a Greenaway plan, libraries receive all books automatically upon publication. Invoice is sent at end of publication season (twice yearly). Books are billed at 50% discount and are non-returnable. Plan is limited to libraries with 10 or more branches.

Watson-Guptill also offers a standing order plan for other libraries for annual publications.

FRANKLIN WATTS, INC.

---

387 Park Avenue South
New York, New York 10016
Telephone: 212-686-7070

ADDRESS FOR ORDERS:

Same as above.

PREPAYMENT:

Publisher requires that all orders under $14 at cost be accompanied by payment.

DISTRIBUTION/IMPRINT:

Bookwright (imprint)
Gloucester Press (imprint)
MacDonald (imprint)

DISCOUNT POLICY:

Publisher's discount schedule for schools and libraries is as follows:

Trade Books (TR):

1 to 9 books	list price
10 to 24 books	20%
25 or more	25%

Reinforced Library Bound Book (RLB):

1 to 24 books	list price
25 or more	5%

Paperback Books (P):

1 to 9 books	list price
10-24 books	20%
25 or more	25%

All editions may be combined for discount. The maximum discount will apply in each discount schedule depending on total number of books.

RETURN POLICY:

No prior authorization is required for returns. The address for returns is: Franklin Watts, Inc., c/o Grolier Enterprises, Sherman Turnpike, Danbury, CT 06816.

SHIPPING AND BILLING POLICY:

Libraries pay postage. Packing slips are enclosed in shipments and invoices are mailed separately unless otherwise instructed by libraries.

BACK ORDER POLICY:

Titles currently unavailable are reported and back ordered unless library requests otherwise.

AUTOMATIC SERVICE AGREEMENT:

Publisher offers an Automatic Service Agreement, a plan whereby libraries receive all new titles upon publication at a 5% discount on RLB books and a 25% discount on trade books.

An annotated list will be sent to libraries twice a year on March and October 1st. All titles appropriate to category selected by library unless library notifies any adjustment within 30 days.

All books in salable condition may be returned. Libraries may discontinue the Automatic Service Plan at any time by notifying publisher in writing at least 30 days prior to either February 1st or October 1st.

STANDING ORDER PLAN:

In the categories selected by library, Franklin Watts sends all new publications immediately upon receipt in the warehouse. Publisher allows a 40% discount for Franklin Watts trade books, 15% on RLB titles, and 40% on paperbacks.

Libraries on standing order plan also receive the same discount for all backlist orders. A one-time reorder privilege of new titles is extended on

titles ordered under the same terms, provided the order is received within 30 days of receipt of original shipment and is marked "Standing Order Customer."

BOOK REVIEW PLAN:

Upon request and under certain conditions, Franklin Watts will send a number of current titles on an approval basis for library selection purposes. For more information on shipping and billing procedures and return procedures, library may call 1-800-433-3411, or write to director of marketing, Franklin Watts, Inc.

WAYFINDER PRESS see JOHNSON BOOKS

WAYNE STATE UNIVERSITY PRESS

5959 Woodward Avenue
Detroit, Michigan 48202
Telephone: 313-577-6120

ADDRESS FOR ORDERS:

Same as above.

PREPAYMENT:

Not required.

DISCOUNT POLICY:

Discounts are as follows:

Trade books, one copy	20%
2 to 4 assorted books	33%
5 to 99 assorted books	40%
Non-trade books, any quantity	20%

RETURN POLICY:

Book returns at 100% credit are permitted within one year of invoice date. Library must request permission, showing quantity and title to be returned, date, and number of invoice under which the books were originally purchased. Out-of-print books are not returnable. Books received without permission or in damaged condition will be returned at sender's expense. Defective books are refundable for credit or exchange without previous correspondence. The address for returns is the same as for orders.

SHIPPING AND BILLING POLICY:

Libraries pay postage for billed orders; publisher pays shipping costs for prepaid orders. Invoices are either sent with shipments or separately, as library requests.

BACK ORDER POLICY:

Titles currently unavailable are either back ordered or cancelled, as library requests.

SPECIAL ORDER PLAN:

Publisher accepts standing orders from libraries at a 20% discount.

JOHN WEATHERHILL, INC. see CHARLES E. TUTTLE COMPANY, INC.

WEINBERG BOOKS see WATER ROW BOOKS, INC.

SAMUEL WEISER, INC

Box 612
York Beach, Maine 03910
Telephone: 207-363-4393
          800-423-7087

ADDRESS FOR ORDERS:

Same as above.

DISTRIBUTION/IMPRINTS:

Publisher distributes its own publications plus those of 200 other small presses, including Nicolas-Hays, Inc. and Aurora Press.

PREPAYMENT:

Prepayment required if library does not have an established account with publisher.

DISCOUNT POLICY:

A 10% discount is given on all books.

RETURN POLICY:

Paperbacks are non-returnable unless damaged or defective. Written

permission, including invoice information, is required for hardcover returns. Books in resalable condition are accepted after 90 days from purchase to one year.

SHIPPING AND BILLING POLICY:

Shipping charges are assessed at library rate. Invoices are sent with the shipments, and monthly statements are issued.

BACK ORDER POLICY:

Items will be placed on back order for a time period established by the library when an account is set up. The back order period can be changed at any time, but requests must be submitted in writing.

WEISER PUBLICATIONS see LLEWELLYN PUBLICATIONS

WESTERN EYE PRESS

Box 917
609 E. Columbia Avenue
Telluride, Colorado 81435
Telephone: 303-728-5178

ADDRESS FOR ORDERS:

Texas Monthly Press
P.O. Box 1569
Austin, Texas 78767
Telephone: 800-288-3288

PREPAYMENT:

Not required.

DISCOUNT POLICY:

1 copy:	no discount
2-9 copies:	20%
10 or more:	30%

RETURN POLICY:

Written permission is not required. Address for returns: Texas Monthly Press/3800 Drosett Drive #H/Austin, TX 78744.

SHIPPING AND BILLING POLICY:

Libraries are charged actual shipping on all orders. Invoices are sent separately.

BACK ORDER POLICY:

Publisher back orders unavailable titles unless the library instructs otherwise.

SPECIAL PLANS:

Library standing order plan is available at a 40% maximum discount.

WESTERN MARINE ENTERPRISES

4051 Glencoe Avenue, Suite 14
Marina Del Rey, California 90292
Telephone: 213-306-2094

ADDRESS FOR ORDERS:

Same as above.

DISTRIBUTION/IMPRINT:

Marketscope
Cruising Classroom
Pacific Search Press
Clymer Publications
Sea Challengers
Helms Publishing

PREPAYMENT:

Prepayment must be made if no credit application is on file.

DISCOUNT POLICY:

Publisher's discount schedule:

1 to 6 books assorted	0%
1 to 6 books assorted, prepaid	20%
6 or more assorted	40%

RETURN POLICY:

All returns are subject to 15% restocking fee. All books must be in salable condition for full credit (less restocking fee). Library must write or call before returning books. Invoice number and date of purchase must accompany all returns.

SHIPPING AND BILLING POLICY:

Library pays shipping costs. There is a handling charge of $1.50. Invoices are

sent with shipment, unless library specifies otherwise.

BACK ORDER POLICY:

Unavailable titles are back ordered and shipped when they become available.

WESTERN RESEARCH HISTORICAL SOCIETY see ASSOCIATED UNIVERSITY PRESSES

WESTVIEW PRESS, INC.

5500 Central Avenue
Boulder, Colorado 80301
Telephone: 303-444-3541

ADDRESS FOR ORDERS:

Same as above.

PREPAYMENT:

Required. Open account available upon completion of credit application.

DISCOUNT POLICY:

Libraries receive a 15% discount on specific mailings.

RETURN POLICY:

Publisher requests libraries to write for written permission before sending returns. Books cannot be returned before 6 months or after 12 months from invoice date. The address for returns is the same as for orders.

SHIPPING AND BILLING POLICY:

Libraries pay shipping charges. The amount is $2.50 for the first book, $.75 for the second, and $.50 for each additional book thereafter.

BACK ORDER POLICY:

Publisher back orders unavailable titles unless requested otherwise by library.

DAVID WHITE, INC. see INDEPENDENT
PUBLISHERS GROUP

WHITE PINE PRESS

Dennis Maloney
76 Center Street
Fredonia, New York 14063
Telephone: 716-672-5743

ADDRESS FOR ORDERS:

Same as above.

PREPAYMENT:

Not required.

DISCOUNT POLICY:

No discount to libraries.

RETURN POLICY:

Returns are accepted within 6 months.
Written permission is required unless
book is defective.

SHIPPING AND BILLING POLICY:

Libraries are charged shipping of about
$1.00-$1.50. Invoices are sent with
shipments unless the library specifies
otherwise.

BACK ORDER POLICY:

Publisher back orders unavailable titles
and ships books when they become
available.

ALBERT WHITMAN & COMPANY

5747 West Howard Street
Niles, Illinois 60648
Telephone: 312-647-1355
         800-255-7675

ADDRESS FOR ORDERS:

Same as above.

PREPAYMENT:

Not required.

DISCOUNT POLICY:

25% discount on orders of 5 or more
books.

RETURN POLICY:

Returns accompanied by complete
information are accepted within one
year.

SHIPPING AND BILLING POLICY:

Libraries are charged actual shipping.
Invoices are sent separately unless the
library specifies otherwise.

BACK ORDER POLICY:

Publisher back orders indefinitely
unless notified otherwise.

SPECIAL PLANS:

Interested libraries should contact
publisher for information regarding
special plans.

WHITNEY LIBRARY OF DESIGN see WATSON-
GUPTILL PUBLICATIONS

WHITSTON PUBLISHING COMPANY, INC.

P.O. Box 958
Troy, New York 12181
Telephone: 518-283-4363

ADDRESS FOR ORDERS:

Same as above.

PREPAYMENT:

Not required.

DISCOUNT POLICY:

No discount to libraries.

RETURN POLICY:

Returns are accepted within 6 months.
Written permission is not required.

SHIPPING AND BILLING POLICY:

Libraries are charged shipping. Invoices are sent with shipments unless the library specifies otherwise.

BACK ORDER POLICY:

Publisher back orders all titles not yet published.

SPECIAL PLANS:

Standing orders are accepted at the same terms as other orders.

BACK ORDER POLICY:

Orders for forthcoming books or out-of-print titles to be reprinted are shipped when available.

STANDING ORDER PLANS:

Standing orders available for the following series: Selected Course Outlines and Reading Lists from Leading American Colleges and Universities in History (16 volumes in 1987; each book updated every two years); Selected Course Outlines in Contemporary Jewish Civilization; Masterworks of Modern Jewish Writing; Course Outlines in American Popular Culture.

MARKUS WIENER PUBLISHING, INC.

2901 Broadway, Suite 107
New York, New York 10025
Telephone: 212-678-7138

ADDRESS FOR ORDERS:

M. Wiener Publishing
c/o M & B Fulfillment Service
540 Barnum Avenue
Bridgeport, Connecticut 06608
Telephone: 203-366-1900

DISTRIBUTION:

Distributes Todd-Wiener Publications (Division for Business Books) and Masterworks of Modern Jewish Writing (imprint of Wiener Publishing).

PREPAYMENT:

Not required.

DISCOUNT POLICY:

No discount to libraries.

RETURN POLICY:

Returns accepted for 30 days. Libraries should write to Bridgeport address for a return label.

SHIPPING AND BILLING POLICY:

Libraries billed $1.50 for the first two titles and $.75 for each additional title. Invoices are sent with shipments unless otherwise requested.

WILDERNESS PRESS

2440 Bancroft Way
Berkeley, California 94704
Telephone: 415-843-8080

ADDRESS FOR ORDERS:

Same as above.

PREPAYMENT:

Not required.

DISCOUNT POLICY:

20% discount to libraries.

RETURN POLICY:

Books, in salable condition and accompanied by the invoice number, may be returned for full credit not sooner than 90 days or more than one year from invoice date. Return authorization is required.

SHIPPING AND BILLING POLICY:

Publisher pays shipping costs on all orders. Invoices are sent with shipments unless the library specifies otherwise.

BACK ORDER POLICY:

Publisher usually back orders unless instructed otherwise.

JOHN WILEY AND SONS, INC.

605 Third Avenue
New York, New York 10158

TELEPHONE INQUIRES:

Book Information Department:

Librarians requesting title information, price, availability, or general bibliographic data, should call: 212-850-6418.

Customer Services Department:

Librarians who wish to place orders, or to make inquiries concerning orders already placed, should call: 201-469-4400.

ADDRESS FOR ORDERS:

John Wiley & Sons, Inc.
Distribution Center
1 Wiley Drive
Somerset, NJ 08875-1272
Telephone: 201-496-4400
FAX: 201-457-0920

PREPAYMENT:

Not required.

DISCOUNT POLICY:

Various plans offered. Contact Library Sales Department for details.

RETURN POLICY:

Time limit: Books must be returned within 18 months of invoice date, except for out-of-print titles which must be returned within 90 days of notification. Notification appears in NACS Confidential Bulletin, Wiley Price List, and General Catalog.

Quantity permitted: 100% of direct purchases from Wiley.

Prior authorization: Not required.

Information required: Returns will not be accepted unless accompanied by invoice or packing list showing invoice number and date, quantity, ISBN, author, title, volume, list price, and discount.

Conditions: Products must be in perfect resalable condition, free of marking, labels, etc. Unsalable items will be returned at library's expense.

Defective products: No permission is necessary. Libraries may return at any time. Publisher requests libraries to clearly indicate reason for being declared defective.

Duplicate shipments: Libraries can return with explanation on copy of invoice.

Non-returnable items: (1) Products not in resalable conditions; (2) Non-book products such as films, tapes, filmstrips, film loops, transparencies, etc.; and (3) out-of-print products.

Address for returns: Same as for orders.

SPECIAL ORDER PLAN:

Standing Order/On Approval Plan:

Library may select from among 68 major subjects and/or 395 minor categories. Additional qualifier, such as price limit, special treatment of series, and other inclusion/exclusions are offered as required by the library's needs.

Shipments are made as new titles are published, and books may be returned after examination for full credit.

There is no purchase volume requirement, and the agreement may be cancelled at any time.

Full details may be obtained from Library Sales Department at New York address, or at 212-850-6705.

Continuations Orders:

Library may enter a Continuation Order for automatic shipment of new volumes in Wiley numbered serials and monograph series. In some cases, a reduced subscription price is offered on Continuation Orders.

Complete list of Wiley series and serials is available on request from Library Sales Department at New York address, or at 212-850-6705.

WILFION BOOKS see DUFOUR EDITIONS, INC.

WILLIAMSON PUBLISHING COMPANY

Box 185, Church Hill Road
Charlotte, Vermont 05445
Telephone: 802-425-2102

ADDRESS FOR ORDERS:

Same as above.

DISTRIBUTION/IMPRINTS:

Distributes: Career Publishing Co;
Cottage Press; Fraser-Research Books.

PREPAYMENT:

Not required.

DISCOUNT POLICY:

25% discount on orders of 5 or more
books; no discount on orders for fewer
than 5.

RETURN POLICY:

Returns in salable condition and
accompanied by invoice information are
accepted within one year. Written
permission is required. Addresses for
returns: (for small returns - fewer than
10 books) Church Hill Road; (for large
returns) c/o American International
Dist. Corp/2 Acorn Ln/Sunderland
Industrial Park/Colchester, VT 05446.

SHIPPING AND BILLING POLICY:

Libraries are charged shipping. Invoices
are sent with shipments unless the
library specifies otherwise.

BACK ORDER POLICY:

Publisher back orders unavailable titles
and ships books when they become
available.

H. W. WILSON COMPANY

---

950 University Avenue
Bronx, New York 10452
Telephone: 212-588-8400

ADDRESS FOR ORDERS:

Same as above.
Telephone: 800-367-6770

PREPAYMENT:

Not required.

DISCOUNT POLICY:

No discount to libraries.

RETURN POLICY:

Books may be returned to Customer
Services Dept. No written permission is
required. CD-ROM products are non-
returnable.

SHIPPING AND BILLING POLICY:

Publisher pays shipping and handling
charges. Invoices are sent separately.

BACK ORDER POLICY:

Almost all titles are currently
available; back orders apply to
forthcoming books.

OTHER:

Libraries must order direct.

B. L. WINCH & ASSOCIATES see JALMAR PRESS

WINGBOW PRESS

P.O. Box 2249
Berkeley, California 94702
Telephone: 415-549-3030

ADDRESS FOR ORDERS:

Wingbow Press
2929 Fifth Street
Berkeley, California 94710
Telephone: 800-227-1516 (in US)
          800-624-4466 (in CA)

DISTRIBUTION/IMPRINTS:

Wingbow Press is a department of
Bookpeople.

PREPAYMENT:

Not required with purchase order.

DISCOUNT POLICY:

For this and other policies, libraries
should contact Bookpeople at the above
address for orders.

WINTERTHUR MUSEUM see UNIVERSITY PRESS OF VIRGINIA

WIZARDS BOOKSHELF

Box 6600
San Diego, California 92106
Telephone: 619-235-0340

ADDRESS FOR ORDERS:

Same as above.

PREPAYMENT:

Required for single copy orders, less 10% for libraries.

DISCOUNT POLICY:

10% discount to libraries.

RETURN POLICY:

Returns are accepted within 6 months on hardcover books only. Paperback books are non-returnable. Written permission is required. Invoice information must accompany returns which should be sent with postage prepaid. 10% restocking charge is applied to all returns. Address for returns (UPS): 2726 Shelter Island Dr/San Diego, CA 92106.

SHIPPING AND BILLING POLICY:

Libraries are charged shipping. Invoices are sent with shipments.

BACK ORDER POLICY:

Publisher notifies library of back orders.

WOMEN'S LEGAL DEFENSE FUND

2000 P Street, N.W.
Suite 400
Washington, DC 20036
Telephone: 202-887-0364

ADDRESS FOR ORDERS:

Same as above.

PREPAYMENT:

All orders must be prepaid.

DISCOUNT POLICY:

1-9 copies:	list price
11-24 copies:	10% discount
25-49 copies:	15% discount
50-100 copies:	20% discount
101+ copies:	negotiable

RETURN POLICY:

Books will be accepted within six weeks if returned in resalable condition with a full explanation of the reason for return.

SHIPPING AND BILLING POLICY:

Shipping and handling charges are included in publication price. Invoices are sent with shipments unless otherwise requested.

BACK ORDER POLICY:

The library is notified of the back order and has the option to wait for availability or receive a refund.

WOODBRIDGE PRESS

815 De La Vina St.
P.O. Box 6189
Santa Barbara, CA 93160
Phone: (805) 965-7039

ADDRESS FOR ORDERS:

Same as above.

PREPAYMENT:

Not required, but larger discount when prepaid.

DISCOUNT POLICY:

25% normally; 40% if prepaid (plus postage)

RETURN POLICY:

Books can be returned within one year. Prior permission not required.

SHIPPING AND BILLING POLICY:

Libraries are charged shipping. Invoices sent separately unless library requests otherwise.

BACK ORDER POLICY:

Publisher will accept back orders and ship when ready at their expense.

WOODENBOAT see INTERNATIONAL MARINE PUBLISHING COMPANY

WORD, INC.

P.O. Box 2518
Waco, Texas 76702-2518
Telephone:

ADDRESS FOR ORDERS:

Word Publishing
Trade Order Processing
7300 Imperial
Waco, Texas 76702-2518

PREPAYMENT:

Not required.

DISCOUNT POLICY:

20% discount to libraries plus postage.

RETURN POLICY:

Returns are accepted two years from date of purchase. Written permission is required. Return to 7300 Imperial address.

SHIPPING AND BILLING POLICY:

Libraries are charged shipping on both billed and prepaid orders. Invoices are sent separately after shipments.

BACK ORDER POLICY:

Back orders are placed and shipped when available unless the library requests cancellation.

SPECIAL PLANS:

Publisher offers standing order plans for certain series, sometimes at extra discount. Interested libraries should address inquiries to Customer Order.

WORLD BANK see UNIFO PUBLISHING, LTD.

WORLD POLICY INSTITUTE

777 United Nations Plaza
New York, New York 10017
Telephone: 212-490-0010

ADDRESS FOR ORDERS:

Same as above.

PREPAYMENT:

Not required with library purchase order.

DISCOUNT POLICY:

No discount to libraries.

RETURN POLICY:

Returns are accepted within 120 days after permission is granted. Written permission is required.

SHIPPING AND BILLING POLICY:

Libraries are charged 15% shipping/handling. Invoices are sent with shipments unless the bill to address is different.

BACK ORDER POLICY:

Publisher does not accept back orders.

WORLD WAR TWO PUBLICATIONS see AVIATION BOOK COMPANY

WORLD WILDLIFE FUND see CONSERVATION FOUNDATION

WORTH PUBLISHERS, INC.

33 Irving Place
New York, New York 10003
Telephone: 212-475-6000

ADDRESS FOR ORDERS:

Same as above.

PREPAYMENT:

Not required.

DISCOUNT POLICY:

10% discount to libraries.

RETURN POLICY:

Returns in salable condition are
accepted within one year. Written
permission is required except for
defective books; requests should include
author, title, quantity, and invoice
number and date. No returns of old
editions will be accepted after 60 days
of the publication date of a new edition
unless the old edition was ordered
afterwards. Address for returns: Worth
Publishers, Inc/c/o T.E. Enterprises/
675 Dell Road/Carlstadt, NJ 07072.

SHIPPING AND BILLING POLICY:

Libraries are not charged shipping if
books are sent via Book Rate or Library
Rate; there is a $0.50 handling charge
on all orders. Invoices are sent
separately unless the library specifies
otherwise.

BACK ORDER POLICY:

Publisher notifies library of back
orders and ships books when they become
available.

THE WRITER, INC.

120 Boylston Street
Boston, Massachusetts 02116
Telephone: 617-423-3157

ADDRESS FOR ORDERS:

Same as above.

PREPAYMENT:

Not required.

DISCOUNT POLICY:

Libraries receive a 20% discount.

RETURN POLICY:

Publisher requests libraries to write for
permission and label before sending
returns. Returns are accepted within six
months of invoice date. The Writer's
Handbook is non-returnable. The address
for returns is the same as for orders.
All returns are credited at 50%.

SHIPPING AND BILLING POLICY:

Libraries pay postage. There is no
handling or billing charge. Invoices are
enclosed with books unless requested
otherwise.

BACK ORDER POLICY:

Publisher back orders on request if
titles will be published within three
months.

SPECIAL ORDER PLAN:

Publisher accepts standing orders for The
Writer's Handbook.

WRITER'S DIGEST BOOKS see F & W
PUBLICATIONS

XENOS BOOKS see BORGO PRESS

YALE UNIVERSITY PRESS

302 Temple Street
New Haven, Connecticut 06520
Telephone: 203-432-0960

ADDRESS FOR ORDERS:

Yale University Press
Order Department
92A Yale Station
New Haven, CT 06520

PREPAYMENT:

Prepayments are not required from libraries having a customer account with publisher. To avoid prepayment delay, libraries are urged to establish customer accounts.

DISCOUNT POLICY:

Libraries pay list price on regular orders. Discount rate for standing orders of titles in a series is 10%; blanket standing orders are granted a 20% discount.

RETURN POLICY:

Written permission is not required for returns. Returns are limited to one year from date of invoice. All books are returnable. The address for returns is: Yale University Press Warehouse, Returns Department, 48 North Branford Road, Branford, CT 06405.

SHIPPING AND BILLING POLICY:

Publisher pays library rate or book rate shipping cost except in cases when libraries receive discount. Invoices are either sent with shipment or separately, as library requests.

BACK ORDER POLICY:

Titles currently unavailable are reported and back ordered unless library requests otherwise.

SPECIAL ORDER PLAN:

Publisher ships one copy of each new title as it is published, following library's instructions for exceptions in certain categories.

YEAR BOOK MEDICAL PUBLISHERS see C. V. MOSBY COMPANY

ZEUS PUBLISHERS see WARREN H. GREEN, INC.

ZONDERVAN BIBLE see ZONDERVAN PUBLISHING HOUSE

ZONDERVAN MUSIC PUBLISHERS see ZONDERVAN PUBLISHING HOUSE

ZONDERVAN PUBLISHING HOUSE

1415 Lake Drive
Grand Rapids, Michigan 49506
Telephone: 616-698-6900
          800-253-1309

ADDRESS FOR ORDERS:

Same as above.

DISTRIBUTION/IMPRINTS:

Distributes: Green Tiger Press; Marshall Pickering Books.
Divisions: Zondervan Publishing House; Zondervan Bible Publishers; Zondervan Music Publishers.

PREPAYMENT:

Not required.

DISCOUNT POLICY:

25% on any quantity.

RETURN POLICY:

Publisher accepts returns of titles that are still in print. Prior permission not required. Address for returns: Zondervan Returns Dept./4444 52nd St./Grand Rapids, MI 49508.

SHIPPING AND BILLING POLICY:

All orders are shipped FOB Grand Rapids. Invoices are sent separately after shipment unless the library specifies otherwise.

BACK ORDER POLICY:

Publisher back-orders unless the library's purchase order states otherwise.

ZONE BOOKS see MIT PRESS
